American History for Beginners

The Ultimate 3-in-1 Guide to United States History, Major Events, and Key Figures That Shaped America's Future

Free Bonus from Captivating History (Available for a Limited time)

Hi History Lovers!

Now you have a chance to join our exclusive history list so you can get your first history ebook for free as well as discounts and a potential to get more history books for free!

Simply visit the link below to join.

Or, Scan the QR code!

captivatinghistory.com/ebook

Also, make sure to follow us on Facebook, X, and YouTube by searching for Captivating History.

Table of Contents

Part 1: The History of the United States for Beginners

The Story of America Simplified for People Who Slept Through History Class

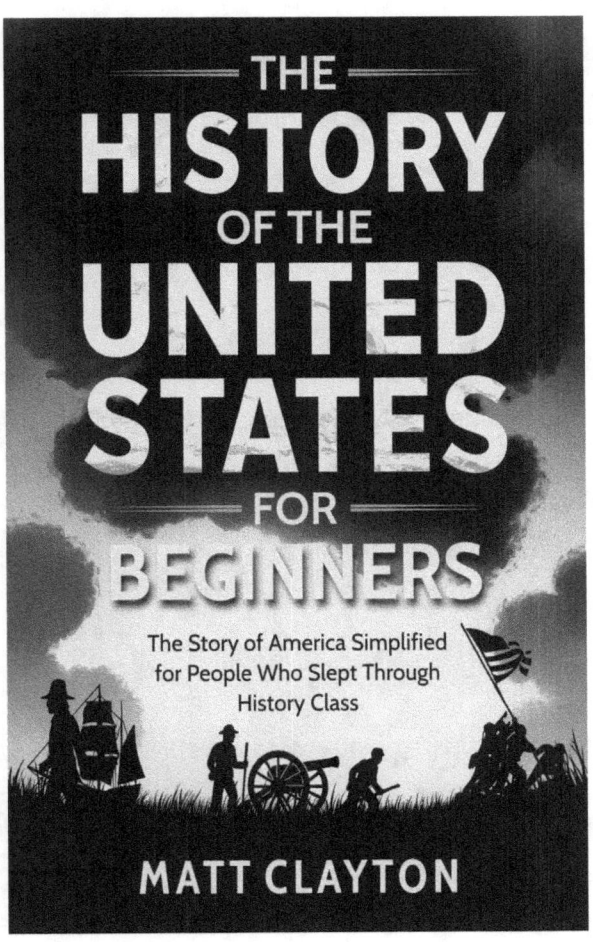

Introduction

Let's be honest. You probably remember history class as that period right after lunch when the teacher droned on about dates and dead people while you tried not to fall asleep. Maybe you passed the tests by memorizing a few key facts, but then forgot everything the next week. If that sounds familiar, this book is for you.

Here's the truth: history isn't boring. Bad history teaching is boring. The actual story of America is packed with drama, conflict, unexpected twists, and characters so interesting you couldn't make them up. We're talking about a place that went from a handful of starving colonists to the world's most powerful nation in less than four centuries. That doesn't happen by accident.

The problem with most history books is that they treat the past like a grocery list. First this happened, then that happened, memorize these dates, moving on. But history isn't a list. It's a story. Better yet, it's thousands of interconnected stories about real people making decisions that shaped the world you live in today.

Every time you vote, you're participating in an experiment that started in 1776. Every time you see a news story about immigration, you're watching a debate that's been happening since before there was a United States. The arguments about government power, individual rights, and who gets to be considered a "real American" have been going on for centuries. Understanding where those arguments came from helps you understand where they're going.

This book won't ask you to memorize dates. Dates matter, but they're not the point. The point is understanding how we got here. Why does the United States look the way it does? Why do Americans think the way they do? Why did some ideas catch on while others failed spectacularly?

American history is a wild ride. There are heroes and villains, though it's not always clear which is which. There are brilliant decisions and catastrophically stupid ones, often made by the same people. There are wars, revolutions, inventions, migrations, disasters, and triumphs. There are moments of incredible courage and periods of shameful injustice. All of it matters. All of it connects.

So forget what you remember from that class after lunch. We're starting fresh. No boring lectures, no pointless memorization—just the story of how America became America. And trust me—it's a story worth knowing.

Chapter 1: The Land Before "America"

The First Migrations: Across the Land Bridge

People lived in America thousands of years before it was even called America. The story of this land doesn't begin with Christopher Columbus or the Pilgrims. It begins with the first humans who walked into a continent that had never seen our species before.

Most scholars once believed these first people arrived during the Last Ice Age, somewhere between fifteen thousand and twenty thousand years ago. However, new evidence, including human footprints discovered in New Mexico, suggests even earlier arrivals, possibly twenty-three thousand years ago or more. Sea levels were lower then. Much of the world's water was locked up in massive glaciers, and a strip of land connected what is now Siberia to Alaska. Scholars call this the Bering Land Bridge, though calling it a bridge makes it sound small. At its widest, this landmass stretched about a thousand miles from north to south. It wasn't a narrow path; it was an entire region, complete with plants, animals, and ecosystems.

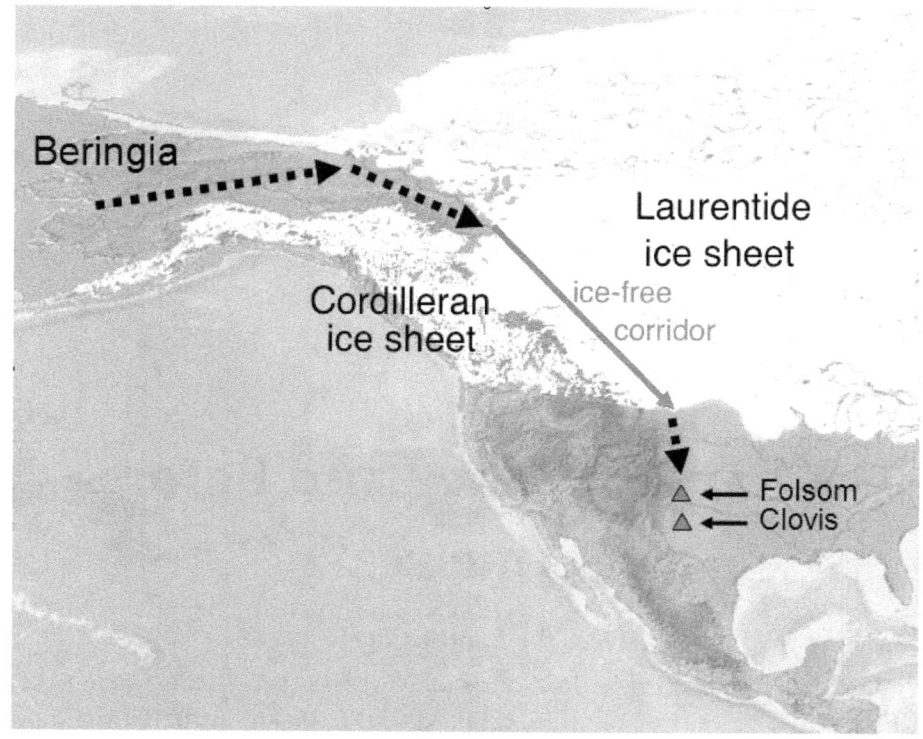

The Bering land bridge.[1]

The people who crossed the bridge weren't on some grand expedition. They were hunting, fishing, and foraging—gathering plants, catching small game, and harvesting marine resources along coastlines. They were doing what humans had always done: moving to where the food was. Over generations, they moved eastward and southward, following river valleys and coastlines, spreading across two continents. Some groups stayed in the north. Others pushed into what would become the United States. Others continued all the way to the southern tip of South America.

This wasn't a single migration. Genetic and linguistic evidence suggest multiple waves of people crossed at different times, likely from different parts of Asia and possibly by different routes. Some might have traveled along the Pacific coast by boat, hugging the shoreline and living off marine resources. The picture is complicated, and archaeologists are still trying to piece it together. New discoveries keep pushing back the dates and adding complexity to what we thought we knew.

What we do know is that by the time sustained European contact began in 1492, people had been living in the Americas for at least twelve thousand years—possibly more than twenty thousand. They had adapted to every environment the continents offered, from arctic tundra to desert to rainforest to prairie. They had developed hundreds of distinct cultures, languages, and ways of life. They had built cities—Cahokia in the Mississippi Valley, Tenochtitlán in Mexico, Caral in Peru—and established complex societies with hierarchies, trade networks, and monumental architecture.

The land shaped them, and they shaped the land. But the degree of this transformation varied enormously. Some societies, like the agricultural communities of the Mississippi Valley, dramatically altered their environments through intensive farming and construction. Others, like the hunter-gatherers of the Great Basin, left a lighter footprint. They burned forests to create better hunting grounds. They cultivated crops and changed the landscape through farming. The "untouched wilderness" that later European colonists claimed to discover was more of a myth than reality. Much of the land had been managed and inhabited by humans for millennia. The story of America doesn't start in 1492; it starts thousands of years earlier, with people whose descendants were still here when the ships arrived.

A Continent of Cultures: From the Iroquois to the Ancestral Puebloans

Here's a mistake almost everyone makes: talking about Native Americans as if they were all one people with one culture. They weren't. Saying "Native American culture" makes about as much sense as saying "European culture" and expecting that to describe both Norway and Greece. The Indigenous peoples of North America were as diverse as the land they inhabited.

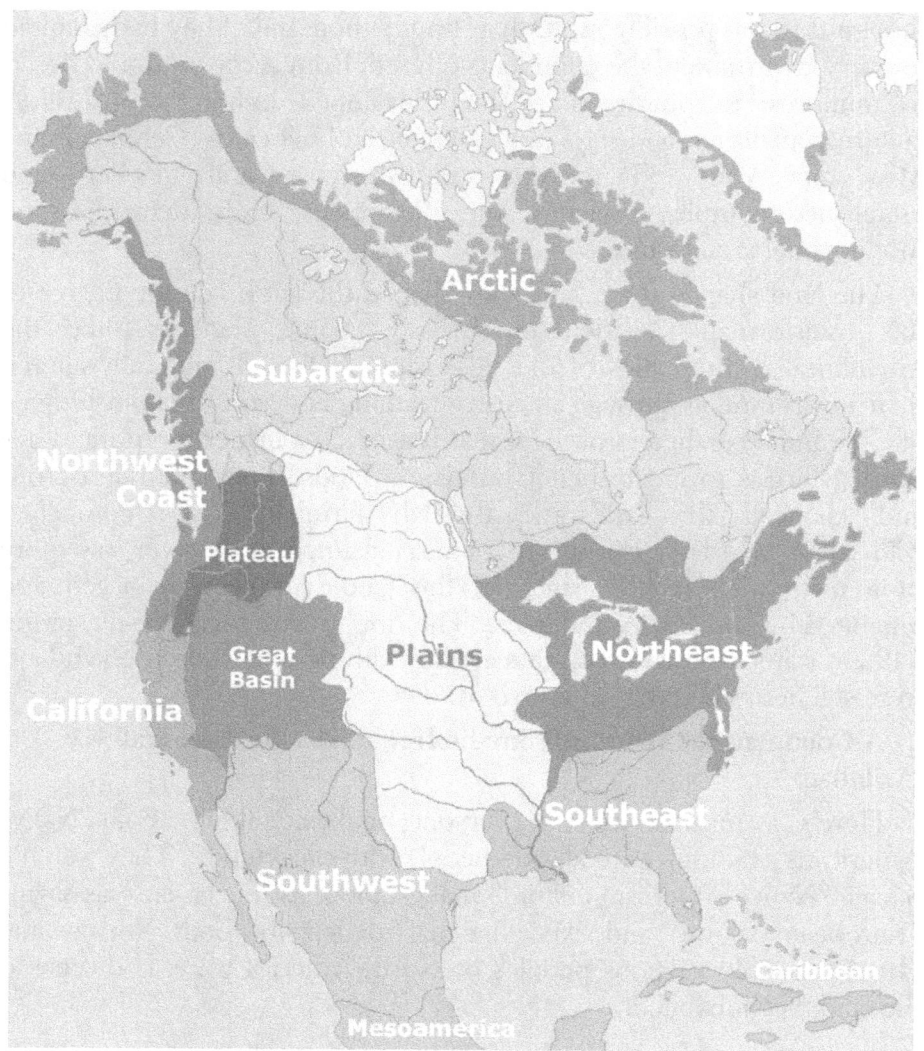

Native American cultural areas.[*]

Let's start in the Northeast, in the forests that stretched from the Atlantic coast to the Great Lakes. Here, several nations formed the Iroquois Confederacy, also called the Haudenosaunee. This alliance brought together the Mohawk, Oneida, Onondaga, Cayuga, and Seneca Nations (and later the Tuscarora). They built longhouses—wooden structures that could hold multiple families—and organized their society through clan mothers who held significant political power. Women owned the land and controlled the food supply. When European colonists arrived, they were shocked to find societies where women had real authority.

The Iroquois Confederacy had a system of governance that impressed many Europeans who encountered it. Representatives from each nation met in councils to make decisions affecting the whole alliance. They had to reach a consensus, not just majority rule.

Move south, and you find entirely different societies. In the Mississippi River Valley and the Southeast, people built massive earthen mounds. We call these cultures the Mound Builders, though that term covers many different groups across more than five thousand years. The most impressive of these was Cahokia, near present-day St. Louis. At its peak, around 1050 CE, Cahokia might have rivaled London in size, with estimates placing both cities at around fifteen thousand to twenty thousand inhabitants. The city featured a massive central plaza, enormous earthen pyramids, and evidence of long-distance trade networks that stretched across the continent.

Shriver Circle and Mound City in Ohio.[3]

Cahokia was a complex urban society with social hierarchies, specialized workers, and organized religion. However, for reasons we still don't fully understand, it declined. By the time European explorers reached the Mississippi Valley, Cahokia was abandoned. The city had been empty for centuries. But the descendants of the Mound Builders were still there, living in other communities and carrying on modified versions of their ancestors' traditions.

Head southwest into what is now Arizona and New Mexico, and the landscape changes dramatically. So do the people. The Ancestral Puebloans adapted to life in the desert. They built incredible cliff dwellings carved into canyon walls. Sites like Mesa Verde and Chaco Canyon show communities that thrived in one of North America's harshest environments. They developed sophisticated irrigation systems to farm corn, beans, and squash in a place with very little rainfall. They built roads connecting distant communities and created a regional trade network.

Like Cahokia, many of these sites were eventually abandoned. Drought, resource depletion, conflict, and climate change all likely played a role. But again, the people didn't disappear. Their descendants are the Pueblo peoples who still live in the Southwest today—the Hopi, Zuni, and others who maintain cultural and spiritual connections to those ancient sites.

On the Great Plains, nations like the Lakota, Cheyenne, and Comanche lived as nomadic hunters, following vast buffalo herds. However, this way of life wasn't ancient. Many Plains tribes moved to the region relatively recently, pushed westward by pressure from other groups and drawn by opportunities created by the horse, which had been reintroduced by the Spanish. Before European contact, the Plains had fewer people. Those who lived there combined hunting with farming along river valleys.

The Pacific Northwest gave rise to yet another distinct set of cultures. Groups like the Tlingit, Haida, and Chinook built their lives around salmon and the sea. They lived in permanent villages of large wooden houses. They carved elaborate totem poles that showed family lineage, social status, clan identity, and spiritual beliefs. They held potlatches— ceremonial gatherings where wealthy leaders gave away possessions to demonstrate their status and redistribute wealth. The mild climate and abundant resources allowed these societies to develop complex social structures without agriculture.

In California, the diversity was staggering. Hundreds of small tribes spoke dozens of unrelated languages. They adapted to environments ranging from coastal redwood forests to inland valleys to deserts. Many groups practiced controlled burning to manage the landscape, encouraging the growth of useful plants and preventing destructive wildfires. Their population density was among the highest north of Mexico.

This diversity mattered. When Europeans arrived, they weren't encountering a unified group that could mount a coordinated response. They were encountering hundreds of separate nations with different languages, different interests, and often long-standing conflicts with each other. Some Native groups allied with Europeans against their traditional enemies. Others resisted fiercely. Still others tried to play different European powers against each other. There was no single Native American response to European colonization because there was no single Native American people.

These societies weren't frozen in time or primitive. They were changed and adapted. They formed alliances and fought wars. They traded over vast distances; seashells from the Pacific coast have been found in burial sites in the Midwest. They developed new technologies and agricultural techniques. They rose and fell, built cities and abandoned them, and conquered neighbors and were conquered in turn. They were doing everything humans everywhere do: trying to survive, competing for resources, creating meaning through art and religion, and building societies that made sense for their environments.

By 1491, North America was home to somewhere between five and ten million people, though estimates vary widely. Some scholars suggest as few as four million, while others argue for more than eighteen million. They spoke hundreds of languages. They had complex histories we can only partially reconstruct. And they were about to experience the most catastrophic disruption any human population has ever faced. But that story belongs to the next chapter.

For now, remember this: before there was an America, there were already Americans. They had been here longer than Rome had existed. They had seen empires rise and fall. They had built civilizations that rivaled European societies in sophistication, though they looked very different. And they had no idea that ships were coming across an ocean largely unknown to most of them.

Chapter 2: The European Invasion Begins

Columbus Didn't Discover America, But He Did Change the World

Christopher Columbus did not discover America. This should be obvious by now. Millions of people already lived there. Vikings reached Newfoundland about five centuries earlier, establishing a short-lived settlement at L'Anse aux Meadows. Columbus wasn't even trying to find a new continent. He was looking for a shortcut to Asia.

However, Columbus did change everything. His voyage in 1492 opened a connection between two worlds that had been separate for thousands of years. What followed transformed both sides of the Atlantic in ways no one could have predicted.

The Spanish monarchs Ferdinand and Isabella had just completed the Reconquista, driving the last Muslim kingdom out of the Iberian Peninsula. They were flush with victory and looking for new projects. Columbus pitched them on reaching Asia by sailing west. The idea wasn't crazy—educated Europeans knew the Earth was round—but Columbus had badly miscalculated the distance. He thought Asia was about where the Caribbean actually is. If the Americas hadn't been there, the voyage would have likely failed due to the long distance and limited provisions.

On October 12, 1492, Columbus's expedition landed in the Bahamas. He thought he'd reached islands off the coast of Asia. He called the people he met "Indians" because he believed he was near India. The name stuck, despite being completely wrong.

Columbus made four voyages to the Caribbean between 1492 and 1504. He explored islands, encountered various Indigenous groups, and established the first Spanish settlements in the Americas. He never realized he'd found continents unknown to Europeans. He died still believing he'd reached Asia.

His legacy is complicated. From a European perspective, he was an explorer who opened up new worlds. From an Indigenous perspective, he began a catastrophe. His men enslaved Native people. They brought diseases. They demanded gold that the islanders didn't have. The Taíno population was decimated within fifty years of Columbus's arrival, with most dying from disease, forced labor, and violence, though some survived through intermarriage or by fleeing.

Columbus was a contradictory figure. He was a skilled navigator and a stubborn visionary who pursued an idea everyone else thought was impossible. He was also a brutal governor who enslaved Indigenous people and oversaw atrocities. Even by the standards of his own time, his treatment of Native populations was harsh enough that he was arrested and briefly imprisoned by Spanish authorities.

But Columbus, the individual, matters less than what he represented. His voyages marked the beginning of sustained contact between Europe and the Americas. And that contact would reshape the world.

The Great Exchange: New Foods, New Diseases, New Peoples

After 1492, plants, animals, diseases, and people began moving between the Eastern and Western Hemispheres on a scale never seen before. Historians call this the Columbian Exchange. It sounds neutral, like a simple trade, but it wasn't. The exchange was profoundly unequal and devastating for the Americas.

Start with disease. This was the biggest killer. Europeans brought smallpox, measles, typhus, influenza, and other diseases to the Americas. Native Americans had no immunity to these illnesses. Within a century of contact, many scholars estimate that between 70 and 95 percent of the Indigenous population of the Americas died. Entire societies disappeared. Villages were abandoned. Complex political systems collapsed. The survivors were left traumatized and dramatically weakened.

The scale of this death is hard to grasp. Imagine nine out of every ten people you know dying within a few generations. The Black Death killed perhaps a third of Europe's population and is remembered as one of history's great catastrophes. The population collapse in the Americas was proportionally far worse.

Disease spread faster than Europeans did. Native people who had never seen a European could catch smallpox from trade goods or from other Natives who had encountered colonists. By the time English colonists reached New England in the 1620s, epidemics had already swept through the region. The "empty" land the Pilgrims found wasn't empty—it was actually full of graves.

The exchange wasn't entirely one-way. Europeans might have contracted syphilis from the Americas, though this remains debated. However, the disease exchange was overwhelmingly harmful to the Americas and beneficial, in a cold demographic sense, to Europeans.

Plants and animals moved too. Europeans brought horses, cattle, pigs, sheep, and chickens to the Americas. Horses had actually lived in the Americas thousands of years earlier, but they had gone extinct. Their reintroduction transformed many Native American societies, particularly on the Great Plains, where horses revolutionized hunting and warfare.

European livestock multiplied rapidly in American environments, often with destructive results. Pigs ran wild and damaged Native crops. Cattle overgrazed fragile ecosystems. But these animals also provided new sources of food and labor.

From the Americas, Europeans gained crops that would transform the world. Potatoes, maize (corn), tomatoes, peppers, cacao, vanilla, and tobacco all came from the Americas. The potato is believed to have played a major role in population growth in Europe and Asia, with some estimates attributing as much as a quarter of that growth to the crop. It was nutritious, grew in poor soil, and could feed more people per acre than traditional European grains. Maize became a staple crop across Africa and Asia. The tomato transformed Italian cuisine, though Europeans initially thought it was poisonous.

The exchange also included people. Europeans began bringing enslaved Africans to the Americas in the early 1500s. The Spanish and Portuguese started this trade, but eventually, all major European powers participated. The transatlantic slave trade expanded because European colonizers demanded large amounts of labor for plantations and mines. The Indigenous population decline accelerated this demand, but the trade was also built on existing systems of African enslavement that the Portuguese had established. Millions of Africans were forcibly transported across the Atlantic in conditions so brutal that a significant percentage died en route. Those who survived faced lives of bondage in mines and on plantations. This traffic in human beings would continue for more than three centuries and shape the development of the entire Western Hemisphere.

The Columbian Exchange transformed ecologies, economies, and societies on both sides of the Atlantic. It enriched Europe and devastated the Americas. It created new hybrid cultures but destroyed old ones. It was not a neutral exchange between equals—it was a collision that benefited one side enormously and cost the other side almost everything.

A Race for North America: St. Augustine, Quebec, and a Lost Colony

Spain dominated early colonization. Spanish conquistadors conquered the Aztec and Inca Empires, gaining access to enormous quantities of gold and silver. Spanish settlers established colonies throughout Central and South America and the Caribbean. But Spain also looked north.

In 1565, Spain founded St. Augustine in Florida. It's the oldest continuously inhabited European-established settlement in what would become the United States. The Spanish built it as a military outpost to protect their treasure fleets from pirates and to counter French attempts to settle in Florida. St. Augustine was never large or particularly prosperous, but it endured. Spanish control of Florida would last, with some interruptions, for more than two centuries.

France entered the race with a different approach. French explorers and settlers were less interested in conquest and more focused on trade, particularly in furs. In 1608, Samuel de Champlain founded Quebec in present-day Canada. The French established a network of trading posts and missions stretching from Canada down through the Great Lakes and eventually to the Mississippi River. They formed alliances with various Native nations, particularly the Huron, who became trading partners and military allies.

The French colonial model relied more heavily on alliances and trade with Indigenous peoples than other European powers, though it still brought disease and conflict. This approach was partly practical. France sent fewer colonists than Spain or England, so the French had to work with Native populations rather than displace them. French traders learned Native languages, married Indigenous women, and integrated themselves into existing trade networks. But this also meant French colonization had a somewhat different character. French settlements remained relatively small, focused on trade rather than agriculture.

England was late to the colonization game. The English had been distracted by religious turmoil at home and wars in Europe. But by the late 1500s, England was ready to try.

In 1585, English settlers landed on Roanoke Island, off the coast of present-day North Carolina. The colony struggled. Supply ships from England were delayed. Relations with the local Native people deteriorated. The colonists returned to England in 1586.

But England tried again. In 1587, a second group of colonists arrived at Roanoke, including women and children. Their leader, John White, sailed back to England for supplies. When he returned in 1590, the colony had vanished. The only clue was the word "CROATOAN" carved into a post. The colonists' fate remains a mystery.

Theories abound. Maybe they moved to nearby Croatoan Island. Maybe they were killed by hostile tribes. Maybe they integrated into Native communities. Archaeologists continue to search for evidence, but the Lost Colony of Roanoke remains one of American history's enduring mysteries.

What's clear is that early colonization was difficult and dangerous. Europeans were entering environments they didn't understand, encountering people whose languages they couldn't speak, and trying to survive with inadequate supplies and little knowledge of local conditions. Many early attempts failed.

But the Europeans kept coming. By 1600, Spain controlled Florida and the Southwest. France was establishing itself in Canada. England was making plans for another attempt at colonization, this time in a place they called Virginia.

The stage was set for the next chapter: permanent English settlement in North America. That settlement would be a disaster that somehow managed to survive.

Chapter 3: The Southern Colonies

Jamestown: The Disastrous First Success

In May 1607, three English ships landed on the coast of Virginia. About a hundred men came ashore and founded Jamestown, the first successful permanent English settlement in North America. "Permanent" is doing a lot of work in that sentence, though. The colony nearly failed a dozen times in its first few years.

The location was terrible. The settlers chose a swampy peninsula because it was easy to defend from Spanish attack. The Spanish had destroyed a French colony in Florida just decades earlier, and the English knew they needed a defensive position. However, the spot they picked on the James River was not great. The water was brackish. Mosquitoes bred in the marshes, spreading what we now know as malaria. The land wasn't good for farming. The soil was poor, and the marsh made drainage impossible. Worse, the area sat in the middle of the Powhatan Confederacy's territory, guaranteeing conflict. The Jamestown colonists had picked one of the worst spots on the entire coast.

The settlers were also the wrong people for the job. The Virginia Company, which organized the expedition, recruited the wrong mix of people. Many were gentlemen who had never done manual labor and considered it beneath their status. They had titles but no practical skills. They expected to find gold, like the Spanish in Mexico and Peru. They didn't expect to spend their time building houses, planting crops, and trying not to starve. Some were craftsmen, but few were farmers. Almost none had experience with wilderness survival. They came from English cities and towns, not agricultural backgrounds. The colony needed people who could grow food and build shelters. Instead, it got people who knew how to wear fancy clothes and expected servants to do the work.

The first winter was brutal. Disease and starvation killed more than half the colonists. By January 1608, only about 38 of the original 105 colonists were still alive. They survived partly because of supplies from England, partly because Captain John Smith imposed strict discipline, and partly because of trade with the Powhatan people. Smith famously declared that anyone who didn't work wouldn't eat. This offended the gentlemen but probably saved lives. The survivors ate horses, then dogs, then rats, and then whatever else they could find.

During what became known as the Starving Time (the winter of 1609–1610), things got even worse. The colony's population had swelled to nearly five hundred people with the arrival of new ships. However, a supply ship had wrecked in Bermuda, and no one knew if help would arrive. The colonists were trapped in the fort by hostile Powhatan warriors outside. They couldn't hunt, fish, or forage. Food ran out. Disease spread. People died by the dozens. They ate leather, shoe soles, and even the starch from their shirt collars. Archaeological evidence has confirmed that some survivors resorted to cannibalism. When spring came, only about sixty colonists were still alive. The rest were dead and buried in the fort.

The survivors decided to abandon Jamestown. They loaded onto ships and started down the river. Then they ran into another English ship coming with supplies and a new governor. The new governor ordered everyone back. Jamestown would survive, though just barely.

Relations with the local Powhatan Confederacy were complicated. The paramount chief, known to the English as Powhatan, led about thirty different tribes in the region. At first, the Powhatan people traded with the English and sometimes helped them. Pocahontas, Powhatan's daughter, became famous for supposedly saving Captain John Smith's life, though many historians believe the event might have been a ritual rather than a literal rescue. What's certain is that she was captured by the English. She converted to Christianity, married an Englishman named John Rolfe, and traveled to England, where she died of disease in 1617.

However, the relationship between the English and the Powhatan was never stable. The English kept expanding. They wanted land. They cut down forests. They expected the Powhatan to supply them with food. The Powhatan had their own needs and weren't interested in supporting a colony of foreigners who took more than they gave. Violence broke out repeatedly. In 1622, the Powhatan launched a major attack that killed about a quarter of the English colonists. The English retaliated with brutal raids. This pattern of uneasy peace broken by violence would repeat throughout colonial history.

Jamestown's survival came down to one crop: tobacco. John Rolfe—the same man who married Pocahontas—figured out how to grow a type of tobacco that English smokers liked. The native tobacco in Virginia was too harsh for English taste, but Rolfe experimented with seeds from Trinidad and the Caribbean, creating a milder variety that became popular in England. A man could make more money growing tobacco in Virginia than he could doing almost anything in England.

Colonists who had been starving suddenly had a way to make money. The transformation was dramatic. Everyone planted tobacco. They planted it in their gardens, in the fort's courtyard, and even in the streets of Jamestown. Fields of tobacco spread along the riverbanks. The Virginia Company might not have found gold, but it had found something almost as valuable.

But tobacco farming was hard work. It required constant attention from planting through harvest. Seedlings needed protection. Plants required careful pruning. Leaves had to be picked at just the right time and then dried and cured properly. Tobacco also exhausted the soil quickly, usually within three years. This meant farmers needed more and more land. They couldn't stay in one place and farm the same fields year after year. They had to clear new land constantly, moving deeper into territory that belonged to Native peoples.

They also needed more workers. One person could only tend so many tobacco plants. At first, they relied on indentured servants—poor English people who agreed to work for several years in exchange for passage to Virginia and the promise of land when their service ended. The terms usually ran four to seven years. During that time, servants worked for their masters, who provided food, shelter, and clothing. Thousands of young men and women came to Virginia as indentured servants. Most were in their teens or early twenties. They came from the bottom rungs of English society. They were desperate enough to gamble on a dangerous voyage and years of hard labor for the chance at a better life.

Life was hard for indentured servants. Masters could be cruel. Work was exhausting. Disease killed many before their terms were up. Those who survived often struggled to get the land they'd been promised. Masters found ways to extend terms, claiming the servant had been disobedient. They added time for sickness or simply cheated them. Even servants who did get land found that the best plots along the rivers had already been claimed by earlier arrivals. They ended up on the frontier, where they were in constant danger from Native peoples whose land they were taking.

Jamestown never became a major city. The Colony of Virginia grew, but it spread out along the rivers rather than concentrating in one place. Planters wanted access to waterways for shipping tobacco. The landscape of Virginia became one of scattered plantations rather than dense towns. This pattern would shape Southern society for centuries.

The Rise of a Plantation Economy

Tobacco made Virginia profitable, and other Southern colonies followed the same model. Maryland, founded in 1632, grew tobacco. The Carolinas, settled in the 1660s, tried various crops before landing on rice and indigo. Georgia, the last British colony on the mainland, was settled in 1733 partly as a buffer against Spanish Florida.

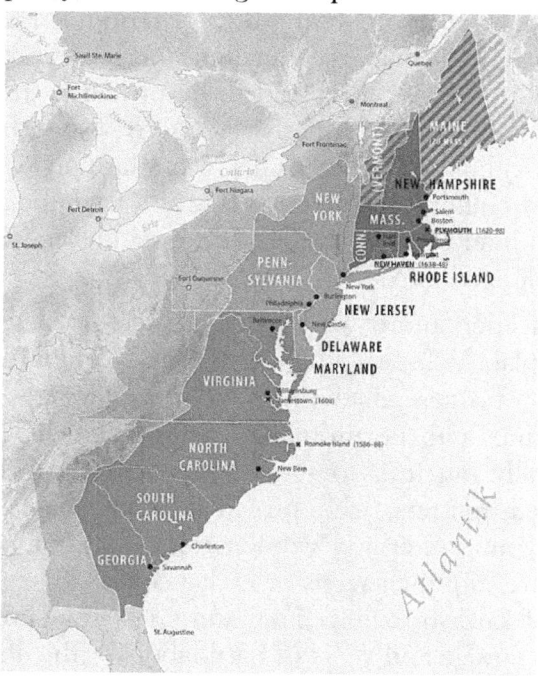

The Thirteen Colonies.'

All these colonies developed plantation economies. A plantation was a large agricultural estate focused on growing cash crops for export. Southern soil and climate were well-suited for crops like tobacco, rice, and eventually cotton. However, these crops needed intensive work, especially at harvest time.

The labor problem became the defining issue of Southern colonial society. Indentured servitude provided some workers but not enough. Indentured servants eventually earned their freedom. They then wanted their own land, which created competition with existing planters. The system was also unreliable. Servants might die, run away, or simply refuse to work as hard as masters wanted.

The solution, from the planters' perspective, was slavery. Enslaved Africans had been in Virginia since 1619, when a Dutch ship sold about twenty captured Africans to Jamestown colonists. At first, the legal status of these people was ambiguous. Some were treated as indentured servants and eventually freed, while others remained enslaved for life. Their children's status was unclear.

But by the 1660s, Virginia and other Southern colonies had passed laws that made slavery permanent and hereditary. If your mother was enslaved, you were enslaved. Slavery became defined by race. Black people could be enslaved for life. White people, no matter how poor, could not. This racial definition was new. Earlier forms of slavery in other societies had been based on conquest, debt, or religion, not skin color. The American system made race the determining factor.

The shift to slave labor happened gradually, but it accelerated quickly. In 1650, there were only a few hundred enslaved people in Virginia. By 1700, there were more than six thousand. By 1750, nearly 40 percent of Virginia's population was enslaved. In South Carolina, where rice plantations required even more labor, enslaved people became the majority of the population.

Slavery was brutal. Enslaved people had no legal rights. They couldn't testify in court against White people. They couldn't legally own property. They couldn't marry legally, though they formed families anyway. They could be bought, sold, beaten, or killed with minimal consequences for the owner. Masters had nearly absolute power over the people they enslaved.

A slave shackle found while digging in New Orleans.[6]

Families were separated when economic needs dictated. A planter might sell a husband to one buyer and a wife to another, or they might keep parents while selling their children. These separations caused a lot of grief, but they were considered normal business transactions. Rape was common, especially of enslaved women by masters and overseers. Children born from these assaults became property, adding to their father's wealth. People who resisted were punished savagely; they were whipped, branded, and mutilated to terrorize others into submission. The point was to break people's spirits and to make them accept their status as property.

Some enslaved people ran away, though where they could run to was limited. The colonies passed laws requiring people to carry passes when traveling. Slave patrols stopped and questioned Black people on the roads. Those caught without papers could be whipped or returned to their owners. A few runaways made it to Spanish Florida, where authorities sometimes granted freedom to fugitives from English colonies. Others tried to disappear into the backcountry or join Native American groups. Most who ran away were caught and returned.

Others resisted in smaller ways that didn't risk immediate death. They broke tools, claiming accidents. They feigned illness or incompetence. They stole food from their masters' supplies. These acts of resistance were dangerous but common. A few slaves led rebellions, though these were rare and brutally suppressed. The 1739 Stono Rebellion in South Carolina saw about twenty enslaved people kill several White people before militia forces killed or captured most of the rebels. The survivors were executed publicly as a warning to others.

The plantation economy created a Southern society unlike anything in the Northern colonies. Wealth was concentrated in the hands of large plantation owners. These planters became a colonial aristocracy. They built large houses, imported luxury goods, and dominated politics. Small farmers still existed, but they had less power and fewer opportunities. Poor Whites often struggled, though they clung to the idea that being White made them superior to enslaved Black people.

The economy was also precarious. Tobacco prices fluctuated. Planters went into debt buying land and enslaved people. If crops failed or prices dropped, fortunes could collapse. However, the system was profitable enough that it persisted and expanded. By the time of the American Revolution, slavery was the foundation of Southern economic and social life.

This had consequences that would shape American history for centuries. The South developed differently from the North. Its economy depended on forced labor. Its society was built on a racial hierarchy. Its political leaders fought to protect slavery. When those protections seemed threatened, the entire system would come apart in the bloodiest war America ever fought. But that's a story for later chapters.

Chapter 4: The New England Colonies

The Pilgrims and Puritans: A "City Upon a Hill"

In November 1620, a small ship called the Mayflower dropped anchor off the coast of Massachusetts. About a hundred passengers had survived the crossing. They are now known as the Pilgrims, though they simply saw themselves as English Separatists seeking religious freedom.

Though we now refer to all of them as "Pilgrims," only about a third of the Mayflower's passengers were Separatists seeking freedom to worship their own way. The rest—farmers, craftsmen, servants, and adventurers—came for economic reasons, not theology. The two groups called each other "Saints" and "Strangers."

The Separatists believed the Church of England was corrupt and beyond reform. They believed the only solution was to separate from it completely. This was illegal and dangerous. English law required everyone to attend Church of England services. The government saw religious uniformity as essential to social order. Separatists were persecuted, fined, and sometimes imprisoned. Some fled to the Netherlands, where religious tolerance was greater. The Dutch Republic allowed different Protestant groups to worship freely—a radical policy for the time.

But after a decade in Holland, the Pilgrims had grown uneasy. Their children were becoming Dutch, losing their English identity. The work available to foreigners was hard and poorly paid. They worried about their community's future. Some decided to try something more radical. They would go to America, where they could build their own society without interference from any government or established church.

They landed far north of their intended destination in Virginia. Bad weather and navigational errors had pushed them off course. Winter was coming. They had no shelter, little food, and no idea how to survive in this place. Before going ashore, forty-one male passengers signed the Mayflower Compact, establishing a framework for self-government. It wasn't a declaration of independence or democracy, but it established the principle that they would govern themselves by agreement rather than by orders from England.

Embarkation of the Pilgrims by Robert Walter Weir.⁶

That first winter killed half of them. Disease, cold, and malnutrition took a steady toll. They lived on the ship while trying to build shelters onshore. The survivors likely would have died too if not for the help from the Wampanoag people. A man named Squanto, who had learned English after being kidnapped and taken to Europe years earlier, taught them how to plant corn, where to fish, and how to survive. Without this help, the Plymouth Colony likely would have failed within its first year.

In fall 1621, the Pilgrims and Wampanoag shared a harvest feast that later inspired the Thanksgiving myth, though at the time it was a diplomatic gathering rather than a formal holiday. The reality was even more complicated. The Pilgrims and Wampanoag had formed an alliance based on mutual need. The Wampanoag had been devastated by disease and needed allies against rival tribes. The Pilgrims needed help surviving.

Plymouth remained small. It never grew into a major colony. The real story of New England actually begins with a different group: the Puritans.

Puritans weren't Separatists. They didn't want to leave the Church of England; they wanted to purify it from within. They wanted to strip away what they saw as Catholic practices and return to simpler, more direct worship. But like the Separatists, they faced pressure in England. King Charles I and his archbishop were cracking down on religious dissent. So, many Puritans decided to leave.

In 1630, about a thousand Puritans arrived in Massachusetts Bay. Their leader, John Winthrop, gave a sermon before landing. He told them they were creating "a city upon a hill"—a model Christian community that would serve as an example to the world. If they succeeded, God would bless them. If they failed, the world would mock them, and their cause would be discredited. The stakes were eternal. They weren't just building a colony; they were also proving that their vision of proper Christianity could work.

The Massachusetts Bay Colony grew quickly. Unlike Virginia, which mainly attracted single men looking for profit, Massachusetts attracted families looking for a godly life. They came prepared, bringing tools, supplies, livestock, and skills. Ministers came with their congregations. Craftsmen brought their trades. They had capital to invest and plans to execute. They established towns, not scattered plantations. Between 1630 and 1642, about twenty thousand Puritans migrated to New England during what became known as the Great Migration. This massive influx gave Massachusetts a strong demographic and economic foundation that Virginia had taken decades to achieve.

The Puritans built a society based on their religious beliefs. Church and state were intertwined. In Massachusetts Bay, only male church members in good standing could vote or hold office. Town meetings handled local government, with male church members making decisions collectively. This wasn't democracy as we understand it—only a minority could participate—but it was more participatory than most European governments at the time.

Puritan life was strict. They believed in hard work, frugality, and discipline. They read the Bible constantly. They watched each other for signs of sin. Dancing was suspect. Theater was forbidden. Fancy clothing was discouraged. The Puritans weren't joyless, though. They drank, celebrated holidays, and enjoyed life's pleasures in moderation. However, they believed every action had moral significance. You couldn't just live; you had to live righteously.

Education mattered deeply to Puritans. They wanted everyone to read the Bible, so they established schools. In 1647, Massachusetts passed the "Old Deluder Satan Act," requiring towns of fifty families or more to hire a schoolteacher. Towns of a hundred families had to establish a grammar school. This was revolutionary. In most of the world, education was reserved for the wealthy. In Puritan New England, it became a community responsibility. In 1636, they founded Harvard College to train ministers. The college would ensure a steady supply of educated clergy to lead congregations. New England would have the highest literacy rates in the colonies. This emphasis on education shaped American culture in profound ways, creating expectations that citizens should be literate and informed.

However, the Puritan vision of a "city upon a hill" had a dark side. They had come to America for their own religious freedom, not to create a society where everyone was free to believe what they wanted. Dissenters weren't tolerated. If you disagreed with Puritan theology or questioned the ministers' authority, you were in trouble.

Dissenters and War: Roger Williams, Anne Hutchinson, and King Philip's War

Roger Williams was a Puritan minister who arrived in Massachusetts in 1631. He quickly became a problem. Williams argued that the government should not enforce religious laws. He said the church and state should be completely separate. He also claimed that the colonists had no right to Native American land unless they bought it fairly. The English charter from the king wasn't enough. These ideas were radical and dangerous to the Puritan leadership.

In 1636, Massachusetts authorities ordered Williams to leave. He fled south with a few followers and founded Providence, which became part of Rhode Island. Rhode Island was different. Williams established religious freedom and the separation of church and state. Anyone could worship as they pleased. Even people with strange or unpopular beliefs were welcome. Other colonies thought Rhode Island was a dangerous mess, but it thrived.

Anne Hutchinson posed a different challenge. She was a midwife and mother of fifteen children who held Bible study meetings in her home. These meetings became popular, sometimes attracting sixty or more people. Hutchinson was smart, well-educated in theology, and charismatic. She taught that people could have direct communication with God through the Holy Spirit. They didn't need ministers as intermediaries. She distinguished between a "covenant of works"—trying to earn salvation through good behavior—and a "covenant of grace"—receiving salvation as a free gift from God. She also suggested that some of Boston's ministers preached a covenant of works and, therefore, weren't among the "elect"—the people God had chosen for salvation.

This was heresy to Puritan leaders. Hutchinson was challenging their authority and suggesting that laypeople, especially women, could interpret scripture like trained ministers. Women in Puritan society were expected to be silent in church and subordinate to male authority. Hutchinson's popular meetings and theological confidence went against these expectations.

In 1637, she was put on trial. The governor and ministers interrogated her for two days. She defended herself skillfully, showing impressive knowledge of scripture and theology. Eventually, she claimed to have received direct revelations from God, declaring that God had spoken to her "by an immediate voice." That sealed her fate. Direct revelation bypassed the authority of ministers and the Bible itself. She was banished and moved to Rhode Island. She was later killed near what is now the Bronx in 1643 during conflicts known as Kieft's War.

These examples showed that Puritan society had limits. You could live there if you accepted their rules and beliefs. If you didn't, you had to leave.

Meanwhile, relations with Native peoples were deteriorating. As more colonists arrived, they took more land. The pattern from Virginia repeated itself in New England. English settlements expanded along rivers and coastlines. Native peoples were pushed back into less desirable territory. Treaties were made and broken. The English legal system didn't recognize Native concepts of land use. Native peoples saw land as something used collectively, not owned individually. English colonists saw land as property to be bought, fenced, and exclusively controlled. These incompatible views led to constant friction.

English livestock made things worse. Pigs and cattle wandered into Native fields and destroyed crops. English colonists expected Native peoples to fence their fields, but this wasn't part of Native agricultural practice. Disputes over damaged crops led to violence. English courts sided with colonists. Native peoples found themselves subject to English law without having agreed to it.

By the 1670s, many Native groups had lost up to 90 percent of their population since European contact, primarily due to disease and displacement. The diseases that had killed so many in earlier decades continued their work. Those who remained faced shrinking territories and increasing English demands for submission.

Metacom, known to the English as King Philip, was the leader of the Wampanoag. His father had made the alliance with the Pilgrims fifty years earlier. But now the situation was different. English colonists vastly outnumbered Native peoples. The English demanded that Native groups disarm and submit to colonial authority. They tried Native people in English courts for crimes while also pushing deeper into Native territory.

In 1675, tensions exploded into King Philip's War. It was the bloodiest conflict per capita in North American colonial history. Native forces attacked English settlements throughout New England. They used guerrilla tactics, hitting towns quickly and disappearing into the forests. They burned dozens of settlements. They killed colonists and destroyed livestock.

The English and their Native allies counterattacked. They burned Native villages and destroyed food supplies. They attacked in winter, when people were most vulnerable. The English sold captured Native people into slavery—some within the colonies and others to plantations in the Caribbean—breaking up families and communities. The war killed thousands on both sides and devastated the New England economy.

The colonists won, but barely. In Plymouth Colony alone, as many as 8 percent of adult male colonists perished in the conflict. Twelve of ninety English towns were completely destroyed, and others were badly damaged. Many families lost homes, livestock, and savings. The colonial government went deep into debt. For Native peoples, the consequences were catastrophic. Thousands died in combat, from starvation after their food supplies were destroyed, or from disease. Survivors were killed, enslaved, or driven from their lands. The Wampanoag, Narragansett, and other groups that had dominated southern New England for thousands of years lost their independence. Metacom was killed in August 1676, and his head was displayed on a pike in Plymouth for decades as a grim warning.

King Philip's War marked a turning point. After 1676, English dominance in New England was secure. Native peoples remained, but they were marginalized populations with little power. The frontier of conflict moved west. The Puritan experiment would continue, but the land it occupied was now permanently in English hands.

Town Halls and Witch Trials: Life in Puritan New England

Puritan New England was built around the town. Unlike Virginia's scattered plantations, New England settlements clustered together. A typical town had a meetinghouse at its center. It served as both a church and a town hall. It would be surrounded by homes, shops, and common land. Beyond the town center lay fields and pastures.

Adult male church members gathered regularly to make decisions. They elected selectmen to handle daily business. They voted on taxes, land distribution, and local laws. They debated issues and settled disputes. Not everyone could participate, but those who could had a lot of influence.

Land was distributed carefully. New towns were granted land by the colonial government. Town leaders then allocated plots to individual families based on their status and usefulness to the community. A minister might get a large lot. A wealthy merchant would get more than a poor farmer. But even poor families got some land. The goal was to create stable communities where families could support themselves.

Life revolved around work, family, and church. Most people were farmers, though towns also had craftsmen, merchants, and professionals. Families were large. Women often bore eight or ten children, though many died young. Everyone worked. Children helped on farms or learned trades. Women managed households, which was exhausting work. They cooked, cleaned, made clothes, preserved food, and often helped in fields or shops.

Church attendance was mandatory. Services lasted for hours. Ministers delivered long sermons analyzing scripture. The congregation sat on hard wooden benches, organized by social status. Falling asleep during services could get you fined.

Puritans believed in witchcraft. They thought Satan was real and active in the world. Witches were people who had made pacts with the devil to gain supernatural powers. Most colonies had laws against witchcraft. Accusations were rare, but they were taken seriously. A few people were executed for witchcraft in various colonies throughout the 1600s.

Then came Salem.

In 1692, several girls in Salem Village began having fits. They screamed, contorted their bodies, and claimed to be tormented by invisible forces. When questioned, they named women they said were witches tormenting them. The accusations spread. More people—mostly women—were accused of witchcraft. Some were seen as outsiders or troublemakers. Some were respectable church members. Fear and hysteria took over.

Colonial authorities took the accusations seriously. They arrested suspects and held trials using special procedures. The usual rules of evidence were relaxed. "Spectral evidence" was allowed—testimony that the accused person's spirit or specter had appeared to the witness and caused harm. This was controversial even at the time. A person's physical body might be in one place while their spirit supposedly tormented someone miles away. How could anyone defend themselves against such charges?

A fanciful illustration of the Salem witch trials.[7]

The accused were pressured to confess and name other witches. Those who confessed and cooperated were spared execution. They might face prison time or some other punishment, but they lived. Those who maintained their innocence were more likely to be convicted and executed. This encouraged false confessions and false accusations.

Nineteen people were hanged between June and September 1692. One man, Giles Corey, was crushed to death under heavy stones for refusing to enter a plea. He was perhaps trying to protect his property from confiscation. Several others died in prison while awaiting trial.

The Salem witch trials revealed the darker side of Puritan society. The trials showed what could happen when religious certainty collided with fear and social tension. Neighbor turned against neighbor. Accusations were based on flimsy evidence—spectral visions, old grudges, or mere suspicion. The legal process broke down, and hysteria overwhelmed reason.

By 1693, the trials had ended. Colonial authorities realized they had made terrible mistakes. Some judges even publicly apologized. The Massachusetts government eventually compensated the victims' families, but the damage was done. Over twenty people were dead. Communities were shattered, and trust had been broken.

New England had been built as a "city upon a hill," a model of righteousness. But like all human societies, it was capable of both great achievement and terrible injustice. The Puritans created towns with strong local governments, built schools, and established traditions of education and civic participation. They also banished dissenters, fought brutal wars, and executed innocent people. Understanding New England means seeing both sides of this story.

Chapter 5: The Middle Colonies

New York, Pennsylvania, and the Melting Pot

Between New England and the South lay a cluster of colonies that didn't fit neatly into either area. New York, New Jersey, Pennsylvania, and Delaware became known as the Middle Colonies. They were middle in geography and middle in character. They were more diverse than New England, less dependent on slavery than the South, and more tolerant than either.

The story starts with the Dutch. In 1624, the Dutch West India Company established New Netherland, with settlements at Fort Orange (present-day Albany) and on Manhattan Island, which soon became the colony's center. The Dutch were interested in trade, especially furs. They wanted to tap into the profitable beaver pelt trade that was making fortunes in Canada. They built New Amsterdam at the southern tip of Manhattan as a trading post and port. The location was perfect. It had a natural harbor with access to the Hudson River, which reached deep into the interior where furs could be obtained.

The settlement was messy and chaotic compared to the orderly Puritan towns of New England. People from many nations lived there—Dutch, English, French, Germans, Scandinavians, Sephardic Jews fleeing persecution, and Africans, both free and enslaved. By the 1640s, observers reported that as many as eighteen languages were spoken in New Amsterdam. No one cared much about religion or ethnicity as long as business got done. If you could trade, you were welcome. This diversity was unusual for the 1600s, when most European settlements tried to maintain religious and ethnic uniformity.

The Dutch never sent many colonists. The company focused on profits, not settlement. Why send farmers when you could just trade for furs? This made strategic sense for business but left the colony weak. By 1664, New Netherland's population was between seven and nine thousand, compared to about sixty thousand in New England.

When England decided it wanted the territory, the Dutch couldn't hold it. The location was too valuable to ignore. It sat between New England and the Southern colonies, controlled access to the interior via the Hudson River, and had an excellent harbor. In 1664, English warships arrived at New Amsterdam. The Dutch governor, Peter Stuyvesant, wanted to fight, but the colonists refused. They saw no point in dying for a company that barely supported them and seemed more interested in obtaining wealth than protecting settlers. The Dutch surrendered New Amsterdam without any serious fighting. England renamed the colony New York after the duke of York, who would later become King James II.

English control didn't change the colony's character much. New York remained diverse and commercial. English law replaced Dutch law, but the mix of peoples and languages continued. The colony attracted merchants, traders, and anyone looking to make money. New York City grew into a major port, handling grain from the Hudson Valley and connecting colonial trade to the Atlantic world.

Pennsylvania started differently. William Penn was an English Quaker, a member of the Religious Society of Friends. Quakers believed in direct spiritual experience without priests or formal liturgy. They rejected violence, refused to swear oaths, and treated women as spiritual equals. They called everyone "thee" and "thou" instead of using titles, which offended people who thought social hierarchy mattered. English authorities hated them. Quakers were fined, imprisoned, and sometimes executed for their beliefs.

Penn was unusual. He was a wealthy, well-connected Quaker. His father had been an admiral, and the king owed the family money. In 1681, Penn convinced King Charles II to grant him land in America to settle the debt. The amount owed was substantial—sixteen thousand pounds, a fortune. The king agreed, probably happy to get rid of some troublesome Quakers and clear the debt simultaneously. Penn received an enormous tract of land—about twenty-eight million acres (roughly forty-four thousand square miles)—one of the largest private land grants in history. The king named it Pennsylvania—"Penn's woods"—over

Penn's objections. Penn thought the name sounded too self-aggrandizing, but the king insisted.

Penn had a vision. He wanted to create a colony based on religious freedom and fair dealing. He called it a "holy experiment." Pennsylvania would welcome people of all Christian denominations and others who believed in God. The government would be elected by property owners. Laws would be made by consensus. Native peoples would be treated fairly and paid for their land. Penn codified his principles in the 1682 Frame of Government, which guaranteed freedom of conscience and an elected assembly.

Penn's Treaty with the Indians by Benjamin West.⁹

Penn advertised throughout Europe. He published pamphlets in English, German, and Dutch, describing Pennsylvania as a land of opportunity where people could worship freely and prosper through hard work. He promised cheap land, good soil, and a government that wouldn't persecute anyone for their beliefs. His timing was perfect. Religious wars and persecution had made life miserable for many Europeans. Economic opportunity was limited for ordinary people. Pennsylvania offered an escape.

Thousands came—English Quakers fleeing persecution, German Lutherans and Pietists seeking religious freedom, Welsh Baptists looking for community, Irish Catholics, Scottish Presbyterians, French Huguenots, and others. Ships arrived regularly carrying families and their possessions. By 1700, Pennsylvania's population was around 18,000, and by 1750, it had grown to roughly 125,000, making it one of the largest colonies. Only Virginia had more people.

Philadelphia, Penn's "city of brotherly love," became the most important city in the colonies. Penn laid it out on a grid pattern with wide streets and public squares. The city attracted craftsmen, merchants, printers, and professionals. Benjamin Franklin would make his career there. The city became a center of colonial intellectual and political life.

Penn's treatment of Native peoples was better than that of most colonists, though his successors often abandoned his policies of fair dealing. He negotiated treaties and insisted on paying for land. He met with Delaware leaders and tried to establish friendly relations.

However, Pennsylvania's rapid growth made conflict inevitable. Settlers pushed westward, and land speculators ignored treaties. After Penn's death, his sons and later colonial leaders often engaged in fraudulent practices, such as the infamous "Walking Purchase" of 1737, which cheated the Delaware out of vast territories. The colony's commitment to pacifism made it hard to defend the frontier. Relations with Native peoples deteriorated.

The "holy experiment" had limits. Religious tolerance didn't extend to atheists, who were seen as a threat to the social order. Most people at the time believed society needed shared religious values to function. Political participation required owning property, which excluded poor laborers and servants. Women could worship freely, but they couldn't vote or hold office.

Slavery existed in Pennsylvania, though Quakers increasingly questioned it. By the mid-1700s, some meetings formally disowned slaveholding members. The contradiction between Quaker beliefs about the "inner light" in every person and the practice of slaveholding troubled many Friends. Some Quakers became early abolitionists, arguing that slaveholding contradicted their beliefs about human equality. However, the colony's economy still depended partly on enslaved labor, especially in Philadelphia, where wealthy merchants owned enslaved people who worked as domestic servants and dockworkers.

Still, Pennsylvania stood out. It offered more freedom and opportunity than most places in the world. Immigrants kept coming. The colony prospered. Penn's vision was imperfect and incomplete, but it influenced American thinking about religious liberty, democratic government, and peaceful coexistence.

Farms, Ports, and a Growing American Identity

The Middle Colonies developed an economy that was different from both the North and the South. They grew grain—wheat, barley, and rye—earning the nickname "breadbasket colonies." The soil was good. The climate was right. Farms were midsized and usually worked by families with perhaps a hired hand or two. This was neither the small subsistence farms of New England nor the large slave plantations of the South.

Grain farming was profitable. Wheat could be exported to other colonies and to Europe, where demand was strong. Caribbean sugar islands needed food for their enslaved workers and couldn't spare land for growing grain. Southern Europe bought American wheat when its harvests failed. Mills processed grain into flour, which shipped even better than raw wheat and commanded higher prices. The Hudson and Delaware Rivers provided easy transportation from farms to ports. Ports like New York and Philadelphia became major export centers, handling not just local grain but also furs from the interior and goods transshipped between colonies. Merchants grew wealthy managing this trade.

The Middle Colonies attracted skilled workers. German immigrants brought advanced farming techniques that had been developed over centuries. They knew how to manage soil fertility, rotate crops to prevent exhaustion, and build barns that protected livestock and stored grain. They introduced the Conestoga wagon, named after the Conestoga River in Pennsylvania. These were sturdy vehicles pulled by teams of horses or oxen that could haul heavy loads over rough roads. The wagons had curved floors to prevent cargo from shifting and white canvas covers for protection. The Conestoga wagon became famous for its durability and design, inspiring the covered wagons used during the 19th-century westward migration. German craftsmen brought skills in metalworking, clockmaking, gunsmithing, and printing. They established workshops that produced high-quality goods.

Diversity was the Middle Colonies' defining characteristic. In Pennsylvania, you might find a German Lutheran village where services were conducted in German, an English Quaker town where plain dress and silent worship were the norm, and a Scots-Irish Presbyterian settlement where fiery sermons and whiskey distilling were common practices, all within a few miles of each other. Each group maintained its language, customs, and religious practices. Germans published newspapers in German. Different churches held services in different languages. Traditional foods, dress, and holidays continued from the old country. People didn't always get along—ethnic tensions flared, religious disputes erupted, and competition over land caused friction—but they learned to live together because they had to.

The Middle Colonies developed more tolerant attitudes by necessity. When your neighbor spoke a different language and worshiped differently, you either learned tolerance or faced constant conflict. Most chose tolerance, at least to a degree. Churches of different denominations stood near each other. People did business across ethnic and religious lines. A German farmer might sell wheat to an English merchant. A Scottish craftsman might work for a Dutch patron. These interactions happened daily. Intermarriage happened too, though it caused controversy. When a German Lutheran married an English Quaker, both families often objected, but such marriages slowly became more common and helped break down barriers.

This environment encouraged a certain practical mindset. Ideology mattered less than getting along. Religious fervor was less intense than in Puritan New England. Social hierarchies were less rigid than in the South. A person's ability mattered more than their background. This wasn't modern equality—women still had limited rights, enslaved people had none, and poor people struggled—but there was more social mobility than in most of the world.

The Middle Colonies also developed stronger town and city life than the South. New York and Philadelphia became cities with complex economies. By the mid-1700s, Philadelphia had about twenty thousand people, surpassing Boston to become the largest city in the colonies. New York wasn't far behind.. Carpenters, shoemakers, silversmiths, tailors, and other craftsmen formed associations to regulate trades and maintain quality standards. Merchants built trading networks that stretched to the Caribbean, Europe, and Africa. Printers published newspapers and books. Benjamin Franklin's Pennsylvania Gazette became one of the most influential newspapers in the colonies. Taverns served as social and political meeting places where men discussed business, politics, and news. Urban culture flourished in ways it didn't in rural Virginia or even in New England's smaller towns.

Education varied. The Middle Colonies lacked New England's public school system but relied on private, church, and community-supported schools to educate children. Literacy rates were high, especially among German and English settlers. The colonies produced their share of educated people, though higher education required going to college in New England or England.

Politics in the Middle Colonies reflected their diversity. No single faction could dominate permanently. Different groups formed coalitions based on economic interests or temporary alliances. Pennsylvania's assembly fought constantly with the Penn family's appointed governors over taxes and defense spending. New York's politics pitted merchants against farmers, English against Dutch, and various factions against each other.

This political messiness frustrated some colonists but created a useful experience. People learned to negotiate, compromise, and form coalitions. They learned that different groups could participate in government without the system collapsing. These lessons would prove valuable later when thirteen very different colonies had to work together.

By the mid-1700s, people from diverse backgrounds were developing a shared colonial identity, though strong ethnic enclaves like the Pennsylvania Germans remained distinct. When a child grew up speaking English in the street, German at home, and traded with Dutch merchants, that child's identity became complex and layered. They were becoming American—a hybrid identity shaped by diversity and the need to cooperate despite differences.

This process was uneven. Many people, especially first-generation immigrants, still identified primarily with their ethnic or religious group. German settlers in Pennsylvania's backcountry maintained the German language and culture for generations. Slowly, however, common interests and shared experiences created bonds across these divisions. Colonial currency, colonial laws, and colonial trade networks all created shared experiences. Young people who had grown up together in diverse communities often cared less about old-country distinctions than their parents did.

The Middle Colonies never attracted the attention that Massachusetts or Virginia did. They weren't founded on grand ideological experiments like the Puritans' "city upon a hill." They weren't built on the dramatic boom-and-bust of tobacco cultivation. They were practical, commercial, diverse, and a bit chaotic. But in many ways, they represented the future of America better than either New England or the South. The nation that would emerge from the Revolution would resemble Pennsylvania—diverse, commercial, and pluralistic (though still limited by inequality and exclusion)—more than any other region.

Chapter 6: The Road to Rebellion

The French and Indian War: A Victory with a Cost

By 1763, Britain's American empire consisted of thirteen colonies stretched along the Atlantic coast. New England had Massachusetts, New Hampshire, Rhode Island, and Connecticut. The middle region had New York, New Jersey, Pennsylvania, and Delaware. The South had Maryland, Virginia, North Carolina, South Carolina, and Georgia. These thirteen colonies had little in common. They competed with each other, distrusted each other, and rarely cooperated. However, Britain's policies after the French and Indian War would force them to choose between unity and submission.

What North America looked like before the French and Indian War.'

In 1754, a young Virginia militia officer named George Washington led a small force into the Ohio River Valley. He was twenty-two years old and ambitious. Virginia claimed the region, but so did France. The French had built a string of forts connecting Canada to Louisiana through the Ohio Valley. Washington's mission was to tell the French to leave. Instead, his men ambushed a small French party, killing the commander, Joseph Coulon de Jumonville. The French called it an assassination. Washington called it a skirmish. Either way, it started a war.

The conflict became known as the French and Indian War in the colonies, though it was part of a larger global struggle called the Seven Years' War. France and Britain were fighting for control of North America and competing for dominance in Europe, India, and the Caribbean. The North American theater was just one front in a world war, but for the colonists, it was everything.

The French had fewer colonists—about sixty thousand in all of New France compared to over one million in the British colonies—but they had strategic advantages. French traders and missionaries had built strong alliances with Native nations like the Huron, Algonquin, and Abenaki, who saw the British as the greater threat to their lands. The French built forts at key locations and controlled the water routes. The British had more colonists but weaker Native alliances. Most British colonists were farmers who wanted Native land, making alliances difficult. Both empires wanted control of the profitable fur trade and the strategic Ohio Valley.

The war went badly for Britain at first. In 1755, General Edward Braddock led a large force to capture Fort Duquesne at the forks of the Ohio River. His army included British regulars and colonial militia, including Washington. Braddock was confident since he had professional soldiers, artillery, and numbers. However, the French and their Native allies ambushed Braddock's army as it marched through the forest. The British soldiers, trained in European warfare, bunched together in formation. The French and their Native allies fired from behind trees. Braddock was killed. His army broke and ran. Washington helped organize the retreat.

French and Native forces won several other victories. They captured British forts like Oswego and William Henry. They raided frontier settlements throughout Pennsylvania, Virginia, and New York. Families fled east. Colonial militias proved unreliable, poorly trained, and unwilling to fight far from home.

Benjamin Franklin proposed a plan for colonial unity at the Albany Congress in 1754, but the colonies rejected it. The Albany Plan of Union would have created a Grand Council with representatives from each colony and a president-general appointed by the Crown. This council could levy taxes, raise armies, and conduct diplomacy with Native nations. However, the colonial assemblies didn't trust each other and didn't want to give up any power to a central authority. The plan died quickly.

William Pitt became the new head of the British war effort in 1757. He understood that North America was crucial. He sent Britain's best generals and thousands of troops. He also changed policy toward the colonies, offering to reimburse them for military expenses. This encouraged colonial cooperation. Pitt poured resources into the war, running up enormous debts but winning victories.

The tide turned in 1758. British forces captured Louisbourg, the fortress guarding the entrance to the St. Lawrence River. In 1759, British forces captured Fort Niagara and drove the French from the Ohio Valley. However, the decisive battle came at Quebec.

General James Wolfe laid siege to Quebec. The city sat on high cliffs above the St. Lawrence River and seemed impregnable. Wolfe spent months trying to find a way in. Finally, he found a narrow path up the cliffs. On the night of September 12, British soldiers climbed up in the darkness. By morning, they were on the Plains of Abraham outside Quebec's walls. The French commander, the Marquis de Montcalm, led his army out to fight rather than wait for reinforcements. The battle lasted about fifteen minutes. British volleys broke the French lines. Both Wolfe and Montcalm were mortally wounded. Wolfe lived long enough to learn he had won. Quebec fell.

By 1760, British forces had captured Montreal, and French resistance collapsed. France was finished in North America.

The Treaty of Paris in 1763 confirmed Britain's victory. France gave up all its territory east of the Mississippi River except New Orleans. Spain, which had allied with France late in the war, gave up Florida to Britain. In compensation, France gave Spain the Louisiana Territory west of the Mississippi. Britain now controlled most of North America east of the river.

British colonists celebrated. The French threat was gone. The colonies could expand westward. However, the war created problems that would eventually tear the empire apart.

First, the war was expensive. Britain's national debt had doubled from £75 million to £133 million. The average British subject paid about twenty-six shillings per year in taxes; the average American colonist paid about one. The government decided that the American colonies should help pay for the war and for the troops that would remain to defend the frontier.

Second, the war changed the relationship between Britain and the colonies. Before the war, Britain had practiced salutary neglect. Colonial assemblies had grown used to running their own affairs. After the war, Parliament decided the colonies needed firmer management.

Third, the war created new conflicts with Native peoples. Britain's victory eliminated France as an ally for Native nations. British colonists started pouring into the Ohio Valley. British officials had promised to protect Native lands, but those promises evaporated.

The British commander, General Jeffrey Amherst, cut off gifts to Native allies and treated them with contempt. He restricted gunpowder and ammunition sales. The message was clear: Britain no longer needed Native allies.

In 1763, an Ottawa leader named Pontiac organized a coalition of tribes. They attacked British forts throughout the frontier. Hundreds of British soldiers and colonists died. Pontiac's War lasted more than a year. Some British officers discussed using biological warfare by giving Native peoples blankets infected with smallpox. At least one documented case occurred at Fort Pitt.

Britain responded with the Proclamation of 1763. King George III drew a line along the Appalachian Mountains. Colonists could not settle west of it. The land was reserved for Native peoples. Britain wanted to avoid expensive frontier wars.

This outraged colonists, who expected to claim that land. Land speculators like George Washington owned claims to millions of acres in the west, but the proclamation threatened those investments. Settlers refused to leave. The proclamation was widely ignored, and it created resentment.

The French and Indian War was a turning point. Britain had won control of North America but lost the trust of its American colonists.

"No Taxation Without Representation!": The Acts That Angered America

Britain needed money because of the crushing war debt. Parliament believed the colonies should contribute. British soldiers had died defending them. British taxpayers had paid enormous sums. The colonies were prosperous because trade was booming. Asking them to pay a share seemed reasonable from the British perspective.

The problem was how Parliament went about it. For decades, the colonies had taxed themselves through their own assemblies. Each colonial legislature voted on its own taxes, decided how to spend the money, and controlled its own finances. This was the English tradition— no taxation without consent of representatives. Now, Parliament was imposing taxes directly without asking the colonial assemblies. This was new and threatening.

The Sugar Act of 1764 came first. Parliament had taxed molasses imports since 1733, but the tax was so high that everyone smuggled it. The new act lowered the tax from six pence to three pence per gallon but promised strict enforcement. The act also expanded vice-admiralty courts, which operated without juries. Accused smugglers would be tried by judges appointed by the Crown, not by sympathetic colonial juries. The act placed new taxes on wine, coffee, and other imports. Merchants were unhappy, but most colonists weren't directly affected.

The Stamp Act of 1765 was different. This tax hit everyone. Every piece of printed paper needed a stamp showing the tax had been paid— newspapers, legal documents, licenses, and even playing cards and dice. The tax wasn't huge—it would have raised about £60,000 per year—but it was direct taxation by Parliament, where colonists had no representatives.

The colonies erupted in anger. The Stamp Act united groups that rarely agreed. Merchants organized boycotts of British goods. Lawyers and writers produced pamphlets arguing against the tax. Groups calling themselves the Sons of Liberty formed in cities and towns. They organized protests, intimidated stamp distributors, and sometimes destroyed property. In Boston, a mob destroyed Lieutenant Governor Thomas Hutchinson's house, breaking furniture, stealing belongings, and burning his manuscript history of Massachusetts. The violence shocked even opponents of the Stamp Act, but it showed how deep people's anger ran.

The core argument was about representation. Colonists insisted that only their own elected assemblies could tax them. Parliament responded that colonists were "virtually represented"—that members of Parliament represented all British subjects everywhere, not just those who elected them. The colonists wanted actual representation—colonists sitting in Parliament with voting power—or no parliamentary taxes at all.

The Virginia House of Burgesses, led by Patrick Henry, passed resolutions denouncing the Stamp Act. Other colonial assemblies followed. In October 1765, delegates from nine colonies met at the Stamp Act Congress in New York. They declared that only colonial assemblies could tax colonists. This was radical. Colonies that couldn't cooperate during the war were now working together against Parliament.

The boycotts worked. British merchants lost money and pressured Parliament to repeal the tax. In 1766, Parliament repealed the Stamp Act. However, Parliament also passed the Declaratory Act, asserting that it had full authority to make laws for the colonies "in all cases whatsoever." Parliament was backing down on tactics while claiming total power in principle.

In 1767, Parliament tried again. The Townshend Acts placed taxes on imported goods like glass, lead, paint, paper, and tea. Charles Townshend, the chancellor of the exchequer, thought these "external" taxes on imports would be more acceptable than the Stamp Act's "internal" taxes. He was wrong. Colonists saw through it. John Dickinson's Letters from a Farmer in Pennsylvania argued that Parliament had no right to tax the colonies for revenue, whether the taxes were internal or external.

Boycotts resumed. Women played a crucial role, organizing non-importation agreements and encouraging domestic production. Groups called Daughters of Liberty promoted American-made cloth. Wearing homespun clothing became a political statement.

The Townshend Acts also reorganized customs enforcement. Britain created the American Board of Customs Commissioners in Boston. Customs officials became more aggressive and corrupt. They seized ships on flimsy pretexts and kept a portion of the proceeds. Colonists hated them.

Tensions rose in Boston. British troops were sent to the city in 1768 to maintain order. Their presence infuriated Bostonians. Soldiers and townspeople clashed repeatedly. On March 5, 1770, a mob harassed soldiers guarding the customs house. Someone threw something. Someone yelled, "Fire!" The soldiers shot into the crowd. Five colonists died.

The incident became known as the Boston Massacre, though "massacre" overstated what happened. It was a tragedy born of tension and confusion, not a planned slaughter. However, colonial propagandists, especially Samuel Adams and Paul Revere, used it to inflame anti-British sentiment. Revere's engraving showed soldiers deliberately firing on peaceful citizens. The image spread throughout the colonies.

The Boston Massacre engraving by Paul Revere.[10]

The soldiers received fair trials. John Adams, Samuel's cousin, defended them in court. Two were convicted of manslaughter; the rest were acquitted. Adams believed in the rule of law even when it wasn't politically convenient. Still, the massacre deepened the divide between Britain and the colonies.

By 1770, Parliament had repealed most of the Townshend duties. Only the tax on tea remained, kept as a symbol of Parliament's right to tax. The crisis seemed to ease. Trade resumed. Prosperity returned. But underneath, resentment continued to build.

Massacre, Tea, and Intolerable Acts: The Point of No Return

For a few years, tensions cooled. Some radicals like Samuel Adams in Boston kept agitating, but most colonists seemed willing to live under British rule as long as Parliament didn't push too hard. Then Parliament made a mistake.

The Tea Act of 1773 wasn't supposed to be controversial. The British East India Company was in financial trouble. Parliament gave it a monopoly on tea sales in America and eliminated the middlemen who had been importing and selling tea. Tea would actually be cheaper than before, even with the Townshend tax. Everyone could save money on tea.

But colonists saw that the act would undercut colonial tea merchants, putting them out of business. Cheap tea would tempt people to buy it, effectively accepting Parliament's right to tax. Once colonists accepted the tea tax, Parliament might impose more.

When ships carrying East India Company tea arrived in colonial ports, resistance organized quickly. In Charleston, the tea was unloaded but locked in warehouses and never sold. In Philadelphia and New York, angry mobs met the ships at the docks. They turned back to England without unloading.

In Boston, Governor Thomas Hutchinson refused to send the ships back. His sons were tea agents. The standoff lasted for weeks. On the night of December 16, 1773, a group of colonists, some disguised as Mohawk Indians, boarded 3 ships and dumped 342 chests of tea into the harbor. The act, known in history as the Boston Tea Party, destroyed property worth about £10,000—equivalent to roughly two million dollars today. It was deliberate defiance and economic sabotage. Some colonists, including Benjamin Franklin, condemned it as vandalism. Others celebrated it as a principled stand against tyranny.

A depiction of the Boston Tea Party.[11]

Britain was furious. In spring 1774, Parliament passed the Coercive Acts. They were called the Intolerable Acts by colonists.

- The Boston Port Act closed Boston Harbor until the city paid for the destroyed tea.

- The Massachusetts Government Act revoked the colony's charter and placed it under direct royal control.

- The Administration of Justice Act allowed royal officials accused of crimes to be tried in Britain.

- The Quartering Act required colonists to house British soldiers.

- The Quebec Act extended Quebec's borders to the Ohio River and granted religious freedom to Catholics, which alarmed Protestant colonists.

These acts united colonial opposition like nothing had before. Even moderates thought Parliament had gone too far. Other colonies rallied to support Massachusetts. Virginia's House of Burgesses called for a day of fasting and prayer. When the royal governor dissolved the assembly, members met anyway and called for a continental congress.

In September 1774, delegates from twelve colonies met in Philadelphia at the First Continental Congress. Only Georgia abstained. The delegates weren't yet radicals seeking independence. Most hoped to remain within the empire, but they were united in opposition to the Intolerable Acts.

The First Continental Congress adopted the Suffolk Resolves, declaring the acts unconstitutional and urging resistance. It created the Continental Association, a complete boycott of British goods.

The First Continental Congress also sent a petition to King George III asking for redress of grievances. Britain ignored it. The king declared the colonies in rebellion. Militias drilled in town squares, and British troops stockpiled weapons in Boston. The question was no longer whether there would be conflict, but when—and where it would start.

Chapter 7: The War for Independence

"The Shot Heard 'Round the World": Lexington and Concord

The war began with an unplanned skirmish at Lexington, but the confrontation itself was no accident. Both sides had been preparing for months.

British General Thomas Gage commanded troops in Boston. He knew the countryside was filling with weapons and ammunition. Colonial militias were training openly. Something had to be done before the situation got worse. Gage decided to seize military supplies stored in Concord, about twenty miles from Boston. He ordered seven hundred soldiers to march there quietly at night, grab the weapons, and get back before anyone could react.

But the countryside was watching. Colonial spy networks tracked every British move. When the soldiers left Boston late on April 18, riders spread the alarm. Paul Revere and William Dawes rode through the night warning towns that British troops were coming. Revere is famous for the ride, but he was captured before reaching Concord. Dawes escaped, but he did not make it to Concord to deliver the news. A third rider, Samuel Prescott, carried the message the rest of the way.

By dawn on April 19, the British column reached Lexington, a small town on the road to Concord. About seventy militia members stood on the town green. Their captain, John Parker, supposedly told them not to fire unless fired upon. The British officer ordered the militia to disperse.

Someone fired a shot. Nobody knows who. Then both sides opened fire.

The fight only lasted minutes. Eight militiamen died. Ten were wounded. One British soldier was injured. The militia scattered, opening the way for the British to march on to Concord.

At Concord, the British found fewer weapons than expected. Colonists had hidden most of them. While British soldiers searched houses and barns, militia companies from surrounding towns gathered. Several hundred men took position at the North Bridge outside town. When British troops tried to cross, the militia fired. This time, the volleys were organized. Several British soldiers fell, and the British retreated across the bridge.

The British faced a problem. They were twenty miles from Boston. Militia were gathering from every direction. The march back became a nightmare. Colonial fighters lined the road, firing from behind trees, stone walls, and buildings. British soldiers in tight formations made easy targets. The soldiers tried to maintain order, but panic spread. Men broke ranks and ran.

British reinforcements met them at Lexington with artillery. This saved the column from complete disaster, but the fighting continued all the way back to Boston. By the time the British reached safety, they had lost 73 men killed, 174 wounded, and 26 missing. Colonial casualties were about 50 killed and 40 wounded.

The British had marched out expecting a quick raid. They came back bloodied and humiliated. The colonial militia had fought well. Armed resistance had begun.

News of Lexington and Concord spread fast. Within days, militia from all over New England converged on Boston. Thousands of armed men surrounded the city. The British were trapped. What started as a police action had become a siege.

The Second Continental Congress met in Philadelphia in May. Delegates faced a crisis. British and colonial forces were fighting. Men were dying. However, most delegates still hoped to avoid full war. They sent another petition to King George, asking him to protect colonial rights. They also created the Continental Army and appointed George Washington as commander.

Washington was a logical choice. He had military experience from the French and Indian War. He was from Virginia, which helped unite Northern and Southern colonies. He looked like a leader—he was tall, dignified, and disciplined. He also owned slaves and had wealth, which reassured conservatives who feared revolution might mean social chaos.

Washington arrived in Massachusetts in July to take command. He found what he considered a disorganized mob rather than a disciplined army. About fifteen thousand men camped around Boston with no uniforms, little organization, and not enough weapons or ammunition. They came and went as they pleased. Officers had no formal authority. Sanitation was terrible. Washington spent months imposing order, building fortifications, and trying to turn farmers into soldiers.

The first shots at Lexington and Concord had been fired by accident, but they started something that couldn't be stopped. The American Revolution had begun.

Declaring Independence: The Power of an Idea

For more than a year after Lexington and Concord, the colonies fought without declaring independence. Congress insisted they were loyal British subjects defending their rights against a corrupt Parliament. Many colonists still hoped the king would intervene, dismiss his ministers, and restore the old relationship. That hope died slowly.

The fighting continued through 1775. In June, the Battle of Bunker Hill showed that colonial militiamen could stand against British regulars even when defeated. The British won the hill but lost more than a thousand men doing it. In March 1776, Washington forced the British to evacuate Boston by placing captured artillery on the heights overlooking the city. The war was spreading, but its purpose remained unclear.

In January 1776, a pamphlet changed everything. Thomas Paine's Common Sense sold 150,000 copies in 3 months—an enormous number for a population of about 2.5 million. Paine wrote in plain language that anyone could understand. He attacked the monarchy itself, not just British policy. Kings were frauds, Paine argued. Hereditary rule was absurd. Why should one man's birth make him better than everyone else? America didn't need Britain. It could govern itself. Independence wasn't just possible—it was common sense.

The pamphlet gave people permission to think the unthinkable. Before Paine, most colonists couldn't imagine life outside the British Empire. After Paine, they couldn't imagine staying in. Paine had taken an idea that seemed radical and made it seem inevitable.

King George declared the colonies in rebellion and hired German auxiliary troops—mainly from Hesse—to fight them. These soldiers were professionals rented from German princes, which was a common practice at the time, but Patriots (colonists who wanted independence) called them "mercenaries" to stir outrage. The use of foreign soldiers against British subjects angered many colonists.

Britain rejected every petition for reconciliation. The Olive Branch Petition, sent by Congress in 1775, begged the king to protect colonial rights. George refused even to receive it. British ships bombarded coastal towns like Falmouth in Massachusetts and Norfolk in Virginia. The king clearly wasn't going to help. He was the enemy.

In June 1776, Virginia's legislature instructed its delegates to propose independence. Richard Henry Lee stood before Congress on June 7 and stated that "these United Colonies are, and of right ought to be, free and independent States."[i] Congress debated for days. Some delegates hesitated. Pennsylvania and New York wanted more time. South Carolina worried about slave rebellions if the empire collapsed. Some delegates still feared permanent separation from Britain. Independence meant real war, not just armed protest. It also meant possible defeat, which would mean execution for treason.

But the momentum was overwhelming. Congress appointed a committee to draft a declaration. The committee included John Adams, Benjamin Franklin, Roger Sherman, Robert Livingston, and Thomas Jefferson. Jefferson did most of the writing. He was thirty-three years old, a Virginia plantation owner and lawyer, and brilliant with words.

Jefferson's draft drew on Enlightenment philosophy, particularly John Locke's ideas about natural rights and government by consent. But Jefferson made those ideas sing. "We hold these truths to be self-evident," he wrote, "that all men are created equal, that they are endowed by their Creator with certain unalienable Rights, that among these are Life, Liberty and the pursuit of Happiness."[ii]

This was radical. Most of the world still lived under kings who claimed to rule by divine right. Jefferson said government existed only to protect people's rights. When the government failed to do that, people could overthrow it. This wasn't just a break with Britain; it was a challenge to monarchies everywhere. It's also important to understand that for most

---

[i] "Lee Resolution." https://www.archives.gov/milestone-documents/lee-resolution

[ii] "Declaration of Independence: A Transcription." https://www.archives.gov/founding-docs/declaration-transcript

people in 1776, the phrase "all men" referred to white, property-owning men. It was not applied to enslaved people, women, or the propertyless. The universal interpretation that seems obvious today was not what most people understood at the time.

The declaration listed grievances against King George. He had dissolved colonial legislatures, maintained standing armies, imposed taxes without consent, cut off trade, and violated basic rights. He had hired foreign mercenaries to kill colonists. He had incited slave rebellions and encouraged Native attacks on frontier settlements. The list went on for paragraphs, building a legal case for separation.

Congress debated the declaration for three days. They cut about a quarter of Jefferson's draft, including a passage condemning slavery and the slave trade. Jefferson had blamed the king for forcing slavery on the colonies, ignoring the colonists' own willing participation in the system. Southern delegates refused to accept any criticism of an institution they depended on. Northern delegates who profited from the slave trade stayed quiet. The final document kept the soaring language about equality while avoiding the contradiction of men who owned slaves declaring all men equal. Abigail Adams would remind her husband, John, that the declaration's principles should apply to women too, but that suggestion went nowhere.

On July 2, 1776, Congress voted for independence. Twelve colonies voted yes. New York abstained but would approve days later. On July 4, Congress approved the final wording of the Declaration of Independence. The date would become the nation's birthday, though the vote for independence happened two days earlier.

Declaration of Independence by John Trumbull.[13]

Not everyone was happy. Some delegates refused to sign. Others signed, knowing they were risking everything. According to a popular story, Benjamin Franklin joked, "We must all hang together, or assuredly we shall all hang separately."[i] It wasn't really a joke. If Britain won, the signers would likely be executed for treason. John Hancock signed first, writing his name large enough, he said, so King George could read it without his spectacles.

The declaration didn't win the war. It didn't create a functioning government. But it did something important. It put the Revolution's purpose in writing. This wasn't just about taxes or representation anymore. It was about universal principles—equality, rights, self-government. Those principles would outlive the men who wrote them and inspire revolutions worldwide.

The declaration also made compromise impossible. Any settlement that didn't include independence was now politically unacceptable for Americans. You couldn't declare independence and then negotiate to stay in the empire. You couldn't proclaim all men equal and then accept subjugation. The declaration committed America to ideas that would take centuries to fulfill, but the commitment was real.

News of independence spread through the colonies. People read it aloud in public squares. Crowds cheered and tore down statues of King George. Church bells rang. Soldiers heard it in camp. Some celebrated. Others worried about the fight ahead. Not everyone wanted to leave the British fold. In New York, Washington had the declaration read to his troops before they faced a massive British invasion. The declaration said America was independent, but Britain still had to be convinced. That would take seven more years of war.

Washington, Valley Forge, and Yorktown: How America Won

Declaring independence was one thing. Winning it was another. On paper, Britain should have crushed the rebellion easily. Britain had the world's most powerful navy, a professional army, and the wealth of an empire. America had farmers with muskets, no navy, and almost no money. The war lasted eight years. America won through persistence, strategy, foreign help, and British mistakes.

---

[i] Keller, Robert Cass. "We Must All Hang Together..."
https://digitalcommons.butler.edu/wordways/vol9/iss1/3/

The first year went badly. In the summer of 1776, British General William Howe landed thirty-two thousand troops on Staten Island. Washington had about twenty thousand men, mostly inexperienced militia. Howe pushed Washington out of New York in a series of battles. At the Battle of Long Island in August, the British nearly trapped and destroyed Washington's entire army. Washington managed a nighttime evacuation across the East River, saving his forces but losing New York City. The Continental Army retreated across New Jersey, losing men through desertion and capture. Enlistments were expiring (many soldiers had signed up for short terms of service). By December, Washington had fewer than three thousand soldiers left. The Revolution looked finished.

Washington needed a victory. On Christmas night 1776, he led his army across the ice-choked Delaware River and attacked Hessian forces in Trenton, New Jersey. The Germans were sleeping off their Christmas celebrations. The Americans surprised them, capturing nearly a thousand prisoners and seizing badly needed supplies. A week later, Washington won another small victory at Princeton. These weren't major battles, but they mattered psychologically. The Continental Army could win. The cause wasn't dead. Men who had been ready to go home signed up for another year.

The war settled into a pattern. The British controlled cities. The Americans controlled the countryside. British armies could win battles, but they couldn't hold territory. Every time they marched into the interior, their supply lines were stretched too thin, and militiamen harassed them constantly. The British also struggled with poor coordination between commanders and changing strategies from London. Some British generals, like Howe, seemed reluctant to press their advantages. Others were aggressive but reckless.

In 1777, British General John Burgoyne led an army south from Canada, planning to cut New England off from the other colonies. The strategy made sense on paper: control the Hudson River Valley and isolate the most rebellious region. Burgoyne captured Fort Ticonderoga easily. But then everything went wrong. His army became bogged down in the wilderness. Loyalist support failed to materialize. American forces under General Horatio Gates blocked his path. At the Battle of Bennington, Americans destroyed a Hessian detachment Burgoyne had sent to find supplies. Burgoyne kept pushing south, deeper into hostile territory. American forces surrounded him at Saratoga, New York. After two battles in September and October, Burgoyne had no choice. On October 17, 1777, he surrendered his entire army—nearly six thousand men. It was the first major American victory.

Saratoga changed everything. France had been secretly helping America with money and weapons since 1776. Benjamin Franklin had gone to Paris as an unofficial ambassador, charming French society and lobbying for support. Now, the French saw a chance to weaken their old enemy, Britain. The Americans had proved they could win. In February 1778, France signed a treaty of alliance with America. The French provided money, troops, and most importantly, a navy that could challenge British control of the seas. Spain joined the war against Britain in 1779. The Netherlands followed in 1780. What had been a colonial rebellion became a global conflict. Britain now faced enemies across Europe, in the Caribbean, in India, and on the high seas. Resources had to be divided. The American theater was no longer Britain's only concern.

The winter of 1777–78 tested the Continental Army's endurance. While the British occupied Philadelphia and lived comfortably, Washington camped at Valley Forge, Pennsylvania, about twenty miles away. The army lacked food, clothing, and shelter. Congress couldn't pay for supplies, and state governments didn't send what was promised. Men wrapped rags around their feet because they had no shoes. They built crude huts, but many lacked blankets. Diseases spread through the camp—typhus, typhoid, dysentery, and pneumonia. About two thousand soldiers died that winter, not from battle but from cold, hunger, and illness. Some deserted. Others barely survived. Washington wrote desperate letters to Congress and state governors, but little help came.

However, Valley Forge also strengthened the army. A Prussian officer, Baron Friedrich von Steuben, arrived. Steuben was a professional soldier who volunteered to train the Continental Army. He spoke little English but used interpreters and demonstrations to drill the troops. He taught them to march in formation, load and fire quickly, and use bayonets effectively. He wrote a training manual that became standard for the army. He turned farmer-soldiers into disciplined troops who could stand in open battle against British regulars. When spring came, Washington's army was smaller but better trained and more confident.

The war moved south in 1778. The British believed Loyalists (those who were loyal to the empire) were stronger in the Southern colonies and that enslaved people might rise up to support the Crown if offered freedom. They captured Savannah, Georgia, in December 1778. In May 1780, they captured Charleston, South Carolina, along with five thousand Continental soldiers—the worst American defeat of the war. British forces under Lord Cornwallis swept through the region, winning major victories.

But British success in battle didn't translate to political control. The Southern countryside became a brutal civil war between Patriots and Loyalists. Militias on both sides burned farms, killed prisoners, and terrorized civilians. Families were divided. Neighbors who had lived peacefully for years turned violent. The British found that winning battles didn't mean controlling territory. As soon as their army moved on, Patriots retook the area.

American General Nathanael Greene took command in the South in October 1780. Greene was a Rhode Island Quaker who had never fired a shot before the war. He became one of Washington's best generals. Greene understood he couldn't defeat the British in open battle, but he didn't need to. He divided his army into mobile units, forcing the British to split their forces to chase them. He retreated when necessary, drawing British armies deep into hostile territory.

At the Battle of Cowpens in January 1781, American General Daniel Morgan used clever tactics to destroy a British force. At Guilford Courthouse in March, Greene fought Cornwallis to a draw. The British technically won, but they lost so many men that they had to retreat. Cornwallis won battles but couldn't pacify the region. His army got smaller and more exhausted with each victory.

Cornwallis moved his army to Yorktown, Virginia, on the coast in 1781. He planned to receive supplies and reinforcements by sea and possibly link up with other British forces. But the French Navy showed up first. A French fleet under Admiral de Grasse sailed from the Caribbean and defeated a British fleet at the Battle of the Chesapeake in September. The British ships limped back to New York for repairs. De Grasse blocked the entrance to Chesapeake Bay. Cornwallis was trapped.

Washington and French General Rochambeau had been camped outside New York, planning to attack the British there. When they learned that de Grasse was sailing for Virginia, they marched their armies south. It was a remarkable feat—moving seven thousand men nearly four hundred miles without the British figuring out where they were going until it was too late. They reached Virginia in September and joined with additional American forces. The combined army of seventeen thousand troops surrounded Yorktown. Cornwallis had about eight thousand men with no way out.

The siege lasted three weeks. American and French artillery pounded British positions day and night. The British tried to dig in, but the bombardment was relentless. Cornwallis sent desperate messages asking for help, but no help came. On October 19, 1781, he surrendered.

Surrender of Lord Cornwallis by John Trumbull.[18]

The British army marched out with their flags furled. Their band reportedly played a tune called "The World Turned Upside Down." It was fitting. The world had turned upside down. A ragtag colonial army had defeated the British Empire. Washington stood silent as the British laid down their weapons. Cornwallis claimed illness and sent a subordinate to surrender his sword. It was a humiliating end for the British.

Yorktown didn't officially end the war. Fighting continued in scattered places. British forces still occupied New York, Charleston, and Savannah. But everyone knew it was over. Britain had lost the will to continue. King George wanted to fight on, but Parliament refused. The war had cost too much money and achieved nothing. Public opinion in Britain had turned against the war.

Peace negotiations took two years. Benjamin Franklin, John Adams, and John Jay represented America in Paris. They negotiated shrewdly, playing European powers against each other. The British wanted to split America from France by offering generous terms. The Americans wanted territory. The Treaty of Paris, signed in September 1783, recognized American independence. Britain gave up all claims to territory east of the Mississippi River except for Canada and Florida, which went back to Spain. The northern boundary was set at the Great Lakes. The southern boundary was set at Spanish Florida. America had won not just independence but a vast territory for expansion.

The Revolution created a new nation, but it left enormous unsolved problems. The Continental Congress had no real power. The Articles of Confederation created a weak central government. The states had issues cooperating with each other. The national debt was massive. Loyalists faced persecution, and many fled to Canada. Native peoples who had allied with Britain lost protection and faced an expanding American nation that wanted their land. And slavery—the great contradiction of a revolution fought for freedom—remained untouched. Building a government that could actually work and resolve these contradictions would be the next challenge.

Chapter 8: Creating a Government

The Articles of Confederation: A Rope of Sand

Winning independence was one thing. Governing the country was another. During the Revolution, the Continental Congress ran the war effort, but it operated without a formal constitution, relying on the cooperation of the states. They needed a real government.

In 1777, Congress drafted the Articles of Confederation. The Articles created a "firm league of friendship" between the states. Each state kept its sovereignty and independence. Congress could declare war, make treaties, and manage foreign affairs. It could borrow money and settle disputes between states. That was about it.

Congress couldn't tax. It could ask states for money, but states could refuse. Congress couldn't regulate commerce between states or with foreign countries. It couldn't enforce its own laws or treaties. It had no executive branch to carry out decisions. It had no national court system. Every significant decision required approval from nine of the thirteen states. Changing the Articles of Confederation required unanimous consent.

The Articles of Confederation reflected what Americans feared most—centralized power. They had just fought a war against a government they saw as tyrannical. They weren't about to create another one. Better a weak central government than a strong one that might become oppressive.

The system didn't work, though. Congress was broke. States refused to pay their share of war debts. Foreign countries wouldn't lend money because America couldn't guarantee repayment. Soldiers who had fought in the Revolution went unpaid. Some received certificates promising future payment, but these certificates quickly lost most of their value, becoming nearly worthless for the soldiers who desperately needed money.

States acted like independent countries. They taxed goods from other states. They printed their own money, causing inflation and confusion. A dollar in Virginia wasn't worth the same as a dollar in Massachusetts. Trade between states was chaotic. Trade with foreign countries was worse because Congress couldn't negotiate favorable terms without the power to enforce agreements.

Foreign countries didn't respect America. Britain refused to evacuate forts in the Northwest Territory as promised in the peace treaty. Spain closed the Mississippi River to American shipping. Pirates from North Africa captured American ships and enslaved their crews. Congress was unable to respond effectively to these threats.

In 1786, the problems exploded in Massachusetts. Farmers were losing their land because they couldn't pay their debts. Courts foreclosed on their farms. Some farmers went to debtor's prison. A Revolutionary War veteran named Daniel Shays led a rebellion. About four thousand farmers closed courthouses to stop foreclosures and threatened to raid a federal armory. The Massachusetts militia eventually put down the rebellion, but it shocked the nation.

Shays' Rebellion showed that the Articles of Confederation couldn't maintain order or protect property. Wealthy Americans, especially merchants and landowners, worried about more uprisings. Something had to change.

George Washington called the government under the Articles "a rope of sand." It looked like a government, but it fell apart when tested. The question was whether the states could create something better without destroying the independence they had just won.

The Constitution: A Bundle of Compromises

In May 1787, delegates from twelve states met in Philadelphia to hold the Constitutional Convention. Rhode Island refused to participate. The meeting was supposed to revise the Articles of Confederation. Instead, the delegates decided to throw them out and start over. They would create an entirely new government based on a constitution.

The convention met in secret. Windows stayed shut despite the summer heat. Delegates agreed not to discuss their debates publicly. They wanted to speak freely without outside pressure. We know what happened because James Madison took detailed notes.

The delegates were not ordinary people. Most were wealthy. Many were lawyers. Some owned slaves. They included George Washington, Benjamin Franklin, James Madison, and Alexander Hamilton. These were men with property and positions to protect. They wanted a government strong enough to maintain order and encourage commerce, but not so strong that it threatened liberty.

Two basic plans emerged. The Virginia Plan, written mainly by James Madison, proposed a strong national government with three branches. Congress would have two houses. Representation would be based on population. Large states liked this plan.

The New Jersey Plan proposed keeping the basic structure of the Articles of Confederation but giving Congress more power. Each state would have equal representation regardless of size. Small states liked this plan.

The debate lasted weeks. Large states insisted that more people meant more representation. Small states refused to be outvoted by Virginia, Pennsylvania, and Massachusetts. The convention nearly collapsed.

The Great Compromise, also called the Connecticut Compromise, solved it. Congress would have two houses. In the House of Representatives, representation would be based on population. In the Senate, each state would have two senators regardless of size. Both houses had to approve laws. Neither large nor small states could dominate.

But the population raised another problem. Southern states wanted enslaved people counted for representation but not for taxation. Northern states said the opposite—count them for taxes but not representation. Neither side wanted to call slavery what it was.

The Three-Fifths Compromise settled this issue. For both representation and taxation, enslaved people would be counted as three-fifths of a person. This was neither moral nor logical. It treated human beings as fractions for political calculation. But it allowed the convention to continue.

The South also demanded protection for slavery. The Constitution prohibited Congress from banning the slave trade until 1808. It required free states to return escaped slaves to their owners. The word "slavery" never appears in the Constitution, but the institution was protected in it.

The delegates created three branches of government. Congress would make laws. The president would enforce laws and conduct foreign policy. Federal courts would interpret laws and settle disputes. Each branch could check the others. Congress could override presidential vetoes. The Senate had to approve treaties and major appointments. The Supreme Court would later establish the power to declare laws unconstitutional, a key check on the other branches that was not explicitly written in the document.

The president would be elected not by popular vote but by an electoral college. Each state would choose electors equal to its number of senators and representatives. The electors would vote for the president. This system gave small states more influence than their population warranted. It also put a barrier between the people and direct election, which many delegates thought was important. They didn't fully trust democracy.

The delegates finished their work in September 1787, but the Constitution needed ratification by nine states. The fight was intense. Federalists supported the Constitution. They argued that a strong national government was necessary to maintain order, pay debts, and defend the country. Anti-Federalists opposed it. They feared the Constitution gave too much power to the central government and threatened state sovereignty and individual liberty.

The Anti-Federalists had strong arguments. The Constitution didn't protect free speech, free press, or trial by jury. To the Anti-Federalists, the new president looked too much like a king, and they feared the office would become a monarchy. The Senate seemed like an aristocracy. In a major and controversial shift from the Articles of Confederation, the federal government could now tax citizens directly without state approval. Where would this power end?

The Federalists fought back in newspapers and pamphlets. Alexander Hamilton, James Madison, and John Jay wrote a series of essays called *The Federalist Papers*, explaining and defending the Constitution. These essays remain the best explanation of the Constitution's design and purpose.

The crucial compromise came during ratification, when Federalists promised to add a bill of rights to address the concerns raised by the Anti-Federalists. This promise won over many skeptics.

The Bill of Rights, ratified in 1791, consisted of ten amendments. The First Amendment protected freedom of religion, speech, the press, assembly, and the right to petition the government. The Second Amendment addressed the right to bear arms. The Third Amendment prevented the government from forcing citizens to house soldiers. The Fourth Amendment protected against unreasonable searches and seizures. The Fifth through Eighth Amendments guaranteed fair legal procedures—the right to due process, trial by jury, protection against self-incrimination, and protection against cruel and unusual punishment. The Ninth and Tenth Amendments stated that rights not listed in the Constitution still belonged to the people, and powers not given to the federal government remained with the states or the people.

By June 1788, nine states had ratified the Constitution, and it was adopted. Virginia and New York ratified soon after, though barely. North Carolina and Rhode Island held out until 1789 and 1790. The new government began operating in 1789.

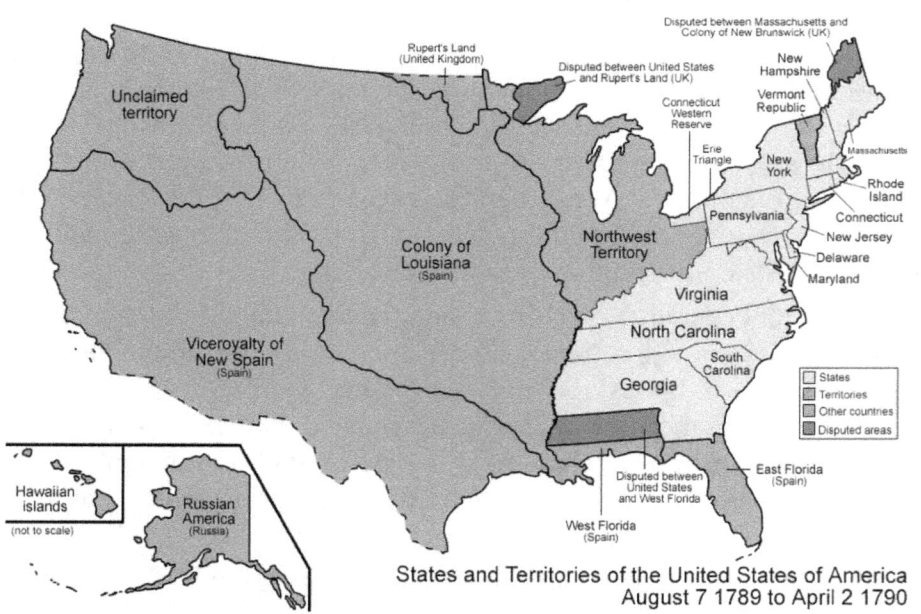

States and Territories of the United States of America
August 7 1789 to April 2 1790

The United States in 1790.[14]

The Constitution was a bundle of compromises. Large states compromised with small states. North compromised with South. But they created a government that proved durable.

Still, the Constitution left enormous questions unanswered. How much power did the federal government really have? Could states nullify federal laws? What happened if states wanted to leave the Union? These questions would be fought over for decades and eventually answered with war.

The Constitution also left the nation's greatest contradiction unresolved. A government based on liberty and equality protected slavery. This compromise allowed the nation to unite, but it planted seeds of future conflict. The Bill of Rights protected individual freedoms but didn't extend them to everyone. Women couldn't vote. Enslaved people had no rights. Native peoples weren't citizens. The Constitution created a framework for government, but the struggle to extend its promises of liberty to everyone would take centuries.

Chapter 9: The First Presidents and a New Capital

President Washington Sets the Standard

In 1789, George Washington became the first president of the United States. Nobody knew what a president should do or how much power the office should have. The Constitution outlined the basics, but the details were unclear. Washington had to figure it out as he went. Every decision he made set a precedent.

Washington didn't want the job. He wanted to retire to Mount Vernon and manage his plantation. However, everyone agreed he was the only person who could unite the country. His reputation from the war made him trusted by both the North and the South, by Federalists and Anti-Federalists. He accepted the presidency as a duty.

The Electoral College voted unanimously for Washington. He took the oath of office on April 30, 1789, in New York City, the temporary capital. He wore a plain brown suit made of American cloth. This symbolic choice promoted domestic manufacturing and sent a message: the president was a citizen, not a king.

An oil painting of George Washington's inauguration.[15]

Washington surrounded himself with talented people. He appointed Thomas Jefferson as Secretary of State to handle foreign affairs. Alexander Hamilton became Secretary of the Treasury to manage finances. Henry Knox took charge of the War Department. Edmund Randolph became Attorney General. These department heads became Washington's Cabinet, though the Constitution didn't mention such a thing. Meeting with advisors to discuss policy became standard practice.

One of Washington's first challenges was what to call him. Some suggested "His Highness" or "His Excellency." Washington rejected titles. "Mr. President" was enough. This established that American leaders wouldn't use royal or aristocratic titles. The president was not above other citizens in rank, only in responsibility.

The most immediate problem was money. The United States was deeply in debt from the Revolution. States owed money. The federal government owed money. Foreign countries and American citizens held bonds and certificates that needed to be repaid. Nobody trusted American credit.

But Hamilton had a plan. He proposed that the federal government assume all state debts. The government would pay off old bonds at full value and issue new federal bonds. This would establish the government's creditworthiness and bind wealthy bondholders to the federal government's success. It would also create a national debt that would tie the states together financially.

Many people hated this plan. States that had already paid their debts didn't want to help states that hadn't. Southern states had paid more of their debts than Northern states. Why should Virginia pay for Massachusetts? Speculators had bought old bonds cheaply from desperate veterans. Now they would profit enormously when the government paid full value. This seemed unfair.

Hamilton didn't care about fairness to individuals; he cared about the nation's credit and financial stability. After intense negotiation, Congress approved his plan. The compromise was that the nation's permanent capital would move south, eventually to a site on the Potomac River between Maryland and Virginia. This new capital would be called Washington. The North got Hamilton's financial plan. The South got the capital.

Hamilton also wanted a national bank. The Bank of the United States would handle government money, make loans, and issue paper currency. It would stabilize the economy and make commerce easier. Jefferson and Madison opposed it. They said the Constitution didn't give Congress the power to create a bank. The government could only do what the Constitution explicitly allowed.

Hamilton argued differently. The Constitution gave Congress power to regulate commerce and collect taxes. A bank helped do both. The Constitution didn't need to list every specific tool Congress could use. This was the first major debate over how to interpret the Constitution. Ultimately, Washington sided with Hamilton. The bank was created.

Washington faced foreign crises too. In 1789, a revolution broke out in France. At first, Americans celebrated. The French were overthrowing their king and fighting for liberty, just like Americans had done.

But the French Revolution turned violent. In 1793, revolutionaries executed King Louis XVI and Queen Marie Antoinette. The Reign of Terror followed. Revolutionary tribunals sent thousands to the guillotine. The violence shocked many Americans.

The French Revolution divided America. Jefferson and his supporters saw it as spreading the fight for freedom. They wore French revolutionary symbols and celebrated French victories. Hamilton and the Federalists were horrified. They saw dangerous mob rule that could destroy civilization. What if the same chaos came to America?

Then, in 1793, Britain and France went to war. France expected American help. The United States had a treaty with France from the Revolutionary War. Many Americans thought America should support France since it had helped them win independence. Others wanted to stay friendly with Britain, America's biggest trading partner.

Washington issued the Neutrality Proclamation. America would trade with both sides but fight for neither. This angered France and pro-French Americans who felt America was betraying an ally. But Washington was actually keeping America out of a war it couldn't afford to fight.

The biggest crisis was domestic. In 1794, farmers in western Pennsylvania refused to pay a federal tax on whiskey. Whiskey was their main product and means of trade. They tarred and feathered tax collectors. They also attacked federal officials. This was called the Whiskey Rebellion.

Washington took it seriously. If people could simply refuse to obey laws they didn't like, the government had no authority. To prove the federal government could enforce its laws, he assembled an impressive force of thirteen thousand militia troops and rode with them partway west to oversee the operation before handing command to General Henry Lee. The rebels dispersed without fighting. Washington had shown that this was no longer a weak government.

Washington served two terms but refused a third. He could have been president for life. Many people wanted him to continue. However, he believed in republican government, not one-man rule. His voluntary retirement set the precedent that presidents serve limited terms. This wasn't written in the Constitution until 1951, but Washington's example made it tradition.

In his Farewell Address in 1796, Washington warned against permanent political parties and foreign entanglements. Americans should stay united and avoid getting pulled into European conflicts. These warnings were ignored almost immediately, but they remained influential ideals.

Washington died in 1799. The nation mourned him as the father of the country. He had used his popularity to establish the presidency as a strong office. He could have been a dictator or a king. Instead, Washington was a citizen who served and then went home. That choice shaped American government forever.

The Birth of Political Parties: Hamilton vs. Jefferson

The Constitution said nothing about political parties. The Founders hoped to avoid them, seeing parties as sources of division and conflict. Washington warned against them in his Farewell Address. But parties formed anyway, growing out of real disagreements over what America should become.

Alexander Hamilton and Thomas Jefferson represented two different visions, and their rivalry created the first American political parties. While this summary simplifies their views, both men were complex, and their followers held a range of opinions.

Hamilton, born illegitimate and poor in the Caribbean, rose by talent and ambition. Serving as Washington's aide during the war, he saw how a weak national government nearly lost the Revolution. He believed America needed a strong federal government and a modern economy built on commerce and manufacturing.

Jefferson, born into Virginia's plantation aristocracy, lived as a gentleman scholar at Monticello. He believed America should remain a nation of independent farmers. He distrusted cities and banks and feared concentrated power. To him, Hamilton's vision resembled the British system they had fought to escape.

Hamilton imagined a commercial and industrial nation with cities, factories, banks, and trade. Tying wealthy citizens to the government through bonds and banks, he argued, would create prosperity and stability. The government should actively promote economic growth.

Jefferson envisioned an agrarian republic of self-reliant farmers who would be independent and virtuous because they owned their own land. Cities, he warned, bred corruption and dependency. The best government was the one that governed least, leaving citizens free to farm their land.

Hamilton distrusted popular rule, believing that the government should be led by the educated and wealthy, people who had the knowledge and stakes to make sound decisions. Jefferson professed faith in the people, though he excluded women, the poor, and enslaved persons. He believed educated citizens could govern themselves and that power should remain with the people in state and local governments.

These philosophical differences soon became political ones. Hamilton's financial plan, the national bank, taxes, and foreign policy all became points of contention. Hamilton's supporters, the Federalists, favored a strong central government, protective tariffs, and close ties with Britain. Jefferson's followers, the Democratic-Republicans, championed states' rights, agriculture, and sympathy with France.

The rivalry grew personal. Hamilton accused Jefferson of radicalism. Jefferson called Hamilton a would-be monarchist. Their allies traded attacks in fiercely partisan newspapers. Politics turned bitter.

The conflict climaxed in the election of 1796. With Washington retiring, John Adams, a Federalist, ran against Jefferson. Adams narrowly won. Under the original Constitution, Jefferson became vice president. Yes, the leader of the opposing party became vice president. This awkward pairing showed that the Founders had never planned for political parties.

Adams's presidency was difficult. He inherited tensions with France. The French were seizing American ships and refusing to negotiate unless America paid bribes. Adams sent diplomats to France, but French officials demanded massive bribes just to meet with them. This became known as the XYZ Affair—the French officials were labeled X, Y, and Z in published reports. Americans were outraged.

War fever swept the nation. Federalists wanted to fight France. As Adams built up the military, Hamilton was appointed to a senior command and personally hoped the army could be used to assert American strength, possibly even against Spanish territories in the future. But Adams pulled back. He sent new diplomats and negotiated peace. The decision probably cost him reelection, but it kept America out of an unnecessary war.

The Federalists, fearing French influence and domestic opposition, passed the Alien and Sedition Acts in 1798. These laws made it harder for immigrants to become citizens and made it illegal to criticize the government. The acts were aimed at Democratic-Republican newspapers and immigrant voters who tended to support Jefferson. Several editors were arrested and jailed for criticizing Adams.

Jefferson and Madison responded with the Kentucky and Virginia Resolutions. These argued that states could nullify federal laws they considered unconstitutional. If the federal government passed unconstitutional laws, states could refuse to enforce them. This was a radical argument that would resurface repeatedly, eventually helping to cause the Civil War.

The election of 1800 was brutal. Federalists called Jefferson an atheist and a radical who would destroy religion and property. Democratic-Republicans called Adams a monarchist and a tyrant.

Jefferson won, and he called his victory the "Revolution of 1800." Indeed, the peaceful transfer of power from one rival party to another was a truly revolutionary moment for the young republic and helped establish a vital democratic norm. Adams left office quietly, though he was bitter about the loss. Many countries at the time saw political transitions end in violence. America managed it through elections and constitutional procedures.

Jefferson believed he had saved the republic from Federalist tyranny. Federalists thought the country was doomed. Neither was right. The political system worked. Parties had formed despite the Founders' wishes, but they provided a way for people with different visions to compete for power without violence. This was the beginning of American democratic politics.

The War of 1812: America's Second War for Independence

We will talk more about what happened during Jefferson's presidency in the next chapter. James Madison became president in 1809. By then, America had been independent for more than twenty-five years, but tensions with Britain never fully disappeared. In June 1812, the United States declared war on Britain. The conflict lasted almost three years and ended in a military draw, with no territorial changes. Yet, it profoundly shaped American identity and politics.

The causes were complex. Britain and France were fighting the Napoleonic Wars, and both sides violated America's neutral trading rights. British ships stopped American vessels and searched for British sailors. They practiced "impressment"—forcing American sailors into British service. Britain claimed these men were deserters from the Royal Navy, but many were actually American citizens. Between 1803 and 1812, about six thousand Americans were impressed.

Britain also supplied and encouraged Native American resistance in the Northwest. Powerful leaders like the Shawnee chief Tecumseh were already organizing a tribal confederacy to defend their lands and sovereignty against American expansion.

Some Americans, especially in the South and West, wanted war. They saw an opportunity to conquer Canada and Spanish Florida. "War Hawks" in Congress, led by Henry Clay and John C. Calhoun, pushed for conflict. New England merchants opposed war because they profited from trade, but they were outvoted.

President James Madison asked Congress to declare war in June 1812. The vote was close, though. New England states nearly refused to participate. Some Federalists derisively called the conflict "Mr. Madison's War" and accused him of serving French interests.

The war began badly. American forces invaded Canada three times in 1812, and each attempt failed. The army was poorly trained and led. State militias refused to cross into Canada, claiming their duty was only to defend their own states. The British and Canadian defenders, though outnumbered, fought effectively.

At sea, things went better. The small American navy won several single-ship duels against British vessels. The USS *Constitution* defeated the HMS *Guerriere*, earning it the nickname "Old Ironsides." These victories lifted morale but did little to change the war's outcome. Britain's navy was simply too large. By 1813, British ships blockaded the American coast, choking off trade.

That year brought some American success. Oliver Hazard Perry defeated a British squadron on Lake Erie, giving the United States control of the lake. Soon after, William Henry Harrison triumphed at the Battle of the Thames, defeating British and Native forces and killing Tecumseh. His death weakened Native resistance throughout the Northwest.

Battle of Lake Erie by William Henry Powell.[16]

By 1814, Britain had defeated Napoleon in Europe and could send veteran troops to America. British forces invaded from Canada, burned Buffalo, and pushed into New York. Another British force landed in Maryland and marched on Washington, DC.

The attack on Washington was humiliating. American forces fled as the British entered the capital and burned the White House, the Capitol, and other public buildings. First Lady Dolley Madison escaped just in time, saving a portrait of George Washington. President Madison fled to Virginia. After burning the city, the British withdrew, having made their point.

They then attacked Baltimore. Fort McHenry defended the harbor as British ships bombarded it through the night of September 13–14, 1814. Watching from a ship in the harbor, American lawyer Francis Scott Key saw the flag still flying at dawn and wrote a poem, "The Star-Spangled Banner," which later became the national anthem.

Meanwhile, Britain prepared a major offensive in the South. A large British force sailed for New Orleans to capture the city and control the Mississippi River. Andrew Jackson, a Tennessee lawyer and plantation owner known for his toughness, commanded the American defense.

Jackson assembled a mixed force of regulars, militia, pirates, free Black troops, and even a few Choctaw warriors. They waited behind hastily built fortifications outside New Orleans. On January 8, 1815, the British advanced across an open field and were met with devastating artillery and rifle fire. More than two thousand British soldiers were killed, wounded, or captured, while American casualties were minimal.

The Battle of New Orleans was a stunning victory that made Jackson a national hero, but it was fought in vain. Two weeks earlier, diplomats in Belgium had signed the Treaty of Ghent. News traveled slowly, and neither side knew the war was over.

The treaty, signed on December 24, 1814, did not force Britain to renounce impressment. The issue simply faded after the Napoleonic Wars ended. The Royal Navy no longer needed so many sailors. The treaty restored conditions to what they had been before the war. No territory changed hands, and neither side could claim victory. Both were exhausted and ready for peace.

Though it accomplished little on paper, the war had lasting effects. It proved the United States could survive a war against a major power. The country had neither collapsed nor been reconquered. Americans increasingly thought of themselves as citizens of one nation rather than of separate states.

The war also destroyed the Federalist Party. Federalists had opposed the conflict, and some radicals even hinted at secession. When news arrived of Jackson's victory and the peace treaty, the Federalists looked unpatriotic and ridiculous. Their party never recovered.

Native Americans' hopes for independence east of the Mississippi also ended. Tecumseh's confederacy and other movements had fought for sovereignty, but the loss of British support left them alone against expanding American settlement. The war cleared the way for westward expansion.

Americans later called it the "Second War of Independence." The phrase is not quite accurate, but the war gave the young republic confidence. Having fought Britain again and survived, the United States was becoming a true nation.

Chapter 10: The Era of Manifest Destiny

The Louisiana Purchase: Doubling the Nation Overnight

In 1803, the United States bought 828,000 square miles of land from France for $15 million, doubling the nation's size overnight. The Louisiana Purchase stretched from the Mississippi River to the Rocky Mountains and from the Gulf of Mexico to Canada, encompassing all or part of fifteen future states.

The acquisition was unexpected, but American interest in controlling New Orleans had long been a strategic goal. The purchase resulted from a mix of war, disease, and diplomatic luck.

France had once owned the Louisiana Territory but lost it to Spain in 1763 after the Seven Years' War. In 1800, Napoleon Bonaparte secretly forced Spain to return it, hoping to rebuild a French empire in the Americas. The territory would supply food and resources to France's Caribbean colonies, especially the wealthy sugar island of Saint-Domingue (modern-day Haiti).

That plan collapsed. Enslaved people in Saint-Domingue rebelled in 1791, fighting for freedom against French, Spanish, and British forces. By 1803, they had won. The Haitian Revolution created the first Black republic in the Americas and the second independent nation in the Western Hemisphere after the United States.

Without his Caribbean colony, Napoleon abandoned his imperial ambitions. Facing renewed war with Britain and desperate for funds, he saw Louisiana as a burden he could sell.

President Thomas Jefferson wanted to secure New Orleans. Western farmers shipped their goods down the Mississippi River to the city's port, the gateway to world markets. When Spain closed the port to Americans in 1802, it threatened the entire western economy. Jefferson sent diplomats to France—James Monroe and Robert Livingston—with instructions to buy New Orleans and perhaps some nearby land. He authorized them to spend up to $10 million.

When Monroe and Livingston arrived in Paris, French Foreign Minister Talleyrand astonished them by asking whether the United States would buy all of Louisiana. They were unprepared. With no authority to purchase the entire territory and no time to seek Jefferson's approval, they had to decide immediately.

They accepted the offer. The price was $15 million—about three cents an acre. It was one of history's greatest bargains.

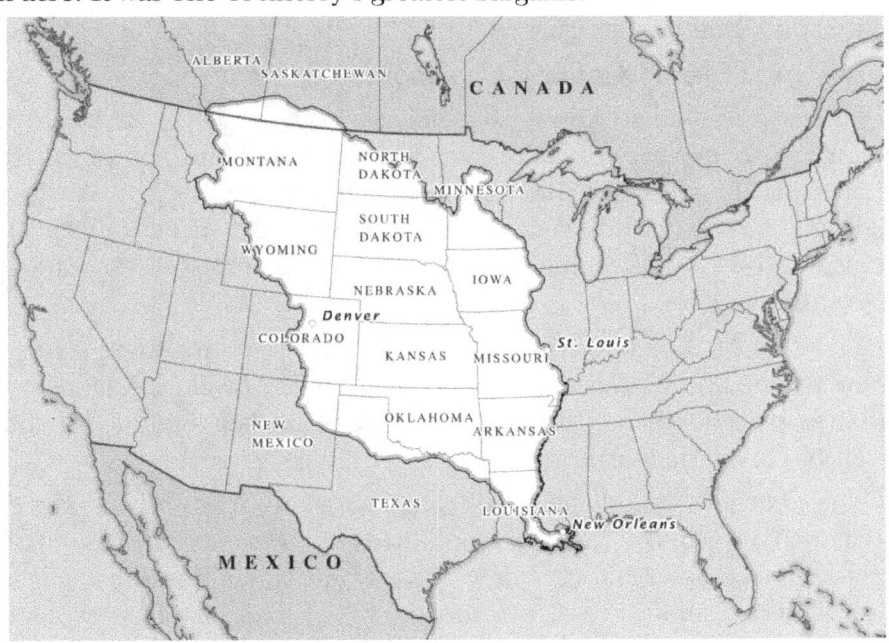

The Louisiana Purchase (overlapped on a current map of the US).[17]

Jefferson received the news in July 1803. He was elated yet uneasy. He believed the federal government could only do what the Constitution explicitly permitted, and it said nothing about acquiring foreign territory. Jefferson considered proposing a constitutional amendment, but he was warned that delay might give Napoleon time to reconsider. He finally decided that the power to purchase land fell within the president's treaty-making authority and chose practicality over principle.

The Senate ratified the treaty. Federalists opposed it, fearing that vast western lands would diminish New England's influence. They were right; the nation's political center soon shifted west and south.

The Louisiana Purchase removed a major European power from the continent's interior, opened space for expansion, and made westward growth seem inevitable. It also ensured future conflict over slavery—whether new territories would be slave or free—a question that would eventually tear the nation apart.

The deal also ignored the fact that the land already belonged to dozens of Indigenous nations who were never consulted about the sale of their homelands. These were not empty lands. The Osage, Pawnee, Sioux, Cheyenne, Arapaho, Comanche, and many others governed vast territories with intricate political systems, trade networks, and alliances. The Louisiana Purchase was, in reality, a transaction between two foreign powers over land neither truly controlled.

Lewis and Clark: Charting the Unknown

Jefferson wanted to know what he had bought, so he organized an expedition to explore the Louisiana Territory and find a route to the Pacific Ocean. He chose his personal secretary, Meriwether Lewis, to lead it. Lewis selected William Clark—a former Army officer and younger brother of Revolutionary War hero George Rogers Clark—to share command.

They left St. Louis in May 1804 with about forty-five men: soldiers, frontiersmen, and Clark's enslaved servant, York. Traveling in a keelboat and two pirogues (small dugout boats), they pushed up the Missouri River into uncharted territory.

The journey was dangerous from the start. The river's current threatened to capsize their boats. Storms, snakes, and disease made survival uncertain. Although they passed through lands inhabited by many Native nations, most encounters were peaceful. The explorers traded goods, gathered information, held councils, and claimed the land for the United States. Native leaders were courteous but unimpressed. These lands were theirs, regardless of European or American claims.

In October 1804, the party reached the Mandan and Hidatsa villages in present-day North Dakota. There, they built Fort Mandan and spent the winter, enduring temperatures of forty below zero.

At Mandan, they hired Toussaint Charbonneau, a French-Canadian trader, as an interpreter. He brought his teenage Shoshone wife,

Sacagawea, who had been captured years earlier by the Hidatsa and sold (or traded) to Charbonneau. She was about sixteen and pregnant.

Sacagawea gave birth in February 1805. When the expedition departed that spring, she went too, carrying her infant son, Jean Baptiste. A war party traveling with a woman and baby signaled peaceful intent, but her contributions went far beyond symbolism. She found edible plants to prevent scurvy, identified landmarks from her childhood, interpreted and negotiated with Shoshone groups, and calmly rescued crucial supplies when a boat capsized. Her composure and knowledge were indispensable.

York, Clark's enslaved servant, was also essential. Many Native peoples had never seen a Black man before. York's presence fascinated them and often aided in diplomacy. A skilled hunter and negotiator, he earned respect and was even regarded by some as spiritually powerful. Despite his service, Clark never freed him.

As the expedition pressed west, the terrain grew harsher. By June, they had reached the Great Falls of the Missouri and were forced to portage, carrying their boats and cargo overland for eighteen miles.

Beyond the falls rose the Rocky Mountains. To cross them, they needed horses. In a remarkable coincidence, the Shoshone band they encountered was led by Cameahwait—Sacagawea's long-lost brother. She had not seen him in five years. Their reunion secured the horses and a guide named Old Toby.

Crossing the Bitterroot Mountains nearly destroyed the expedition. Snow fell early, food ran out, and some men wanted to turn back. They melted tallow from candles and ate portable soup to survive. Old Toby led them to the Nez Perce villages, where they were fed and helped to build new canoes.

Following the Clearwater, Snake, and Columbia Rivers, the explorers reached the Pacific on November 7, 1805. "Great joy in camp. We are in view of the ocean," Clark wrote in his journal.[i]

---

[i] "O Joy Day." https://www.nps.gov/articles/o-joy-day-november-7-1805.htm

Lewis and Clark on the Lower Columbia, 1905 by Charles Marion Russell.[18]

They built Fort Clatsop near present-day Astoria, Oregon, and endured a miserable winter of rain, sickness, and scarcity. They saw the sun only six times in four months. In March 1806, they began the return journey.

The trip home was faster. Dividing into groups, they explored more territory. Lewis's party clashed with Blackfeet warriors. Two were killed in a struggle over horses and guns; it was the only deadly encounter of the expedition.

Reunited, the explorers reached St. Louis in September 1806—two years and four months after their departure. They had traveled roughly eight thousand miles, mapped the route, and established contact with dozens of Native nations. Scientifically, the expedition identified 178 plant species and 122 animals previously unknown to American scientists. They provided the first detailed descriptions of grizzly bears, prairie dogs, and pronghorn antelope, as well as valuable data on the Great Plains, the Rockies, and the Pacific Northwest.

Their journey also opened the West to American expansion. Fur traders followed, then settlers. The expedition strengthened US claims to Oregon and made the West seem accessible.

For Native peoples, it was a warning. More Americans would follow. The Lewis and Clark Expedition marked the beginning of the end of Native control of the West.

The Trail of Tears: The Human Cost of Expansion

The federal government pledged to respect Native sovereignty but rarely kept its word. State governments ignored federal treaties, and settlers simply seized the land they wanted.

In the Southeast, five major nations—the Cherokee, Chickasaw, Choctaw, Creek, and Seminole—occupied millions of acres in Georgia, Alabama, Mississippi, Tennessee, and Florida. White settlers called them the "Five Civilized Tribes" because they had adopted many European-American customs. The label itself revealed assumptions that Native cultures had to resemble White society to be deemed acceptable.

The Cherokee, in particular, had adapted extensively. They developed a written language created by Sequoyah in 1821, published a bilingual newspaper (the *Cherokee Phoenix*), and established a formal government with a constitution. They built schools, mills, and plantations. Some even enslaved Black people. They had done nearly everything White Americans claimed was necessary to be "civilized."

It made no difference. White Georgians coveted Cherokee land, and when gold was discovered there in 1829, the pressure to remove them became overwhelming.

That same year, Andrew Jackson became president. Jackson had defeated the Creek Nation in 1814 at the Battle of Horseshoe Bend, in which around eight hundred Creek warriors were killed. He believed Native peoples could not coexist with White civilization—they must move west or disappear.

In 1830, Jackson pushed the Indian Removal Act through Congress. The law authorized the president to negotiate treaties exchanging Native lands in the East for territory west of the Mississippi. It claimed removal would be voluntary and peaceful. It was neither.

The Cherokee fought the removal in court, hiring lawyers and suing the state of Georgia. In *Cherokee Nation v. Georgia* (1831) and *Worcester v. Georgia* (1832), the Supreme Court ruled partly in their favor. Chief Justice John Marshall wrote that the Cherokee were a "domestic dependent nation" with rights to their land and that Georgia's laws did not apply there.

Jackson reportedly sneered, "John Marshall has made his decision. Now let him enforce it."[i] Whether he said those words or not, his actions

---

[i] "The First Hundred Years." https://www.thirteen.org/wnet/supremecourt/antebellum/history2.html

showed he had no intention of obeying the Supreme Court's ruling. The federal government refused to protect Cherokee rights.

Georgia divided Cherokee territory into parcels and distributed them by lottery to White settlers. The Cherokee government was declared illegal, its leaders arrested, and the *Cherokee Phoenix* shut down. White settlers occupied Cherokee farms.

A small faction of Cherokee was convinced that resistance was futile. They signed the Treaty of New Echota in 1835. It ceded all Cherokee land east of the Mississippi in exchange for $5 million and land in Indian Territory (now Oklahoma). The signers represented only a tiny minority. The Cherokee government and thousands of Cherokees petitioned against it, but Congress ratified the treaty anyway.

The Cherokee were given two years to move voluntarily. Most refused. In 1838, President Martin Van Buren sent General Winfield Scott with seven thousand troops to remove them by force.

Soldiers arrived at Cherokee homes with bayonets drawn. Families had minutes to gather what they could. Many took nothing. They were herded into stockades, where disease spread and people died while awaiting deportation.

Removal began in spring 1838 and continued into winter. About sixteen thousand Cherokee were forced to walk more than a thousand miles to Indian Territory in poorly planned, undersupplied groups.

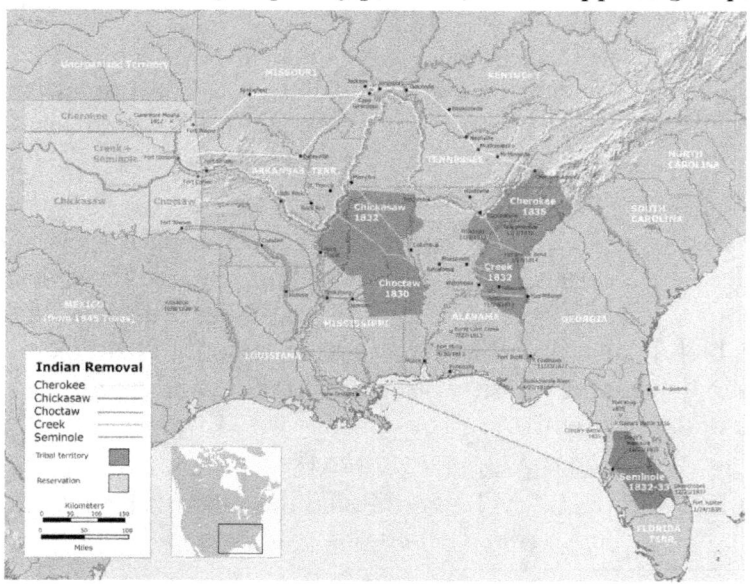

A map of the process of the Indian Removal Act.[19]

Winter brought brutal conditions. People lacked clothing, food, and shelter. They trudged through freezing rain and snow. Whooping cough, typhus, dysentery, and measles ravaged the columns. Food was scarce and often spoiled. Some walked barefoot. The elderly and sick rode in wagons, but there were never enough.

Roughly four thousand Cherokee died from disease, starvation, and exposure during the march or soon after arriving in Indian Territory. Families were torn apart, and communities were destroyed. The Cherokee called it *Nunna daul Tsuny*—"The Trail Where They Cried." Americans remember it as the Trail of Tears.

The Cherokee were not alone. The Choctaw were removed beginning in 1831. About 15,000 were forced west, suffering some 2,500 deaths. The Creek followed in 1836, losing thousands to disease and starvation. The Chickasaw negotiated better terms and financed their own removal, yet they still suffered heavy losses.

The Seminole in Florida resisted. When the federal government tried to remove them, they fought back. The Second Seminole War (1835–1842) became the longest and costliest of all the American Indian Wars. Led by Osceola and other chiefs, the Seminole waged guerrilla warfare in the swamps. The US Army never truly defeated them. Most were killed, captured, or removed, but a few hundred retreated into the Everglades and never surrendered.

By 1840, most of the Five Civilized Tribes had been expelled. The federal government seized roughly twenty-five million acres. White settlers poured into the Southeast, and cotton plantations spread across former Native lands.

The government promised that Indian Territory would remain Native land "for as long as the grass grows"—a guarantee written into treaties that were broken within a generation. White settlers soon wanted that land too.

The removals set a lasting pattern. Native peoples had no rights that White Americans were bound to respect, regardless of treaties, laws, or Supreme Court rulings. When White Americans wanted Native land, they took it. The government either helped or looked away.

Texas, Oregon, and the Mexican-American War

By the 1840s, many Americans believed westward expansion was their destiny. Journalist John O'Sullivan coined the phrase "Manifest Destiny" in 1845, writing that it was America's "manifest destiny to overspread the continent allotted by Providence." The idea held that God intended the United States to control all land from the Atlantic to the Pacific, justifying the seizure of any territory Americans desired, regardless of who lived there.

Westward the Course of Empire Takes Its Way by Emanuel Leutze.[20]

Texas was the first test. Though it belonged to Mexico, Americans had been moving there since the 1820s. Mexico had initially encouraged immigration, offering land grants to attract settlers. Empresarios (people who had been given grants to settle land), such as Stephen F. Austin, brought hundreds of American families to Texas. By 1830, they outnumbered Mexican Tejanos.

The Mexican government grew alarmed. Settlers ignored Mexican laws. They were expected to convert to Catholicism and learn Spanish, but most refused. When Mexico abolished slavery in 1829, Americans in Texas defied the ban. Mexico tried to halt further immigration in 1830, but by then, the frontier was beyond its control.

Tensions deepened as President Antonio López de Santa Anna centralized power, weakening local autonomy. Texans—both Anglo settlers and some Tejanos—rebelled in 1835, demanding independence.

The Texas Revolution was brief but brutal. In February 1836, Santa Anna's army besieged about two hundred Texan defenders, including Davy Crockett and Jim Bowie, at the Alamo mission in San Antonio. After thirteen days, the defenders were overrun. Almost all of them were killed.

"Remember the Alamo" became the Texans' rallying cry. The next month, Santa Anna ordered the execution of about 350 prisoners captured at Goliad.

In April, Sam Houston led his outnumbered army against Santa Anna at San Jacinto. Attacking during the Mexican army's siesta, Houston's men routed their enemies in eighteen minutes, killing over six hundred and capturing Santa Anna himself. To save his life, Santa Anna signed treaties recognizing Texas independence.

Mexico never accepted those treaties but lacked the strength to reconquer the province. The Republic of Texas remained independent from 1836 to 1845.

Annexation to the US proved divisive. Texas permitted slavery, and admitting it would upset the fragile balance between free and slave states. Northern politicians resisted, seeing annexation as a scheme to expand slavery. Abolitionists—people who wanted to end slavery entirely—were especially vocal, arguing that the Texas Revolution itself had been driven by slaveholders protecting their "property" from Mexican law. The issue remained unresolved for nearly a decade.

Meanwhile, thousands of Americans moved to Oregon Country, which included modern Oregon, Washington, Idaho, and parts of Montana and Wyoming. Both the United States and Britain claimed the region and had agreed to joint occupation in 1818.

By the 1840s, settlers following the Oregon Trail demanded that the region become American. The slogan "Fifty-four Forty or Fight!" called for US control up to latitude 54°40'—the southern boundary of Russian Alaska.

James K. Polk won the presidency in 1844 on an expansionist platform, promising to acquire both Texas and Oregon. Congress annexed Texas in 1845, and it became the twenty-eighth state that December.

Polk then settled the Oregon question with Britain. Despite fiery rhetoric, he had no wish for war. In 1846, the two nations agreed to divide the territory at the 49th parallel. The United States gained the southern portion, and Britain retained the north, which later became part of Canada.

Conflict with Mexico soon followed. The two nations disputed the southern border of Texas. Mexico claimed the Nueces River. The United States insisted on the Rio Grande, 150 miles farther south.

President Polk also coveted California. It belonged to Mexico, but it was sparsely populated by Mexican settlers. American traders and pioneers were already arriving there. Polk sent diplomats to offer to purchase California and New Mexico, but the Mexican government refused. Having just lost Texas, it would not sell more territory.

To provoke a confrontation, Polk ordered General Zachary Taylor to move US troops into the disputed zone between the Nueces and the Rio Grande—a step Mexico viewed as an invasion. In April 1846, Mexican forces attacked an American patrol. Polk used the incident to claim that Mexico had "shed American blood upon American soil." Congress declared war.

The conflict was controversial from the outset. Many Americans, especially in the North, denounced it as a war of aggression to expand slavery. Congressman Abraham Lincoln demanded proof that the clash had occurred on US soil. Poet and philosopher Henry David Thoreau refused to pay taxes to support the war and was jailed. Abolitionist Frederick Douglass condemned it as a war "to extend and sustain slavery."

Mexico was divided and poorly led, and it suffered defeat after defeat. US forces invaded from multiple directions. General Stephen Kearny seized Santa Fe and marched on to California, where John C. Frémont and American settlers staged the short-lived Bear Flag Revolt before joining US troops. Zachary Taylor was triumphant in northern Mexico. General Winfield Scott landed at Veracruz and advanced inland. In September 1847, he captured Mexico City after a series of victories. The war was over.

The Treaty of Guadalupe Hidalgo, signed in February 1848, ended the conflict. Mexico ceded California, Nevada, Utah, most of Arizona and New Mexico, and parts of Colorado and Wyoming to the United States. In return, the US paid $15 million and assumed $3.25 million in claims by American citizens against Mexico. Roughly 525,000 square miles were added to the nation.

The treaty guaranteed rights for Mexicans living in the ceded territories, including citizenship and property protection. These promises were quickly broken. Many lost their land through fraud, violence, or legal manipulation. Courts demanded proof of ownership under American standards, but most Mexican titles were based on older Spanish grants without formal documentation. Legal proceedings were conducted in English and were very expensive. Even when Mexican landowners won, squatters refused to leave, and local officials sided with White settlers. Within a generation, most Mexicans had been dispossessed. Mexican Americans became second-class citizens in a land that had once been theirs.

The war left deep resentment in Mexico. Many Mexicans viewed it as naked aggression by a stronger nation. Ulysses S. Grant, who fought in the campaign, later called it "one of the most unjust wars ever waged by a stronger against a weaker nation."[i]

By 1850, the United States stretched from the Atlantic to the Pacific. Manifest Destiny seemed fulfilled, but it came at an immense cost. Native Americans had been killed or driven from their homelands, Mexico dismembered, and the debate over slavery's expansion was about to tear the country apart. The land had been conquered. Now, Americans had to decide what kind of nation it would become.

---

[i] Fleek, Sherman. "Grant in Mexico."
https://www.army.mil/article/216806/grant_in_mexico_one_of_the_most_unjust_wars_ever_waged

Chapter 11: A House Dividing

King Cotton and the Southern Way of Life

By 1850, the American South had become a region unlike any other in the nation. Its economy, society, and politics all revolved around a single crop: cotton. And cotton depended entirely on enslaved labor.

Cotton had not always dominated the South. In the late 1700s, tobacco was the chief cash crop. Cotton, though profitable to grow, was hard to process. Each boll contained seeds that had to be removed by hand, and a person could clean only a single pound in a day.

That changed in 1793. Eli Whitney, a Yale graduate visiting a Georgia plantation, invented the cotton gin, a machine that used rotating teeth to separate cotton fibers from seeds. One person operating a gin could process fifty pounds of cotton a day. Within a generation, the invention transformed Southern agriculture.

A model of a cotton gin.[21]

Production exploded. In 1790, the South produced about 3,000 bales of cotton; by 1820, 335,000; by 1850, 2.13 million; and by 1860, on the eve of the Civil War, 3.8 million bales annually.

The cotton boom made the South wealthy. Cotton became America's most valuable export. Textile mills in Britain and the Northern United States depended on Southern cotton. The phrase "Cotton is King" was not idle boasting; cotton gave the South economic power and political confidence.

But the crop demanded immense labor. Fields had to be plowed, planted, weeded, and harvested. Cotton plants required constant attention throughout the growing season, and the bolls ripened at different times, forcing repeated passes through the fields. Workers picked cotton in brutal heat, often from sunrise to sunset, filling sacks that weighed fifty pounds or more.

The cotton economy rested on slavery. Planters bought enslaved people to work the expanding fields. As cotton cultivation moved west into Alabama, Mississippi, Louisiana, Arkansas, and Texas, the demand for enslaved labor soared. The domestic slave trade became a vast industry. More than a million people were forcibly moved from the Upper South (states like Maryland and Kentucky) to the Deep South (states like Georgia and Alabama) between 1790 and 1860. Families were torn apart. Children were sold away from their parents. Husbands and wives were separated.

By 1860, nearly four million people were enslaved in the United States. Most of them lived in the South, and most worked on cotton fields. Slavery was legal in fifteen states.

The system created a rigid social hierarchy. At the top stood the planters. Only about a quarter of White Southerners owned any enslaved people, and just 12 percent owned more than twenty slaves—the usual threshold for being called a "planter." A tiny elite—less than 1 percent—owned over a hundred. These elites owned the best land, dominated state politics, and set the tone of Southern life.

Most White Southerners were small farmers who owned no enslaved people. They worked their own land, grew their own food, and lived modestly. Some rented land or served as overseers on plantations. They were not rich, but they were free and White—and that distinction defined their social status.

Below them were poor Whites with no land at all. They worked as laborers, hired hands, or tenant farmers, with little opportunity or power. Yet Southern society taught them that Whiteness alone made them superior to enslaved people. This racial hierarchy preserved the system, even though slavery chiefly benefited the wealthy elite.

At the bottom were the enslaved. They were denied freedom, rights, and legal protection. They were property under the law. Slaves could be bought, sold, inherited, or used to pay debts. Masters held near-total authority. Enslaved people could not legally marry, own property, or testify against Whites. Most states forbade them to learn to read or write.

Life under slavery was brutal. Enslaved people worked long hours in harsh conditions, lived in crude cabins, and often lacked adequate food, clothing, and medical care. Punishment was constant. Whipping was routine, and other forms of torture—branding, mutilation, or selling family members away—were used to enforce obedience. Sexual violence against enslaved women was widespread and unpunished.

Still, enslaved people resisted in countless ways. Some fled north, though few reached freedom. Others slowed work, broke tools, or feigned illness. Many practiced religion in secret, preserved African traditions, and built families despite having no legal right to do so. In 1831, Nat Turner led a rebellion in Virginia that killed about sixty White people before being suppressed. Turner and his followers were executed, and Southern Whites responded with harsher laws and greater violence.

Despite everything, enslaved communities created rich cultures. They developed a spiritual form of Christianity emphasizing deliverance. They also forged new family bonds and created music that later shaped blues, jazz, and gospel. Even within bondage, they preserved their humanity.

Southern Whites defended slavery with increasing fervor. Some claimed it was sanctioned by the Bible. Others argued that Black people were naturally inferior and benefited from "civilization." They began calling slavery a "positive good" rather than a necessary evil, insisting that enslaved people were content and well cared for. They claimed slaves were better off than Northern factory workers. These statements were repeated so often that many White Southerners came to believe them.

The South grew defensive. Any criticism was seen as an attack on its way of life. States passed laws restricting free speech, banning abolitionist writings, and punishing dissent. The South became a closed society, intolerant of any challenge to slavery.

The cotton economy shaped Southern politics as well. Planters dominated legislatures and Congress. They used political power to defend slavery, demanding enforcement of the Fugitive Slave Act (the return of escaped people) and the right to expand slavery into new territories. They viewed any restriction on the institution of slavery as a threat to their wealth, status, and survival.

By 1850, the South had tied its future to slavery and cotton. The system enriched a few but impoverished the region as a whole. The South had few factories, little infrastructure, and limited education. It depended on the North for manufactured goods and on Britain for markets. Yet Southern leaders could imagine no alternative. Cotton was king—and slavery was its foundation.

Compromises Over Slavery: Kicking the Can Down the Road

From the beginning, slavery divided the nation. The Constitution had sidestepped the issue, allowing each state to decide for itself. However, as the country expanded west, a problem emerged: would new states allow slavery or prohibit it? The answer would determine the balance of power in Congress.

By 1819, there were eleven free states and eleven slave states, giving each side equal representation in the Senate. That balance was about to break.

Missouri applied for statehood in 1819, seeking to enter as a slave state. Northern congressmen objected. Missouri lay north of the latitude where slavery had traditionally existed. If it entered as a slave state, slavery would spread into new regions, and the North would lose its influence in the Senate.

The debate in Congress was fierce. Southern representatives said Congress had no power to restrict slavery in new states. Northern representatives said slavery was immoral and must not spread. Some threatened disunion. The young nation seemed ready to tear itself apart.

Senator Henry Clay of Kentucky crafted a compromise. Missouri would enter as a slave state. Maine, which had been part of Massachusetts, would enter as a free state, preserving the balance at twelve free and twelve slave states. Additionally, slavery would be prohibited in the rest of the Louisiana Purchase territory north of latitude 36°30', Missouri's southern border. South of that line, slavery would be permitted.

The Missouri Compromise was passed in 1820. It appeared to solve the problem. Each side got something, and the crisis passed.

However, the compromise revealed how deeply divided the country had become. Thomas Jefferson, retired at Monticello, called the debate "a fire bell in the night" that filled him with terror.[i] He understood that the slavery question would one day destroy the Union. The Missouri Compromise did not resolve the conflict; it had merely postponed it.

For thirty years, the compromise held. New states often entered in pairs—one free, one slave—to preserve the balance: Arkansas and Michigan, Florida and Iowa, Texas and Wisconsin. The Senate remained even.

Then came the Mexican-American War. The new territories it added reopened the question. In 1846, even before the war ended, Pennsylvania Congressman David Wilmot proposed that slavery be prohibited in any territory acquired from Mexico. His proposal—the Wilmot Proviso—passed the House but failed in the Senate. Though never enacted, it showed that many Northerners were determined to stop slavery's expansion.

Southerners saw the Wilmot Proviso as an attack on their rights. They argued that Congress could not prohibit citizens from taking their property—meaning enslaved people—into the territories. Slaveholders, they said, had as much right to settle there as anyone else. Excluding slavery was unfair discrimination against the South.

The election of 1848 brought the crisis to a head. Zachary Taylor, a Louisiana plantation owner and hero of the Mexican-American War, won the presidency as a Whig (one of the major political parties of the time). But Taylor surprised everyone. He opposed slavery's expansion. He encouraged California and New Mexico to apply for statehood quickly, bypassing the territorial stage. Both were expected to prohibit slavery.

California's application for statehood in 1850 triggered another national crisis. It had grown rapidly after gold was discovered in 1848. By 1850, its population justified statehood. California's constitution prohibited slavery. If it were admitted, free states would outnumber slave states sixteen to fifteen. The South would lose its Senate veto.

---

[i] "Fire Bell in the Night." https://www.monticello.org/research-education/thomas-jefferson-encyclopedia/fire-bell-night-quotation/

Southern politicians threatened secession. Some spoke openly of forming an independent nation. The Union once again seemed on the verge of collapse.

And once again, Henry Clay stepped forward. Elderly and in poor health, he proposed another compromise with multiple parts:

- California would enter as a free state.
- The rest of the territories seized from Mexico would be organized into the New Mexico and Utah Territories, with no restrictions on slavery. Settlers would decide for themselves whether to permit it—a policy called "popular sovereignty."
- The slave trade, but not slavery itself, would be abolished in Washington, DC.
- A stronger Fugitive Slave Act would require Northern states to return escaped enslaved people and force ordinary citizens to assist in their capture.
- Texas would give up its disputed claims in New Mexico in exchange for federal assumption of its debts.

The debate lasted eight months and became one of the most dramatic in Senate history. Clay, John C. Calhoun of South Carolina, and Daniel Webster of Massachusetts—the "Great Triumvirate" of American politics—made their final appearances on the national stage.

Calhoun was dying. Too weak to deliver his speech, he sat wrapped in blankets while another senator read it for him. He warned that the North must cease attacking slavery and grant the South equal rights in the territories or else the Union would dissolve. He died a month later.

Webster gave his famous "Seventh of March" speech. He supported the compromise, including the Fugitive Slave Act, to save the Union. A native of Massachusetts and an opponent of slavery, Webster's position outraged Northern abolitionists. They called him a traitor. But Webster believed preserving the Union was more important than halting slavery's expansion.

President Taylor opposed the compromise, insisting that California should be admitted immediately without concessions to the South. But Taylor died suddenly in July 1850. Vice President Millard Fillmore became president and supported Clay's plan.

Clay's health failed before the legislation passed, and Senator Stephen Douglas of Illinois took over. Douglas broke the proposal into separate bills and built different coalitions to pass each one. By September 1850, all parts had been enacted. Together, they became known as the Compromise of 1850.

The compromise appeared to work. The crisis passed. Business revived. Politicians congratulated themselves for saving the Union.

However, the Fugitive Slave Act created new turmoil. It required federal commissioners to return escaped enslaved people and denied the accused the right to trial by jury or to testify on their own behalf. Commissioners were paid $10 if they ruled in favor of a slaveholder but only $5 if they ruled in favor of freedom, creating an obvious financial bias. The law also required citizens to help capture fugitives when ordered. Refusal could mean fines or imprisonment.

Northerners hated the law. They saw it as the federal government forcing them to participate in slavery. Several states passed "personal liberty laws" to obstruct enforcement.

Abolitionists became more active and organized. They formed vigilance committees to help fugitives escape to Canada. Figures like Frederick Douglass, a formerly enslaved man who became a powerful speaker and writer, spoke out against the law. Harriet Tubman, who had escaped slavery herself, made repeated dangerous trips into the South as part of the Underground Railroad—a secret network of safe houses and routes that helped enslaved people reach freedom in the North and Canada. Tubman personally led about seventy people to freedom and was never caught.

When slave catchers came north, mobs sometimes freed captives by force. In Boston, activists stormed a courthouse to rescue an escaped slave and spirited him to Canada.

The Fugitive Slave Act radicalized Northern opinion. People who had once been indifferent to slavery became opponents. Harriet Beecher Stowe's novel *Uncle Tom's Cabin*, published in 1852, dramatized slavery's cruelty and the Fugitive Slave Act's evil. It became a sensation, selling 300,000 copies in its first year. The book turned millions of Northerners against slavery. Southerners banned it and denounced it as lies.

The Compromise of 1850 bought time, but it solved nothing. The divisions only deepened.

Bleeding Kansas and John Brown's Raid: The Point of No Return

In 1854, Senator Stephen Douglas sought to organize the Nebraska Territory to promote settlement and build a transcontinental railroad. To gain Southern support, he proposed repealing the Missouri Compromise line. Instead of a fixed boundary, settlers in Kansas and Nebraska would decide the question of slavery themselves through popular sovereignty.

The Kansas-Nebraska Act, passed in May 1854, outraged the North. The Missouri Compromise had been treated as sacred for thirty-four years. Now, it was gone, and slavery could spread into territories that had long been considered free.

The act shattered the old political order. The Whig Party collapsed, unable to bridge its Northern and Southern wings. Out of the chaos, a new party rose in the North—the Republican Party—and it was dedicated to halting slavery's expansion. It drew former Whigs, anti-slavery Democrats, and reformers of many kinds. The Republican Party would never win a single electoral vote in the South before the Civil War, but the North's growing population made it a national force without Southern support.

Kansas quickly became a battleground. Pro-slavery and anti-slavery settlers poured in to shape its future. Missouri slaveholders crossed the border to cast illegal votes, while Northern emigrant aid societies sent settlers opposed to slavery, determined to make Kansas a free state. Both sides arrived armed and ready for conflict.

Violence soon followed. Pro-slavery forces attacked the town of Lawrence, Kansas, destroying printing presses and burning buildings. In retaliation, radical abolitionist John Brown led a gruesome counterattack. He and his followers dragged five pro-slavery settlers from their homes and hacked them to death with swords. Neither side was innocent, but Brown's massacre crossed a line. It was calculated terror meant to drive slavery's supporters from Kansas.

The territory descended into guerrilla warfare. Armed bands raided settlements, burned homes, and murdered opponents. At least fifty-six people were killed. Newspapers called it "Bleeding Kansas." The territory became a violent preview of the national conflict to come.

Even Congress was not immune. In May 1856, Senator Charles Sumner of Massachusetts delivered a blistering speech attacking pro-slavery leaders and mocking Senator Andrew Butler of South Carolina. Two days later, Butler's cousin, Congressman Preston Brooks, entered the Senate chamber and brutally beat Sumner with a cane. Trapped at his desk, Sumner was struck again and again until he collapsed, bleeding and unconscious. He suffered head injuries so severe that he did not return to the Senate for three years.

The North was horrified. A United States senator had been assaulted for speaking his mind on the Senate floor. The South, however, celebrated. Brooks received hundreds of new canes from admirers. One was engraved with the words "Hit him again."

In 1857, the Supreme Court deepened the crisis. Dred Scott, an enslaved man, had been taken by his owner into free territory. He sued for his freedom, arguing that living on free soil made him free. Chief Justice Roger Taney, writing for the majority, issued one of the most infamous decisions in American history.

Taney ruled that Black people—whether enslaved or free—could never be American citizens and had "no rights which the white man was bound to respect."[i] Scott, therefore, had no standing to sue in federal court. Taney went further, declaring that Congress had no power to prohibit slavery in the territories. The Missouri Compromise, he said, had been unconstitutional from the beginning. Slaveholders could take their "property" anywhere in the nation. Popular sovereignty was meaningless.

The South rejoiced, but the North was enraged. Republicans denounced the decision as judicial tyranny. Abraham Lincoln, a rising Republican lawyer in Illinois, argued that the ruling was morally wrong and could not stand as the nation's final word.

Meanwhile, Kansas remained in chaos. Pro-slavery forces wrote a constitution at Lecompton allowing slavery and held a vote to approve it. The election was fraudulent—anti-slavery settlers boycotted, and pro-slavery voters rigged the results. President James Buchanan, a Pennsylvania Democrat sympathetic to the South, supported the constitution anyway and urged Congress to approve it.

Stephen Douglas broke with Buchanan, insisting that if Kansas voters truly opposed slavery—and most did—their will must prevail. Congress ultimately rejected the Lecompton Constitution. Kansas entered the Union as a free state in 1861, but the struggle had poisoned national politics.

---

[i] Magnusson, Martin. "No Rights Which the White Man Was Bound to Respect." https://www.acslaw.org/expertforum/no-rights-which-the-white-man-was-bound-to-respect/

Then, in October 1859, John Brown returned to the stage. Convinced that slavery would never end without bloodshed, he planned to seize the federal arsenal at Harpers Ferry, Virginia, arm enslaved people, and ignite a general uprising.

Brown and eighteen followers—thirteen White men and five Black men—attacked on the night of October 16. They captured the arsenal but were quickly surrounded. No enslaved people joined them; Brown's plan had been doomed from the start. By morning, the local militia had trapped them inside.

Colonel Robert E. Lee led a detachment of US Marines that stormed the building. Ten of Brown's men were killed, including two of his sons. Brown himself was wounded and captured.

He was tried for treason, murder, and inciting slave insurrection. Found guilty, he faced execution. At his trial and in his final statements, Brown was calm, eloquent, and unrepentant. He declared that slavery was an evil so monstrous that violence was justified to destroy it. On December 2, 1859, John Brown was hanged. His last written words were prophetic: "I, John Brown, am now quite certain that the crimes of this guilty land will never be purged away but with blood."[i]

Many Northerners condemned Brown's violence but admired his courage and conviction. Henry David Thoreau compared him to Christ; Ralph Waldo Emerson called him a saint. Brown became a martyr to the anti-slavery cause.

The South was terrified. Brown had attempted to spark the nightmare they most feared—a slave rebellion. Southerners saw him as a terrorist and blamed Republicans for inspiring him. They began forming militias and stockpiling weapons, convinced that Northern abolitionists were preparing for war.

John Brown's raid did not start the Civil War, but it made the conflict feel inevitable. The South believed the North sought to destroy its way of life. The North believed the South was a violent, lawless society built on human bondage. Trust was gone. Compromise was dead.

In 1860, Americans would elect a new president—a choice that would decide whether the nation held together or fell apart.

---

[i] "John Brown's Last Note." https://www.marxists.org/archive/brown-john/1859/last-note.htm

Chapter 12: The Civil War: A Nation at War with Itself

Secession and the Firing on Fort Sumter

The election of 1860 tore the country apart. The Democratic Party split along sectional lines. Northern Democrats nominated Stephen Douglas, while Southern Democrats chose John C. Breckinridge of Kentucky. A fourth group, the Constitutional Union Party, nominated John Bell of Tennessee and tried to ignore the slavery question entirely.

The Republican Party nominated Abraham Lincoln, a lawyer from Illinois with little political experience. He had served one term in Congress and lost a Senate race to Douglas in 1858. However, he was moderate, articulate, and from a crucial swing state. The Republicans knew they needed only the North to win.

Lincoln's position on slavery was clear but cautious. He opposed its expansion into new territories and believed it was morally wrong, yet he pledged not to interfere where it already existed. He would enforce the Fugitive Slave Act and preserve the Union above all else.

Southerners didn't believe him. They saw Lincoln and the Republican Party as mortal enemies. To them, stopping slavery's spread meant slowly strangling the institution itself. Many feared he would encourage slave revolts and destroy their way of life. They would not accept a Republican president.

Lincoln won the election with just under 40 percent of the popular vote, but he secured a decisive Electoral College victory, earning 180 votes. He carried every free state except New Jersey, which he split with Douglas. He did not win a single Southern state and wasn't even on the ballot in ten of them. The nation had voted along rigid sectional lines.

South Carolina moved first. On December 20, 1860, a state convention voted unanimously to secede. The delegates declared that the Union was dissolved and that South Carolina was now a free and independent state.

Others followed swiftly: Mississippi on January 9, Florida on January 10, Alabama on January 11, Georgia on January 19, Louisiana on January 26, and Texas on February 1. Seven states had left the Union before Lincoln even took office.

In February 1861, delegates from the seceded states met in Montgomery, Alabama, to form a new nation—the Confederate States of America. They adopted a constitution modeled on that of the United States but with explicit protections for slavery. Jefferson Davis of Mississippi became president, and Alexander Stephens of Georgia became vice president. Stephens proclaimed that the Confederacy rested upon "the great truth that the negro is not equal to the white man" and that slavery was its "cornerstone."[i]

President James Buchanan did nothing. He declared secession illegal but insisted he had no constitutional power to stop it. He left the crisis for Lincoln, who would not take office until March 4. The country drifted toward war.

The immediate crisis centered on federal property in the South. Most forts, arsenals, and customhouses had already been seized by local forces, but a few remained under US control. The most important was Fort Sumter in Charleston Harbor, South Carolina.

Major Robert Anderson commanded fewer than ninety men inside the fort. South Carolina demanded that he surrender, but Anderson refused. He was a federal officer on federal soil and would not yield without orders from Washington.

Lincoln took office on March 4, 1861. In his inaugural address, he again reassured the South that he would not interfere with slavery where it existed. However, he declared secession both illegal and void. The Union, he said, was perpetual; no state could lawfully leave it. He

---

[i] "Cornerstone Speech." https://www.battlefields.org/learn/primary-sources/cornerstone-speech

pledged to enforce federal law everywhere. He closed with an appeal: "We are not enemies, but friends. We must not be enemies."[i]

The South was unmoved. Confederate leaders wanted Fort Sumter. As long as the US flag flew over it, their independence was incomplete.

By April, the garrison was running out of food. Lincoln faced a terrible choice: abandon the fort, which would seem to recognize secession, or resupply it, which might provoke war. He chose a middle course. He announced he would send provisions—food only, no arms—and informed South Carolina in advance. If the Confederates allowed the ships through, there would be no conflict. If they fired, they would start the war.

Confederate President Jefferson Davis made his decision. He ordered General P. G. T. Beauregard to demand the fort's surrender. If it refused, he was to open fire.

Anderson refused. At 4:30 a.m. on April 12, 1861, Confederate guns roared to life. For thirty-four hours, they hammered Fort Sumter with some four thousand shells. The fort's walls shuddered under the bombardment, but remarkably, no one on either side was killed during the attack. The first deaths of the war came only after the surrender, when a cannon exploded during a ceremonial salute, killing two Union soldiers.

The attack on Fort Sumter.[ii]

[i] "First Inaugural Address of Abraham Lincoln."
https://avalon.law.yale.edu/19th_century/lincoln1.asp

On April 13, Anderson surrendered. His men marched out with flags flying and drums beating, as they were allowed to evacuate with full honors. The Confederate banner was raised over the fort. The Civil War had begun.

Lincoln called for seventy-five thousand volunteers to suppress the rebellion. The call forced the Upper South to choose sides. Virginia, Arkansas, Tennessee, and North Carolina—states that had resisted secession after Lincoln's election—refused to fight against their Southern neighbors. Within weeks, all four joined the Confederacy.

Four slave states remained loyal: Delaware, Maryland, Kentucky, and Missouri. These border states were crucial. If Maryland seceded, Washington, DC, would be surrounded. If Kentucky left, the Confederacy would control the Ohio River. Lincoln used a mix of political persuasion and military authority to hold them. He suspended habeas corpus in Maryland and arrested suspected Confederate sympathizers.

By summer 1861, eleven states had seceded. The Confederate capital moved from Montgomery to Richmond, Virginia—just one hundred miles south of Washington. The war everyone had feared, and many had thought impossible, had come at last.

Blue vs. Gray: Strengths, Weaknesses, and Strategies

The Union and the Confederacy entered the war with different strengths, weaknesses, and strategies.

The Union held overwhelming advantages in population and resources. About 22 million people lived in the North compared to roughly 9 million in the South—and 3.5 million of those were enslaved people who would not fight for the Confederacy. The North could raise larger armies and replace its losses more easily.

It also possessed nearly all of the nation's industry. Northern factories produced 97 percent of the country's firearms, 94 percent of its cloth, and 90 percent of its boots and shoes. The North had about 110,000 factories, while the South had about 18,000. Its industrial power could equip vast armies with weapons, uniforms, and supplies, while the South had to import most of what it needed.

The Union also had 22,000 miles of railroad track, compared to 9,000 in the South. Northern transportation lines were more extensive, better maintained, and more efficiently connected, allowing troops and supplies to move quickly and reliably.

The Union Navy dominated the seas. The Confederacy began the war with virtually no navy at all. Meanwhile, the Union could impose a blockade that cut off trade and imports. Since the South relied heavily on exporting cotton to buy weapons and goods from Europe, the blockade slowly strangled its economy.

Yet the Confederacy possessed important strengths of its own. It fought a defensive war and did not need to conquer the North. It only had to survive until the North gave up. Its armies could operate on familiar ground, using shorter interior lines of supply and communication, and they enjoyed the support of local populations.

The South also had a strong military tradition. Many of the US Army's finest officers were Southerners who resigned their commissions when their states seceded. Robert E. Lee, for instance, was offered command of the Union Army but refused to fight against Virginia. Generals such as Lee, Joseph E. Johnston, and Thomas "Stonewall" Jackson gave the Confederacy skilled leadership and high morale.

The Confederate strategy relied on endurance. Southern leaders believed that if their armies could win enough battles and make the war costly and unpopular, the North might choose peace. Many Northerners had opposed abolition before the war and might not support a long, bloody conflict to force the South back into the Union. Confederate leaders believed that time favored them.

They also counted on foreign help. Britain and France depended on Southern cotton for their textile industries, and Confederate officials hoped that "King Cotton" would compel those nations to recognize the Confederacy or even intervene militarily. However, the plan failed. Britain had large cotton reserves and found new suppliers in Egypt and India. Its mills also relied on Northern grain. Public opinion in Europe was strongly anti-slavery. Neither Britain nor France ever recognized the Confederacy.

The Union's overall strategy came from General Winfield Scott, the aging hero of the Mexican-American War. Known as the Anaconda Plan, it aimed to suffocate the South by blockading its ports to cut off trade, seizing control of the Mississippi River to split the Confederacy in two, and capturing Richmond, the Confederate capital. The Union would strike from multiple directions and use its greater resources to wear down resistance. The plan would take time, but Scott believed patience and pressure would prevail.

Most Northerners, however, expected a quick victory. They assumed the South would collapse after one or two decisive battles. They were wrong. The war would last four years and claim more than 600,000 lives—more than all other American wars combined until Vietnam. It would become the bloodiest conflict in American history.

From Bull Run to Gettysburg: The Turning Points

The first major battle of the Civil War came in July 1861. A Union force marched from Washington toward Richmond. About thirty thousand Union soldiers met twenty thousand Confederates near Manassas Junction, Virginia, along a creek called Bull Run.

At first, Union forces pushed the Confederates back, and victory seemed certain. Spectators from Washington—congressmen, journalists, and their families—came to watch the battle as if it were a grand show. They brought picnic baskets and carriages.

Then, Confederate reinforcements arrived by railroad. General Thomas Jackson's brigade held firm on a hill. Another Confederate general shouted, "There is Jackson standing like a stone wall!" The name stuck—"Stonewall" Jackson—and the Confederates rallied behind him.

The Confederate line held and then counterattacked. The Union Army's retreat turned into a chaotic rout. Soldiers dropped their weapons and ran toward Washington, clogging the roads with wagons, artillery, and terrified spectators fleeing alongside them.

The Battle of Bull Run—called First Manassas in the South—shocked the North. It was clear this would not be a short or easy war. The Confederacy had proven its determination and skill. Lincoln called for more volunteers and appointed General George B. McClellan to command the Army of the Potomac, the Union's primary land army.

McClellan was a gifted organizer and trainer. He built the Army of the Potomac into a disciplined, well-equipped force. But he was also cautious—too cautious. He constantly overestimated enemy strength and hesitated to attack. Lincoln grew frustrated. "If General McClellan does not want to use the army," he said, "I would like to borrow it."[i]

In the spring of 1862, McClellan finally acted. He transported his army by sea to the Virginia Peninsula and marched toward Richmond. The Peninsula Campaign brought Union forces within six miles of the

---

[i] "George B. McClellan." https://www.thirteen.org/wnet/historyofus/web06/features/bio/B06.html

Confederate capital. But on May 31, Confederate General Joseph E. Johnston attacked at Seven Pines. Johnston was wounded in battle, and Robert E. Lee took command of the Confederate Army.

Lee was everything McClellan was not. He was bold, aggressive, and willing to take risks. In late June, he launched a series of attacks known as the Seven Days' Battles. Lee's army took heavy losses but pushed McClellan back to the James River. The Peninsula Campaign had failed.

Lincoln then gave command of the Army of Virginia to General John Pope, but Pope fared no better. In August 1862, Lee defeated him decisively at the Second Battle of Bull Run. Lee then invaded Maryland, hoping a victory on Northern soil would encourage foreign recognition of the Confederacy and persuade Maryland to join the South.

McClellan, who had been restored to command, moved to intercept Lee. On September 17, 1862, the two armies clashed near Sharpsburg, Maryland, at Antietam Creek. The Battle of Antietam became the bloodiest single day in American history. More than twenty-two thousand soldiers were killed, wounded, or missing. The carnage was unimaginable—fields littered with bodies and a sunken road filled with corpses that earned the name Bloody Lane.

Tactically, the battle was a draw, but Lee was forced to retreat back into Virginia. For Lincoln, that was enough. Five days later, he issued the preliminary Emancipation Proclamation.

In the West, the Union enjoyed greater success. General Ulysses S. Grant captured Fort Henry and Fort Donelson in Tennessee in February 1862, opening the way into the Deep South. At Shiloh in April, Grant's army was surprised by a Confederate attack but rallied to win a bloody victory. Grant's determination earned him a reputation as a fighter who refused to quit.

The Union Navy captured New Orleans in April 1862 under Admiral David Farragut, giving the Union control of the Mississippi River's mouth. By mid-1863, Union forces controlled most of the river except for Vicksburg, Mississippi, and Port Hudson, Louisiana. Grant laid siege to Vicksburg, bombarding the city for six weeks. Civilians hid in caves, and food ran out. On July 4, 1863, Vicksburg surrendered. Port Hudson fell days later. The Union now controlled the entire Mississippi River, cutting the Confederacy in two.

At the same time, Lee launched a second invasion of the North. In June 1863, his army marched into Pennsylvania, hoping to relieve pressure on Vicksburg, threaten Northern cities, and perhaps force Lincoln to negotiate peace. The Union Army of the Potomac, now led by General George Meade, moved to intercept him.

The two armies met by chance at the small town of Gettysburg, Pennsylvania. Neither side intended to fight there, but a skirmish on July 1 escalated as both sides called in reinforcements. Confederate forces pushed Union troops back through the town, but the Union held the high ground—Cemetery Hill and Cemetery Ridge—south of town.

On July 2, Lee attacked both Union flanks. The fighting was ferocious. On the Union left, at Little Round Top, the 20th Maine Regiment under Colonel Joshua Chamberlain held the line in desperate hand-to-hand combat. When they ran out of ammunition, they fixed bayonets and charged downhill, driving the Confederates back.

On July 3, Lee made his boldest gamble. He ordered a frontal assault on the Union center. About 12,500 Confederate soldiers under General George Pickett marched across nearly a mile of open ground under relentless artillery and rifle fire. It was a slaughter. Union guns tore gaps in the Confederate ranks. A few reached the Union lines, but they were overwhelmed. Pickett's Charge failed disastrously—more than half of the attacking force was killed, wounded, or captured.

Pickett's Charge.[28]

Lee retreated to Virginia on July 4. The Battle of Gettysburg cost about fifty-one thousand casualties in total—the bloodiest battle of the war. Lee would never again invade the North. The Confederacy's best chance for victory was gone.

Gettysburg and Vicksburg marked the turning point of the Civil War. The Confederacy could no longer win militarily. From then on, it could only fight to survive and hope the North would eventually tire of war.

The Emancipation Proclamation and Lincoln's Leadership

When the war began, Lincoln said its purpose was to preserve the Union, not to end slavery. Many Northerners were willing to fight for the Union but not for emancipation. Lincoln needed to keep the border states loyal and couldn't afford to make the war about slavery—at least not yet.

Still, slavery was always at the center of the conflict. The Confederacy had seceded to protect it. The war's fundamental cause was slavery and its expansion.

As the fighting continued, Northern attitudes began to shift. Union soldiers encountered slavery firsthand as they advanced through the South. They saw families separated, people whipped and starved, and human beings treated as property. Many who had once been indifferent to slavery came to see it as evil.

Enslaved people themselves pushed the issue. Whenever Union troops approached, enslaved people fled to Union lines, seeking freedom. Some Union commanders were unsure how to handle them. A few even returned them to slaveholders.

General Benjamin Butler found a legal solution. He declared that escaped slaves were "contraband of war"—enemy property that could be seized. The idea spread quickly. Soon, thousands of "contrabands" sought refuge in Union camps, where they provided labor and information about Confederate movements. Many later enlisted when the Union began accepting Black soldiers.

Lincoln moved cautiously toward emancipation. In August 1861, Congress passed the First Confiscation Act, freeing enslaved people used to support the Confederate war effort. In April 1862, Congress abolished slavery in Washington, DC. In June, it banned slavery in all federal territories—an act that directly challenged the Supreme Court's Dred Scott decision.

Lincoln initially proposed gradual, compensated emancipation. Border states could voluntarily free enslaved people over time, and the federal government would pay slaveholders for their loss. Freed people would be resettled in Africa or the Caribbean. However, the border states refused, and the plan went nowhere.

By mid-1862, Lincoln had decided that slavery had to end—not only because it was wrong but because it was necessary for victory. Ending slavery would weaken the Confederacy by removing its labor force and preventing Britain or France from supporting a nation fighting to preserve human bondage. It would also allow Black men to join the Union Army.

Lincoln waited for a Union victory before acting. He didn't want emancipation to look like an act of desperation. Antietam provided that opportunity.

On September 22, 1862, Lincoln issued the preliminary Emancipation Proclamation. It declared that on January 1, 1863, all enslaved people in states still in rebellion would be freed. The Confederacy had one hundred days to return to the Union and keep slavery. None did.

On January 1, 1863, Lincoln signed the final Emancipation Proclamation. It did not apply to the border states or to areas of the Confederacy already under Union control since those regions were not considered to be "in rebellion." Critics mocked the document for freeing enslaved people where Lincoln had no power while leaving them enslaved where he did.

However, the proclamation changed the war's meaning. The Union was now fighting to end slavery as well as to preserve the nation. The war had become a moral crusade. The proclamation also ensured that Britain and France would not intervene since neither government would support a war to preserve slavery.

The proclamation allowed Black men to serve in the Union Army and Navy. By the end of the war, about 180,000 Black soldiers and 19,000 sailors had served. They fought in segregated units under White officers and were paid less than White soldiers, but they fought bravely. At Fort Wagner, South Carolina, the 54th Massachusetts Infantry led a courageous but doomed assault. Their valor earned widespread respect and helped shift public opinion.

Black soldiers faced deadly risks if captured. The Confederacy refused to treat them as prisoners of war. Many were executed or sold into slavery. At Fort Pillow, Tennessee, Confederate troops under Nathan Bedford Forrest massacred surrendering Black soldiers. Still, tens of thousands continued to fight for freedom and the Union cause.

Lincoln's leadership throughout the war was tested constantly. He struggled with hesitant generals, political opposition, and personal grief. Abolitionists accused him of moving too slowly, while conservatives said he moved too fast. "Copperhead" Democrats demanded peace at any cost.

Lincoln never lost sight of his ultimate goal—the preservation of the Union. His personal views were clear—he hated slavery—but he acted with political caution and constitutional restraint. Once he concluded that emancipation was necessary to save the Union, he used his wartime powers as commander in chief to make it happen.

Lincoln also sought to make emancipation permanent. The Emancipation Proclamation was a war measure that could be reversed. To end slavery everywhere, he pushed for a constitutional amendment. The Thirteenth Amendment, which abolished slavery in all states, was passed by Congress in January 1865 and sent to the states for ratification. Lincoln would not live to see it completed, but he had set freedom in motion.

By 1864, Union victory was within reach. Grant, now general in chief, launched coordinated offensives across the South. In Virginia, his army hammered Lee's forces in brutal, grinding battles, such as the Wilderness, Spotsylvania, and Cold Harbor, to name a few. Grant refused to retreat. Meanwhile, General William Tecumseh Sherman captured Atlanta in September 1864 and marched to the sea, destroying railroads, factories, and farms to break the South's ability to fight.

Lincoln faced reelection that fall. Many feared he would lose. His opponent, George McClellan, promised to negotiate peace. But Sherman's capture of Atlanta revived Northern morale, and Lincoln won easily.

In his second inaugural address in March 1865, Lincoln spoke of reconciliation and responsibility. He acknowledged that slavery had caused the war and urged Americans to rebuild "with malice toward none, with charity for all." He sought "to bind up the nation's wounds" and achieve a lasting peace founded on justice and freedom.[i]

Five weeks later, the war was nearly over, but Lincoln was dead. He had preserved the Union and struck down slavery. His steady vision and moral courage carried the nation through its darkest hour and made him, in the eyes of history, one of America's greatest leaders.

---

[i] "Lincoln's Second Inaugural Address." https://www.nps.gov/linc/learn/historyculture/lincoln-second-inaugural.htm

Chapter 13: Reconstruction: An Unfinished Revolution

Rebuilding a Broken Nation: Presidential and Radical Reconstruction

The Civil War ended in April 1865. General Robert E. Lee surrendered to Ulysses S. Grant at Appomattox Court House, Virginia, on April 9, and other Confederate forces followed in the weeks that came. The war had claimed an estimated 620,000 to 750,000 American lives. The South lay in ruins—its cities burned, railroads destroyed, and fields devastated. Four million formerly enslaved people were now free. The Southern economy had collapsed.

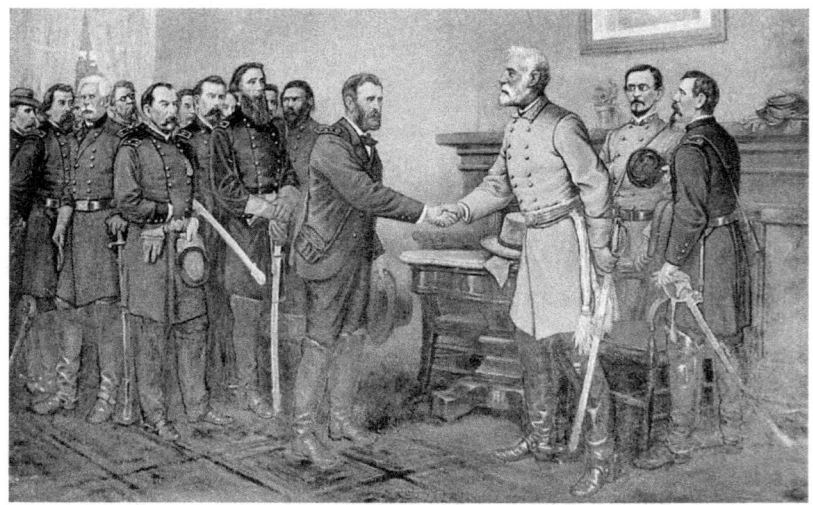

The surrender of General Robert E. Lee.[24]

The question was what to do next. How would the South rejoin the Union? What would happen to former Confederate leaders? What rights would freed people have? These questions defined the era known as Reconstruction, which lasted from 1865 to 1877.

Lincoln had already begun thinking about Reconstruction during the war. In December 1863, he announced his "Ten Percent Plan." When 10 percent of voters in a Confederate state took an oath of loyalty to the Union, that state could form a new government and rejoin. The new government had to abolish slavery, but Lincoln's plan said nothing about voting rights for freed people. It was deliberately lenient toward former Confederate states.

Radical Republicans in Congress considered the plan far too forgiving. They wanted to punish Confederate leaders and safeguard the rights of freed people. In July 1864, Congress passed the Wade-Davis Bill, which required 50 percent of voters to swear loyalty and demanded stronger guarantees of equality. Lincoln refused to sign it before Congress adjourned.

The debate soon became moot. On April 14, 1865—five days after Lee's surrender—Lincoln went to Ford's Theatre in Washington to see a play. John Wilkes Booth, a Confederate sympathizer and popular actor, entered Lincoln's box and shot him in the head. Lincoln died the next morning. He was fifty-six years old.

THE ASSASSINATION OF PRESIDENT LINCOLN,
AT FORD'S THEATRE WASHINGTON.D.C.APRIL 14th 1865.

A depiction of Lincoln's assassination.[25]

Booth escaped, but he was hunted down and killed twelve days later. Eight conspirators were arrested, tried, and convicted. Four, including Mary Surratt—the first woman executed by the federal government—were hanged. Three received life sentences, and one was imprisoned for six years.

Lincoln's assassination shocked the nation. Many Southerners feared harsh retribution. However, Vice President Andrew Johnson, who became president, pursued a surprisingly lenient course.

Johnson was a Democrat from Tennessee and the only Southern senator to remain loyal to the Union when his state seceded. Lincoln had chosen him as his 1864 running mate to appeal to Democrats and border-state voters. Johnson despised the Southern planter aristocracy—he had been poor and resented wealthy slaveholders—but he also believed in White supremacy and states' rights.

His Reconstruction plan closely resembled Lincoln's. Johnson offered amnesty to most Confederates who swore loyalty. High-ranking officials and wealthy planters had to apply to him personally for pardons, yet he issued thousands, restoring much of the old elite's influence. He appointed provisional governors in Southern states. Once they drafted new constitutions abolishing slavery and renouncing secession, they could rejoin the Union.

Southern states moved quickly under his plan. They ratified the Thirteenth Amendment, which abolished slavery nationwide in December 1865. They also enacted laws known as Black Codes to restrict the freedom of Black people. Though details varied by state, the intent was the same—to keep freed people subordinate. Black citizens were barred from owning guns, serving on juries, or testifying against Whites in court. They needed written permission to travel or gather in groups, and many states required yearly labor contracts. Those without contracts could be arrested for vagrancy and forced to work.

The Black Codes effectively re-created slavery in all but name, proving that the South intended to maintain White control despite emancipation.

Elections in the fall of 1865 made matters worse. Southern voters returned many former Confederate leaders to power. Georgia even sent Alexander Stephens, the Confederacy's former vice president, to the US Senate. When Congress convened that December, dozens of ex-Confederates arrived to claim seats.

Republicans in Congress were outraged. The South had lost the war but behaved as if it had won. Southern governments were defiant, their laws were repressive, and Johnson's leniency seemed to reward rebellion. Congress refused to seat the Southern delegates and created a Joint Committee on Reconstruction to investigate conditions in the South. Reports from the Freedmen's Bureau, a federal agency aiding freed people, revealed thousands of violent attacks and murders had been committed with impunity.

In early 1866, Congress passed the Civil Rights Act, declaring that all people born in the United States were citizens with equal rights under the law. Designed to nullify the Black Codes, it was the first major civil rights law in US history. Johnson vetoed it, claiming it violated states' rights, but Congress overrode his veto—the first override of a major presidential veto in American history.

Freedmen voting in New Orleans.[36]

That same year, Congress proposed the Fourteenth Amendment, defining citizenship as being born within the United States and guaranteeing equal protection and due process under the law. It also reduced representation for states that denied voting rights to adult males and barred former Confederate officials from holding office unless Congress granted amnesty.

Tennessee ratified the amendment and was readmitted to the Union. The other Southern states, urged on by Johnson, rejected it. Johnson campaigned openly against both the amendment and the Republican majority in the 1866 congressional elections.

The results were disastrous for him. Republicans won overwhelming control of Congress, gaining enough seats to override any veto. Radical Reconstruction had begun.

In March 1867, Congress passed the Reconstruction Acts over Johnson's veto. These laws divided the South into five military districts governed by Union generals until new governments were established. To rejoin the Union, states had to write new constitutions guaranteeing Black male suffrage and ratify the Fourteenth Amendment. Former Confederate leaders who had held office before the war were excluded from the process.

Congress also moved to limit Johnson's power. The Tenure of Office Act required Senate approval for the removal of certain officials. It was aimed specifically at protecting Secretary of War Edwin Stanton, a Radical Republican ally.

When Johnson tried to fire Stanton in February 1868, the House of Representatives impeached him for violating the act and other offenses—the first presidential impeachment in US history. The Senate trial took place that spring. Republicans fell one vote short of the two-thirds needed to convict. Seven Republican senators voted to acquit, believing Johnson's actions did not meet the constitutional standard for removal. He remained in office but was politically powerless.

Meanwhile, Reconstruction continued under military supervision. Hundreds of thousands of Black men registered to vote and helped elect delegates to state constitutional conventions. The new constitutions created public school systems, reformed taxes, and guaranteed civil rights.

By 1868, six southern states—Arkansas, Alabama, Florida, Louisiana, North Carolina, and South Carolina—had ratified new constitutions and the Fourteenth Amendment. They were readmitted to the Union. The remaining four—Georgia, Mississippi, Texas, and Virginia—followed by 1870 after ratifying the Fifteenth Amendment, which prohibited denying the right to vote on the basis of race.

The End of an Era: The Compromise of 1877 and the Rise of Jim Crow

The presidential election of 1876 brought Reconstruction to an end. It became one of the most disputed contests in American history.

Republican Rutherford B. Hayes of Ohio faced Democrat Samuel J. Tilden of New York. Tilden won the popular vote by about 250,000, but the Electoral College was unresolved. Tilden had 184 electoral votes—one short of the 185 needed to win—while Hayes had 165. Twenty votes were disputed: one from Oregon and a total of nineteen from Florida, Louisiana, and South Carolina, the three Southern states still under Republican control.

Both parties claimed victory in those states and submitted conflicting sets of electoral votes, each accusing the other of fraud. Both were right to some degree. Democrats had used intimidation to keep Black citizens from voting, while Republicans had manipulated vote counts.

The Constitution offered no clear procedure for resolving such a dispute. Congress had to decide, but with Democrats controlling the House and Republicans controlling the Senate, neither side trusted the other's judgment.

To break the deadlock, Congress created a special Electoral Commission of fifteen members: five senators, five representatives, and five Supreme Court justices. It was meant to be balanced—seven Republicans, seven Democrats, and one independent. When the independent justice declined to serve and a Republican replaced him, the commission ended up with eight Republicans and seven Democrats.

Every disputed vote was decided strictly along party lines. Hayes won each contest, giving him 185 electoral votes to Tilden's 184.

Democrats were outraged. If they controlled the House, they could have blocked the count. Talk of armed resistance spread. The nation seemed on the brink of another crisis.

Behind the scenes, a deal was struck. Though details remain debated, Southern Democrats agreed to accept Hayes's election. In return, Republicans promised to withdraw federal troops from the South, effectively ending Reconstruction. Hayes also pledged federal support for Southern infrastructure projects and the appointment of at least one Southern Democrat to his Cabinet.

This arrangement, known as the Compromise of 1877, was finalized in February. Hayes took office on March 4, and in April, he ordered the last federal troops to withdraw from South Carolina and Louisiana. The remaining Reconstruction governments collapsed immediately. Democrats took control. Reconstruction was over.

The consequences for Black Southerners were devastating. Without federal protection, White-dominated state governments began systematically dismantling Black rights.

Unable to overtly violate the Fourteenth and Fifteenth Amendments, Southern lawmakers found indirect ways around them. They passed "race-neutral" measures designed to suppress Black voting. Poll taxes required payment to vote, barring many poor citizens. Literacy tests demanded that voters interpret sections of the state constitution—tests graded subjectively by White officials, who failed Black college graduates while passing illiterate Whites. Some states added grandfather clauses, exempting men from such tests if their grandfathers had been eligible to vote. This ensured poor White men could vote while Black men, whose ancestors had been enslaved, could not.

The results were staggering. In Louisiana, around 130,000 Black men were registered to vote in 1896; by 1904, only around 1,300 remained. Across the South, Black political power vanished almost overnight.

At the same time, Southern legislatures enacted segregation acts known as Jim Crow laws, named after a racist minstrel character. These laws mandated racial separation in nearly every sphere of life—schools, hospitals, railroads, streetcars, restaurants, theaters, hotels, parks, and public facilities. "Whites Only" and "Colored" signs marked the new racial order.

These laws were not about separation but domination. Facilities for Black citizens were always inferior. Schools were starved of funds, railroad cars were decrepit, and waiting rooms were cramped and neglected. The intent was unmistakable. The laws were meant to enforce the idea of Black inferiority.

In 1896, the Supreme Court gave constitutional sanction to segregation. In *Plessy v. Ferguson*, the Supreme Court ruled that segregation was legal as long as facilities were "separate but equal." The case arose when Homer Plessy, a Black man in Louisiana, was arrested for sitting in a Whites-only train car. The Supreme Court upheld his conviction. Only Justice John Marshall Harlan dissented, declaring that "the Constitution is color-blind" and that segregation violated the

Fourteenth Amendment—a view that would not prevail for over sixty years.

Violence reinforced White supremacy. Lynching—murder by mob, usually by hanging—became a tool of terror. Between 1877 and 1950, thousands of Black Americans were lynched, often on false accusations or for trivial "offenses," such as speaking disrespectfully to a White person, looking at a White woman, or achieving economic success.

Many lynchings were public spectacles. Crowds of hundreds or even thousands gathered to watch, taking photographs and selling them as postcards. Victims were tortured, mutilated, and killed. Local authorities rarely intervened. The federal government did nothing.

White supremacist terrorist organizations helped maintain this system. The Ku Klux Klan, founded in Tennessee in 1866, was the most infamous. Klan members wore white robes and hoods to hide their identities. They rode at night, attacking Black people and White Republicans who supported them. They whipped, tortured, and murdered. They burned homes, schools, and churches. The Klan's goal was to terrorize Black people into submission and restore White Democratic control of the South.

Federal efforts temporarily broke the Klan's power in the early 1870s, but it had already helped destroy Reconstruction. Though the original Klan faded, the violence and intimidation it represented continued. White mobs attacked Black communities, burned homes and businesses, and drove successful Black families out of towns. The system that emerged was white supremacy enforced by law and terror. Black Americans became second-class citizens in their own country. They were denied the right to vote, denied equal education, denied justice, and lived under constant threat of violence.

This was not a return to slavery, though. It introduced a rigid racial caste system more sweeping and institutionalized than what came before. Slavery had been about labor and property; Jim Crow was about race and power.

Despite the odds, Black Southerners resisted. They built communities, churches, schools, and businesses. They preserved their dignity, family, and faith. They never ceased demanding justice. But without the support of the federal government and the courts, the struggle for equality would last nearly a century.

Reconstruction had sought to fulfill the promises of the Declaration of Independence and the Constitution. For a brief time, it seemed possible. Black men voted, held office, and sent their children to school. Then it ended. The North lost the will to continue, the South regained control, and the promise of equality was postponed. The failures of Reconstruction demanded another movement, another generation, and new sacrifices to correct them. That struggle would come, but not for a long time.

Chapter 14: The Gilded Age: Robber Barons and Railroads

The Industrial Revolution, American Style

Between 1870 and 1900, the United States transformed from a farming nation into an industrial power. New technologies, vast natural resources, and millions of workers created an economic boom unlike anything the world had seen.

The numbers tell the story. In 1860, America trailed the great industrial powers in manufacturing output, but by the end of the century, it had overtaken them. Steel production exploded, from tens of thousands of tons in the 1870s to over eleven million tons by 1900. Railroads expanded severalfold. And the US population soared, increasing more than two times over those four decades.

Several forces drove this growth. The nation possessed immense natural wealth—coal in Pennsylvania and West Virginia, iron ore in Minnesota, oil in Pennsylvania and later Texas, and timber across the continent. These resources fed the new industries.

Innovation reshaped daily life. Thomas Edison didn't invent the first light bulb, but he perfected a practical one and, more importantly, created the entire system of power generation and distribution that illuminated cities. His Menlo Park laboratories produced invention after invention—the phonograph, the motion-picture camera, and an improved telephone transmitter. Edison held more than one thousand patents.

Alexander Graham Bell introduced the telephone in 1876. Within two decades, wires connected cities nationwide. Christopher Sholes devised the typewriter. Nikola Tesla developed the alternating-current system that powered long-distance transmission, and George Westinghouse built the infrastructure to use it. Together, these technologies created new industries and millions of jobs.

The railroad knit it all together. Trains carried raw materials to factories and finished goods to markets, opening the West to settlement. Railroads also created employment in steel, coal, and transport. In 1869, the transcontinental railroad united the country when the Union Pacific, building west from Omaha, met the Central Pacific from Sacramento at Promontory Summit, Utah. The "golden spike" driven that May cut travel from New York to San Francisco from months to a single week.

The celebration of the completion of the transcontinental railroad.[17]

To spur construction, the federal government granted railroad companies between 130 and 175 million acres of land—an area larger than Texas. Companies sold this land to settlers to raise capital, founding towns along their routes.

But corruption was rampant. Executives bribed politicians, inflated construction costs, and manipulated stocks. The Crédit Mobilier scandal exposed how insiders overcharged the Union Pacific by millions while bribing congressmen with shares. A few tycoons amassed fortunes while laborers lived in poverty.

New corporate forms fueled expansion. Corporations could raise capital by selling stock, and limited liability encouraged investment. John D. Rockefeller, through Standard Oil (founded in 1870), used secret railroad rebates, predatory pricing, and takeovers to control about 90 percent of US oil refining by 1880. His "trust" centralized dozens of firms under one board, creating the nation's first great monopoly.

Andrew Carnegie built a steel empire from humble beginnings. Born poor in Scotland, he immigrated as a child and rose from mill worker to industrialist. Adopting the Bessemer process, he made steel faster and cheaper. By owning iron mines, coal fields, railroads, and ships, he controlled every stage of production—a system of "vertical integration" that made his company more efficient and profitable than any rival. By 1900, Carnegie Steel produced more than all of Britain's mills.

J. P. Morgan, the banker, financed railroads and industries, reorganizing companies in distress and consolidating them for profit. In 1901, he bought Carnegie Steel for $480 million, merging it into U.S. Steel, the first billion-dollar corporation.

To admirers, these men were "captains of industry." To critics, they were "robber barons." They built modern America but also crushed competition, exploited workers, and corrupted politics. They amassed vast fortunes while millions labored in poverty.

Factory life was harsh. Laborers worked ten to twelve hours a day, six days a week, for low pay and little safety. Industrial accidents maimed thousands. Children as young as eight toiled in mines and mills. By 1900, nearly two million children worked for wages.

Workers tried to organize for better conditions, but employers fought unionization with firings, blacklists, private guards, and court injunctions. Major strikes often ended in bloodshed.

The Great Railroad Strike of 1877 erupted after wage cuts spread through the industry. Strikes paralyzed dozens of cities. In Pittsburgh, militia units fired on crowds, and buildings burned. More than one hundred people died before President Hayes sent troops to restore order—the first major federal intervention in a labor dispute.

The Haymarket Affair of 1886 began as a protest for an eight-hour workday in Chicago. When police attacked demonstrators, a bomb exploded, killing seven officers. Police fired back, killing four workers. Eight anarchists were convicted despite flimsy evidence; four were executed. The event turned public opinion against organized labor.

An engraving of the Haymarket Affair.[38]

The Pullman Strike of 1894 spread across the rail network after George Pullman cut wages but not rents in his company town. The American Railway Union, led by Eugene V. Debs, refused to handle Pullman cars. Rail traffic west of Chicago halted until President Grover Cleveland sent troops. The strike was broken, and Debs was jailed.

Laborers lost most of these confrontations. Corporate wealth and government power were overwhelming. Yet, the labor movement endured, eventually winning the eight-hour workday, safety laws, and collective bargaining rights, but only after decades of struggle.

The Gilded Age—a term coined by Mark Twain—glittered on the surface. America grew rich and powerful, but beneath the gold lay poverty, corruption, and inequality. A small elite controlled vast wealth and influence, while millions of workers lived on the edge of survival. The gap between rich and poor widened, dividing industrial America.

The Rise of the City and the Flood of Immigration

In 1860, most Americans lived on farms or in small towns. By 1920, most lived in cities. Urbanization happened faster in America than almost anywhere else in history.

Cities grew because of industry. Factories needed workers. Workers needed housing, food, and services. Small cities became large cities, and large cities became enormous. New York had 800,000 people in 1860 and 3.4 million by 1900. Chicago grew from 112,000 to 1.7 million in the same period.

Cities changed how Americans lived. Skyscrapers rose after the elevator was invented in the 1850s and steel-frame construction was developed in the 1880s. Electric streetcars replaced horse-drawn carriages. Telephones, electric lights, and indoor plumbing arrived in wealthy neighborhoods first but eventually spread. Cities built water systems, sewers, and bridges.

Chicago around 1900.[39]

However, cities had terrible problems. Housing couldn't keep up with population growth. Immigrants and poor workers crowded into tenements—apartment buildings with tiny, dark rooms. Jacob Riis, a journalist and photographer, documented tenement life in New York. His book *How the Other Half Lives* shocked middle-class readers with images of families living in airless rooms, children sleeping in alleys, and people crammed into spaces unfit for animals. In some tenements, ten people lived in rooms meant for two.

Lodgers in a Crowded Bayard Street Tenement, photographed by Jacob Riis.[80]

Cities lacked proper sanitation. Garbage piled in the streets. Open sewers bred disease. Cholera, typhoid, and tuberculosis killed thousands. Fires were common in crowded wooden buildings. Crime thrived in poor neighborhoods. Political machines controlled city governments through corruption and patronage.

Immigration fueled urban growth. Between 1870 and 1920, more than twenty-five million immigrants came to America. They came from all over Europe—Italy, Poland, Russia, Greece, and Hungary, to name a few. They also came from China, Japan, and Mexico. People came seeking opportunity, fleeing poverty, and escaping persecution.

Black Americans also migrated to Northern cities in large numbers, especially after 1910. This movement, later called the Great Migration, saw hundreds of thousands of Black Southerners leave the Jim Crow South for cities like Chicago, Detroit, New York, and Philadelphia. They were fleeing racial violence, segregation, and a lack of economic opportunity. They hoped to find factory jobs, better schools for their children, and freedom from the constant threat of lynching. Northern cities offered more opportunities than the South, though Black migrants still faced discrimination in housing, employment, and daily life. They were often restricted to certain neighborhoods and given the lowest-paying, most dangerous jobs. Still, they built vibrant communities, established churches and businesses, and created cultural movements like the Harlem Renaissance. By 1970, more than six million Black Americans had moved north and west, fundamentally changing the regions they left and the cities where they settled.

Earlier immigrants had primarily come from northern and western Europe, places like Germany, Ireland, Britain, and Scandinavia. The new immigrants came from southern and eastern Europe. They spoke different languages, practiced different religions, and had different customs. Many native-born Americans feared and resented them.

The journey was hard. Most immigrants traveled in steerage—the cheapest accommodations at the bottom of ships. Conditions were crowded, dirty, and dangerous. The voyage across the Atlantic took one to two weeks.

After arriving in America, immigrants faced processing at Ellis Island in New York Harbor beginning in 1892. Officials checked them for diseases, asked questions about their background and plans, and decided whether to admit them. About 2 percent were turned away. The rest entered America.

Immigrants arriving at Ellis Island, 1915.[81]

Most immigrants settled in cities. They took jobs in factories, mines, and construction. They worked long hours for low pay in dangerous conditions. Many couldn't speak English and had no skills for industrial work. They took whatever jobs they could find.

Immigrants formed ethnic neighborhoods, like Little Italy, Chinatown, Polish neighborhoods, and Jewish neighborhoods. These communities helped newcomers adjust. People spoke their native language, ate familiar food, and attended churches or synagogues with others from their homeland. Benevolent societies helped immigrants find jobs and housing.

However, ethnic neighborhoods also isolated immigrants from mainstream American society. They became targets for prejudice. Native-born Americans accused immigrants of taking jobs, lowering wages, spreading disease, and refusing to assimilate. Political cartoons depicted immigrants as criminals, anarchists, or subhuman creatures.

A political cartoon of American men out of work while immigrants find work easily.[33]

Anti-immigrant sentiment led to restrictions. The Chinese Exclusion Act of 1882 banned Chinese immigration. It was the first federal law restricting immigration based on nationality. The ban lasted until 1943. Japanese immigration was later restricted through diplomatic agreements.

Southern and eastern Europeans faced discrimination, but they weren't banned until the 1920s. They were accused of being too different, too poor, too radical, and too foreign. Some employers refused to hire certain nationalities. Signs said "No Irish Need Apply" or "Italians Keep Out."

Immigrants transformed American culture despite the hostility. They brought new foods, like pizza, bagels, and tacos. They brought new music, art, and traditions. Their labor built American industry. Their children became Americans while keeping connections to their heritage. The process was difficult and often painful, but immigration made America more diverse and dynamic.

Cities became centers of culture and innovation. Newspapers multiplied. Theaters offered plays and vaudeville shows. Department stores like Macy's and Marshall Field's changed how people shopped. Professional sports grew, with baseball becoming a national pastime. Libraries, museums, and universities were founded. Cities were exciting, dangerous, crowded, and full of possibilities.

The Wild West: Myth vs. Reality

While cities expanded in the East, the West was being settled. The popular image of the Wild West—cowboys, gunfights, outlaws, and frontier justice—captured the national imagination. Some of it reflected reality, but much was myth and exaggeration.

For decades, the Great Plains had been called the "Great American Desert." It was believed to be too dry for farming. That assumption was partly true. Yet after the Civil War, settlers poured in. The Homestead Act of 1862 offered 160 acres of free land to anyone who would live on and farm it for five years. Thousands of families took the chance.

Life on the plains was grueling. With little timber, settlers built sod houses—walls of thick earth and grass that were dark, damp, and crawling with insects. Winters were brutal, and summers were scorching. Droughts killed crops, and grasshoppers devoured fields by the acre. Many homesteaders simply gave up and left.

Technology eventually made prairie life more feasible. Barbed wire made fencing land cheaper. Steel plows cut the tough prairie sod. Windmills drew water from underground wells. Railroads delivered supplies and carried crops to market. By the 1880s, wheat farms and cattle ranches covered the plains.

The cattle industry exploded after the Civil War. Texas held millions of wild cattle descended from Spanish herds. Cowboys drove them hundreds of miles north to railheads in Kansas, where towns like Dodge City and Abilene became shipping centers for Eastern markets.

The cowboy soon became an American icon. In truth, he was a poorly paid ranch hand doing hard, dirty, dangerous work. Roughly a third were Mexican vaqueros, and many others were formerly enslaved men seeking freedom and wages in the West. Cowboys spent months on the trail, living on beans and hardtack, enduring heat, cold, and dust. At the end of a drive, they often celebrated recklessly, spent their pay, and signed up for another.

The open range disappeared within a generation. Barbed wire fenced off grazing land. Farmers and ranchers fought over water and grass. Severe winters in the late 1880s killed millions of cattle. By 1890, the great cattle drives were history.

Mining towns sprang up wherever gold or silver was found. People flocked to Nevada, Colorado, Montana, and the Dakotas to strike it rich. Settlements like Virginia City and Deadwood appeared almost overnight. Most prospectors failed to find precious metals, and wage laborers soon replaced independent miners. Mining was perilous too. They had to deal with cave-ins, explosions, and poisonous gases.

Boomtowns were rough places filled with saloons, gambling halls, and brothels. Violence was frequent, and law enforcement was scarce or corrupt. Still, the popular image of constant gunfights is overstated.

A few figures—Wild Bill Hickok, Wyatt Earp, Jesse James, and Billy the Kid—became legends through dime novels and later Hollywood films. Their real lives were far less glamorous.

The deeper story of the West, however, was the destruction of Native American nations. As settlers claimed land, they displaced Native peoples. The US Army waged decades of war across the plains.

The Plains Indians—the Sioux, Cheyenne, Comanche, Apache, and others—fought fiercely to defend their land and culture. They won notable victories. For instance, Red Cloud's warriors destroyed a cavalry detachment in 1866. Ten years later, Sitting Bull and Crazy Horse led Lakota and Cheyenne fighters to annihilate Custer's regiment at the Battle of the Little Bighorn.

Yet Native nations could not prevail. The US Army was larger, better armed, and supplied. More devastating still was the slaughter of the buffalo. Once numbering in the tens of millions, the herds that sustained the Plains tribes were wiped out by commercial and sport hunters. Railroads even promoted buffalo shooting from train windows. By 1890, fewer than one thousand remained.

Forced onto reservations, Native peoples endured starvation, disease, and poverty. Traditional life became impossible. The Dawes Act of 1887 tried to turn Native people into farmers by dividing tribal land into individual plots. The policy was disastrous. Much of the land was unsuitable for farming, and speculators cheated many families out of their allotments. Within a generation, tribes lost about two-thirds of their territory.

Cultural suppression followed. Native children were taken from their families and sent to distant boarding schools, where they were forbidden to speak their languages or practice their religions. The schools' motto— "Kill the Indian, save the man"—summed up their policy of cultural destruction.

A photograph of Native American students at a boarding school, 1879.[88]

The Ghost Dance movement of 1890 revealed the desperation of Native communities. A Paiute prophet named Wovoka preached that a sacred dance would restore Native lands, bring back the buffalo, and drive away White settlers. Although peaceful, the movement alarmed US authorities.

That winter, soldiers surrounded a group of Lakota Ghost Dancers at Wounded Knee Creek, South Dakota. A shot rang out, and troops opened fire. At least 150 Lakota—possibly 300—were killed, including women and children. Wounded Knee was a massacre, not a battle, and it marked the end of armed Native resistance.

By 1890, the Census Bureau had declared the frontier was closed; no clear line separated settled from unsettled land. The West had been conquered. Native nations were confined to reservations, and White settlers controlled the territory. Even as the reality ended, the myth of the Wild West was just beginning.

Chapter 15: The Progressive Era: Reforming the Nation

The Muckrakers: Exposing the Dirt

By 1900, many Americans sensed that something was deeply wrong. Corporations had grown too powerful. Politicians were corrupt. Workers were exploited. Cities were filthy and dangerous. The gap between the rich and the poor seemed to widen without limit. A growing number of citizens demanded reform.

The movement that answered that call was Progressivism. It was not a single organization or ideology but a broad coalition of middle-class reformers, social workers, labor activists, farmers, ministers, and politicians. They often disagreed about methods but shared a conviction that the government had a duty to address social problems and restrain corporate power for the public good.

Journalists became key allies in that crusade. Through fearless investigation, they exposed corporate greed, corrupt politicians, unsafe workplaces, and social injustice. President Theodore Roosevelt dubbed them "muckrakers," borrowing from a character in *Pilgrim's Progress* who raked filth from the ground. He meant it as a criticism, but the label became one of honor.

Among the most influential was Ida Tarbell, whose father had been ruined by John D. Rockefeller's Standard Oil monopoly. After years of research, Tarbell published a series in *McClure's Magazine* detailing how Standard Oil crushed rivals through secret railroad rebates, predatory pricing, and industrial espionage. Her meticulous reporting turned public opinion against monopolies and helped lead to federal antitrust action against Standard Oil.

Lincoln Steffens, another *McClure's* writer, took on political corruption in *The Shame of the Cities.* Investigating municipal governments across the nation, he revealed the same pattern everywhere—politicians trading contracts and favors for bribes, city funds siphoned off for cronies, and public resources exploited for private gain. His work forced Americans to confront corruption.

In 1906, Upton Sinclair aimed to expose the misery of immigrant labor in Chicago's meatpacking industry. His novel *The Jungle* portrayed families crushed by poverty, injuries, and exploitation. However, readers were more horrified by his descriptions of diseased animals, filth, and even body parts ending up in the nation's food supply. "I aimed at the public's heart," Sinclair later said, "and by accident I hit it in the stomach."[i]

Public outrage reached Washington. President Roosevelt ordered an investigation of Chicago's packinghouses, whose findings confirmed Sinclair's claims. Within months, Congress passed the Meat Inspection Act and the Pure Food and Drug Act, establishing federal oversight of food and medicine.

Ida B. Wells, a pioneering Black journalist, had been fighting a different battle since the 1890s. Investigating lynchings in the South, she documented hundreds of cases in which Black men, women, and children were murdered by White mobs. Her reports revealed that accusations were often fabricated and that lynching served as a weapon of terror to uphold White supremacy. Despite death threats that forced her to leave the South, Wells continued writing and organizing, laying early foundations for the civil rights movement.

Ida B. Wells.[ii]

[i] "Upton Sinclair and the Pure Food and Drug Act."
https://pmc.ncbi.nlm.nih.gov/articles/PMC1653522/

Jacob Riis, mentioned earlier, used photography to expose urban poverty. His 1890 work *How the Other Half Lives* revealed the squalid tenement conditions endured by immigrant families in New York. The haunting images spurred public demand for housing reform and new building codes.

Together, these journalists forced comfortable Americans to confront realities they had long ignored. Their investigations informed and outraged the public, shifted opinion, and compelled lawmakers to act. Magazines such as *McClure's*, *Collier's*, and *Cosmopolitan* carried muckraking stories to millions, proving that investigative journalism could become one of the most powerful engines of democratic reform.

Teddy Roosevelt and the Trust Busters

Theodore Roosevelt became president by accident. In 1900, Republicans renominated William McKinley for a second term and chose Roosevelt, then governor of New York, as his running mate. Party bosses hoped to sideline the young, energetic, and unpredictable reformer by putting him in the vice presidency, a position with little real power at the time.

McKinley won easily. Six months later, an anarchist shot him at the Pan-American Exposition in Buffalo. McKinley died eight days later. On September 14, 1901, Theodore Roosevelt—just forty-two years old—became the youngest president in American history.

Roosevelt was unlike any of his predecessors. Energetic, intellectual, and outspoken, he had been a sickly child who remade himself through rigorous exercise. He had worked as a rancher in the Dakotas, served as New York City's police commissioner, and become a national hero in the Spanish-American War. He loved boxing, hunting, and debate. A voracious reader, he could discuss literature, history, and science with ease. He had strong opinions about nearly everything, and he never hesitated to express them.

Unlike earlier presidents who deferred to Congress, Roosevelt believed in an active, powerful executive branch. He called the presidency a "bully pulpit," a platform for leading public opinion and promoting reform. His energetic style transformed the office and thrilled progressives.

Big business became his first major test. Roosevelt was not anti-business; he viewed corporations as essential to modern life. However, he believed some had grown so powerful that they threatened the public good. Government, he insisted, must regulate them to protect ordinary citizens.

In 1902, he directed the attorney general to sue the Northern Securities Company, a railroad holding company controlled by J. P. Morgan and other financiers, under the Sherman Antitrust Act of 1890, a federal law designed to break up monopolies and prevent companies from restricting competition. Morgan offered to "fix it up" privately, but Roosevelt refused. He wanted to prove that corporations answered to the government, not the other way around.

Two years later, the Supreme Court ruled five to four that Northern Securities had violated antitrust law and ordered it dissolved. The victory earned Roosevelt the nickname "trust buster." His administration filed more than forty antitrust suits, including one against Standard Oil.

Roosevelt distinguished between "good trusts" and "bad trusts." The former operated efficiently and served the public; the latter exploited consumers or crushed competition. He believed the government should regulate or dismantle only the bad ones—a pragmatic policy that pleased both reformers and moderates.

In 1902, he faced a nationwide coal strike in Pennsylvania. Miners worked long hours in dangerous conditions for low pay. They demanded higher wages and shorter hours. When mine owners refused to negotiate, the nation faced a winter fuel crisis. Roosevelt felt compelled to intervene. He threatened to seize the mines with federal troops unless both sides accepted arbitration. The compromise granted miners a 10 percent wage increase and a nine-hour workday—the first time a president had intervened in a labor dispute on behalf of workers.

Conservation became one of Roosevelt's passions. A lifelong outdoorsman, he feared that unregulated development was destroying the nation's natural resources. Using executive power, he protected land on an unprecedented scale, creating 5 national parks, 18 national monuments, and 150 national forests, totaling 230 million acres. He established wildlife refuges and preserved landmarks such as the Grand Canyon for future generations.

Part of Yellowstone National Park, the first national park in the world.⁵⁵

Western business interests and some politicians protested, arguing that resources should be open for mining, logging, and grazing. Roosevelt ignored them. Natural resources, he declared, belonged to all Americans, not just those who could profit from them. His conservation legacy reshaped the American landscape.

In foreign affairs, Roosevelt pursued an assertive policy. He believed the United States should act as a global power. "Speak softly and carry a big stick" was his motto. He expanded the Navy, mediated international disputes, and was willing to use force when necessary. Under his leadership, the United States emerged as an imperial power, a development discussed in the next chapter.

Roosevelt declined to seek another term in 1908, having served nearly two full terms. Confident his policies would continue, he endorsed his friend William Howard Taft as his successor and departed for an African safari.

Taft proved more cautious and conservative than Roosevelt had expected, disappointing progressives. Frustrated, Roosevelt challenged him for the Republican nomination in 1912. When Taft prevailed, Roosevelt formed the Progressive—or "Bull Moose"—Party, declaring himself "as strong as a bull moose." The split divided Republican votes and handed victory to Democrat Woodrow Wilson.

Roosevelt had brought energy, idealism, and moral conviction to the presidency. Though his own party fractured, the progressive movement he helped inspire would endure.

Votes for Women: The Long Fight for Suffrage

In 1900, most American women could not vote or serve on juries. In many states, they still faced legal restrictions that limited their control over wages and property. Married women had few rights. Society expected them to remain at home, raise children, and defer to men.

Yet, women had been fighting for equality for decades. The organized suffrage movement—the campaign for voting rights—began at Seneca Falls, New York, in 1848, when Elizabeth Cady Stanton and Lucretia Mott convened the first women's rights convention. About three hundred people attended. The meeting issued a Declaration of Sentiments modeled on the Declaration of Independence: "We hold these truths to be self-evident, that all men and women are created equal."

The declaration listed injustices. Women could not own property on equal terms or attend most colleges. They were excluded from many professions and lacked custody rights in divorce. The convention demanded full equality, including the right to vote.

Even among reformers, suffrage was controversial. Many thought it too radical. Stanton and her allies insisted that without political power, women could not secure other rights. The vote, they argued, was essential.

Progress came slowly. After the Civil War, the movement split over the Fifteenth Amendment, which gave voting rights to Black men but not to women. Stanton and Susan B. Anthony opposed it for excluding women. Others, including Lucy Stone and Frederick Douglass, supported it as a necessary step toward broader equality.

Two rival organizations emerged. Stanton and Anthony led the National Woman Suffrage Association, which pressed for a federal amendment. Stone helped found the American Woman Suffrage Association, which pursued state-by-state reform. The groups reunited in 1890 as the National American Woman Suffrage Association (NAWSA).

The Western territories led the way. Wyoming granted women the vote in 1869 and retained it upon statehood in 1890. Colorado, Utah, and Idaho followed in the 1890s. Western states were newer, less rigid, and more open to women's public roles. After all, women had helped build frontier communities as ranchers, business owners, and civic leaders.

By 1900, only four states allowed women to vote. A new generation revitalized the cause. Carrie Chapman Catt applied disciplined organization and political strategy, focusing on referendums and coalitions. Alice Paul, drawing on the militant tactics of British suffragists, staged parades, protests, hunger strikes, and acts of civil disobedience.

A parade for women's suffrage.[86]

Between 1910 and 1914, seven more states—all in the West—granted suffrage. In 1913, Paul organized a massive parade in Washington, DC, on the eve of Woodrow Wilson's inauguration. Thousands of women marched down Pennsylvania Avenue. Hostile crowds attacked them while police stood by. The violence shocked the nation and drew sympathy to the movement.

World War I accelerated change. Women filled factory, office, and hospital jobs, proving they could do "men's work." They bought war bonds, volunteered, and kept the economy running. President Wilson, once opposed to suffrage, gradually shifted his position, calling it "vital to the winning of the war."

Paul and her followers continued to picket the White House—a bold act during wartime. Arrested and jailed, they went on hunger strikes and were force-fed by guards, a brutal procedure that drew national outrage. Public opinion turned decisively in their favor.

In 1919, Congress passed the Nineteenth Amendment. It stated that "the right of citizens of the United States to vote shall not be denied or abridged by the United States or by any State on account of sex." Ratification required approval by three-fourths of the states.

The final battle came in Tennessee. In August 1920, the state legislature split evenly. A young representative, Harry Burn, had intended to vote no until he received a letter from his mother urging him to "help Mrs. Catt put the 'rat' in ratification."[i] Burn switched sides, and the amendment passed by a single vote.

On August 26, 1920, the Nineteenth Amendment was ratified. Seventy-two years after Seneca Falls, women finally won the vote. About twenty-six million women could now participate in national elections.

The victory, though monumental, was incomplete. Many women, especially Black women in the South, remained effectively disenfranchised by poll taxes, literacy tests, and intimidation. Native American women (and men) lacked citizenship until 1924, and Asian American women faced legal exclusion. The fight for universal suffrage would continue for decades.

The movement itself revealed divisions. Some White suffragist leaders, especially in the South, appealed to racist arguments, claiming that White women's votes would preserve White supremacy. Black activists such as Mary Church Terrell and Ida B. Wells fought for suffrage while also confronting racism within the movement, forming

[i] Kratz. Jessie. "Putting the 'Rat' in Ratification." https://prologue.blogs.archives.gov/2017/08/01/putting-the-rat-in-ratification-tennessees-role-in-the-19th-amendment/

their own organizations to pursue both racial and gender equality.

Still, the Nineteenth Amendment was a landmark achievement. Women gained the political voice that reformers had long demanded. They could vote, influence policy, and hold office. Stanton and Anthony did not live to see it, but the women who won the vote in 1920 stood on the foundation they had built.

Chapter 16: America on the World Stage

"A Splendid Little War": The Spanish-American War

For most of its history, the United States avoided foreign entanglements. George Washington had warned against permanent alliances, and the nation focused on continental expansion and economic growth. By the 1890s, however, some Americans believed it was time to play a larger role in world affairs.

European powers controlled vast colonial empires across Africa, Asia, and the Pacific. Many Americans argued that the United States needed colonies of its own for raw materials, markets, and naval bases. Others claimed it was America's duty to spread "civilization" and Christianity to so-called "backward" peoples. This blend of economic ambition, strategic interest, and racial ideology came to be known as imperialism.

Cuba provided such an opportunity. Only ninety miles from Florida, the island remained under Spanish rule, and Cubans had been fighting for independence since 1868. When rebellion flared again in 1895, Spain's General Valeriano Weyler forced civilians into concentration camps, where thousands died of disease and starvation.

American newspapers sensationalized the conflict. Rival New York publishers William Randolph Hearst and Joseph Pulitzer competed for readers with lurid stories of Spanish atrocities—many exaggerated or invented. This "yellow journalism," named after a popular comic strip (the Yellow Kid), inflamed public opinion and stirred sympathy for the Cuban cause.

Many Americans saw parallels to their own revolution against colonial rule, while investors feared for their Cuban sugar interests. President William McKinley resisted calls for war, preferring diplomacy.

That restraint ended on February 15, 1898, when the battleship USS *Maine* exploded in Havana Harbor, killing more than 260 sailors. The ship had been sent to protect American citizens during the unrest. Although later evidence suggested an internal accident, a Navy inquiry blamed a mine, and the public blamed Spain. "Remember the Maine!" became a rallying cry. Newspapers demanded war.

McKinley asked Congress for authorization to use force, and on April 25, 1898, Congress declared war on Spain. The conflict was brief and one-sided. Spain's military was outdated. The United States was industrial, confident, and eager to prove itself.

The first major battle occurred thousands of miles away in the Philippines, a Spanish colony in the Pacific. On May 1, Commodore George Dewey sailed into Manila Bay with the US Asiatic Squadron and destroyed the Spanish fleet within hours and without losing a single American sailor. Dewey became a national hero overnight.

The campaign in Cuba proved harder. The US Army was unprepared for tropical warfare. Soldiers wore heavy wool uniforms and suffered from poor supplies. Diseases like yellow fever, malaria, and typhoid killed far more than combat.

The most famous engagement came on July 1 at San Juan Hill near Santiago. American troops, including the volunteer cavalry known as the Rough Riders, stormed Spanish positions. Theodore Roosevelt, who had resigned as assistant secretary of the Navy to fight, led his men up nearby Kettle Hill. Though he fought on foot and the Spanish had begun to retreat, newspapers celebrated him as a hero. Two days later, the US Navy destroyed the Spanish fleet attempting to flee Santiago Harbor. Spain surrendered soon after.

Illustration of the Rough Riders at San Juan Hill.[97]

The war lasted less than four months. Secretary of State John Hay called it "a splendid little war."

The Treaty of Paris, signed in December 1898, formally ended the conflict. Spain relinquished Cuba and ceded Puerto Rico, Guam, and the Philippines to the United States in exchange for $20 million. Practically overnight, the nation had become an imperial power.

Annexing the Philippines sparked fierce debate. Anti-imperialists argued that colonial rule violated America's founding principles. The Declaration of Independence proclaimed government by the consent of the governed, yet Filipinos had not consented to American control. Figures such as Mark Twain, Andrew Carnegie, and William Jennings Bryan denounced annexation.

Imperialists countered that America needed Pacific bases for trade with Asia and that Filipinos were unprepared for self-rule. Some cloaked expansion in racial and civilizing rhetoric, claiming Americans had a duty to uplift "inferior" peoples. The Senate ratified the treaty by a single vote.

Filipinos, who had fought Spain with American encouragement, felt betrayed. In February 1899, war broke out between US forces and Filipino independence fighters led by Emilio Aguinaldo. The Philippine-American War dragged on for three years. American troops used brutal tactics—burning villages, torturing prisoners, and killing civilians—while Filipinos waged a fierce guerrilla war. About 4,200 American soldiers died. Filipino losses were far heavier—an estimated 20,000 fighters and as many as 200,000 civilians from violence, famine, and disease.

By 1902, the United States had secured its empire, but at a terrible moral cost. The nation that had once championed liberty and self-determination now ruled distant colonies—an empire won in what many had called a "splendid little war."

World War I: The War to End All Wars

On June 28, 1914, a Serbian nationalist assassinated Archduke Franz Ferdinand, heir to the Austro-Hungarian throne, in Sarajevo. Within weeks, Europe was at war.

The continent's web of alliances, which were intended to prevent conflict, helped ignite it instead. Austria-Hungary blamed Serbia and declared war. Russia mobilized to defend Serbia. Germany then declared war on Russia and France and invaded Belgium to strike at France. Britain entered the war to defend Belgium. Soon, the Ottoman Empire and Bulgaria joined Germany and Austria-Hungary as the Central Powers, while Italy, Japan, and others sided with Britain, France, and Russia as the Allied Powers.

Both sides expected a short conflict. Instead, the war descended into a stalemate. On the Western Front, armies dug trenches stretching from Switzerland to the North Sea. Soldiers lived in mud under constant fire. Attacks across no man's land met with machine guns, artillery, and barbed wire. The 1916 Battle of the Somme alone resulted in more than one million casualties and changed almost nothing.

New technology made killing more efficient and more terrible. Machine guns fired hundreds of rounds per minute. Artillery shattered entire landscapes. Poison gas choked and blinded, and tanks and airplanes appeared for the first time. The war became a slaughter on an industrial scale.

President Woodrow Wilson declared American neutrality in August 1914. Most Americans approved. The war seemed like a distant European struggle. However, true neutrality proved impossible.

Americans had ties to both sides, and the US economy boomed through trade with the Allies, who bought American food, weapons, and supplies. Banks loaned billions to Britain and France.

Germany viewed this trade as aiding its enemies. In 1915, it declared the waters around Britain a war zone and warned that submarines, or U-boats, would sink ships without warning. This violated international law, which required prior notice and evacuation.

On May 7, 1915, a U-boat torpedoed the British passenger liner *Lusitania* off Ireland. The ship sank in 18 minutes, killing 1,198 people, including 128 Americans. Outrage swept the United States. Germany claimed the *Lusitania* carried ammunition, making it a legitimate target, but the deaths of civilians pushed the country closer to war.

Wilson protested, and Germany temporarily restricted submarine attacks. Tensions eased, and Wilson won reelection in 1916 under the slogan "He kept us out of war."

That peace was short-lived. In January 1917, Germany resumed unrestricted submarine warfare, hoping to starve Britain before the US could intervene. Wilson severed diplomatic ties. Then British intelligence intercepted the Zimmermann Telegram, in which German Foreign Minister Arthur Zimmermann proposed a military alliance with Mexico, promising to help it reclaim Texas, New Mexico, and Arizona if the US decided to enter the war. When the telegram became public, American outrage exploded.

In March, German submarines sank three American merchant ships. On April 2, Wilson asked Congress for a declaration of war, saying the world must be made "safe for democracy." Congress approved on April 6, 1917.

The US was unprepared. The army numbered just 200,000 men. Congress passed the Selective Service Act, requiring registration for military service. A draft lottery filled the ranks. By war's end, 2.8 million men had been drafted, and 2 million had volunteered.

Training and transport took months. The first American troops—called "Doughboys"—arrived in France in June 1917. General John J. Pershing commanded the American Expeditionary Forces and insisted they fight as a unified army rather than as reinforcements for British or French units.

American forces saw major combat in 1918. Russia had left the war after the Bolshevik Revolution of November 1917. Lenin's new government signed a separate peace with Germany, freeing German divisions for a final offensive in the west.

In March 1918, Germany launched that offensive, breaking through Allied lines and advancing toward Paris. The Allies barely held. US troops helped stem the tide. At Belleau Wood in June, Marines fought ferocious battles, and at Château-Thierry and the Second Battle of the Marne in July, American reinforcements stopped German advances.

In September, Pershing led his army in its first large-scale assault at St. Mihiel, capturing a key German position. Later that month, Americans joined the massive Meuse-Argonne offensive, the largest in US history. The fighting lasted until the armistice and cost more than twenty-six thousand American lives, but the advance forced Germany to retreat.

American troops on the Western Front.[88]

By autumn, Germany was collapsing. The British blockade had caused starvation, soldiers mutinied, and civilians protested. On November 9, Kaiser Wilhelm II abdicated. Two days later, at 11:00 a.m. on November 11, 1918, the guns fell silent. The Great War was over.

About 116,500 American soldiers died—roughly half from disease, including the global influenza pandemic of 1918–1919. Another 204,000 were wounded. For Europe, the losses were staggering. France lost about

1.4 million men, Britain nearly one million, Germany around two million, and Russia almost two million. An entire generation was scarred or gone.

President Wilson sought a peace that would prevent future wars. In January 1918, he outlined his vision in the Fourteen Points: open diplomacy, freedom of the seas, arms reduction, self-determination for nationalities, and, most importantly, a League of Nations to resolve disputes peacefully.

When Wilson traveled to Paris for the peace conference—the first sitting president to go to Europe—he was hailed as a hero. Europeans hoped his idealism would reshape the world. However, Britain's David Lloyd George, France's Georges Clemenceau, and Italy's Vittorio Orlando wanted to punish Germany and secure their national interests.

The Treaty of Versailles, signed in June 1919, was harsh. Germany had to accept full responsibility for the war, pay reparations of $33 billion, surrender territory and colonies, and reduce its military to a token force. The terms humiliated Germany and sowed resentment that would fester into another war.

Wilson secured his League of Nations but compromised on other ideals. The treaty was far more punitive than Wilson had wanted. Self-determination wasn't granted to colonized peoples. Secret deals among the Allies remained. Many idealists who had supported Wilson's Fourteen Points felt betrayed.

Wilson returned home to fight for Senate ratification of the treaty. He needed two-thirds support, but opposition formed quickly. Some senators thought the treaty was too harsh on Germany. Others thought it was too lenient.

The main opposition came from Republican Senator Henry Cabot Lodge. Lodge wanted amendments to protect American sovereignty. He particularly opposed Article X of the League Covenant, which required members to defend any nation attacked by another. Lodge feared this gave the League too much power over American foreign policy and would drag America into foreign wars.

Wilson refused to compromise, convinced the treaty was humanity's best hope for peace. He toured the country by train to rally public support, but the exhausting schedule led to a severe stroke in September 1919. Partially paralyzed, he withdrew from public life as his wife, Edith, managed access to him.

In November 1919 and again in March 1920, the Senate rejected the Treaty of Versailles. The United States never joined the League of Nations.

Wilson's dream of a new world order collapsed. Americans, disillusioned by the cost and outcome of the war, turned inward again.

The Roaring Twenties: Jazz, Flappers, and Prohibition

After World War I, Americans longed for "normalcy." They were weary of sacrifice and reform. The 1920s became a decade of prosperity, innovation, and cultural change. It was also a time of conflict and contradiction.

The economy boomed. New technologies created new industries and mass consumer markets. Automobiles, once luxuries for the rich, became affordable for millions. Henry Ford's assembly line revolutionized manufacturing. Each worker performed one small task as cars moved past on a conveyor belt, dramatically increasing efficiency. The Model T, which cost $850 in 1908, sold for just $260 by 1924.

Automobiles transformed daily life. People could live farther from work, fueling the growth of suburbs. Young people gained new independence. Entire industries—gas stations, motels, repair shops, roadside diners—sprang up to serve motorists. Roads improved, and tourism expanded.

Other technologies changed life just as dramatically. Radio broadcasting began in 1920, and by 1929, more than ten million homes had radios. Families gathered to listen to news, music, sports, and dramas, hearing the same voices and advertisements across the nation. It brought the nation together in new ways.

Movies became the decade's most popular entertainment. Silent films gave way to "talkies" in 1927 with *The Jazz Singer.* Lavish movie palaces opened in every major city. Hollywood became the world's film capital, and movie stars became idols. Audiences filled theaters for comedies, romances, westerns, and gangster stories.

The era's exuberance earned it the name "the Roaring Twenties." Jazz, created by Black musicians in New Orleans and carried north to Chicago and New York, defined the sound of the decade. Artists like Louis Armstrong, Duke Ellington, and Bessie Smith made jazz a national obsession. It was just like the decade itself—syncopated, improvisational, and alive.

Youth culture flourished. Women, in particular, embraced new freedoms. "Flappers," with their short skirts, bobbed hair, and cigarettes in hand, defied traditional standards of dress and behavior. They danced to jazz, drove cars, and claimed the right to pleasure and independence.

Josephine Baker dancing the Charleston.[39]

The Harlem Renaissance celebrated Black art, music, and literature. Harlem, in New York City, became a center of creativity. Writers such as Langston Hughes and Zora Neale Hurston, musicians like Ellington and Armstrong, and thinkers including W. E. B. Du Bois helped forge a new sense of racial pride and artistic achievement. The movement showed that Black artists were equal to any in the world and demanded recognition on their own terms.

Yet beneath the glamour, the decade revealed deep anxieties. The Red Scare of 1919–1920 reflected postwar fear of revolution. After the Bolshevik takeover in Russia, Attorney General A. Mitchell Palmer ordered raids that arrested thousands of suspected radicals—mostly immigrants—many of whom were deported without trial. The hysteria faded, but it left a legacy of suspicion and repression.

Nativism took political form in new immigration restrictions. The quota laws of 1921 and 1924 sharply limited arrivals from southern and eastern Europe—groups nativists deemed "undesirable"—and banned immigration from Asia entirely. The quotas would remain in place until 1965.

Racism also found expression in the reborn Ku Klux Klan. The new Klan, founded in 1915, targeted not only Black Americans but also Catholics, Jews, immigrants, and anyone it saw as un-American. Claiming as many as four million members by the mid-1920s, it wielded power in states far beyond the South, including Indiana and Oregon. Marches, rallies, and acts of intimidation spread its message until internal scandals and public backlash brought about its decline.

The nation's boldest social experiment was Prohibition. The Eighteenth Amendment, ratified in 1919, outlawed the manufacture, sale, and transport of alcohol. Temperance reformers hoped it would reduce crime and poverty and strengthen families.

Prohibition agents destroying alcohol.⁴⁰

It did the opposite. Americans kept drinking—just illegally. Speakeasies flourished, homemade liquor circulated, and organized crime took control of the alcohol trade. Gangsters like Al Capone built empires on bootlegging and bribery. Violence surged as rival mobs battled for territory. Law enforcement was underfunded and often corrupt. The ban bred cynicism toward government and made ordinary citizens lawbreakers. By the early 1930s, most Americans saw Prohibition as a failure. The Twenty-First Amendment repealed it in 1933.

The 1920s glittered with prosperity and excitement, but the shine hid serious problems, including economic inequality, racial division, cultural conflict, and reckless speculation in the stock market. The good times would not last. When the bubble burst, the crash would bring a reckoning.

Chapter 17: The Great Depression and the New Deal

The Stock Market Crash of 1929 and the Dust Bowl

The prosperity of the 1920s rested on fragile foundations. Wealth was concentrated at the top: the richest 5 percent of Americans earned about one-third of all income. Farmers faced low crop prices and mounting debt, and workers' wages rose slowly while corporate profits soared. Many families could not afford the very goods they produced.

Credit masked the weakness. Installment buying—paying for cars, radios, and furniture over time—created the illusion of affluence. However, families were going into debt to maintain their standard of living. When incomes fell, they missed payments and stopped buying. Consumer spending collapsed, and businesses that depended on it followed.

Global conditions made matters worse. Europe was still reeling from World War I. Germany struggled under huge reparation payments, and other nations lacked the means to buy American goods. Tariffs choked what trade remained. The Smoot-Hawley Tariff of 1930 raised import taxes to protect US industries, but foreign governments retaliated. International commerce plunged as a result.

Speculation in the stock market was the final, most visible danger. Throughout the 1920s, stock prices rose far beyond companies' actual worth. Investors bought shares on credit—"on margin"—putting down only 10 percent and borrowing the rest. As long as prices climbed, profits looked endless. Banks lent freely, fueling the bubble.

In September 1929, prices began to fall. Nervous investors sold; others panicked and joined them. On October 24—Black Thursday—trading on the New York Stock Exchange exploded, with nearly thirteen million shares changing hands. Bankers tried to restore calm by buying stock, but confidence was gone. Five days later, on October 29—Black Tuesday—sixteen million shares were sold. Prices collapsed, wiping out billions in wealth.

The crash did not cause the Great Depression by itself, but it exposed and intensified deep economic weaknesses. Banks that had loaned money for stock purchases failed when borrowers defaulted. Without federal insurance, depositors lost their savings overnight. As banks closed, credit vanished. Businesses could not borrow, production slowed, workers were laid off, and unemployment spread in a downward spiral.

By 1933, one in four Americans was out of work—around fifteen million people. Factories stood silent, stores were shuttered, and families lost homes to foreclosure. Breadlines formed in every city. Shantytowns made of scrap wood and metal—called "Hoovervilles" after President Herbert Hoover—appeared on the edges of cities. Men who had once been middle-class professionals sold apples on street corners or begged for odd jobs.

The psychological toll was immense. Men who had supported families felt humiliated by joblessness. Divorce and suicide rates rose. Malnutrition spread as children went hungry and schools closed due to a lack of funds. Families sometimes sent children to relatives who were better able to feed them. The Depression frayed not only the economy but also the nation's social fabric.

Women often became the primary earners when men could not find work, taking jobs as cleaners, seamstresses, or factory hands for meager pay. The crisis challenged traditional gender roles but brought little lasting change in women's economic status.

Farmers suffered even more. Overproduction and falling prices had already hurt them in the 1920s; now, demand collapsed completely. Corn that had sold for $1.50 a bushel in the early 1920s brought 32 cents in 1932. Cotton fell from 18 cents to 6 cents a pound. Unable to pay mortgages, many lost their land to foreclosure. Neighbors sometimes held "penny auctions," bidding a few cents to return foreclosed property to its owners.

Then nature turned against them. During World War I, farmers had plowed up millions of acres of Great Plains grassland to plant wheat. The deep-rooted prairie grass that held the soil together disappeared. When drought hit in the early 1930s, the land dried out. Winds carried away the topsoil in giant dust storms.

The Dust Bowl engulfed parts of Oklahoma, Texas, Kansas, Colorado, and New Mexico. "Black blizzards" blotted out the sun and buried farms. People stuffed rags around doors and windows, but fine dust still coated every surface. Breathing became dangerous, and "dust pneumonia" was common. The worst storm—Black Sunday, April 14, 1935—lifted three hundred million tons of soil into the air and carried it east to the Atlantic Ocean.

About 2.5 million people left the Great Plains during the 1930s, many heading west along Route 66 toward California. They became known as "Okies," whatever their state of origin. Packing all they owned into cars and trucks, they sought farm work but found little. Growers exploited the oversupply of labor, paying starvation wages. Migrants lived in camps without sanitation or clean water. Some towns posted signs reading, "Okies and Dogs Not Allowed." Police tried to block their entry at state lines. John Steinbeck's *The Grapes of Wrath* captured their suffering and resilience.

Migrant mother, Nipomo, California by Dorothea Lange.[41]

The Great Depression and the Dust Bowl produced human misery on a scale the nation had never seen. President Hoover believed recovery would come naturally. Viewing the crash as a temporary correction, he opposed direct federal aid, convinced it would foster dependency and undermine self-reliance. He urged voluntary cooperation among businesses and charities instead.

Hoover was not idle, though. He created the Reconstruction Finance Corporation to lend money to banks and industries and supported limited public works projects. But private and local relief collapsed under the crisis's scale. Charities ran out of funds, cities went bankrupt, and hunger spread. To many Americans, Hoover seemed indifferent. His name became synonymous with hardship—Hoovervilles, "Hoover blankets" for newspapers used as covers, and "Hoover flags" for empty pockets turned inside out.

By 1932, desperation turned to anger. Democrat Franklin D. Roosevelt, governor of New York, ran against Hoover, promising a "New Deal" for Americans. He projected confidence and optimism. Voters responded overwhelmingly: he won forty-two of forty-eight states.

When Roosevelt took office in March 1933, the nation was on the brink of collapse. More than five thousand banks had failed, unemployment was near 25 percent, and industrial production had fallen by nearly half. In his inaugural address, Roosevelt sought to restore faith, saying, "The only thing we have to fear is fear itself."

Franklin D. Roosevelt and the New Deal

Franklin D. Roosevelt brought energy and experimentation to the presidency. He surrounded himself with advisors—his "Brain Trust"— who proposed bold solutions to the Great Depression. Roosevelt believed the government had to act directly to relieve suffering and revive the economy. If one program failed, he was willing to try another. It was a revolutionary shift from the hands-off policies of earlier presidents.

His first challenge was the banking crisis. On March 6, 1933, he declared a national bank holiday, closing all banks for inspection. Federal examiners reviewed their finances. Sound banks reopened, while weak ones remained closed. Roosevelt explained the plan in his first "fireside chat," speaking by radio in calm, direct language that reassured the public. When banks reopened, depositors lined up to return their savings. The panic was over.

During Roosevelt's first hundred days, Congress passed an extraordinary series of laws. The Emergency Banking Act restored stability to the financial system. The Federal Deposit Insurance Corporation (FDIC) insured deposits up to $2,500, ensuring that people would never again lose all of their savings when banks failed. Confidence in the banks returned.

To fight unemployment, the administration launched public works programs. The Civilian Conservation Corps (CCC) employed young men on environmental projects. They planted trees, built trails, fought forest fires, and developed parks. Over nine years, about three million men worked in the CCC, earning $30 a month and sending most of it home to their families.

The Tennessee Valley Authority (TVA) transformed one of the poorest regions of the country. Covering parts of seven states, the TVA built dams to control floods, generate hydroelectric power, improve navigation, and provide jobs. It brought electricity to rural areas for the first time and became a model for regional planning.

Farmers received aid through the Agricultural Adjustment Act (AAA), which sought to raise crop prices by reducing supply. The government paid farmers to plant fewer acres or destroy surplus livestock. Though controversial—critics denounced destroying food while people went hungry—the plan succeeded in lifting farm incomes.

Industrial recovery came through the National Industrial Recovery Act (NIRA), which encouraged businesses to set voluntary codes for prices, wages, and hours. Firms that complied displayed a Blue Eagle symbol. The program proved complicated and unpopular, and in 1935, the Supreme Court struck it down as unconstitutional.

Roosevelt's second wave of reforms between 1935 and 1938 was broader and more lasting. The Works Progress Administration (WPA), established in 1935, became the largest jobs program in US history, employing 8.5 million people to build roads, bridges, schools, hospitals, and airports—over 650,000 miles of roads and 125,000 public buildings. The WPA also supported artists, writers, and musicians who painted murals, recorded oral histories, and gave free performances, preserving culture as well as creating work.

The Social Security Act of 1935 established a permanent safety net. It provided old-age pensions funded by payroll taxes, unemployment insurance for workers who lost jobs, and aid to children and people with disabilities. Before Social Security, most elderly Americans lived in poverty; now, they had a guaranteed income in retirement. The act excluded many agricultural and domestic workers—jobs held largely by Black Americans—but it laid the foundation for future social welfare policy and remains central to American life today.

The National Labor Relations Act (Wagner Act) of 1935 strengthened organized labor. It guaranteed workers the right to form unions and bargain collectively, and it created a board to enforce those rights. Union membership surged. The newly formed Congress of Industrial Organizations (CIO) organized mass-production workers in steel and automobile plants. When General Motors workers staged a sit-down strike in 1936–37, they won union recognition. By 1945, about one-third of non-farm workers belonged to unions, up from less than one-tenth in 1930.

The Fair Labor Standards Act of 1938 capped the New Deal's labor reforms. It established a federal minimum wage, set a forty-hour workweek, required overtime pay, and restricted child labor—protections that became basic expectations for American workers.

Boys working in a coal mine in Pennsylvania.[43]

Roosevelt's activism alarmed many business leaders and conservatives. They accused him of socialism and of destroying free enterprise. The

Supreme Court became an obstacle, striking down the NIRA in 1935 and the AAA the next year. Furious, Roosevelt proposed in 1937 to expand the Supreme Court by adding up to six new justices—one for each member over seventy who refused to retire. He claimed it would ease the Supreme Court's workload, but few believed him. Critics from both parties denounced the plan as a power grab that threatened judicial independence. Congress rejected it, handing Roosevelt his greatest political defeat.

Yet the controversy might have achieved its aim. Soon after, the Supreme Court began upholding New Deal legislation. Justice Owen Roberts, previously a consistent opponent, switched sides in key cases—a shift dubbed "the switch in time that saved nine." Meanwhile, retirements allowed Roosevelt to appoint new justices sympathetic to his programs. By 1940, he had named seven of the nine justices, ending the Supreme Court's resistance.

Opposition also came from the left. Senator Huey Long of Louisiana proposed a "Share Our Wealth" plan to heavily tax the rich and guarantee every family a basic income. Father Charles Coughlin, a popular radio priest, attacked bankers and demanded government control of industry. Both men condemned Roosevelt for doing too little, not too much.

The New Deal's record on race was mixed. Many programs excluded or segregated Black Americans. CCC camps and TVA towns were segregated, and Social Security omitted occupations that employed most Black workers. Roosevelt, who was dependent on Southern Democrats in Congress, avoided challenging segregation directly. Even so, New Deal programs provided jobs for hundreds of thousands of Black Americans, and First Lady Eleanor Roosevelt emerged as a strong advocate for civil rights, working with Black leaders and urging reform.

Despite the sweeping reforms, the New Deal did not fully end the Depression. By 1939, unemployment still hovered around 17 percent. When Roosevelt tried to cut spending in 1937 to balance the budget, the economy slipped back into recession, and unemployment rose again. Only with the vast government spending of World War II did full recovery arrive.

Economists later argued that Roosevelt's programs worked but were too limited; larger deficits and more spending might have restored prosperity sooner. Nevertheless, the New Deal transformed the relationship between government and citizens. It established the idea that the federal government bears responsibility for economic security and social welfare. It created lasting institutions—Social Security, unemployment insurance, bank deposit protection—and modernized the nation's infrastructure. Above all, it restored hope.

Roosevelt went on to win four elections—1932, 1936, 1940, and 1944—more than any other president. His long tenure led to the Twenty-Second Amendment in 1951, limiting presidents to two terms. Through crisis and war, Roosevelt redefined the presidency, expanded federal power, and reshaped Americans' expectations of what government should do.

Chapter 18: World War II

From Pearl Harbor to D-Day: America Joins the Fight

War returned to Europe in September 1939 when Adolf Hitler's Nazi Germany invaded Poland.

Hitler had come to power in 1933. The Nazis blamed Germany's problems on the Treaty of Versailles, Jews, communists, and other scapegoats. Hitler promised to restore German greatness. He rearmed the nation in defiance of the treaty, occupied the Rhineland in 1936, and annexed Austria in 1938.

At Munich in September 1938, Britain and France agreed to let Germany take part of Czechoslovakia, hoping appeasement would prevent war. It didn't. In March 1939, Germany seized the rest of the country. That August, Hitler shocked the world by signing a non-aggression pact with the Soviet Union. The two dictators secretly agreed to divide Poland between them.

On September 1, 1939, Germany invaded Poland using a tactic called *blitzkrieg*, or "lightning war." Tanks, aircraft, and infantry advanced together in coordinated attacks that overwhelmed Polish defenses. Within weeks, Poland was defeated. The Soviet Union invaded from the east. Britain and France declared war, but they could do little to help.

In spring 1940, Germany attacked Western Europe. Denmark and Norway fell first. In May, German forces invaded Belgium, the Netherlands, and France, bypassing the French Maginot Line (a system of fortifications) by driving through the Ardennes Forest. German tanks raced to the English Channel, trapping Allied troops. More than 300,000

British and French soldiers were rescued from Dunkirk by military and civilian boats. France surrendered in June. Hitler had conquered Western Europe in six weeks.

Britain stood alone. Winston Churchill, who became prime minister in May 1940, vowed, "We shall fight on the beaches ... we shall never surrender."[i] Germany launched an air campaign—the Battle of Britain—to destroy the Royal Air Force and prepare for an invasion. Though outnumbered, British pilots fought with determination. Germany eventually abandoned daylight bombing but continued nightly raids on British cities. London was devastated, yet Britain endured.

In June 1941, Hitler made his greatest mistake: invading the Soviet Union with over three million troops. Expecting a quick victory, Germany instead faced a brutal war of attrition that would kill tens of millions and ultimately destroy the Nazi regime.

Americans watched the war with alarm but wanted to stay out. Isolationism was strong. Congress had passed the Neutrality Acts in the 1930s to keep the nation out of foreign conflicts. Many believed the US entry into World War I had been a mistake.

President Franklin D. Roosevelt disagreed. He believed Nazi Germany threatened US security and democratic values. In September 1940, he traded fifty old destroyers to Britain for naval bases. In March 1941, Congress passed the Lend-Lease Act, allowing Roosevelt to lend or lease weapons to any country vital to American defense. The United States became "the arsenal of democracy," supplying Britain and later the Soviet Union.

In August 1941, Roosevelt and Churchill met off Newfoundland and issued the Atlantic Charter, outlining shared goals for a postwar world—self-determination, freedom of the seas, disarmament, and collective security through a new international organization. Though still neutral, the United States was preparing for war.

Then Japan forced the issue.

Japan had been at war with China since 1937, committing atrocities such as the Rape of Nanking, where hundreds of thousands of civilians were killed. Seeking an empire in Asia, Japan joined Germany and Italy in the 1940 Tripartite Pact. In 1941, it occupied French Indochina. The

---

[i] "We Shall Fight on the Beaches." https://winstonchurchill.org/resources/speeches/1940-the-finest-hour/we-shall-fight-on-the-beaches/

United States responded with economic sanctions, including an oil embargo. Japan depended on American oil; without it, its military would grind to a halt.

Japanese leaders faced a choice: abandon expansion or go to war. They chose war, planning a surprise attack on the US Pacific Fleet at Pearl Harbor, Hawaii. By crippling the fleet, they hoped to secure Southeast Asia before the United States could recover.

On December 7, 1941, Japanese aircraft launched a devastating surprise attack on Pearl Harbor. The first wave of 183 planes appeared over Oahu at 7:55 a.m. on a peaceful Sunday morning. American servicemen were eating breakfast, attending church, or still asleep in their bunks. Within minutes, the harbor erupted in chaos.

Torpedo bombers skimmed low across the water, releasing specially designed shallow-water torpedoes that slammed into the battleships moored along "Battleship Row." Dive bombers screamed down from above, their payloads ripping through steel decks and human bodies. Fighters strafed airfields, destroying planes parked wingtip to wingtip. These were easy targets; they had been arranged that way to guard against sabotage.

At 8:10 a.m., the USS *Arizona* took a direct hit. An armor-piercing bomb penetrated the deck and ignited the forward ammunition magazine. The explosion lifted the 32,000-ton battleship out of the water. Within nine minutes, the *Arizona* sank, taking 1,177 sailors and Marines with her—nearly half of all American deaths that day.

The sinking of the USS Arizona.[48]

The USS *Oklahoma* capsized after multiple torpedo strikes, trapping more than 400 men inside her hull. Burning oil spread across the water, turning the bay into an inferno. Men leapt from sinking ships into flaming seas.

A second wave of 171 planes struck at 8:50 a.m., hammering ships that had survived the first assault and smashing the already-ruined airfields. By the time the attack ended shortly after 9:00 a.m., eight battleships had been sunk or damaged, nearly 200 aircraft had been destroyed, and more than 2,400 Americans were dead. Another 1,000 were wounded.

However, for all its tactical success, Pearl Harbor was Japan's greatest strategic blunder. The attack failed to achieve its key objectives. All three of the Pacific Fleet's aircraft carriers were at sea and escaped unscathed. Japanese commanders also left Pearl Harbor's infrastructure largely intact; the fuel tanks, repair docks, and submarine base survived, enabling the US Navy to recover and strike back far sooner than Japan expected.

Most importantly, the attack unified a divided nation. Isolationism vanished overnight. The next day, Roosevelt addressed Congress, calling December 7 "a date which will live in infamy." Congress declared war on Japan with only one dissenting vote. When Germany and Italy honored their alliance with Japan by declaring war on the United States, America was fully committed to a global war.

The first months went badly for the Allies—the coalition fighting against Germany, Italy, and Japan. Japan conquered the Philippines, Malaya, Singapore, the Dutch East Indies, and Burma. General Douglas MacArthur withdrew from the Philippines in March 1942, vowing, "I shall return."

The soldiers left behind fought on until May 1942, when they were forced to surrender—the largest capitulation in American military history. What followed was one of the war's worst atrocities. Some seventy-five thousand American and Filipino prisoners of war were forced to march sixty miles through the sweltering jungle from Bataan to prison camps. During the Bataan Death March, Japanese guards brutally beat, bayoneted, or shot anyone who fell behind. Prisoners received no food or water and were denied medical care. Those who stopped to help fallen comrades were executed. Between 5,000 and 10,000 Filipino soldiers and 600 to 650 Americans died during the march or in the first weeks of captivity from disease, starvation, and execution.

By May 1942, Japan controlled an empire stretching from the borders of India to the central Pacific, encompassing the Dutch East Indies (modern Indonesia) with its vital oil resources, Burma (cutting off supply routes to China), and countless strategic islands. American military planners feared Japan might even threaten Australia or invade Hawaii.

The Turning Point: Midway

Japan's string of victories came to a dramatic end in June 1942 at the Battle of Midway, a tiny atoll in the central Pacific. Admiral Isoroku Yamamoto planned to lure what remained of the US Pacific Fleet into a trap and destroy it, eliminating the last obstacle to Japanese dominance. He dispatched a massive armada.

What Yamamoto didn't know was that American codebreakers had cracked Japan's naval communications. Admiral Chester Nimitz, commander of the Pacific Fleet, knew the Japanese plan. He positioned his three available carriers northeast of Midway and waited.

The battle began on June 4, 1942. Japanese aircraft bombed Midway Island while US torpedo squadrons launched desperate, near-suicidal attacks against the Japanese fleet. Wave after wave of slow, vulnerable torpedo planes were cut to pieces. The sacrifice seemed futile.

Then, at 10:22 a.m., everything changed. While Japanese fighters were still at low altitude finishing off the torpedo planes, American dive bombers appeared high above the fleet. The Japanese carriers were at their most exposed, caught at a vulnerable moment in their flight operations. In five catastrophic minutes, American bombs found their targets. *Akagi*, *Kaga*, and *Sōryū* erupted in flames; the fourth carrier, *Hiryū*, was fatally hit later that afternoon and scuttled the next morning.

Japan lost four carriers, a heavy cruiser, and more than three thousand men, including many of its most experienced pilots, veterans who could not be replaced. The United States lost the carrier *Yorktown*, a destroyer, and over three hundred men. It was the most decisive naval victory in American history.

Midway shattered Japan's naval power and left Tokyo on the defensive. In August 1942, US Marines landed on Guadalcanal in the Solomon Islands. After six months of fierce jungle fighting, malaria, and heavy losses on both sides, the Americans prevailed.

The Allies adopted an "island hopping" strategy, capturing key islands, building airfields, and moving closer to Japan while bypassing heavily defended outposts. Each victory cost thousands of lives as

Japanese troops fought to the death.

Back in Europe

While American forces battled Japan in the Pacific, Stalin demanded that Britain and America open a second front in Europe to relieve pressure on the Soviet Union. Churchill and Roosevelt agreed the Allies were not yet ready for a direct assault on Nazi-occupied France. Instead, they would strike at Germany's vulnerable southern flank through North Africa.

In November 1942, American and British forces launched Operation Torch—the largest amphibious invasion in history up to that point—landing at Casablanca, Oran, and Algiers. Commanded by General Dwight D. Eisenhower, more than 100,000 Allied troops came ashore, catching the Vichy French defenders off guard. The operation marked America's first major offensive against Nazi Germany and the beginning of a hard-fought North African campaign.

American troops heading to North Africa.⁴

The landings succeeded, but the men's early enthusiasm faded quickly. American forces, untested in battle, soon faced Germany's seasoned Afrika Korps under Field Marshal Erwin Rommel, the legendary "Desert Fox." In February 1943, at Kasserine Pass in Tunisia, Rommel and General Hans-Jürgen von Arnim struck American positions with devastating effect. German tanks smashed through inexperienced units, inflicting heavy casualties and sending GIs into chaotic retreat. It was a humiliating baptism by fire. Poor coordination and underestimation of the enemy had cost dearly.

The defeat, however, became a turning point for the US Army. Eisenhower replaced weak commanders and brought in aggressive leaders like General George S. Patton Jr., who imposed strict discipline and revitalized morale. American forces adapted quickly, refining their tactics, logistics, and coordination. The humiliation hardened them.

By May 1943, the tide had turned. Trapped between Patton's advancing army from the west and British forces under General Bernard Montgomery pushing from the east, more than 250,000 German and Italian troops surrendered in Tunisia. The Allies now controlled North Africa, securing vital Mediterranean shipping lanes and opening the way to invade southern Europe.

More importantly, America's once-inexperienced army had become a capable, confident fighting force. It was ready for brutal campaigns in Sicily, Italy, and France.

The Allies invaded Sicily in July and mainland Italy in September. Italy surrendered, but German forces occupied the country and fought bitterly. Progress up the Italian Peninsula was slow and costly.

Meanwhile, the Soviets gained the upper hand in the east. At Stalingrad in 1942-43, an entire German army was destroyed. At Kursk, the next summer, the Soviets won the largest tank battle in history. Pushing west, they liberated their territory and advanced toward Germany. Stalin kept demanding a true second front in France.

That front finally opened in June 1944. Operation Overlord—the Normandy invasion—was the largest amphibious operation in history. Eisenhower commanded nearly 160,000 troops, which landed on five beaches in northern France.

At dawn on June 6, 1944—D-Day—Allied forces stormed ashore. Paratroopers had dropped behind enemy lines overnight. At Omaha Beach, Americans faced devastating fire; some units suffered 90 percent casualties. Yet they pressed forward. By day's end, about 150,000 Allied troops were ashore. Over 4,000 were dead, but the invasion had succeeded.

It took two months to break out of Normandy. German defenses were strong, but Allied air power and numbers prevailed. In late July, General George Patton's Third Army broke through and raced across France. Paris was liberated on August 25. By September, Allied armies had reached Germany's border.

Victory seemed close. Some believed the war would end by Christmas. They were wrong. Germany wasn't finished yet.

The Home Front: Rosie the Riveter and Japanese Internment

World War II transformed American society. The war effort required everyone to contribute.

Industry converted to war production. Automobile factories built tanks and aircraft. Shipyards turned out warships and cargo vessels at astonishing speed. Henry Kaiser's yards produced Liberty Ships—cargo vessels—in about forty-five days; one was built in just about four days as a publicity stunt. By war's end, American industry had produced about 300,000 aircraft, approximately 90,000 tanks and armored vehicles, thousands of ships, and millions of tons of supplies.

The war ended the Great Depression. Factories needed workers, so unemployment practically vanished, and wages rose. Millions of Americans who had struggled through the 1930s now had steady jobs and new prosperity.

Women entered the workforce in unprecedented numbers. About six million took jobs during the war, many in heavy industry—shipyards, aircraft plants, and munitions factories. "Rosie the Riveter" became the symbol of women war workers, portrayed in posters flexing her arm under the slogan "We Can Do It!" Women proved they could handle work once reserved for men.

Women at work in factories.*

Most women left these jobs when the war ended, as society expected them to make way for returning veterans. Yet it proved that women could do any job and helped lay the foundation for the women's movement of the 1960s and 1970s.

African Americans also found new opportunities. About one million served in the military, though in segregated units. The Tuskegee Airmen—Black fighter pilots—earned distinction in Europe. On the home front, Black workers filled industrial jobs but faced discrimination and were often given the hardest, dirtiest tasks. In 1941, A. Philip Randolph, leader of the Brotherhood of Sleeping Car Porters, threatened a march on Washington to protest discrimination in defense industries. Roosevelt responded with Executive Order 8802, banning such discrimination and creating the Fair Employment Practices Committee. The war began to erode racial barriers, though segregation remained.

Prosperity was widespread, but so was injustice. On February 19, 1942, Roosevelt signed Executive Order 9066, authorizing the military to exclude people from designated areas. The order was used to remove about 120,000 Japanese Americans—two-thirds of them US citizens—from the West Coast.

The government claimed it was for national security, fearing espionage or sabotage. There was no evidence of either. The true causes were racism, wartime hysteria, and pressure from West Coast politicians and business interests who wanted to eliminate Japanese American competition.

Families had only days to sell their homes and possessions, often at ruinous prices. They were sent to internment camps—barren compounds ringed with barbed wire and guard towers—in remote areas of California, Arizona, Utah, Idaho, Wyoming, Colorado, and Arkansas. Families lived in cramped, unheated barracks with no privacy, enduring harsh climates.

These were prisons in all but name. People were held without trial or charge, guilty only of having Japanese ancestry.

Many still served their country. The 442nd Regimental Combat Team, composed almost entirely of Japanese Americans, fought in Italy and France and became the most decorated unit in US military history for its size and length of service. These soldiers fought for the very nation that had imprisoned their families.

Legal challenges failed. In *Korematsu v. United States* (1944), the Supreme Court upheld internment as a valid wartime measure. The camps closed in 1945, but returning families found their homes and businesses gone. No compensation was offered until 1988, when Congress formally apologized and provided small payments to surviving internees. The episode revealed how easily fear and prejudice could override constitutional rights.

On the home front, gasoline, rubber, meat, sugar, and coffee were rationed. Families received coupon books and planted "victory gardens" to supplement food supplies. People collected scrap metal, rubber, and paper for recycling. Everyone was expected to contribute to the war effort.

The war reshaped American culture. Movies, music, and radio promoted patriotism and morale. Hollywood stars sold war bonds, and entertainers performed for troops overseas. News focused almost entirely on the war.

Unlike later conflicts, World War II enjoyed overwhelming public support. Americans believed they were fighting for freedom and survival against tyranny. The war was widely remembered as "the Good War."

The Atomic Bomb and the Dawn of the Nuclear Age

By early 1945, Germany was collapsing. Soviet forces were pushing from the east, and American and British forces were advancing from the west. In December 1944, Germany launched one final offensive—the Battle of the Bulge—in Belgium. After brutal winter fighting, American troops held their ground. It was Germany's last gasp.

In March 1945, Allied forces crossed the Rhine River into Germany. Hitler retreated to a bunker in Berlin. Soviet troops surrounded the city. On April 30, Hitler committed suicide. A week later, on May 7, Germany surrendered unconditionally. The war in Europe was over.

President Franklin D. Roosevelt did not live to see victory. He died of a cerebral hemorrhage on April 12, 1945, after twelve years in office. Vice President Harry S. Truman became president. He knew little of Roosevelt's plans or the war's secrets. Now, he had to finish the war and shape the peace.

Japan fought on. American forces had captured islands ever closer to the Japanese homeland—Iwo Jima in March and Okinawa in June 1945. Both battles were horrifically costly. At Iwo Jima, about seven thousand Americans died to capture an island only eight square miles in size. At Okinawa, more than twelve thousand Americans were killed. Japanese troops fought to the death. On Okinawa, thousands of civilians committed suicide, convinced by propaganda that Americans would torture or kill them.

Raising the flag at Iwo Jima.⁴⁶

Meanwhile, American bombers were devastating Japan's cities. Firebombing raids killed hundreds of thousands. The March raid on Tokyo alone killed about 100,000 people. Japanese cities, built largely of wood, burned easily. Yet Japan refused to surrender. Its government, dominated by military leaders, vowed to fight to the end.

The US military planned to invade Japan in November 1945. Operation Downfall was expected to cost hundreds of thousands of American lives and perhaps millions of Japanese military and civilian casualties. Japan had two million soldiers defending the home islands and had mobilized civilians to resist with any weapon they could find.

Then came a new weapon. In July 1945, American scientists successfully tested the first atomic bomb in New Mexico. The Manhattan Project, a secret program that began in 1942, developed the weapon at a cost of $2 billion. Directed by physicist J. Robert Oppenheimer, it produced a weapon of unprecedented destructive power.

Truman now faced a momentous decision: should he use the atomic bomb against Japan?

Supporters argued that using it would end the war immediately and save countless American lives. It would also demonstrate America's power to the Soviet Union, which was emerging as a postwar rival. Many Americans felt Japan, which had begun the war with a surprise attack and committed terrible atrocities, deserved no mercy.

Others disagreed. Some scientists and officials warned that using the bomb on cities would be immoral and could trigger a nuclear arms race. They wanted to demonstrate the weapon on an uninhabited island to compel Japan's surrender. Truman rejected that idea. A demonstration might fail, and Japan might believe the United States had only one bomb. After four years of total war, Truman felt no obligation to spare Japan's cities.

He authorized its use.

On August 6, 1945, a B-29 bomber, *Enola Gay*, dropped an atomic bomb on Hiroshima, a city of about 350,000 people. The blast, equal to about 15,000 tons of TNT, destroyed the city in seconds. A blinding flash and fireball leveled buildings and vaporized people near the center. About 70,000 to 80,000 died instantly; by the end of 1945, roughly 140,000 were dead from burns and radiation.

Japan still refused to surrender. On August 8, the Soviet Union declared war on Japan and invaded Manchuria, crushing Japanese forces there. The next day, a second atomic bomb destroyed Nagasaki, killing about 40,000 people instantly and 70,000 by year's end.

Japan's government was paralyzed. Military leaders wanted to fight on, but civilians urged surrender. Emperor Hirohito broke the deadlock. In an unprecedented move, he personally ordered surrender.

On August 15, 1945, Japan announced its capitulation. Millions celebrated around the world. World War II was over. On September 2, Japan formally surrendered aboard the USS *Missouri* in Tokyo Bay—V-J Day, Victory over Japan Day.

The atomic bomb had ended the war but opened a new and perilous era. Within a few years, the Soviet Union developed its own bomb. The nuclear arms race scientists had feared became reality, and humanity now lived under the shadow of annihilation.

The debate over Truman's decision endures. Some argue the bombings saved lives by preventing invasion; others contend Japan was already defeated and that the bombs were used to intimidate the Soviets more than to defeat Japan. The question will never be settled.

What is clear is that World War II changed everything. It killed an estimated sixty to eighty-five million people worldwide—about 3 percent of humanity. The Holocaust murdered six million Jews and millions of others in Nazi camps. Cities were destroyed, empires fell, and the world was divided between two superpowers: the United States and the Soviet Union. The atomic bomb created the possibility of human extinction.

The world emerged from the war transformed, entering a new age of power, fear, and uncertainty that would define the rest of the 20th century.

Chapter 19: The Cold War: A 45-Year Standoff

The Iron Curtain, Containment, and the Red Scare

World War II created two superpowers: the United States and the Soviet Union. They had been allies against Nazi Germany, but their partnership was uneasy. The two nations had opposite political systems and incompatible visions for the postwar world. Their rivalry would dominate international affairs for the next forty-five years.

The conflict began over Europe's future. As Soviet forces pushed west in 1944 and 1945, they occupied Poland, Romania, Bulgaria, Hungary, Czechoslovakia, and eastern Germany. Stalin installed communist governments in these countries, canceling elections and eliminating opposition. The Soviet Union built a buffer zone of satellite states to protect itself from future invasion.

At Yalta in February 1945, Roosevelt, Churchill, and Stalin met to plan the postwar order. Stalin promised free elections in Eastern Europe, but broke that promise. When Roosevelt died two months later, the hope of continued cooperation died with him.

President Truman took a harder line with the Soviets. At Potsdam in July 1945, tensions were clear. Germany was divided into four occupation zones controlled by the United States, Britain, France, and the Soviet Union. Berlin, deep inside the Soviet zone, was also divided. What were meant as temporary arrangements became permanent boundaries.

In March 1946, Winston Churchill warned of the new division, saying, "An iron curtain has descended across the Continent." Behind that curtain, Soviet domination was complete. Europe was now split between East and West, communist and democratic.

Containment became the foundation of US foreign policy. In March 1947, Truman announced what became known as the Truman Doctrine. Greece and Turkey faced communist insurgencies, and Britain could no longer support them. Truman asked Congress for $400 million in aid, declaring that it must be US policy "to support free peoples who are resisting attempted subjugation by armed minorities or by outside pressures."[i] The United States was now committed to opposing communism anywhere in the world.

In June 1947, Secretary of State George Marshall unveiled the Marshall Plan, a massive program to rebuild Western Europe's economy. The United States offered billions in aid to restore prosperity and prevent communist influence. The Soviet Union rejected the offer and forced its satellites to do the same. Over four years, the Marshall Plan provided about $13 billion to Western Europe. It worked—Europe recovered, and democracy endured.

The first major Cold War crisis came in Berlin. In June 1948, the Soviets blocked all road and rail access to West Berlin, hoping to force the Allies out. Truman refused to retreat. The United States and Britain organized the Berlin Airlift, flying supplies into the city around the clock for nearly a year. At its peak, planes landed every few minutes, delivering 2.3 million tons of food, fuel, and supplies. In May 1949, the Soviets lifted the blockade. The Allies had won without firing a shot.

---

[i] "Truman Doctrine." https://www.archives.gov/milestone-documents/truman-doctrine

German children watching a plane land during the Berlin Airlift.⁷

That same year, the United States, Canada, and ten Western European nations formed the North Atlantic Treaty Organization (NATO), pledging mutual defense if attacked. The Soviet Union responded in 1955 with the Warsaw Pact, its alliance with Eastern European satellites. Europe was now divided into two armed camps.

In August 1949, the Soviet Union detonated its first atomic bomb—years earlier than expected. America's nuclear monopoly was over, and the arms race had begun. Both sides built thousands of weapons, enough to destroy the world many times over.

Meanwhile, communism spread to Asia. In China, Mao Zedong's communist forces defeated Chiang Kai-shek's Nationalist government after years of civil war. Despite massive US aid, Chiang's regime was corrupt and unpopular, while Mao's forces gained peasant support. In 1949, the communists triumphed. Chiang fled to Taiwan, and China— home to one-fifth of the world's population—became communist.

Americans were stunned. Politicians asked, "Who lost China?" Republicans blamed Truman and the Democrats. Some accused the State Department of harboring communist sympathizers, creating a climate of fear.

That fear exploded into the Red Scare. In 1950, Senator Joseph McCarthy of Wisconsin claimed to have a list of communists in the State Department. He never produced evidence, but his accusations terrified the nation. People accused of communist ties could lose their jobs, reputations, and friends.

McCarthy targeted government officials, Hollywood figures, teachers, and union leaders. Congressional committees investigated suspected communists. Those who refused to cooperate were blacklisted and couldn't work. The House Un-American Activities Committee (HUAC) pursued alleged communist influence in Hollywood. The "Hollywood Ten"—writers and directors who refused to testify—were jailed for contempt of Congress, and studios barred them from employment.

Some espionage cases were real. Julius and Ethel Rosenberg were convicted of passing atomic secrets to the Soviets and executed in 1953. Julius was guilty, though Ethel's role was minor (she just typed the notes). Alger Hiss, a State Department official, was convicted of perjury for denying espionage. These cases fueled fears of communist infiltration.

But McCarthy's accusations soon went far beyond any real threat. His reckless charges and bullying tactics—guilt by association, innuendo, and character assassination—became known as McCarthyism.

His downfall came in 1954, when he accused the US Army of harboring communists. The televised Army-McCarthy hearings exposed his cruelty and bluster. When McCarthy attacked a young lawyer, Army counsel Joseph Welch famously asked, "Have you no sense of decency, sir, at long last?" The spell was broken. The Senate censured McCarthy later that year. He died in 1957, ruined by alcoholism.

The Cold War also changed America's map. The vast territory had been purchased from Russia in 1867 for $7.2 million—about two cents an acre. At the time, critics mocked the deal as "Seward's Folly" and "Seward's Icebox," named after Secretary of State William Seward, who negotiated it. What use did America have for a frozen wasteland covered with glaciers, icebergs, and polar bears? The purchase seemed like a colossal waste of money.

But Alaska proved its worth. The discovery of gold in 1896 brought thousands of prospectors north. In the Cold War, Alaska's proximity to the Soviet Union made it strategically vital. Military bases and radar stations transformed the frozen frontier into America's northern shield. What had once seemed like folly now looked like a bargain.

Hawaii followed as the fiftieth state. However, Hawaii's path to statehood was darker. In 1893, American businessmen—sugar planters who controlled the islands' economy—overthrew Queen Lili'uokalani with help from US Marines. The queen surrendered under protest, believing the United States government would restore her throne. It did not. President Grover Cleveland called the overthrow illegal and immoral, but Congress refused to act. Hawaii became a US territory in 1898. It was annexed because of its strategic location in the Pacific.

Statehood came after decades of debate. Some opposed it because Hawaii's population was majority non-White—Japanese, Native Hawaiian, Filipino, and Chinese called the islands home. Others worried about admitting a territory so far from the mainland. But Pearl Harbor had proven Hawaii's strategic importance, and Hawaiian soldiers had fought bravely in World War II, including Japanese American units. The islands' multiethnic population voted overwhelmingly for statehood.

For the first time, the American flag flew over territory beyond the continent, and there were fifty stars instead of forty-eight.

The Space Race: Competition Beyond Earth

The Cold War reached beyond Earth's atmosphere. In October 1957, the Soviet Union shocked the world by launching *Sputnik*, the first artificial satellite. The beach-ball-sized sphere orbited the planet every ninety-six minutes, transmitting radio beeps that anyone could hear. Americans listened with awe and dread. If the Soviets could launch satellites, they could launch nuclear missiles that might reach American cities in minutes.

The "Sputnik crisis" triggered a wave of national anxiety. How had America fallen behind? Critics blamed complacent leadership and weak science education. President Eisenhower responded by boosting defense spending and establishing NASA—the National Aeronautics and Space Administration—in 1958 to coordinate the US effort in what is known as the Space Race.

The Soviets extended their lead. In 1961, cosmonaut Yuri Gagarin became the first human in space, orbiting Earth aboard *Vostok 1*. His triumphant flight made him an international hero and a symbol of communist progress. Weeks later, American astronaut Alan Shepard made a brief suborbital flight, but the United States still trailed.

Determined to restore American prestige, President John F. Kennedy made a bold commitment. In May 1961, he announced that the US would land a man on the moon and return him safely before the decade's end. It was an audacious goal—the technology didn't yet exist—but Kennedy understood that the Space Race was about more than science. It was a contest to prove that democratic capitalism could outpace Soviet communism.

Both superpowers poured billions into their space programs. NASA's Mercury missions sent the first Americans into orbit, followed by Gemini, which tested the skills needed for a lunar mission. The Soviets achieved more firsts—the first woman in space (Valentina Tereshkova, 1963) and the first spacewalk (Alexei Leonov, 1965)—but America was closing the gap.

The Apollo program aimed for the moon, driven by the massive Saturn V rocket, the most powerful ever built. Tragedy struck in January 1967 when a fire during a ground test killed three Apollo 1 astronauts—Gus Grissom, Ed White, and Roger Chaffee. NASA overhauled spacecraft design and safety procedures but pressed on.

On December 24, 1968, Apollo 8 became the first manned mission to orbit the moon. Astronauts Frank Borman, Jim Lovell, and William Anders photographed Earth rising over the lunar horizon—an image that became iconic. Their Christmas Eve broadcast from lunar orbit captivated millions worldwide.

Finally, on July 20, 1969, Apollo 11 fulfilled Kennedy's dream. Neil Armstrong stepped onto

Earthrise.⁴⁸

the lunar surface, saying, "That's one small step for man, one giant leap for mankind." Buzz Aldrin joined him while Michael Collins orbited above. After two and a half hours of exploration, they returned home as heroes.

America had won the Space Race. Achieved just months before Kennedy's deadline, the moon landing restored national confidence and prestige. It showed that democracy and innovation could surpass the Soviets and inspired a generation to pursue science and engineering. Kennedy, assassinated in 1963, never saw his vision realized.

After Apollo, the rivalry eased. In 1975, American and Soviet spacecraft docked in orbit in a gesture of détente. The Space Race ended not in confrontation but in cooperation, proving that even Cold War rivals could find common ground among the stars.

The Cuban Missile Crisis and the Brink of Nuclear War

However, the 1950s were a decade of tension and fear. Both superpowers built vast nuclear arsenals. The United States tested the hydrogen bomb in 1952, and the Soviet Union followed in 1953. These weapons were a thousand times more powerful than those dropped on Japan. Entire cities could vanish in seconds.

Atmospheric testing spread radioactive fallout. Americans built backyard bomb shelters. Schools held "duck and cover" drills, teaching children to hide under desks as if that might save them. The threat of nuclear annihilation became part of everyday life.

In 1959, revolutionaries led by Fidel Castro overthrew Cuba's US-backed government. At first, Washington tried to work with him, but Castro soon nationalized American businesses and aligned with Moscow. In 1961, the CIA organized an invasion of Cuba by exiles at the Bay of Pigs. It was a disaster. The invaders were quickly defeated, embarrassing the new Kennedy administration and driving Castro further into the Soviet camp.

The following year brought the most dangerous confrontation of the Cold War. In October 1962, American U-2 spy planes discovered Soviet nuclear missiles in Cuba—just ninety miles from Florida. The missiles could reach US cities within minutes. Kennedy faced an impossible choice: accept Soviet missiles in the Western Hemisphere or act and risk nuclear war.

He chose a middle course. On October 22, Kennedy announced a naval "quarantine" of Cuba, blocking further Soviet shipments and demanding that the missiles already there be removed. Soviet ships were en route. If they tried to run the blockade, US warships would stop them—possibly by force.

For thirteen tense days, the world held its breath. Kennedy and Soviet Premier Nikita Khrushchev exchanged urgent messages while both sides searched for a way out that avoided surrender or catastrophe. On October 27, a Soviet missile battery in Cuba shot down an American U-2, killing the pilot. US generals urged retaliation, but Kennedy held back, giving diplomacy one last chance.

That same day, a Soviet submarine armed with nuclear torpedoes was cornered by US warships near the blockade line. Cut off from Moscow and running out of air, the captain prepared to launch a nuclear torpedo. Two officers agreed, but one, Vasili Arkhipov, refused. His decision likely prevented a global nuclear war.

The next morning, October 28, Khrushchev agreed to withdraw the missiles. Publicly, Kennedy promised not to invade Cuba; privately, he also agreed to remove US missiles from Turkey. Both leaders could claim victory. The crisis was over.

The Cuban Missile Crisis brought the world closer to nuclear war than ever before. It also led to new safeguards. In 1963, Washington and Moscow established a direct "hotline" for crisis communication and signed the Limited Test Ban Treaty, banning nuclear tests in the atmosphere, underwater, and in space.

But the fear did not fade. The crisis spurred both nations to expand their nuclear arsenals. By the 1980s, the United States and the Soviet Union each possessed enough warheads to destroy the planet many times over. This deadly balance was called mutual assured destruction, or MAD. Neither side dared strike first, knowing both would perish. It was a fragile peace, maintained not by trust but by fear of the end of the world.

The Korean and Vietnam Wars: Hot Wars in a Cold Conflict

The Cold War spread beyond Europe. In June 1950, communist North Korea invaded South Korea. Korea had been divided after World War II, with Soviet forces in the north and American forces in the south. Both superpowers later withdrew, leaving rival governments.

North Korean leader Kim Il-sung, backed by the Soviet Union and China, sought to reunify the peninsula by force. His troops swept across the border and quickly overran most of South Korea. President Truman saw this as a test of containment and committed American forces under the United Nations flag.

General Douglas MacArthur commanded the UN forces, most of them American. In September 1950, he launched a daring amphibious landing at Inchon, cutting North Korean supply lines. UN troops recaptured Seoul and advanced deep into North Korea, nearing the Chinese border.

China warned it would intervene if UN forces approached. MacArthur ignored the threat. In November, hundreds of thousands of Chinese soldiers poured across the Yalu River, driving UN forces into retreat. The war settled into a stalemate near the original border.

MacArthur urged bombing China and even using nuclear weapons. Truman refused. When MacArthur publicly criticized him, Truman fired him for insubordination.

The Korean War dragged on. Armistice talks began in 1951 but stalled for two years. The fighting finally ended in July 1953 with a ceasefire that restored the prewar boundary. Korea remained divided. About thirty-seven thousand Americans were killed, along with millions of Koreans and Chinese. The conflict had preserved the status quo at a terrible cost.

Korea had shown that the Cold War could turn hot. Vietnam proved it could become a quagmire.

Vietnam had been a French colony called French Indochina. During World War II, Japan occupied it. Vietnamese nationalists led by Ho Chi Minh fought the Japanese and declared independence in 1945. But France wanted its colony back, so war broke out between French forces and Ho's communist-led Viet Minh.

The United States supported France, seeing the conflict through the lens of the Cold War. If Vietnam fell to communism, other Southeast Asian nations might follow. Despite massive US aid, France lost. In 1954, Viet Minh forces defeated the French at Dien Bien Phu, forcing France to withdraw.

The Geneva Accords temporarily divided Vietnam along the 17th parallel. Ho's communists controlled the north. A pro-Western government led by Ngo Dinh Diem ruled the south. Elections meant to reunify the country were never held; US leaders feared Ho would win. The division became permanent.

Throughout the 1950s, communist insurgents in South Vietnam—the Viet Cong—fought Diem's regime, supported by North Vietnam. The US sent military advisors to train South Vietnamese forces. President Kennedy increased their number to about sixteen thousand by 1963.

Diem's government was corrupt and repressive. He favored Catholics in a mostly Buddhist country. Buddhist monks protested, some burning themselves alive in public—images that horrified Americans. In November 1963, the South Vietnamese military overthrew and killed Diem with tacit US approval, plunging the country into political chaos.

After Kennedy's assassination, Lyndon Johnson inherited a deteriorating situation. In August 1964, after reports that North Vietnamese patrol boats attacked US destroyers in the Gulf of Tonkin, Johnson asked Congress for authorization to use force. The Gulf of Tonkin Resolution passed overwhelmingly, giving him broad war powers.

In 1965, Johnson sent combat troops to Vietnam. By 1968, more than 500,000 Americans were fighting there. US forces used massive firepower—bombing, artillery, and advanced weapons—but the Viet Cong and North Vietnamese Army fought as guerrillas. They avoided large battles, relied on ambushes and tunnels, and blended into the civilian population. The US won battles but couldn't win the war.

American troops looking for Viet Cong soldiers.⁴⁰

At first, most Americans supported the war, trusting official claims that victory was near. However, as casualties rose and the war dragged on, opposition grew. Many questioned whether Vietnam truly threatened US security. Young men were being drafted to fight in a distant jungle for unclear goals.

The anti-war movement expanded. Students protested on college campuses. Civil rights leaders like Martin Luther King Jr. condemned the war. The movement included pacifists, clergy, and ordinary citizens who saw the war as immoral or unwinnable.

An anti-war protester giving a flower to armed police.[50]

In January 1968, during Tet—the Vietnamese New Year—communist forces launched massive attacks across South Vietnam. Militarily, the Tet Offensive failed; communist forces suffered heavy losses. Politically, it was a disaster for the US government. Americans had been told the enemy was nearly defeated, yet they saw fighting in every major city, even the US Embassy in Saigon.

Tet shattered public confidence. CBS news anchor Walter Cronkite declared the war unwinnable. "If I've lost Cronkite," Johnson reportedly said, "I've lost Middle America."[i] In March 1968, Johnson announced he would not seek reelection. The war had destroyed his presidency.

Richard Nixon won the 1968 election, promising "peace with honor." His policy of "Vietnamization" aimed to train South Vietnamese forces to take over the fighting while US troops withdrew. At the same time, Nixon secretly expanded the war, bombing Cambodia and Laos to destroy communist sanctuaries.

The conflict dragged on. American casualties mounted, and protests intensified. In May 1970, National Guard troops shot and killed four students at Kent State University in Ohio during an anti-war protest, shocking the nation. In 1971, the *Pentagon Papers*—secret government documents—were leaked to the press, revealing that successive administrations had misled the public about the war. Trust in government collapsed.

Nixon and his advisor, Henry Kissinger, negotiated with North Vietnam. In January 1973, they signed the Paris Peace Accords. American forces would withdraw, and North Vietnam would release US prisoners of war. The agreement left North Vietnamese troops in the South, so everyone knew the peace was temporary.

The last American troops left Vietnam in 1973. In 1975, North Vietnamese forces captured Saigon. Desperate South Vietnamese tried to flee as helicopters evacuated people from the roof of the US Embassy—an image that came to symbolize American defeat. Vietnam was formally unified under communist rule.

About fifty-eight thousand Americans died in Vietnam. Vietnamese casualties, civilian and military, numbered in the millions. The war cost billions of dollars and divided American society. Veterans returned home to a country that was uncertain how to receive them. Many suffered from PTSD and felt forgotten.

The experience left deep scars and made future leaders wary of foreign interventions—the so-called "Vietnam Syndrome." It would take decades for the United States to regain its confidence in global leadership.

---

[i] Dunwoody, Dave. "1968, Year Of Discontent: LBJ Declines To Run For Second Term." https://www.wuwf.org/local-news/2018-03-29/1968-year-of-discontent-lbj-declines-to-run-for-second-term

The Fall of the Berlin Wall and the End of an Era

The Cold War lasted through the 1970s and 1980s. Relations between the superpowers alternated between tension and détente (periods of relaxation). In the 1970s, détente produced arms control agreements and increased trade, but tensions returned in 1979 when the Soviet Union invaded Afghanistan.

Ronald Reagan became president in 1981 and took a hard line against Moscow, calling the Soviet Union an "evil empire." He launched a massive military buildup, increasing defense spending to pressure the Soviet economy, and supported anti-communist movements worldwide, including guerrillas fighting Soviet forces in Afghanistan.

Reagan's most controversial initiative was the Strategic Defense Initiative (SDI), nicknamed "Star Wars." It aimed to develop a system to shoot down incoming missiles from space. Scientists doubted it would work, but the Soviets feared it could undermine mutual assured destruction. They could not afford to compete in such an expensive arms race.

By the 1980s, the Soviet system was crumbling. Its economy was stagnant, its political structure corrupt and inefficient, and the war in Afghanistan a costly disaster. Eastern European satellite states were becoming increasingly rebellious. The system was collapsing under its own weight.

In 1985, Mikhail Gorbachev became the Soviet leader. Young and pragmatic, he recognized that reform was essential. He introduced *glasnost* (openness) and *perestroika* (restructuring), allowing limited free speech and attempting to modernize the economy. He withdrew Soviet troops from Afghanistan and negotiated arms reduction treaties with Reagan.

But Gorbachev's reforms unleashed forces he couldn't control. Once people could criticize the regime, they demanded more. In Eastern Europe, communist governments began to fall. Poland's Solidarity movement challenged Soviet rule, and Hungary opened its border with Austria, letting East Germans escape to the West.

The Berlin Wall, the Cold War's starkest symbol, had divided the city since 1961. On November 9, 1989, after weeks of protests, East Germany announced that citizens could cross freely. Crowds surged to the wall. Guards, confused and without orders, opened the gates. People climbed atop the wall, celebrating, and began tearing it down with hammers and pickaxes. The Berlin Wall fell.

Within a year, Germany reunified. Communist governments across Eastern Europe collapsed. The Soviet empire was gone.

Gorbachev's reforms had failed to preserve the Soviet Union. The republics declared independence, and Boris Yeltsin emerged as Russia's leader. On December 25, 1991, Gorbachev resigned. The Soviet Union ceased to exist.

The Cold War was over. The United States had won without fighting World War III. The threat of nuclear annihilation that had loomed for forty-five years was lifting. Democracy and capitalism had triumphed over communism.

Victory came with costs. The arms race had consumed trillions of dollars. Proxy wars in Korea, Vietnam, Afghanistan, Africa, and Latin America had killed millions. The nuclear arsenals built during the Cold War still existed, posing new dangers as the Soviet Union's weapons were scattered among successor states. The euphoria of victory soon gave way to new challenges in a post–Cold War world.

But in 1991, the sense of relief and triumph was real. The long struggle was over. The Cold War had ended not with a bang but with a whimper, and for a time, the world seemed safer.

Chapter 20: The Civil Rights Movement

From Segregation to Montgomery: The Fight Begins

After Reconstruction ended in 1877, Black Americans in the South lived under Jim Crow segregation. Their right to vote was stripped away through poll taxes, literacy tests, and intimidation. They attended inferior schools and faced violence and discrimination. The system was designed to keep them subordinate. For decades, change seemed impossible.

Yet Black Americans never stopped resisting. They built their own communities, churches, and institutions. They organized, protested, and fought in courts for their rights.

The National Association for the Advancement of Colored People (NAACP), founded in 1909, led the legal fight. Thurgood Marshall, one of its leading attorneys, challenged school segregation across the South. Marshall and his team argued that separate schools for Black children violated the Fourteenth Amendment's guarantee of equal protection.

Segregated waiting rooms at the train station.[51]

Their efforts culminated in *Brown v. Board of Education of Topeka*. On May 17, 1954, the Supreme Court unanimously ruled that segregation in public schools was unconstitutional. The decision overturned *Plessy v. Ferguson* and struck at the foundation of legal segregation.

The *Brown* decision was a landmark victory, but enforcing it proved difficult. In *Brown II* (1955), the Supreme Court ordered desegregation "with all deliberate speed"—language that allowed Southern states to delay. Some districts closed public schools rather than integrate. White Citizens' Councils formed to oppose desegregation, and politicians pledged to resist.

In 1957, the crisis came to a head in Little Rock, Arkansas, where nine Black students sought to attend Central High School. The governor ordered the National Guard to block them. On September 4, an angry White mob surrounded fifteen-year-old Elizabeth Eckford as she tried to enter the school.

Elizabeth Eckford trying to go to school.[5]

President Eisenhower, usually cautious on civil rights, could not ignore open defiance of federal authority. He sent the 101st Airborne Division to escort the Little Rock Nine into the school. They attended under military protection for the rest of the year. The confrontation proved that the federal government would enforce desegregation, but it also revealed the depth of Southern resistance.

Meanwhile, a new phase of the struggle began in Montgomery, Alabama. On December 1, 1955, Rosa Parks, a seamstress and NAACP member, refused to surrender her bus seat to a White passenger. Parks's arrest sparked the Montgomery Bus Boycott.

Black residents organized the boycott and chose a young minister, Martin Luther King Jr., to lead it. The protest lasted 381 days. Boycotters walked to work or organized carpools despite harassment and violence. King's home was bombed, but he preached perseverance and nonviolence.

In November 1956, the boycott ended in victory. The Supreme Court ruled in *Browder v. Gayle* that bus segregation was unconstitutional. The boycott showed that nonviolent mass protest could defeat segregation. King emerged as a national leader, and the modern civil rights movement had begun.

King's philosophy of nonviolent resistance, inspired by Gandhi, emphasized peaceful defiance of unjust laws. Protesters would accept arrest and suffering without retaliation, appealing to the nation's conscience. Peaceful demonstrators faced beatings, arrests, and sometimes death, but their actions exposed the brutality of Jim Crow to the world.

In 1957, King and other ministers formed the Southern Christian Leadership Conference (SCLC) to coordinate civil rights efforts across the South. The movement was growing, but most of the region remained segregated, and Black citizens still faced enormous barriers to voting in the Deep South.

"I Have a Dream": The Height of the Civil Rights Movement

The civil rights movement gained momentum in 1960. On February 1, four Black college students in Greensboro, North Carolina, sat at a Woolworth's lunch counter and politely asked to be served. They were refused but stayed until closing. They returned the next day with more students.

The sit-in movement spread across the South. Black students sat at segregated lunch counters, libraries, and parks, refusing to move even when cursed, spat on, or attacked. By August, lunch counters in twenty-seven Southern cities had been integrated. The sit-ins energized the movement and drew in a new generation of activists.

In April 1960, the students formed the Student Nonviolent Coordinating Committee (SNCC). Its young members organized protests and voter registration drives, risking their lives for justice.

In 1961, integrated groups of activists began Freedom Rides to challenge segregation in interstate travel. In Alabama, mobs attacked riders. One bus was firebombed outside Anniston, and others were beaten in Birmingham as police stood aside. Attorney General Robert Kennedy sent federal marshals to protect them. By autumn, the Interstate Commerce Commission banned segregation in interstate bus terminals.

In 1963, Martin Luther King Jr. and the SCLC launched a campaign in Birmingham, Alabama, one of the nation's most segregated cities. King was jailed and wrote his "Letter from Birmingham Jail," defending nonviolent protest and condemning White moderates who urged patience. "Injustice anywhere is a threat to justice everywhere."

As protests grew, Birmingham's police chief unleashed fire hoses and dogs on peaceful demonstrators, including children. Images of the brutality shocked the world. Under pressure, Birmingham business leaders agreed to desegregate stores and hire Black employees. The campaign marked a major victory and convinced President Kennedy that civil rights legislation was necessary.

On June 11, 1963, Kennedy called civil rights "a moral issue" in a televised address. That night, NAACP leader Medgar Evers was murdered outside his home in Mississippi.

To build support for the legislation, civil rights groups organized the March on Washington. On August 28, 1963, more than 250,000 people gathered at the Lincoln Memorial to demand jobs and freedom. Martin Luther King Jr. delivered the final speech. Setting aside his prepared text, he spoke from the heart. "I have a dream that my four little children will one day live in a nation where they will not be judged by the color of their skin but by the content of their character." His words became immortal.

MLK leading the March on Washington.[58]

Three months later, on November 22, 1963, President Kennedy was assassinated in Dallas, Texas. He was riding in an open-top limousine through Dealey Plaza, waving to cheering crowds, when shots rang out. Kennedy was struck twice and died within half an hour. Texas Governor John Connally, riding in the same car, was seriously wounded but survived. The motorcade raced to the hospital, but doctors could do nothing. At 1:00 p.m., Kennedy was pronounced dead. He was forty-six years old.

Within hours, police arrested Lee Harvey Oswald, a twenty-four-year-old former Marine who had once lived in the Soviet Union and supported pro-Castro causes. Oswald worked at the Texas School Book Depository, the building from which the shots were fired. He denied killing the president, insisting he was a "patsy."

Two days later, as he was being transferred between jails, Oswald was shot and killed by Jack Ruby, a Dallas nightclub owner, in front of television cameras. Millions watched in shock. The accused assassin would never stand trial.

The nation was traumatized. Kennedy was young, charismatic, and symbolized hope and change. His death felt like the theft of the future. Americans watched the funeral on television. The images were seared into the nation's memory.

Vice President Lyndon Johnson took the oath of office aboard Air Force One, still parked in Dallas, with a bloodstained Jackie Kennedy at his side. The transition of power was swift and constitutional, but the shock lingered. Conspiracy theories spread almost immediately. How could one man with a cheap rifle kill the president? Was Oswald part of a larger plot? The Warren Commission was created to investigate and concluded in 1964 that Oswald acted alone. Many Americans never accepted its findings.

Kennedy's death left his civil rights bill unfinished. President Lyndon Johnson, using his mastery of Congress and invoking Kennedy's legacy, made it his top priority. "No memorial oration or eulogy could more eloquently honor President Kennedy's memory than the earliest possible passage of the civil rights bill for which he fought so long," Johnson told Congress.[i]

---

[i] "Address Before a Joint Session of the Congress."
https://www.presidency.ucsb.edu/documents/address-before-joint-session-the-congress-0

The Civil Rights Act of 1964 was passed that July. It outlawed segregation in public accommodations and prohibited employment discrimination based on race, color, religion, sex, or national origin. It also gave the federal government power to enforce desegregation.

Yet most Black Southerners still could not vote. Literacy tests, poll taxes, and intimidation kept them from registering. In 1964, activists launched Freedom Summer in Mississippi, led largely by local Black organizers and joined by Northern volunteers. Three workers—James Chaney, Andrew Goodman, and Michael Schwerner—were murdered by the Ku Klux Klan, including local law enforcement. Their deaths drew national outrage and exposed the violence that upheld White supremacy.

In 1965, King and the SCLC launched a voting rights campaign in Selma, Alabama, where only 2 percent of Black residents were registered to vote. Peaceful protests met brutal repression. On March 7—"Bloody Sunday"—state troopers attacked marchers at the Edmund Pettus Bridge with clubs and tear gas. Television cameras captured the violence, horrifying the nation.

The images from Selma galvanized public support. Under federal protection, thousands marched from Selma to Montgomery. On August 6, 1965, Johnson signed the Voting Rights Act, banning literacy tests and empowering the federal government to oversee elections in areas with histories of discrimination. Black voter registration in the South rose dramatically. The act was the movement's greatest legislative triumph.

A Shifting Movement: From Black Power to New Challenges

By the mid-1960s, the civil rights movement was changing. The focus shifted from the South to the North, from ending legal segregation to confronting economic inequality, and from strict nonviolence to more militant tactics.

Northern cities weren't segregated by law, but they were in practice. Black residents were confined to poor neighborhoods with underfunded schools, scarce jobs, and tense relations with police. Housing and employment discrimination were widespread. Poverty and frustration ran deep.

In August 1965, riots erupted in Watts, a Black neighborhood in Los Angeles, after a confrontation between police and a Black motorist. For six days, Watts burned. Thirty-four people died, more than a thousand were injured, and damage reached $40 million. Similar uprisings followed in Newark, Detroit, and dozens of other cities, revealing that racial injustice was not just a Southern problem.

Many younger activists grew impatient with nonviolence. In 1966, Stokely Carmichael of SNCC popularized the slogan "Black Power." It meant different things to different people—racial pride, self-defense, economic independence, political control. To some, it called for Black communities to govern themselves; to others, it justified armed self-defense.

The Black Panther Party, founded in Oakland in 1966 by Huey Newton and Bobby Seale, embodied this new militancy. The Panthers armed themselves and patrolled Black neighborhoods, monitoring police. They launched free breakfast programs for children and community health clinics. They preached pride and self-determination, but they also clashed violently with police. The FBI targeted them as a threat, and several leaders were killed in raids and confrontations. The movement splintered into factions with different strategies and philosophies.

Martin Luther King Jr. remained committed to nonviolence but broadened his mission. He spoke out against the Vietnam War in 1967, arguing that money spent on war should be used to fight poverty at home. He planned a Poor People's Campaign to unite poor Americans of all races. Critics said he was spreading himself too thin, but King believed racism, poverty, and militarism were inseparable.

On April 4, 1968, while in Memphis supporting striking sanitation workers, King was shot on the balcony of the Lorraine Motel. He died an hour later. He was thirty-nine. James Earl Ray, a White supremacist, was convicted of the murder.

King's death shattered the movement and the nation. Riots broke out in more than one hundred cities. The movement had lost its bridge between factions, the voice that White America had listened to.

The civil rights movement transformed the nation. It ended legal segregation, secured voting rights, and opened doors once closed to Black Americans. Thurgood Marshall became the first Black Supreme Court justice in 1967, and more Black politicians were elected to office than ever before.

But victory was incomplete. Legal equality did not bring economic equality. Black Americans still faced discrimination, poverty, segregated schools, and police brutality. The Second Reconstruction, like the first, remained unfinished. The work of justice continued.

The Rights Revolution Spreads

The civil rights movement inspired other Americans to challenge inequality and discrimination. During the late 1960s and 1970s, marginalized groups adopted the same tactics—marches, sit-ins, legal challenges, and appeals to American ideals of equality and justice.

The women's liberation movement gained momentum. Betty Friedan's *The Feminine Mystique* (1963) challenged the notion that women could find fulfillment only as wives and mothers. Women demanded equal pay, access to education and careers, and control over their own bodies. The National Organization for Women (NOW), founded in 1966, fought for legal equality. Gloria Steinem and other feminists launched *Ms.* magazine in 1972 to challenge sexist portrayals in the media. Women pushed for the Equal Rights Amendment, which Congress passed in 1972 but which ultimately failed to be ratified by enough states.

Gloria Steinem.[a]

Despite that defeat, women made major gains. More entered the workforce, legal barriers fell, and Title IX of the 1972 Education Amendments banned sex discrimination in education, opening doors in sports and academics.

Other movements also emerged. Cesar Chavez and Dolores Huerta organized farmworkers, forming the United Farm Workers union. The American Indian Movement (AIM) fought for Native rights and sovereignty. AIM gained attention with the 1973 occupation of Wounded Knee, protesting broken treaties and government abuses. Gay rights activists resisted police harassment during the 1969 Stonewall riots in New York City, launching the modern LGBTQ movement.

These movements faced fierce opposition and often won only gradual victories. Yet they transformed American society, expanding the nation's understanding of equality and citizenship. The civil rights movement had shown that ordinary people could change the country, and others took that lesson to heart.

Chapter 21: From Crisis to Triumph: America After the 1960s

Watergate and the Crisis of Trust

The social upheavals of the 1960s—civil rights protests, anti-war demonstrations, urban riots, and cultural rebellion—had deeply divided the nation. Richard Nixon won the presidency in 1968 by promising to restore "law and order" and represent the "silent majority" of Americans who were weary of turmoil and rapid change.

Nixon achieved notable successes. In 1972, he opened diplomatic relations with communist China and pursued détente with the Soviet Union, easing Cold War tensions. At home, he created the Environmental Protection Agency and signed landmark environmental legislation. He won reelection that year in a landslide.

However, his presidency ended in disgrace, destroyed by a crime that began small and grew into a constitutional crisis.

On June 17, 1972, five men were arrested breaking into the Democratic National Committee headquarters at the Watergate complex in Washington, DC. They were caught installing wiretaps and photographing documents. At first, it seemed like a minor burglary. The Nixon administration denied involvement, dismissing it as a "third-rate burglary attempt."

Two *Washington Post* reporters, Bob Woodward and Carl Bernstein, kept digging. Guided by a secret source known only as "Deep Throat," they uncovered a web of illegal activity tied to Nixon's reelection campaign. The burglars had received campaign funds, and the White House was implicated.

Nixon tried to cover it up, ordering aides to obstruct the FBI investigation, authorizing hush money payments, and lying to the public. For months, he succeeded.

Then the scandal erupted. In 1973, one burglar confessed. Televised Senate hearings exposed a pattern of corruption, abuse of power, and contempt for the law. Investigators discovered Nixon had secretly recorded Oval Office conversations. When they demanded the tapes, he refused, claiming executive privilege.

The "Saturday Night Massacre" in October 1973 shocked the nation. Nixon ordered Attorney General Elliot Richardson to fire the special prosecutor. Richardson refused and resigned. His deputy also refused and resigned. The third-ranking official finally carried out the order. The blatant obstruction deepened public outrage.

Under mounting pressure, Nixon released edited transcripts of the tapes. They revealed a crude, vindictive president who routinely discussed illegal acts. In July 1974, the Supreme Court unanimously ordered him to release all the tapes. One recording, from June 23, 1972—just days after the break-in—proved Nixon had tried to block the FBI investigation.

Facing certain impeachment and removal, Nixon resigned on August 8, 1974—the first president to do so. Vice President Gerald Ford became president and, a month later, pardoned Nixon, arguing the country needed to move on. The pardon was unpopular but likely spared the nation more division.

Watergate shattered trust in the government. It revealed that the president had betrayed his oath of office. Millions concluded that politicians were corrupt and the system was rigged.

The 1970s brought further crises. In 1973, Arab oil producers imposed an embargo on nations supporting Israel during the Yom Kippur War. Oil prices quadrupled, gas stations ran dry, and Americans waited for hours in long lines. Inflation surged while economic growth stalled—a toxic mix called "stagflation." Factories closed as competition from Japan and Europe grew. The long postwar boom was over.

Jimmy Carter, a former Georgia governor and Washington outsider, won the 1976 election promising honesty and competence after Watergate. Intelligent, moral, but politically inept, Carter struggled to inspire confidence. He told Americans hard truths. The energy crisis was real, and conservation was necessary. In 1979, he warned of a "crisis of confidence." Though accurate, the speech reinforced the perception of national decline.

That same year, Iranian revolutionaries stormed the US Embassy in Tehran, taking fifty-two Americans hostage. They demanded the return of the deposed shah, who was receiving medical care in the US. The hostages remained captive for 444 days. A rescue mission failed disastrously, killing eight servicemen. They were released only on January 20, 1981—the day Ronald Reagan took office.

By 1980, inflation topped 13 percent, gas lines stretched for blocks, and the Soviet Union had invaded Afghanistan. Americans felt humiliated and adrift.

Cars waiting in line for gas, 1979.[55]

They were ready for a change.

The Reagan Revolution

Ronald Reagan, a former actor and California governor, radiated optimism and faith in free markets, limited government, and American greatness. In 1980, he defeated Carter in a landslide.

Reagan's message was simple. Government wasn't the solution; it was the problem. He argued that cutting taxes, reducing regulations, and unleashing private enterprise would revive prosperity. Americans, tired of stagnation and pessimism, embraced his vision.

"Reaganomics" had three pillars: massive tax cuts, deregulation, and higher military spending. The top income tax rate fell from 70 to 28 percent. Reagan deregulated industries, from banking to telecommunications, and poured billions into defense. Critics called it "trickle-down economics," arguing it favored the rich and worsened inequality. Reagan claimed growth would offset tax cuts. Instead, the national debt nearly tripled.

The early years were painful. To crush inflation, Federal Reserve Chairman Paul Volcker raised interest rates to nearly 20 percent, triggering a deep recession. Unemployment hit 10 percent in 1982. But by 1984, inflation had been tamed, jobs returned, and the economy boomed. Reagan won reelection in a landslide.

The 1980s became a decade of wealth and ambition. Wall Street thrived, and "yuppies"— young urban professionals—chased riches. Success was celebrated, even glorified. However, inequality widened. Industrial cities like Detroit and Pittsburgh declined as factories closed or moved overseas. Family farms failed. The savings and loan crisis cost taxpayers over $100 billion.

Reagan also declared a "War on Drugs," emphasizing punishment over treatment. Harsh sentencing laws swelled the prison population, disproportionately affecting Black communities. Meanwhile, the AIDS epidemic devastated the gay community. The administration's slow response fueled outrage and spurred new LGBTQ activism.

Reagan reshaped American politics. He united economic conservatives, Cold War hawks, and religious traditionalists into a powerful coalition that redefined the Republican Party. Evangelical Christians, mobilized by his defense of "family values," became a dominant political force.

Abroad, Reagan escalated the arms race but later worked with Soviet leader Mikhail Gorbachev to reduce nuclear weapons. By the late 1980s, the Cold War was ending. The Berlin Wall fell in 1989, and the Soviet Union collapsed in 1991. Supporters credited Reagan's military buildup with forcing the Soviet surrender, although others cited internal Soviet decay. Either way, the United States stood alone as the world's superpower.

Gorbachev and Reagan signing a treaty.[56]

Reagan left office in 1989 as one of the most popular presidents in modern history. He restored American confidence after years of doubt and shifted politics decisively to the right. Yet his legacy was mixed. The deficit soared, inequality widened, and social problems—from drugs to homelessness—deepened. Deregulation contributed to future financial instability.

Still, by 1990, the economy was strong. The Cold War was over. America felt triumphant.

The "End of History?": America in the 1990s

Political scientist Francis Fukuyama famously argued that the end of the Cold War marked "the end of history"—not literally, but in the sense that liberal democracy had triumphed and the great ideological struggles were finished. The United States stood as the world's sole superpower. The future looked bright.

The 1990s seemed to confirm that optimism. The economy boomed. The internet revolutionized communication and commerce. America was prosperous and at peace. Yet beneath the surface, new problems were forming that would erupt in the next century.

George H. W. Bush was president when the Cold War ended. He managed the transition skillfully, overseeing the peaceful breakup of the Soviet Union and the reunification of Germany. But his biggest challenge came from an unexpected quarter.

In August 1990, Iraq invaded Kuwait. Dictator Saddam Hussein sought Kuwait's oil wealth and access to the Persian Gulf, threatening Saudi Arabia and global energy supplies. Bush assembled an international coalition of thirty-five nations to drive Iraq out. The United Nations authorized force.

Operation Desert Storm began in January 1991. A massive air campaign crippled Iraqi forces, followed by a swift ground assault. The campaign lasted just one hundred hours. Kuwait was liberated, and Iraqi forces were routed. Fewer than three hundred Americans died in combat. Bush chose not to invade Iraq or topple Saddam, believing that would lead to chaos. The war showcased US military dominance—high-tech precision weapons, rapid deployment, and overwhelming firepower.

US aircraft flying over Iraq during the Gulf War.[57]

But Bush couldn't turn military victory into political success. The economy slipped into a recession, and after breaking his "no new taxes" pledge, he lost support. In 1992, Arkansas Governor Bill Clinton defeated him.

Clinton, the first baby boomer president, was young, charismatic, and politically skilled. His presidency coincided with extraordinary economic growth. The economy expanded for eight straight years. Unemployment fell to 4 percent. The stock market soared. The federal budget shifted from deficit to surplus. New technologies, such as personal computers, cell phones, and the internet, transformed business and daily life.

The internet truly revolutionized the economy. Tim Berners-Lee created the World Wide Web in 1989. By the mid-1990s, millions of Americans were going online. Startups like Amazon, eBay, and Google emerged. Investors poured money into anything ending in ".com." The stock market exploded in what became known as the dot-com boom—a speculative frenzy built on faith in a "new economy."

It was a bubble. In 2000, it began to burst. Hundreds of companies failed, and trillions in paper wealth vanished. Yet the internet endured, permanently reshaping communication, commerce, and culture.

Clinton's presidency was marked by both accomplishment and controversy. He failed to reform health care but embraced centrist policies after Republicans won Congress in 1994. Declaring "the era of big government is over," he balanced the budget and signed welfare reform, which critics said harmed the poor.

His personal misconduct nearly destroyed his presidency. In 1998, revelations of an affair with White House intern Monica Lewinsky led to charges of perjury and obstruction of justice. The House impeached him, but the Senate acquitted him. Despite the scandal, Clinton left office with high approval ratings. The economy was booming, and most Americans separated his personal failings from his performance in office.

Foreign policy in the 1990s was mixed. The US intervened in Somalia, where a humanitarian mission turned tragic when eighteen American soldiers were killed in Mogadishu in 1993. The shock led Clinton to pull US forces out and become cautious about future interventions. The US failed to act during the 1994 Rwandan genocide, in which about 800,000 people were killed—something Clinton later called his greatest regret.

In the Balkans, however, America and NATO intervened decisively. Ethnic cleansing in Bosnia and later in Kosovo prompted airstrikes and peacekeeping missions that helped end the wars. Though controversial, the interventions are credited with halting genocide and restoring stability.

Meanwhile, terrorism was emerging as a global threat. In 1993, terrorists bombed the World Trade Center in New York, killing six. In 1998, al-Qaeda, led by Osama bin Laden, bombed US Embassies in Kenya and Tanzania, killing more than two hundred. In 2000, al-Qaeda attacked the USS *Cole* in Yemen, killing seventeen sailors. These attacks were warnings few recognized.

The 2000 presidential election exposed deep divisions. Vice President Al Gore faced Texas Governor George W. Bush, the son of the former president. The race was so close that it came down to Florida, where disputes over ballots and recounts left the outcome uncertain for thirty-six days. In *Bush v. Gore* (2000), the Supreme Court voted five to four to halt the recount, effectively awarding Florida—and the presidency—to Bush. Gore conceded, but many Democrats felt the election had been stolen. The bitterness deepened political polarization.

The 1990s had been years of prosperity and peace, but the optimism of the "end of history" would not last. The new century would bring challenges that shattered the illusion of American invulnerability and tested the nation's confidence once again.

September 11, 2001: The Day That Changed Everything

Tuesday, September 11, 2001, began as an ordinary day. By nightfall, nearly three thousand people were dead, and America had changed forever.

At 8:46 a.m., American Airlines Flight 11 crashed into the North Tower of the World Trade Center in New York City. The Boeing 767 struck near the top of the 110-story building, creating a massive fireball. Many thought it was a tragic accident—until, seventeen minutes later, United Airlines Flight 175 hit the South Tower. America was under attack.

The Twin Towers after the planes struck.⁵⁸

Both towers burned. People trapped above the impact zones faced impossible choices. Some leaped from windows rather than burn. At 9:37 a.m., American Airlines Flight 77 slammed into the Pentagon, killing 184 people. A fourth plane, United Flight 93, was also hijacked. Passengers, learning of the other attacks, decided to fight back. They stormed the cockpit, forcing the plane down in a Pennsylvania field at 10:03 a.m., saving countless others at the cost of their own lives.

At 9:59 a.m., the South Tower collapsed. The North Tower followed at 10:28. Lower Manhattan became a wasteland of smoke and dust. Thousands ran for their lives; others rushed toward danger. Among the dead were 343 firefighters and 72 police officers. Nearly 3,000 people from more than 90 countries were killed—office workers, flight crews, first responders, and ordinary citizens beginning an ordinary morning.

The nation was in shock. Flights were grounded. Stock markets closed. That evening, President George W. Bush addressed the nation: "Today, our fellow citizens, our way of life, our very freedom came under attack."[i]

Investigators soon identified the perpetrators: nineteen men, mostly from Saudi Arabia and members of al-Qaeda, a terrorist network led by Osama bin Laden. A wealthy Saudi who had turned to radical Islamic extremism, bin Laden had already orchestrated the 1998 US Embassy bombings in Africa and the 2000 attack on the USS *Cole*. Now, from his base in Afghanistan under Taliban protection, he had struck the United States itself.

Bush demanded that the Taliban hand over bin Laden. They refused. On October 7, 2001, the United States launched airstrikes in Afghanistan. Working with Afghan allies known as the Northern Alliance, US forces quickly toppled the Taliban, though bin Laden escaped into the mountains. The war to find him and stabilize Afghanistan would last twenty years.

Congress swiftly passed the USA PATRIOT Act, vastly expanding government surveillance powers. Supporters said it was vital to prevent future attacks, while critics warned it endangered civil liberties. In 2002, the Department of Homeland Security was created, merging twenty-two agencies to coordinate domestic protection. Airport security became federalized and far stricter.

For a moment, America was united. Flags flew everywhere. Political divisions faded. Bush's approval rating reached 90 percent. Yet, that unity would soon fracture.

Convinced that Iraqi dictator Saddam Hussein possessed weapons of mass destruction and supported terrorism, the Bush administration turned its attention to Iraq. In his 2002 State of the Union Address, Bush labeled Iraq, Iran, and North Korea an "axis of evil." Many allies and Americans were skeptical. UN inspectors found no active weapons programs. Still, in March 2003, the US and a "coalition of the willing," led by Britain, invaded Iraq.

---

[i] "Darkest Day." https://www.baylor.edu/content/services/document.php/89472.pdf

Baghdad fell within weeks. Bush declared "mission accomplished" aboard an aircraft carrier that May. However, no weapons were found. Iraq descended into insurgency and a religious war. Thousands of Americans died, and Iraqi casualties—both military and civilian—numbered in the hundreds of thousands. The war divided Americans and discredited US intelligence abroad. It drained resources, cost trillions, and destabilized the Middle East.

The Afghanistan war also dragged on, becoming America's longest conflict. Generations of soldiers fought and died with no clear end. The "War on Terror" became a permanent feature of American life.

At home, security and surveillance expanded. Civil liberties seemed to diminish. Muslims and Arab Americans faced discrimination and suspicion. The unity formed around September 11 gave way to polarization. By the end of Bush's presidency, the nation was mired in two wars and reeling from the 2008 financial crisis—the worst since the Great Depression.

The optimism of the 1990s had vanished. September 11 shattered the sense of safety that once seemed unshakable. The attacks killed thousands and launched wars that killed hundreds of thousands more. Even two decades later, the country still lived in their shadow—divided, wary, and forever changed.

Conclusion: The Unfolding Story

From the first migrations across the land bridge thousands of years ago to the terror attacks of September 11, 2001, American history has been a story of conflict and struggle over the meaning of freedom and equality.

The United States was built on revolutionary ideals: liberty, equality, democracy, and opportunity. The Declaration of Independence proclaimed that all men are created equal and have unalienable rights. The Constitution established a democratic government with checks on power.

However, from the beginning, America failed to live up to its ideals. Slavery existed alongside liberty. Native peoples were displaced and destroyed. Women were excluded from political rights and most civic participation. Immigrants faced discrimination. The gap between American ideals and American reality has always been vast.

American history is the story of the struggle to close that gap—abolitionists demanding freedom, suffragists demanding votes, workers demanding fair treatment, civil rights activists demanding equality, and immigrants demanding acceptance. Progress has never been inevitable. Every advance required conflict and sacrifice. Slavery ended only after a civil war. Women won the vote after seven decades of activism. Segregation fell only through years of protest and federal intervention.

The pattern repeats: injustice, resistance, struggle, change, new injustices to fight.

The Unfinished Chapter

In the 21ˢᵗ century, old problems persist in new forms. Economic inequality has reached levels unseen since the Gilded Age. Racial tensions sparked the largest protests in American history after George Floyd's murder in 2020. Americans remain divided over the causes of racial disparities and the best path forward. Some see systemic racism as the primary barrier to equality; others emphasize individual responsibility, cultural factors, or economic class. Debates over policing, criminal justice, and how to teach racial history in schools have become flashpoints.

Climate change poses what many scientists consider an existential threat. America's industrial growth and reliance on fossil fuels have contributed to global warming. Americans disagree about the urgency of the threat, the role human activity plays, and how to balance environmental concerns with economic growth and energy independence. The consequences—fires, floods, storms, and rising seas—are reshaping communities and sparking debates about adaptation and responsibility.

Political polarization has deepened so sharply that Americans consume different news, believe different facts, and question shared democratic norms. Trust in institutions has fallen to historic lows.

Technology has transformed life in unsettling ways. The internet democratized information but spread misinformation. Social media connects people while deepening division. Artificial intelligence promises innovation but threatens jobs and privacy. The speed of change leaves Americans struggling to adapt.

America's role in the world has shifted. China has emerged as a rival superpower. Global challenges like climate change, migration, and pandemics demand cooperation, yet domestic debates about America's proper role abroad—whether to lead, to cooperate, or to prioritize domestic needs—complicate US foreign policy. The wars in Iraq and Afghanistan left Americans questioning the costs and benefits of military intervention.

Yet, American history offers many reasons for hope. The nation has survived crises before—revolution, civil war, depression, world wars, and the Cold War. Each time, Americans argued, adapted, and endured. The Constitution has lasted for more than 230 years. It is flexible enough to allow reinvention while preventing tyranny. Despite its failures, it has enabled reform.

Americans have repeatedly shown the capacity for renewal. They ended slavery, expanded suffrage, confronted segregation, and advanced rights. The belief that change is possible remains America's most radical idea.

The story is not over. Americans will continue to disagree—often bitterly—about what needs to change and how to achieve it. But that argument—angry, hopeful, and likely unending—is what makes America, America.

Part 2: The American Revolution for Beginners

The Story of the Revolutionary War Simplified for People Who Slept Through History Class

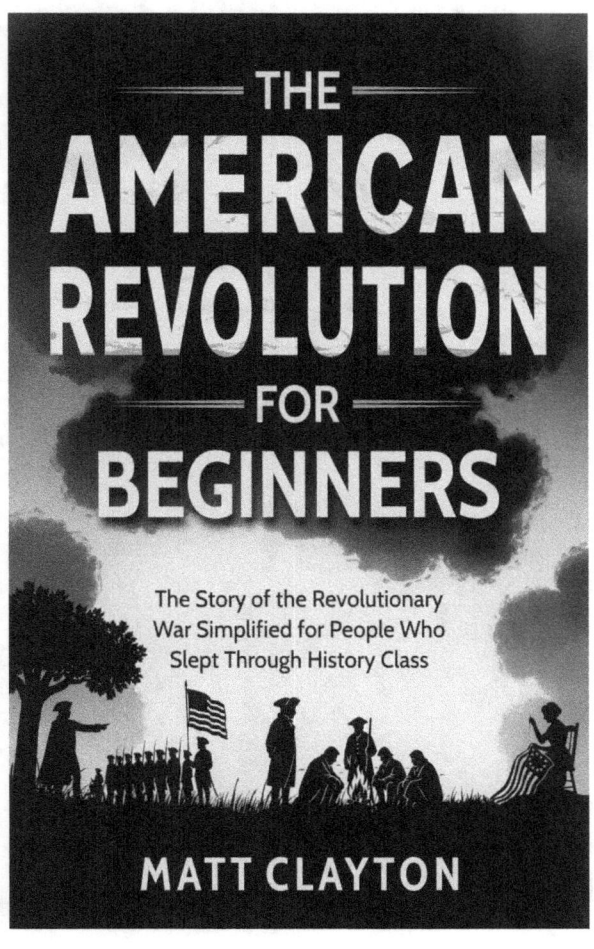

Introduction:
Waking Up to a Revolution

Let me guess. You fell asleep during history class. Or maybe you were there, but your mind was somewhere else entirely. Perhaps you passed the tests by memorizing a few dates and names, then promptly forgot everything the moment you walked out the door. If any of this sounds familiar, I wrote this book for you.

Here's the thing about the American Revolution: it's one of the most important events in human history. Yet for many people, it's just a blur of powdered wigs, old paintings, and half-remembered phrases like "Give me liberty or give me death." It happened a long time ago. The people involved seem distant and formal. And if we're being honest, most history books don't help. They're dense, filled with military jargon, and written like stuffy textbooks.

But here's what they don't tell you in school: the American Revolution is an incredible story. It's a story about impossible odds, about farmers facing down the most powerful military on Earth. It's about a group of colonies that had every reason to fail but somehow didn't. It's about real people making difficult choices, taking enormous risks, and changing the world in the process.

This wasn't inevitable. Britain was a superpower with the world's most powerful navy and a professional army. The colonies had no standing army or navy in the traditional sense, though they did have experienced local militias and a growing network of coordination through groups like the Committees of Correspondence. Still, the odds were heavily against them. Britain had every advantage, and most observers expected the rebellion to fail. The fact that it succeeded is genuinely remarkable.

So why should you care about something that happened over two hundred years ago? Because the ideas that emerged from this revolution still shape your life today. The concept that government exists to serve the people, not the other way around. The idea that citizens have fundamental rights that no authority can take away. The belief that ordinary people should have a say in the laws that govern them. These weren't obvious truths in the 1770s. They were radical and dangerous ideas that people died for.

Whether you're picking up this book because you want to finally understand what you missed in school, because you're curious about American history, or because someone told you that you should know this stuff, welcome. You're about to discover that the story of the American Revolution is far more interesting than you probably thought. It's messy, complicated, and absolutely fascinating.

Let's start at the beginning, before anyone was talking about revolution, back when the American colonies were proud parts of the British Empire. Because to understand why people would risk everything to break away, we first need to understand what they were breaking away from.

Chapter 1: A Tale of Two Worlds: Britain and Her American Colonies

More Than a King's Possession

In 1750, if you had asked free colonists living in British North America who they were, most would not have said "American." They would have called themselves British subjects. A Virginian tobacco planter, a Boston merchant, and a Pennsylvania farmer all considered themselves part of the British Empire. Many were proud of it. Britain was the most powerful nation on Earth, and they belonged to it.

Of course, this identity was not universal. The hundreds of thousands of enslaved Africans and African Americans in the colonies were denied any such status or rights. Indigenous peoples also had their own identities and allegiances.

But here's what made the Thirteen Colonies unusual: they were three thousand miles away from the king who claimed to rule them. In an age when the fastest form of communication was a ship crossing the Atlantic, that distance created space and room to develop their own way of doing things.

By the mid-eighteenth century, roughly 1.5 million people of European and African descent lived in the Thirteen Colonies, which stretched along the eastern seaboard of North America. (This number doesn't include the many Indigenous peoples who still inhabited these lands and the territories beyond.) They were not a unified group. The colonies had distinct identities, different economies, and sometimes conflicting interests.

New England, the northernmost region, consisted of Massachusetts, Connecticut, Rhode Island, and New Hampshire. The climate was cold, the soil was rocky, and large-scale farming was difficult. So, New Englanders turned to other pursuits. They fished the rich waters off their coast. They built ships and traded goods over the Atlantic. Towns were the center of life here, and town meetings gave ordinary property-owning men a direct voice in local government. Puritan religious heritage also shaped the region, creating communities that valued education and literacy. By 1750, New England had the highest literacy rates in the colonies.

The Middle Colonies—New York, New Jersey, Pennsylvania, and Delaware—were the most diverse region. Here, you found English settlers alongside Dutch, Germans, Scots-Irish, and others. Multiple languages filled the streets of Philadelphia and New York City. Religious diversity matched ethnic diversity. You had Quakers in Pennsylvania, Dutch Reformed congregations in New York, Presbyterians, Catholics, Jews, and more. This region produced grain in abundance, earning it the nickname "the breadbasket colonies." Large port cities like Philadelphia and New York became commercial hubs where merchants grew wealthy on trade.

The Southern Colonies—Maryland, Virginia, North Carolina, South Carolina, and Georgia—had a different character. Here, the climate was warmer, the growing season longer, and plantation agriculture dominated the economy. They grew tobacco in Virginia and Maryland and rice and indigo in South Carolina and Georgia. These crops required intensive labor, so Southern planters relied on chattel slavery.

By 1750, enslaved Africans and African Americans made up about 40 percent of the South's population. In South Carolina, they were actually the majority. This created a society with a small planter elite at the top, a middle group of small farmers, and a large enslaved population with no rights at all at the bottom. Slavery existed in every colony. Northern colonies used enslaved labor in households, on farms, and in port cities, though in smaller numbers.

Despite these differences, the colonies shared some common features. Most colonists made their living from the land. Even in commercial New England, the majority of people were farmers. Society was more fluid than in Europe. There were still wealthy elites and poor laborers, but the middle class was broader. A man with ambition and a bit of luck could acquire land and improve his status. This was harder to do in Europe, where centuries-old social hierarchies were more rigid.

Life in the colonies was physically demanding. Most people lived on farms or in small villages. Families produced much of what they needed. They grew food, made clothes, and built furniture. Women ran households, managed farms when men were away, and often produced goods to sell or trade. When families needed something they couldn't make, they traded with neighbors or traveled to the nearest town. Roads were often just dirt paths that turned to mud in the rain. A journey of fifty miles could take days.

Colonial cities, though small by European standards, were growing and prosperous. Boston, the largest city in New England, had about fifteen thousand people by 1750. Philadelphia, founded much later, was growing rapidly and would soon surpass Boston. New York, Charles Town (later Charleston), and Newport were other important urban centers. These cities connected the colonies to the wider Atlantic world through trade.

The colonial economy was tied to Britain, but it was not entirely dependent on it. Colonists traded extensively with each other and with other parts of the world. New England merchants shipped fish and lumber to the Caribbean, where they traded for sugar and molasses. They turned the molasses into rum, which they sold throughout the colonies and even back across the Atlantic. This is often called the triangular trade, though in reality, Atlantic commerce was more complex, with ships following many different routes and trading patterns. This trade operated partly outside British regulations, and British officials largely ignored it.

Colonial politics followed a similar pattern. Each colony had a governor, usually appointed by the king or the colony's proprietor (the person who had been granted ownership of the colony). Each also had an elected assembly, where colonists who met property requirements could vote for representatives. These assemblies controlled taxation and spending. Over time, they gained considerable power. They weren't democracies by modern standards—women and enslaved people couldn't vote, and even among free men, one usually needed to own property to participate. However, most people in the world in 1750 had no say in how they were governed. The colonists had far more control over their own affairs.

The property requirements for voting varied by colony, but typically, a man needed to own a certain amount of land or have assets worth a certain value. This excluded many people, but land was more available in America than in Europe. A larger percentage of men met the voting requirements than they would have in Britain. In some colonies, perhaps 50 to 60 percent of White adult males could vote. Tenant farmers, landless laborers, indentured servants, and sailors were excluded, along with all women and all people of color, whether free or enslaved.

Colonial political life was often combative. Elections could be rowdy affairs. Candidates provided food and alcohol to potential voters. Arguments broke out. However, colonists took politics seriously because it mattered to their daily lives. The assembly decided how much to spend on roads, whether to issue paper money, how to deal with Native American relations, and countless other practical matters.

The distance from Britain meant these assemblies operated with considerable independence. If a governor tried to enforce an unpopular policy, the assembly could refuse to pay his salary until he backed down. This tactic worked because months would pass before London even heard about the dispute, and more months would pass before instructions arrived. By then, the situation had often resolved itself.

The key point is that by 1750, the colonists had grown used to running their own affairs. They paid taxes to their colonial governments, which they elected. They obeyed local laws, which their own assemblies passed. Britain existed as a distant but generally benevolent presence. The colonists traded with British merchants, fought alongside British soldiers when needed, and were proud to be part of the empire. Britain didn't interfere much in their daily lives. This was about to change.

The Mother Country

To understand why Britain eventually tried to tighten its grip on the colonies, you need to understand Britain itself in the mid-eighteenth century. This was a nation at the height of its power, confident in its place as a dominant force in European and world affairs.

In 1750, Britain had a population of about 7 million in England and Wales, with another 1.2 million in Scotland. London was one of the largest cities in Europe, a bustling center of commerce, politics, and culture. The British economy was growing, driven by trade, manufacturing, and the early stirrings of what would become the Industrial Revolution.

Britain was a constitutional monarchy. Unlike absolute monarchies in France or Spain, where the king's word was law, British kings ruled within limits set by Parliament. This arrangement came from the Glorious Revolution of 1688, when Parliament had essentially hired a new king after removing the old one. The message was clear: the monarch served at Parliament's pleasure, not the other way around.

Parliament consisted of two houses. The House of Lords was filled with hereditary nobles and bishops. The House of Commons was "elected," though "elected" is misleading by modern standards. Only property-owning men could vote, and many seats were controlled by wealthy patrons. Towns with tiny populations had representatives, while growing industrial cities sometimes had none. This system was riddled with corruption and inequality, but it was still more representative than most governments of the time.

Real power in Britain rested with Parliament, particularly the House of Commons, which controlled taxation and spending. The monarch still held significant authority but needed Parliament's cooperation to govern effectively and to fund policies.

The king in 1750 was George II, the second monarch from the German House of Hanover. The Hanoverians had taken the British throne in 1714 when the previous royal line died out without an heir. George II, like his father before him, spoke German as his first language and spent considerable time in Hanover. This made him less connected to his British subjects and more dependent on his ministers to manage British politics. Real governing power increasingly rested with the prime minister and Cabinet, who needed the support of Parliament to remain in office.

British society had a rigid class structure. At the top sat the aristocracy—dukes, earls, and other titled nobles who owned vast estates and wielded enormous political and economic power. Below them came the gentry, wealthy landowners without titles. Then came the middle class—merchants, lawyers, doctors, and prosperous farmers. At the bottom were laborers, servants, and the poor. Moving between these ranks was difficult. Birth determined most people's station in life.

Now here's where the colonies fit into British thinking. Britain subscribed to an economic theory called mercantilism. The core idea was simple: a nation's power came from accumulating wealth, particularly gold and silver. To get wealthy, you needed to export more than you imported.

Colonies played a crucial role in this system. They existed to benefit the mother country. The colonies provided raw materials that Britain couldn't produce itself—tobacco, rice, indigo, timber, and furs. They also served as markets for British-manufactured goods. The colonists would buy British textiles, tools, and other products. This arrangement, in theory, made Britain wealthier and more powerful.

Parliament passed laws to enforce this system. The Navigation Acts, first enacted in the 1650s and expanded over the decades, required that certain colonial goods could be shipped only to Britain or British possessions. Colonial trade had to be carried on British or colonial ships. Britain also tried to limit some colonial manufacturing that competed with British industries, though many colonial enterprises like shipbuilding and rum production thrived.

These laws had real consequences when enforced. Virginia tobacco planters, for instance, could sell their crop only to British merchants, who then resold it to European buyers at a markup. The planters couldn't deal directly with French or Dutch buyers, even if they offered better prices.

The Iron Act of 1750 banned new finishing mills for making tools and other finished iron products, though it encouraged the production of raw iron for export to Britain. Britain wanted to channel colonial industry, not eliminate it entirely, but the goal was clear: colonies should provide raw materials and buy finished goods.

The theory was that everyone benefited. The colonies got protection from the British military and guaranteed markets for their raw materials. Britain got the raw materials it needed and customers for its manufactured goods. In practice, it meant wealth flowed toward Britain, and the colonies remained economically subordinate.

Salutary Neglect: The Unspoken Agreement

Here's the important part, though. For most of the colonial period, Britain didn't enforce these laws very strictly. Yes, the laws existed on paper, but British officials in the colonies were often corrupt, easily bribed, or simply looked the other way. Colonial merchants routinely traded with French and Spanish colonies in the Caribbean. This was technically illegal, but it was incredibly profitable. Britain knew this was happening but largely ignored it.

This informal arrangement came to be called "salutary neglect." The term was coined by British politician Edmund Burke in 1775, but he was describing something that had been reality for generations. Britain made laws governing the colonies, but it didn't vigorously enforce them. The Navigation Acts existed, but colonial merchants found ways around them. Customs officials were supposed to collect duties on imports, but they were frequently bribed or simply ineffective. Colonial assemblies passed local laws and governed local affairs with minimal interference from London.

Why did this happen? Several reasons. First, Britain was busy fighting wars in Europe. Wars against France over succession and trade routes consumed Britain's attention and resources. The colonies seemed quiet and generally loyal. They required little military presence. They contributed to Britain's economy through trade. Why rock the boat?

Second, enforcing laws across the Atlantic was expensive and difficult. A letter from London to Boston took six to eight weeks in good weather, longer in winter. Instructions might arrive months after they were relevant. British officials couldn't simply call London with questions. By the time a question was asked and answered, the situation had often changed. Tight control was nearly impossible.

Third, British officials in the colonies were often appointed as rewards for political loyalty back home, not for competence or dedication. Many saw their positions as opportunities for personal enrichment. They collected their salaries, took bribes, and caused minimal trouble. The system was corrupt, but from the colonial perspective, corruption had an upside: corrupt officials left you alone.

Fourth, British merchants trading with the colonies actually benefited from lax enforcement. They made money from colonial trade while colonial merchants evaded regulations that would have hurt commerce. It was an arrangement that worked for the people actually involved, even if it violated the letter of the law.

During this period of minimal oversight, colonial assemblies gradually accumulated real power. They gained control over tax collection and spending. They determined how much to pay the governor and other officials. They passed laws regulating everything from land sales to tavern licenses. When governors tried to assert royal authority, assemblies pushed back, and the assemblies often won because they held the purse strings.

Governors found themselves in an awkward position. They were appointed by the Crown to represent royal authority, but they depended on the colonial assemblies for their salaries and the money to run the government. If a governor pushed unpopular policies, the assembly could simply refuse to pay him or fund his initiatives. Many governors learned to compromise and avoid confrontation. They kept London happy with optimistic reports while giving the assemblies much of what they wanted. It was easier than fighting.

Some colonies had more power than others. Rhode Island and Connecticut elected their own governors, making them nearly independent. Pennsylvania and Maryland were owned by private families who appointed governors, but these governors still depended on assemblies for funding. Even the royal colonies, where the Crown appointed governors directly, saw their assemblies gain increasing authority.

Think of it like this. Imagine you rent an apartment. The lease says your landlord can enter at any time for inspections. But your landlord is busy and never actually shows up. For years, you live as if the apartment is entirely yours. You paint the walls, rearrange everything, and forget that, legally, the landlord has rights you're ignoring. Then one day, the landlord decides to start enforcing the lease. You're shocked and angry. The landlord is confused and angry. You've both been operating under different assumptions.

That's essentially what happened between Britain and the American colonies. The colonists grew accustomed to a high degree of autonomy. They began to see self-government as normal, even as their right. Meanwhile, British officials back in London believed, legally and theoretically, that Parliament held supreme authority over the colonies. Parliament could make any law it wanted regarding the colonies. The colonists were subjects, not partners.

The colonists still identified as British. They took pride in British military victories. They consumed British culture and goods. They saw themselves as participants in the British Empire, sharing in its glory. When Britain called for colonial militia to help in wars against France or Spanish colonies, the colonists usually contributed. They fought alongside British regulars (British soldiers) in conflicts like King William's War, Queen Anne's War, and King George's War.

The colonists saw their military contributions as proof of their loyalty and value to the empire. Colonial militias fought to defend their homes and to help Britain defeat its enemies. They took casualties and spent money on military endeavors. They saw themselves as full partners in the imperial project.

However, there was a disconnect. When colonists thought about their relationship with Britain, they focused on their contributions and loyalty. When British officials thought about the colonies, they saw subordinate territories that existed to serve British interests. Both sides thought they understood the relationship, but they were thinking about it in fundamentally different ways.

The colonies also developed their own political culture during this time. They valued property rights, representative government, and resistance to arbitrary authority. These values came partly from their English heritage; English political thought emphasized rights going back to the Magna Carta. However, the colonial experience shaped these values in distinctive ways. Colonists saw themselves as defending traditional English liberties, but they interpreted those liberties more broadly than officials in London did.

By 1750, the Thirteen Colonies had been operating under this system for generations. The oldest colonies—Virginia and Massachusetts—had been around since the early 1600s. That was 150 years of developing their own institutions and their own ways of doing things. Several generations of colonists had been born who had never even seen England. America was their home, not just a temporary settlement.

The seeds of future conflict were being planted, but in 1750, no one saw revolution on the horizon. The system seemed stable. Both sides benefited from the relationship. The colonies prospered. Britain gained wealth and power from colonial trade and resources.

Then came a war that would shatter this comfortable arrangement and set in motion events no one could have predicted. The French and Indian War would force Britain to pay attention to America in new and unprecedented ways. And once Britain started paying attention, the long period of salutary neglect would end. The consequences would transform the colonies, transform Britain, and ultimately change the world.

Chapter 2: The War That Changed Everything: The French and Indian War

A Clash of Empires in the New World

In 1754, a young Virginia militia officer led a small group of men through the forests of the Ohio Valley. His name was George Washington. He was twenty-two years old, ambitious, and eager to prove himself. His mission was to deliver a message to French forces who had built forts in territory that Virginia claimed. The message was simple: leave.

The French refused.

What followed was a series of skirmishes that would spiral into a massive war stretching across multiple continents. The British called it the Seven Years' War. In America, it became known as the French and Indian War. Whatever you call it, this conflict changed everything. It redrew the map of North America and left Britain with a staggering debt. It also set in motion the events that would lead, within two decades, to the American Revolution.

To understand why this war mattered so much, you need to understand what Britain and France were fighting over. Both nations had claims in North America. Britain controlled the Thirteen Colonies along the Atlantic coast. France controlled Canada to the north and had claimed the vast interior of the continent—the Mississippi River Valley and the lands beyond. Between these empires lay the Ohio Valley, a region of forests and rivers that both sides wanted.

The Thirteen Colonies in 1775.[39]

The Ohio Valley was valuable. The land was fertile. The rivers provided transportation routes. Most importantly, it was rich with fur-bearing animals, and the fur trade was enormously profitable. Both

British colonists and French traders wanted access to this territory and to the Native American tribes who lived there and controlled the fur trade.

The Indigenous peoples of the region—the Shawnee, the Delaware, the Miami, and others—were not passive bystanders in this conflict. They had their own interests and their own power. European success in North America depended on alliances with Native nations. The French had cultivated these relationships carefully. French traders lived among Native communities, learned their languages, and married into their families. The French presence was smaller and less threatening to Native ways of life than British colonial expansion, which brought farmers who cleared forests and displaced Indigenous peoples from their lands.

Britain's American colonists, particularly those in Virginia and Pennsylvania, saw the Ohio Valley as the future. Land speculators had already formed companies to claim and sell territory there. Farmers wanted new land for their families. To them, the French presence was an obstacle to colonial expansion.

In 1753, Virginia's governor sent young George Washington to tell the French to withdraw from the Ohio Valley. Washington delivered the message, and the French commander politely declined. Washington returned to Virginia and reported their refusal. Virginia decided to send soldiers to force the issue.

In the spring of 1754, Washington led a small force back to the Ohio Valley. His instructions were to build a fort at the strategic junction where the Allegheny and Monongahela Rivers meet to form the Ohio River. But when he arrived, he found that the French had already built Fort Duquesne on that exact spot. With his modest force, Washington couldn't challenge a fortified position. He retreated and built a small, hastily constructed fort called Fort Necessity.

On May 28, 1754, Washington's men encountered a small French party. What happened next is disputed. Washington claimed the French fired first. French accounts say Washington's men ambushed them. Either way, there was a brief fight. Ten French soldiers died, including the commanding officer. This skirmish in the Pennsylvania wilderness was the first shot of what would become a global war.

The French response was swift. A larger French and Native American force surrounded Fort Necessity. Washington's position was weak. His fort sat in a low meadow that flooded when it rained, and his men were outnumbered. On July 4, 1754, after a day of fighting in pouring rain,

Washington surrendered. The French allowed him and his men to march away, and Washington returned to Virginia. His first military command had ended in defeat.

However, the war was just beginning. The skirmishes in the Ohio Valley convinced British officials that they needed to confront French expansion in North America. In 1755, Britain sent General Edward Braddock with two regiments of regular army soldiers to capture Fort Duquesne. Washington joined as a volunteer aide, eager for another chance at military glory.

Braddock's expedition was a disaster. He marched his men through the wilderness using European tactics designed for European battlefields. His force was large and well equipped but slow. On July 9, 1755, as Braddock's column approached Fort Duquesne, French and Native American forces ambushed them. Fighting from behind trees in the forest, they devastated the British ranks. Braddock was mortally wounded. Nearly two-thirds of his officers were killed or wounded. The survivors, including Washington, who had two horses shot out from under him, retreated in disorder.

The defeat shocked the British and terrified the colonists. The frontier was now exposed to French and Native American raids. Settlements in Pennsylvania, Maryland, and Virginia came under attack. Families fled eastward.

For the next two years, the war went badly for Britain. The French and their Native allies won victories in the northern colonies, capturing British forts. In 1756, the conflict officially expanded to Europe, where Britain and France fought alongside their respective allies. This was now a world war, with fighting in Europe, North America, the Caribbean, Africa, and India.

In 1757, Britain's fortunes changed. William Pitt became the effective leader of the British government. Pitt was a brilliant strategist who understood that Britain's strength was its navy. He decided to pour resources into the North American campaign while using the navy to cut off French reinforcements. He sent more troops, more ships, and more money to America. He also called on the colonies to raise their own troops, promising that Britain would reimburse them for the costs.

The colonies responded. Thousands of colonial men joined militia units and fought alongside British regulars. George Washington commanded a Virginia regiment defending the frontier. Other colonies contributed men, money, and supplies. This was a joint effort, and the colonists saw themselves as full partners in the British cause.

The tide of war turned. In 1758, British and colonial forces captured Fort Duquesne. They rebuilt it and renamed it Fort Pitt (it later became the city of Pittsburgh). In 1759, British forces achieved an even more stunning victory. They captured Quebec, the capital of French Canada, in a battle that saw both the British and French commanders killed. The following year, Montreal fell. French power in North America had been broken.

The war extended far beyond North America. British forces captured French sugar islands in the Caribbean. They seized French trading posts in Africa and India. The Royal Navy dominated the seas, strangling French maritime trade. Britain's allies in Europe kept French armies occupied on the continent. By 1762, France was exhausted and ready for peace. Spain, which had foolishly entered the war late on France's side, quickly discovered that Britain could strike Spanish possessions as well. The British captured Havana in Cuba and Manila in the Philippines.

The war officially ended with the Treaty of Paris in 1763. The terms were devastating for France. Britain gained all of French Canada and all French territory east of the Mississippi River. Spain ceded Florida to Britain. France was left with almost nothing in North America. On paper, Britain had won a complete victory.

The colonists celebrated. They had fought alongside British soldiers and contributed to this great triumph. The French threat was gone. The Ohio Valley and the lands beyond were open for settlement. The future looked bright.

Colonial contributions to the war had been substantial. Massachusetts alone raised over seven thousand troops at the war's height. Overall, tens of thousands of colonists served in militia units during the conflict. They garrisoned forts, scouted wilderness routes, supplied British armies, and fought in major battles. The human cost was real—thousands of colonial soldiers died from combat, disease, and the hardships of wilderness campaigns.

The colonial assemblies had also borrowed heavily to fund their war efforts. They issued paper money and ran up debts to pay and supply their troops. William Pitt had promised that Parliament would reimburse the colonies for their military expenses, and after the war, Britain did pay back a significant portion of these costs. However, the reimbursements were often delayed and didn't cover everything. Many colonies emerged from the war carrying substantial debts of their own.

But this victory came with more costs that no one fully understood yet.

A Costly Victory

Britain had won the war, but the victory left the empire in a difficult position. The war had been staggeringly expensive. Britain's national debt nearly doubled during the conflict, rising from roughly 75 million pounds to about 133 million pounds—an astronomical sum for the time. The annual interest payments alone consumed much of the government's revenue.

The British people were already heavily taxed. They paid taxes on land, windows, candles, paper, and dozens of other everyday items. Parliament couldn't raise taxes further without risking unrest at home. British subjects in England felt they had borne the burden of defending the empire, including the American colonies. Many believed it was only fair that the colonists should help pay for the war they had benefited from.

The tax burden in Britain was genuinely heavy. An average British citizen paid roughly twenty-six shillings per year in taxes. By comparison, colonists in Massachusetts, one of the more heavily taxed colonies, paid about one shilling per year to their colonial government. British taxpayers knew this disparity existed, and many resented it. Why shouldn't the colonists contribute more?

Britain also planned to keep about ten thousand troops stationed in North America after the war. These soldiers would defend the new territories, maintain peace with Native nations, and enforce British authority. The annual cost of maintaining this force would be roughly 300,000 pounds. British officials thought it reasonable that the colonies should help pay for their own defense.

From the British perspective, this seemed sensible. The war had been fought partly to protect the colonies. British soldiers had died defending colonial frontiers. Britain had spent enormous sums of money. Now that the war was over, Britain faced the ongoing cost of defending its vastly expanded North American territories. Thousands of British troops would need to remain in America to secure the new borders and maintain order. Someone had to pay for this.

The colonists saw things very differently. They had contributed to the war effort. They had raised militia forces and supplied food and materiel. They had taken casualties. Colonial assemblies had voted for funds for the war, going into debt themselves. They felt they had done their part. From their perspective, they had helped Britain expand its empire, and they expected to enjoy the fruits of victory without additional burdens.

There was another cost to consider, one that would prove even more problematic than money. The relationship between British regular soldiers and colonial militia had not always been smooth. British officers often looked down on colonial troops as undisciplined and unreliable. Colonial officers resented being outranked by British officers regardless of experience or ability. George Washington, who had proven himself a capable leader, was irritated that any British regular officer, no matter how junior, technically outranked him as a colonial.

These tensions didn't seem crucial in 1763. The war was over, and both sides had won. However, these different perceptions—about who had contributed what to the victory, about who deserved credit, about who should pay the costs going forward—would fester and grow.

The war had also changed how the colonists saw themselves. Thousands of colonists from different colonies had fought together. A Massachusetts man and a Virginia man who might never have met otherwise had shared campfires and battles. They discovered they had more in common than they might have thought. The experience created a sense of a broader American identity beyond individual colonies.

This emerging identity wasn't strong or clear yet. Men still identified primarily with their home colonies. A Virginian felt more loyalty to Virginia than to some abstract idea of America. But the war had created connections that hadn't existed before. Officers from different colonies had worked together. Soldiers had discovered that colonists from other regions weren't so foreign after all. They spoke the same language, mostly shared the same Protestant religion, and faced the same challenges. These thin threads of connection would strengthen over time.

At the same time, colonists had seen British military power up close. They had fought alongside British regulars and watched how the British army operated. They had seen its strengths—discipline, training, and professional leadership. They had also seen its weaknesses—rigid tactics, arrogant officers, and the difficulties of supplying and moving large forces in the American wilderness. The British military no longer seemed quite so invincible.

Britain, meanwhile, had drawn its own conclusions. British officials had been frustrated by what they saw as colonial foot-dragging during the war. Colonial assemblies had argued about how many men to raise and how much money to spend. Some colonies had contributed more than others. To British eyes, this looked like selfishness and a lack of commitment to the empire. The colonies, British officials concluded, needed to be governed more firmly. The era of lax supervision needed to end.

The Proclamation of 1763: Don't Cross the Mountains

In October 1763, just months after the Treaty of Paris officially ended the war, the British government issued a royal proclamation that stunned the American colonists. The Proclamation of 1763 established a boundary line following the crest of the Appalachian Mountains—essentially the sources of rivers flowing into the Atlantic. Colonists were forbidden from settling west of that line without royal permission. Land grants in that territory were suspended. Traders needed special licenses to operate there. In effect, Britain had placed western settlement under direct royal control.

This made no sense to the colonists. They had just fought a war to secure these territories. Young men had died to push the French out of the Ohio Valley. Land companies already had claims there, and families had plans to move there. Now Britain was telling them they couldn't go.

From the British perspective, the proclamation was a practical measure to prevent conflict with Native Americans. The war with France was over, but Britain now faced the challenge of managing relationships with the Indigenous peoples who lived in the newly acquired territories. These nations had not been defeated. They remained powerful military forces. Many had been allied with France and were suspicious of British intentions.

In the spring and summer of 1763, even before the Treaty of Paris was signed, a massive Native American uprising had broken out. Warriors from the Ottawa, Ojibwa, Potawatomi, Seneca, Delaware, Shawnee, and other nations rose up against British control. An Ottawa leader named Pontiac led the siege of Fort Detroit and became the most prominent figure in the conflict. The Native Americans attacked British forts and settlements across the frontier. Hundreds of colonists were killed—possibly more than a thousand—though exact numbers are uncertain given the scattered nature of frontier settlements. The violence shocked British officials, who realized they couldn't simply take over the western territories without consequences.

Pontiac's War, as it became known, demonstrated the military power of Native American confederacies. Warriors laid siege to Fort Detroit for months. They captured Fort Sandusky, Fort St. Joseph, Fort Miami, Fort Ouiatenon, Fort Venango, Fort Le Boeuf, and Fort Presque Isle. Only a few major posts, like Fort Pitt and Fort Niagara, held out. British forces struggled to respond. The wilderness warfare that Native fighters excelled at negated many advantages of British military training and equipment.

The uprising finally subsided in 1764, not because Britain defeated the Native forces, but through a combination of negotiation, exhaustion, and the realization by Native leaders that the French were not coming back to help them. Pontiac eventually made peace, but the conflict had shown British officials that they needed to manage Native relations carefully. They couldn't afford another widespread frontier war.

The proclamation was designed to calm this crisis. By forbidding colonial settlement west of the mountains, Britain hoped to reassure Native nations that their lands would be protected. The Crown would negotiate with tribal leaders directly for any land transfers, which would prevent the chaotic, fraudulent, and often violent way that colonists had been acquiring Native lands.

There was another reason for the proclamation. Westward expansion was expensive to manage. Scattered settlements needed military protection. Britain would have to build forts and station troops across a vast territory. It was far easier and cheaper to keep the colonists concentrated along the coast, where they could be protected and governed with fewer resources.

The colonists didn't care about British reasoning. They saw the proclamation as a betrayal. The Ohio Valley represented opportunity. The proclamation denied them opportunities. It felt like Britain was placing the interests of Native peoples above those of its own colonists.

Land speculators were particularly angry. Wealthy colonists, including George Washington, had invested in companies planning to acquire and sell western land. The proclamation threatened to make these investments worthless. If they couldn't sell land in the west, they would lose money.

These land companies represented significant capital and powerful colonial elites. The Ohio Company, for instance, had been formed before the war, with investors including members of the Washington and Lee families of Virginia. They had been granted rights to 200,000 acres in the Ohio Valley. Similar companies existed in other colonies. These men had political influence and were accustomed to getting what they wanted. The proclamation directly threatened their economic interests, and they would spend the next decade trying to get around it or overturn it.

In practice, the proclamation was difficult to enforce. The Appalachian Mountains were long and wild. Britain didn't have enough soldiers to patrol the entire frontier. Colonists ignored the line and moved west anyway. Settlers continued to cross the mountains, take land, and dare British officials to stop them. By the late 1760s, large numbers of colonists had settled in violation of the proclamation, particularly in the backcountry of Pennsylvania and Virginia.

But even though the proclamation failed as a practical measure, it succeeded in making colonists resentful and suspicious. It was one of the first signs that the postwar relationship between Britain and the colonies would be very different from what had come before.

The war that was supposed to secure British dominance in North America had instead created new problems. Britain had debts to pay and territories to defend. The colonists had expectations that Britain seemed determined to deny. Both sides were looking at the same victory and drawing opposite conclusions about what should come next.

Chapter 3: "No Taxation Without Representation!": The Acts of Anger

Paying the Piper: The Sugar and Stamp Acts

In 1764, Parliament faced an enormous problem. The national debt stood at roughly 133 million pounds. Annual interest payments consumed over half the government's revenue. Britain needed money, and Parliament decided the American colonies should help pay for their own defense and administration.

George Grenville, the prime minister, believed he had found a solution that would raise revenue without imposing too heavy a burden on the colonies. He would enforce existing trade duties that had been ignored for decades, and he would introduce new taxes that British subjects at home already paid. The colonists would finally contribute their fair share to the empire that protected them.

Parliament's first move came in April 1764 with the American Revenue Act, commonly called the Sugar Act. This law actually reduced the tax on molasses imported into the colonies, cutting it from six pence per gallon to three pence. That sounds like good news, right? A tax cut?

Not quite. The old six-pence tax had rarely been collected. Colonial merchants routinely smuggled molasses or bribed customs officials. The tax existed on paper but not in practice. The new three-pence tax, however, would be rigorously enforced. The law expanded the jurisdiction of vice admiralty courts, where cases would be tried without juries. It gave customs officials new powers to search ships and warehouses. Ships could be seized for violations. The burden of proof shifted to the accused—you had to prove you hadn't smuggled goods rather than the government proving you had.

The Sugar Act also added duties on other imports, including wine, coffee, certain textiles, and indigo. It prohibited the importation of foreign rum entirely. It also included provisions to crack down on smuggling, requiring detailed documentation for all shipments and imposing harsh penalties for violations.

For New England merchants who depended on the molasses trade to make rum, this was a crisis. The three-pence tax, even though lower than the old rate, would be expensive if actually collected. More importantly, the aggressive enforcement threatened their entire business model, which had operated outside British regulations for generations.

New England merchants imported molasses from the French Caribbean islands because it was cheaper than from the British islands. They distilled the molasses into rum. They then sold the rum throughout the colonies, to Africa in the slave trade, and even back to Europe. This was a hugely profitable business. The Sugar Act's enforcement would either make this trade unprofitable or force merchants to comply with regulations they had ignored for decades.

Colonial assemblies protested. They sent petitions to Parliament arguing that the Sugar Act would harm colonial trade and hurt the colonial economy. They also began to question Parliament's authority to tax the colonies at all. The Massachusetts assembly argued that colonists, as British subjects, had the right to be taxed only by their own elected representatives. Parliament, where colonists had no representatives, shouldn't be able to tax them.

This constitutional argument didn't get much attention in 1764. The Sugar Act was primarily seen as a trade regulation, and Parliament clearly had authority to regulate imperial trade. However, the seeds of a larger disagreement were being planted.

Then came the Stamp Act—and everything exploded.

In March 1765, Parliament passed the Stamp Act. This law provoked a firestorm that shocked everyone involved. The Stamp Act was different from the Sugar Act. It required that many printed materials in the colonies carry an embossed revenue stamp purchased from official distributors. Newspapers needed stamps. So did pamphlets, legal documents, licenses, college diplomas, almanacs, dice, and playing cards. Even advertisements required stamps. Any document used in legal or commercial transactions needed to be on stamped paper or carry a stamp. The stamps cost money, from a halfpenny for a newspaper to ten pounds for certain legal documents.

The cost wasn't enormous for most items. Most legal documents required stamps costing a few shillings. The total revenue Parliament expected to raise was about sixty thousand pounds per year—a small sum compared to Britain's massive debts but enough to offset some of the costs of keeping troops in America.

From Parliament's perspective, this was a reasonable and moderate tax. Britain had used stamp taxes since 1694. British subjects paid stamp duties on all sorts of documents. The tax was easy to collect, and it applied broadly across society, so everyone contributed. It seemed like an efficient, fair way to raise revenue.

Parliament debated the Stamp Act but passed it easily. Few members of Parliament anticipated serious resistance. Some colonial agents in London, including Benjamin Franklin, warned that the colonists might object, but these warnings were largely ignored. Parliament believed it had the right to tax the colonies, and most members saw no reason the colonists would think otherwise.

They were catastrophically wrong.

The colonists reacted with fury that caught British officials completely off guard. The anger wasn't really about the money. Most colonists could afford the stamp taxes. It was about the principle behind the tax and what it represented.

Parliament was imposing a direct tax on the colonies. This was not a trade regulation like the Sugar Act, nor was it an external duty on imports coming into colonial ports. This was an internal tax. Parliament was reaching into colonial society to tax colonists for activities within their own communities. They were now being taxed for buying newspapers, filing legal documents, getting married, or playing cards. And Parliament had done this without asking the colonial assemblies or seeking colonial consent.

This violated what many colonists believed was a fundamental right of British subjects. They had grown up hearing that British liberty meant you couldn't be taxed without your consent. This principle was central to

British constitutional history. The English Civil War in the 1640s had been fought partly over this issue. The Glorious Revolution of 1688 had affirmed it. Parliament could tax British subjects only because British subjects elected members of Parliament.

However, colonists didn't elect members of Parliament. They had no representatives there. How, then, could Parliament tax them? By what right could a body where they had no representation reach across the ocean and demand money from them?

Some British officials argued that the colonists had "virtual representation" in Parliament. Members of Parliament, they claimed, represented all British subjects everywhere, not just the people in their particular districts. Many British towns and cities sent no members to Parliament, yet they were considered virtually represented. Why should the colonies be different?

The colonists rejected this argument. Virtual representation was a fiction, they said. Real representation required actual elected representatives who answered to voters and could be removed by them. Members of Parliament didn't know what was going on in the colonies, didn't answer to colonial voters, and couldn't be removed by colonists. That wasn't representation—it was taxation by a foreign legislature.

"No taxation without representation" became a rallying cry. The phrase captured an argument that went straight to the heart of the imperial relationship. If Parliament could tax the colonies without their consent, what else could Parliament do? Could Parliament seize colonial property? Quarter soldiers in colonial homes? Shut down colonial assemblies? What limits existed on British power over America?

The colonists began to fear that they were becoming subjects without rights, governed by a distant legislature where they had no voice. They saw themselves sliding toward the status of conquered peoples, ruled by force rather than by consent. Everything their ancestors had fought for in England's constitutional struggles was being denied to them in America.

The reaction wasn't uniform across the colonies. Some people thought the Stamp Act, while unwelcome, was legal and should be obeyed. Many wealthy colonists worried that resistance might lead to chaos and mob rule. Some argued that protesting would only make things worse and that colonists should work within the system to get the act repealed.

However, a significant portion of the colonial population, particularly in port cities where people were more politically engaged and where the economic impact would be most directly felt, was outraged. Merchants, lawyers, printers, and artisans all faced direct costs from the Stamp Act. Newspapers, which had become important vehicles for political debate, would have to pay for stamps on every issue. Lawyers needed stamps for legal documents. Merchants needed stamps for shipping papers and contracts.

Colonial assemblies passed resolutions condemning the act. The Virginia House of Burgesses, led by a young lawyer named Patrick Henry, passed resolves in May 1765 declaring that only the Virginia assembly could tax Virginians. Henry's resolves went further than many Virginia leaders were comfortable with, and some were rescinded after he left town. However, newspapers throughout the colonies printed the full set of resolves, and they inspired similar declarations elsewhere. Other colonial assemblies followed Virginia's lead, asserting their sole right to tax their own people.

But the resistance went far beyond formal legislative protests. It spilled into the streets in ways that alarmed both British officials and colonial elites, who feared losing control of the situation. The Stamp Act crisis was about to get violent.

Sons of Liberty and Boiling Streets

In the summer of 1765, as the November date for the Stamp Act to take effect approached, organized resistance emerged throughout the colonies. Groups calling themselves the Sons of Liberty appeared in Boston, New York, Philadelphia, Charleston, and other cities. These organizations coordinated opposition to the Stamp Act and targeted the officials appointed to distribute the stamps.

The Sons of Liberty were not a single organization but rather loosely connected groups in different colonies who shared information and tactics. Their members included merchants, artisans, shopkeepers, and laborers. Some were wealthy and respectable; others were working men of modest means. What united them was their opposition to the Stamp Act and a willingness to take direct action.

The name came from a speech by an Irish member of Parliament, Isaac Barré, who had defended the colonists during debates over the Stamp Act. He called the colonists "sons of liberty" who had been planted in America by British oppression. Colonial protesters adopted the name proudly. They saw themselves as defenders of British liberty against parliamentary tyranny.

In Boston, a lawyer and political organizer named Samuel Adams became a key figure in coordinating resistance. Adams came from a prominent Boston family but had failed in business and lived modestly. What he lacked in wealth, he made up for in political skill. Adams was a master propagandist who understood how to mobilize public opinion. He wrote articles for newspapers under various pen names and organized meetings at taverns and coffeehouses. He helped coordinate the Sons of Liberty's activities and connected Boston's resistance to similar movements in other colonies.

Adams worked closely with other Boston radicals, including his second cousin John Adams, merchant John Hancock, physician Joseph Warren, and silversmith Paul Revere. These men formed a network that could quickly organize protests, spread information, and coordinate action. They operated openly in some ways—holding meetings and publishing in newspapers—but also covertly, planning actions that would intimidate British officials while maintaining some level of deniability.

The Sons of Liberty targeted the stamp distributors—the men who would actually sell the stamps and collect the revenue. If they could force these men to resign, the Stamp Act would be unenforceable. Without distributors, there would be no stamps. And without stamps, no one could comply with the law even if they wanted to.

On August 14, 1765, a Boston crowd made its move against Andrew Oliver, the wealthy merchant appointed as the Massachusetts stamp distributor. Early that morning, someone hung an effigy of Oliver from a large elm tree at the corner of Essex Street. The tree would become known as the Liberty Tree, a rallying point for protests. The effigy wore a sign identifying it as the stamp distributor.

Lieutenant Governor Thomas Hutchinson ordered the sheriff to remove the effigy. The sheriff looked at the crowd that had gathered around the tree and wisely declined to interfere. The effigy hung all day, and crowds came to see it. That evening, as darkness fell, the crowd cut down the effigy and carried it through the streets in a mock funeral procession. They marched to Olive's counting house—a building where money for a business was kept—and tore it to pieces.

The crowd, which had grown to several thousand by this point, then moved to Oliver's house. They beheaded the effigy on his lawn. They broke windows, destroyed his garden, and damaged his coach. Oliver and his family fled. The crowd eventually dispersed, but the message was clear.

The next day, Oliver resigned his position as stamp distributor by writing to the local authorities. But the Sons of Liberty weren't satisfied. They wanted a public resignation. They wanted to humiliate him so badly that no one else would want to take the position. On August 17, under pressure, Oliver appeared in person at the Liberty Tree and swore an oath before a large crowd that he would not distribute stamps. The crowd cheered.

Twelve days later, violence erupted again, this time targeting Lieutenant Governor Thomas Hutchinson. Hutchinson was a native-born Massachusetts man, but he had defended Parliament's right to tax the colonies. His own relatives had been appointed to positions enforcing British policies, including Andrew Oliver (Hutchinson's brother-in-law). To the Sons of Liberty, Hutchinson represented everything wrong with British rule. He was an American who had sold out his countrymen for personal gain.

On the night of August 26, a crowd attacked Hutchinson's elegant Boston home. What followed was not a protest but destruction. The crowd broke down the doors. They destroyed furniture, scattered papers and books, stole money and belongings, drank the wine from his cellar, and tore the house apart. They chopped down the fruit trees in his garden. They ripped off the cupola on the roof. They even tore up the floorboards looking for hidden money. Hutchinson and his family barely escaped. By dawn, the house was a shell.

The destruction of Hutchinson's house shocked many colonists, including some who opposed the Stamp Act. This went beyond intimidation into lawless violence. Even Samuel Adams, who had encouraged resistance, publicly condemned the attack as going too far. Several men were arrested and charged, though getting convictions proved difficult because witnesses were reluctant to testify.

But the violence worked. Similar scenes played out across the colonies, though most didn't reach the level of destruction seen at Hutchinson's house. In Newport, Rhode Island, three men connected to stamp enforcement saw their houses attacked. In New York, Lieutenant Governor Cadwallader Colden, who had defended the Stamp Act, saw an effigy of himself paraded through the streets and burned. His carriage was destroyed. The crowd threatened his house, but troops intervened before any serious damage occurred.

In Charleston, South Carolina, stamp distributor George Saxby resigned after effigies were burned and his house was threatened. In every colony, stamp distributors faced intimidation. Some resigned immediately. Others tried to hold out but eventually gave in to the pressure. By November 1, when the Stamp Act was supposed to take effect, not a single stamp distributor in the colonies was willing to perform his duties.

The resistance wasn't just violent. It was also economic and strategic. Colonial merchants agreed to boycott British goods until the Stamp Act was repealed. They called it "non-importation." If Parliament wanted revenue from America, the colonists would cut off the trade that generated that revenue. Merchants in Boston, New York, and Philadelphia signed agreements not to order British goods. They pressured other merchants to join. Those who refused faced public shaming—and sometimes worse.

The boycotts hurt. British merchants who depended on American markets began losing money. Ship orders declined, and warehouses filled with unsold goods. British merchants began pressuring Parliament to repeal the act.

The Stamp Act also couldn't function without cooperation. The law required stamps, but if no one would sell or buy them, the law was meaningless. Newspapers refused to use stamped paper and published anyway, daring authorities to shut them down. Courts in some colonies closed rather than use stamps on legal documents, bringing legal business to a halt. In other places, courts operated without stamps. Ships left port without stamped clearance papers. The law was unenforceable without widespread violence, and Britain didn't have the troops or the will to force compliance in its colonies.

In October 1765, delegates from nine colonies met in New York for the Stamp Act Congress. This was a remarkable development. The colonies had never voluntarily coordinated their actions on such a scale before. The Stamp Act Congress had no legal authority, as no one had given them permission to meet. But they met anyway, recognizing that united action was more powerful than individual protests.

The Stamp Act Congress drafted a Declaration of Rights and Grievances. The language was carefully crafted to be respectful but firm.

The delegates acknowledged their allegiance to the Crown and their subordination to Parliament in matters of imperial policy. However, they insisted that taxation was different. Only bodies where the colonists were represented could tax them. They sent petitions to King George III, the grandson of George II, and to both houses of Parliament, requesting repeal of the Stamp Act.

The Stamp Act Congress demonstrated that the colonies could work together. It also strengthened the network of resistance leaders across colonial boundaries. Men who met in New York would correspond afterward, sharing information and tactics. When the next crisis came, these connections would prove valuable.

By early 1766, the combination of colonial resistance, economic pressure from British merchants, and the practical impossibility of enforcement convinced many in Parliament that the Stamp Act had been a mistake. The act was generating no revenue. Instead, it was creating chaos. It cost Britain money as trade declined, and it united the colonies in opposition to British authority.

In March 1766, Parliament repealed the Stamp Act. The news reached America in May, and the celebrations were jubilant. Colonists lit bonfires and rang church bells. They felt their resistance had justified their rights and their place in the empire.

But Parliament had not conceded the constitutional point. On the same day it repealed the Stamp Act, Parliament passed the Declaratory Act, which asserted that Parliament had "full power and authority" to make laws binding the colonies "in all cases whatsoever." Parliament was saying that it was repealing the tax as a matter of practical politics and to restore peace, but that it absolutely had the right to tax the colonies if it so chose. It was not giving up any authority.

The colonists mostly ignored or downplayed the Declaratory Act. They had won the battle, and that seemed more important than abstract declarations. Few colonists wanted to pick a fight over theoretical questions of constitutional authority when they had just achieved a victory.

So, the constitutional disagreement remained unresolved. Parliament believed it had supreme authority over the colonies in all matters. The colonists believed they had rights that Parliament couldn't violate, including the right to tax themselves. Both sides thought they had won.

The Stamp Act crisis had changed things. The colonists had learned they could successfully resist British policy through coordinated action. They had organizations in place to mobilize protests. They had also discovered a sense of common cause across colonial boundaries.

Britain had learned something too: the colonies were more difficult to govern than anticipated, more unified than expected, and willing to use violence to resist policies they opposed. However, rather than accept colonial autonomy or work out a new constitutional arrangement, British officials became more determined to assert their authority and make the colonies submit to parliamentary supremacy.

The Boston Massacre: A Clash in the Snow

After repealing the Stamp Act, Parliament waited a year before trying again. In June 1767, Chancellor of the Exchequer Charles Townshend introduced a new set of taxes, known as the Townshend Acts. Townshend thought he had learned from the Stamp Act debacle. The colonists had objected to internal taxes, so he would impose external taxes—duties on imports. These taxes would fall on glass, lead, paint, paper, and tea brought into the colonies.

Townshend assumed these external taxes would be more acceptable than the internal Stamp Act tax. The colonists had always accepted Parliament's right to regulate trade, which included imposing duties on imports. This seemed like a safe approach that would raise revenue without provoking another crisis.

Parliament was wrong. The colonists argued that the purpose of these duties was to raise revenue, not to regulate trade. That made them taxes, and taxes without colonial consent were unconstitutional regardless of what form they took. The colonists had spent a year clarifying their constitutional position, and they weren't about to concede the point just because Parliament changed tactics.

The Townshend Acts did more than impose duties. They created new systems for enforcement that the colonists found deeply threatening. The acts established an American Board of Customs Commissioners based in Boston to collect duties and crack down on smuggling. These commissioners had broad powers and reported directly to London, not to colonial governors. They brought a new level of British authority into colonial ports.

The acts also allowed customs officials to use writs of assistance—general search warrants that let them search any ship, warehouse, or building for smuggled goods without showing specific cause. These writs had existed before, but the Townshend Acts made them more common and more aggressively used. To colonists who valued their property rights and privacy, this felt like an intolerable invasion.

Finally, the Townshend Acts stated explicitly that the revenue raised would pay the salaries of colonial governors and judges. This was a direct attack on colonial political power. Remember, colonial assemblies had gained leverage over governors by controlling their salaries. If a governor didn't need the assembly's money, he didn't need to listen to the assembly. Parliament was trying to make royal officials financially independent of colonial control.

The colonial response followed the patterns established during the Stamp Act crisis. Merchants organized boycotts of British goods. The Sons of Liberty coordinated resistance. Newspapers published angry essays condemning Parliament's actions. Colonial assemblies passed resolutions asserting their rights. John Dickinson, a Pennsylvania lawyer, wrote a series of essays called *Letters from a Farmer in Pennsylvania* that articulated the colonial constitutional position. The essays were widely reprinted and read throughout the colonies.

John Dickinson by Charles Willson Peale.[80]

This time, the conflict lasted longer and grew more bitter. The Townshend Acts remained in effect for three years. The boycotts strained colonial economies, and political tensions infected personal relationships. Loyalists who supported British authority faced social ostracism and sometimes harassment. The Sons of Liberty became more aggressive, intimidating merchants who broke the boycott and customs officials who tried to do their jobs.

One of their most brutal tactics was tarring and feathering. Victims were stripped, covered in hot tar, and then coated with feathers. The tar burned the skin, and removing it often tore off flesh. It was painful, humiliating, and sometimes deadly. The Sons of Liberty used this punishment to terrorize anyone who cooperated with British authorities. The threat of tarring and feathering was often enough to force compliance.

Boston became the center of resistance and tension. The city had a reputation for radicalism and disorder. British customs officials stationed there found their jobs difficult and dangerous. Crowds harassed them. They faced threats and occasional violence. The customs commissioners lived in fear—and with good reason.

In June 1768, customs officials in Boston seized the *Liberty*, a ship belonging to wealthy merchant John Hancock, for smuggling. Hancock was one of the richest men in Massachusetts and a prominent member of the resistance movement. The seizure was probably legal—Hancock likely had been smuggling—but it was also political. The customs officials wanted to demonstrate their authority and hit a leading patriot where it hurt.

The seizure triggered a riot. A crowd attacked the customs officials, beating some of them and forcing them to flee to Castle William, a fort on an island in Boston Harbor. For days, the customs commissioners stayed at the fort, too afraid to return to the city. They sent desperate messages to London pleading for military protection.

The British government decided Boston needed to be brought under control. In October 1768, British troops arrived in Boston—two regiments, about one thousand soldiers in bright red uniforms. They marched through the streets with flags flying, drums beating, and bayonets fixed. It was a show of force designed to intimidate the population and protect British officials.

The soldiers set up camps on Boston Common. Some were quartered in buildings around the city. Their presence was impossible to ignore—armed soldiers in a civilian city during peacetime. To many colonists, this was a violation of their rights and a dangerous precedent.

The Bill of Rights of 1689, one of the foundational documents of British liberty, had declared that keeping a standing army in peacetime without Parliament's consent was illegal. But Parliament had consented to troops in Boston—the colonial assemblies had not. The soldiers were there not to defend against external enemies but to enforce British authority over British subjects. This felt like a military occupation.

The Quartering Act, passed by Parliament in 1765, required colonists to provide housing and supplies for British troops when needed. Boston's leaders resisted. They refused to provide adequate quarters, forcing soldiers to camp outdoors or stay in makeshift accommodations. The dispute over quartering added another layer to the conflict.

Tensions between soldiers and civilians were constant. The soldiers were poorly paid—eight pence a day, barely enough to survive. Many took part-time jobs during their off hours, competing with local workers for employment. In a port city where many men worked as day laborers, rope makers, or dock workers, this competition for jobs created deep resentment.

Soldiers and civilians exchanged insults on the streets. Brawls broke out in taverns. Boston's young men, especially sailors and apprentices, seemed to delight in provoking the soldiers. They threw things at them, mocked them, and allegedly called them "lobsterbacks" because of their red coats. The soldiers, trained for military discipline but not for urban policing, didn't know how to handle this kind of low-level harassment.

On March 2, 1770, several days before the famous massacre, a serious brawl erupted at a rope-making establishment between workers and soldiers looking for part-time jobs. The workers insulted the soldiers. The soldiers fought back. More men joined on both sides. The fight was eventually broken up, but both sides nursed grudges. The city felt like a powder keg waiting for a spark.

On the evening of March 5, 1770, the spark came.

The day had been tense, with several scuffles between soldiers and civilians. As darkness fell, a cold wind blew through the streets. Snow and ice covered the ground. A crowd began to gather near the customs house on King Street. The exact sequence of events that followed is disputed. Eyewitnesses gave contradictory accounts, and both sides had reason to shape the narrative to their advantage. However, the basic facts are clear.

A British soldier stood guard alone at the customs house. A crowd of Bostonians confronted him, throwing snowballs and chunks of ice and shouting insults. The soldier called for help. Captain Thomas Preston arrived with seven or eight soldiers to reinforce the guard. The soldiers formed a semicircle, their muskets loaded, facing the crowd.

The crowd grew larger and more aggressive. They weren't armed with guns, but they weren't peaceful either. They threw more snowballs, ice, oyster shells, and pieces of wood. They dared the soldiers to fire. They pressed closer. Some accounts say the crowd numbered several hundred. It was dark, cold, and chaotic. The soldiers were nervous, surrounded by hostile civilians in unfamiliar streets.

Someone—accounts differ on who—yelled something that sounded like "Fire!" One soldier discharged his musket. Then others fired, either on command or in panicked response. Smoke filled the air. When it cleared, five Bostonians lay dead or dying in the snow. Several others were wounded.

Crispus Attucks, the first to fall, was a man of African and Native American descent who worked on the docks and on whaling ships. Samuel Gray was a rope maker. James Caldwell was a sailor. Samuel Maverick was a seventeen-year-old apprentice. Patrick Carr was an Irish immigrant leather worker. These men weren't wealthy merchants or educated lawyers. They were ordinary people, and they became martyrs to the cause of colonial liberty.

The aftermath could have been catastrophic. Boston was on the verge of exploding into greater violence. Thousands of armed colonists from surrounding towns began gathering, ready to march on the city. British troops prepared for battle. One more spark might have ignited a full-scale conflict right there in 1770, five years before the American Revolution actually began.

But cooler heads prevailed. Lieutenant Governor Thomas Hutchinson, still bitter from having his house destroyed five years earlier but trying to prevent worse bloodshed, addressed the crowd. He promised that justice would be done and urged people to go home. Captain Preston and his soldiers were arrested and charged with murder. More importantly, the British commander agreed to move the troops out of the city center. The soldiers were withdrawn to Castle William in the harbor.

What happened next showed both the rule of law and the complexity of the situation. Captain Preston and his soldiers needed lawyers to defend them. In a highly charged atmosphere where public opinion ran against the soldiers, finding defense attorneys was difficult. But two men stepped forward: John Adams and Josiah Quincy Jr.

John Adams, Samuel Adams's cousin, was a respected lawyer who opposed British policy. He had written against the Townshend Acts. However, he believed in the legal process and the right to a fair trial. He believed that even British soldiers accused of murder deserved competent legal representation. Adams took the case despite knowing it would hurt his reputation and cost him clients.

The trials didn't begin until months later, in the fall of 1770. In separate trials, Captain Preston was acquitted; the jury found that he had not ordered his men to fire. Six of the soldiers were acquitted entirely. Two soldiers were convicted of manslaughter rather than murder. They were branded on the thumb as punishment and released. The trials demonstrated that colonists could distinguish between their political grievances and individual justice—that they valued legal procedures even in a highly charged situation.

But the propaganda value of the "Boston Massacre" was enormous. Patriot leaders, especially Samuel Adams, used the event to inflame anti-British sentiment. Paul Revere, a Boston silversmith and member of the Sons of Liberty, created an engraving depicting the event. The engraving showed British soldiers in a neat line, firing on the orders of Captain Preston into a peaceful, orderly crowd of well-dressed civilians. It was inaccurate on nearly every detail—the crowd had not been peaceful, Preston hadn't ordered the firing, and the scene wasn't as orderly as depicted—but it was powerful propaganda.

A printed copy of Paul Revere's engraving.[61]

Copies of Revere's engraving spread throughout the colonies, shaping how people understood what had happened. The image reinforced the narrative patriots wanted to tell: British soldiers were murderers who would kill Americans on the streets of their own cities. The troops were an occupying army. British rule would only lead to blood in the snow.

Ironically, by the time of the Boston Massacre, the Townshend Acts were already being repealed. The boycotts had worked again. British merchants were losing money and pressuring Parliament to back down. On March 5, 1770—the same day as the Boston Massacre—Parliament voted to repeal most of the Townshend duties. They kept only the tax on tea, a symbolic assertion of Parliament's right to tax the colonies.

So, once again, the colonists seemed to have won. Most of the taxes were gone. British troops had left Boston's streets. Trade resumed. The crisis appeared to be passing. For a few years, things were relatively calm. Some historians call this period from 1770 to 1773 the "quiet years."

However, the constitutional question remained unresolved. What authority did Parliament have over the colonies? Could Parliament tax them? Could it make laws governing their internal affairs? The colonists said no—only their own assemblies could do those things. Parliament said yes—it had complete authority over all parts of the British Empire.

The relative peace of the early 1770s was deceptive. Both sides had backed down from the immediate fight, but neither had changed their minds about the core issue. The fundamental disagreement remained. The organizations for resistance remained in place. People still remembered their grievances. It would only take another spark to ignite the conflict again.

Chapter 4: The Point of No Return

The Tea Act and a Famous Party

The years from 1770 to 1773 were relatively quiet compared to the turbulent 1760s. The Townshend duties were gone, except for the symbolic tax on tea. British troops had withdrawn from Boston's streets. Trade resumed. But beneath the surface, tensions remained. Pamphlets still circulated debating constitutional questions. Local protests continued. The quiet was more of a lull than a true peace, and many colonists realized that the underlying constitutional disagreement hadn't been resolved.

In May 1773, Parliament passed the Tea Act. This seemingly minor piece of legislation would trigger a crisis that made all previous conflicts look modest by comparison. Parliament's primary intent was to help the British East India Company, which was in financial trouble, not to punish the colonies. But patriot leaders immediately saw it as something more sinister—a political trap designed to trick colonists into accepting parliamentary taxation.

The East India Company was one of Britain's most important commercial enterprises. It controlled British trade with India and had a monopoly on importing tea to Britain. But by 1773, the company was drowning in debt. It had warehouses full of unsold tea—millions of pounds of it. The company owed money to the British government and was on the verge of bankruptcy. If it collapsed, it would damage the British economy and embarrass the government.

Parliament decided to help. The Tea Act allowed the East India Company to sell tea directly to the American colonies without paying certain duties it had previously paid in Britain. The company could also bypass colonial merchants who normally imported and sold tea, selling instead through its own agents. This would allow the company to sell tea in America more cheaply than before, undercutting smugglers who brought in Dutch tea illegally. The cheaper price would attract customers, the company would sell its surplus tea, and everyone would benefit.

That was the theory. In practice, the Tea Act created a firestorm.

The tea tax itself—the one remaining Townshend duty—was still in place. The Tea Act didn't impose a new tax. It kept the existing three-pence-per-pound duty that had been there since 1767, a tax colonists had long disputed as illegitimate. However, the act made this existing tax more enforceable by making legally imported British tea cheaper than smuggled alternatives. Colonists who had been avoiding the tax by buying smuggled tea would now have an incentive to buy the cheaper legal tea, but they would have to pay the disputed duty.

Colonial merchants who had been importing tea saw the Tea Act as a direct attack on their livelihoods. The East India Company's agents would control the tea trade, cutting out the middlemen. Established merchants would lose business to the company's chosen agents, who were often wealthy men with political connections. In cities like Boston, New York, and Philadelphia, this looked like corruption and a monopoly. The British government was rigging the market to benefit a powerful corporation and a few privileged individuals.

Colonial leaders saw the Tea Act as a trap. If colonists bought the East India Company's cheap tea, they would be paying the tea tax. By accepting the tea and paying the tax, they would be implicitly accepting Parliament's right to tax them. The constitutional principle they had fought for would be surrendered for the sake of cheap tea.

The patriots organized resistance. They held meetings in taverns and town halls. They published essays in newspapers. They used the newly formed Committees of Correspondence to coordinate action between colonies. These committees had first appeared in Massachusetts in 1772 to maintain organized opposition. The Tea Act crisis made them spread rapidly. Many towns formed committees. They wrote letters to each other, sharing information and strategies. For the first time, the colonies had a permanent, organized network for coordinating resistance.

The message was clear: the tea must not be accepted. It must not be sold, and it must not be taxed. Ships carrying East India Company tea were already headed to colonial ports. When they arrived, colonists would have to decide what to do.

In some ports, resistance succeeded through different means and local circumstances. In Charleston, South Carolina, the tea was unloaded but stored in a warehouse where it sat unsold and untaxed, rotting. In Philadelphia and New York, determined crowds and political pressure convinced the tea ships' captains to turn around and sail back to Britain without unloading.

But Boston was different.

Three ships carrying East India Company tea arrived in Boston Harbor in late November 1773—the *Dartmouth*, the *Eleanor*, and the *Beaver*. The ships docked, but patriot leaders warned the captains not to unload. The captains were in an impossible situation. Massachusetts law required ships to unload their cargo and pay customs duties within twenty days of arrival or be seized. But the Sons of Liberty and a growing crowd of Bostonians were demanding that the ships leave with their cargo.

Governor Thomas Hutchinson—yes, the same man whose house had been destroyed in 1765—refused to let the ships leave without unloading and paying the tax. Hutchinson was determined to enforce the law and break the back of colonial resistance. He used his authority to prevent the ships from leaving the harbor, creating a legal and political standoff. The deadline was December 16. After that, customs officials would seize the ships and unload the tea.

Boston was at an impasse. The ships couldn't leave. The tea couldn't be unloaded without triggering massive resistance. The twenty-day deadline was approaching. Something had to give.

On the afternoon of December 16, thousands of Bostonians gathered at Old South Meeting House. The crowd was enormous—estimates suggest several thousand people. They had been meeting for days, debating what to do. Samuel Adams and other patriot leaders addressed the crowd. They sent one final message to Governor Hutchinson, pleading with him to let the ships leave. Hutchinson refused.

As darkness fell, Samuel Adams stood before the crowd and reportedly said, "This meeting can do nothing more to save the country." It might have been a signal. It was certainly the end of legal options.

What happened next became one of the most famous acts of political protest in history.

A group of men, some poorly disguised as Mohawk Indians with faces darkened by soot and blankets wrapped around their shoulders, left the meeting house. They marched to Griffin's Wharf, where the three tea ships were docked. This was not a random mob; they were organized and disciplined. Estimates suggest 100 to 150 men participated directly, while thousands watched from the shore.

The men boarded the ships, and the ships' crews didn't resist. The men broke open the tea chests. By most accounts, there were 342 chests in total, containing roughly 90,000 pounds of tea. The value is often estimated at about £10,000 sterling, a fortune. They dumped the tea into Boston Harbor. It took three hours. The men were careful not to damage the ships themselves or steal anything. This was about the tea and what it represented, not vandalism or theft.

The Boston Tea Party.[68]

The next morning, Boston Harbor was choked with tea leaves. The tide had washed them up on shore. For weeks, the smell of tea hung over the waterfront. The destruction was complete. The tea would never be sold, and the tax would never be collected.

The Boston Tea Party, as it came to be called, was not actually called that at the time. Participants referred to it as "the destruction of the tea." The term "tea party" came later and had an ironic, mocking tone; after all, this was no genteel party but a revolutionary act. The name stuck, though.

Colonial reactions were mixed. In Boston and other centers of patriot activity, many people celebrated openly. They had struck a blow against British tyranny. They had defended the principle of no taxation without representation.

However, many other colonists disapproved, some strongly. Destroying private property worth thousands of pounds seemed to cross a line from legitimate protest into lawlessness. Moderate colonists who opposed British taxes but valued order and property rights worried that the movement was spiraling out of control. Benjamin Franklin, who was in London representing Pennsylvania, was among those who expressed disapproval when he heard the news. He believed the tea should be paid for. He and others like him feared the destruction would give Parliament an excuse for harsh retaliation.

A portrait of Benjamin Franklin by Joseph-Siffred Duplessis.[68]

He was right to worry. The Boston Tea Party would provoke the most severe British response yet. Parliament would crack down on Massachusetts with a vengeance—and that response would unite the colonies in a way nothing else had.

The Empire Strikes Back: The Intolerable Acts

When news of the Boston Tea Party reached London in January 1774, King George III and members of Parliament were outraged. Even British politicians who had previously sympathized with colonial grievances felt the colonists had gone too far. The tea belonged to the East India Company. It had been destroyed deliberately. Someone had to pay, and someone had to be punished. Britain's authority had to be reasserted, or the empire would dissolve into chaos.

Parliament moved quickly to punish Massachusetts and reassert control. Between March and June 1774, the British Parliament passed a series of laws called the Coercive Acts. In America, they became known as the Intolerable Acts. The name reveals how colonists saw them—not as legitimate governance but as intolerable tyranny.

The first was the Boston Port Act, which became law in March 1774. This act closed Boston Harbor to all commercial shipping until the destroyed tea was paid for and the town demonstrated its submission to British authority. No ships could enter or leave except for military vessels and ships carrying food and fuel, which required special permits. The closure would remain in effect until the governor certified that order had been restored and compensation had been paid.

This was an economic death sentence for Boston. The city's economy depended on its port. Merchants couldn't receive goods or send products to market. Sailors and dockworkers lost their jobs. Shipowners faced ruin. Thousands of Bostonians depended directly or indirectly on the port for their livelihoods. The closure hurt everyone, not just the men who had destroyed the tea.

The punishment was collective on purpose. British officials knew perfectly well that the destruction had been carried out by a small group, but they blamed all of Boston for tolerating and celebrating the act. The message was clear: if you support resistance, you will all suffer the consequences.

The Massachusetts Government Act, passed in May, was even more radical. The colony's charter, which had granted significant self-government, was essentially revoked. The council, which had been elected by the assembly, would now be appointed by the king. Town meetings—the heart of New England's local democracy—were severely restricted. They could meet only once a year to elect officials unless the governor gave specific permission for additional meetings. Many local offices that had been elected would now be appointed by the governor.

This attacked the very foundations of colonial self-government. Town meetings had existed in Massachusetts since the 1600s. They were where ordinary citizens discussed local affairs, debated issues, and made collective decisions. They were noisy, contentious, and deeply democratic. To British officials, town meetings were where radicals like Samuel Adams stirred up trouble and organized resistance. Shutting them down would, Parliament hoped, silence the radicals and restore order.

The Administration of Justice Act allowed the governor to transfer trials of British officials accused of capital crimes to Britain or to another colony. The law was meant to protect British officials from hostile colonial juries. If a customs official or a soldier was accused of murder while doing his duty, he could be tried in Britain, where he might get a fair trial, rather than in Massachusetts, where a local jury might convict him regardless of the evidence.

Colonists called this the "Murder Act." They saw it as a license for British officials to commit violence without consequences. If a soldier killed a colonist, he could simply be shipped to Britain, where no colonial witnesses could afford to travel and testify. The soldier would walk free. Justice would be denied. Officials could act with impunity, knowing they would never face punishment from colonial courts.

The Quartering Act, also passed in 1774, expanded the requirements for housing British troops. The law specified that troops should first be housed in barracks and public buildings, but if those were insufficient, the governor could require the use of uninhabited buildings, barns, and other structures. While the act didn't explicitly authorize quartering in occupied private homes, colonists feared this was the inevitable next step and saw the act as a threat to their property rights and personal liberty.

Parliament also passed the Quebec Act in 1774. This act was technically separate from the Coercive Acts and addressed the government of Quebec, which Britain had acquired from France. Colonists lumped it together with the Intolerable Acts because of its timing and because they saw it as part of the same pattern of authoritarian overreach.

The Quebec Act extended Quebec's boundaries south to the Ohio River, encompassing lands that several colonies claimed. It allowed Catholics in Quebec to worship freely and hold public office, alarming

Protestant colonists who harbored deep anti-Catholic prejudices. It established French civil law in Quebec rather than English common law. And it made no provision for an elected assembly, placing power instead in an appointed governor and council.

To colonists, the Quebec Act looked like a blueprint for their own future under British rule. Here was a territory with no elected assembly, no English legal protections, and no religious restrictions on Catholics. If Britain governed Quebec this way, might it eventually govern all the colonies this way? The act fed fears that Britain intended to strip away colonial rights and impose authoritarian rule.

The cumulative effect of these laws was devastating to colonial morale and unity, but not in the way Britain intended. Rather than isolating Massachusetts and dividing the colonies, the Intolerable Acts united them. Colonists throughout America saw Massachusetts's fate as a warning of what could happen to any colony that defied British authority.

A patriot cartoon depicting the Intolerable Acts as the forcing of tea on a Native American woman (symbolizing the American colonies)."

Britain had made a mistake. If it had targeted only the individuals who destroyed the tea, it might have divided colonial opinion. Many colonists who opposed British taxes still valued property rights and opposed mob violence. But by punishing an entire city, revoking a colonial charter, and imposing what looked like military rule, Parliament confirmed the patriots' worst fears about British tyranny.

Boston didn't stand alone. Other colonies sent food and supplies to help the city survive the port closure. Cartloads of grain arrived from Connecticut. Rice came from South Carolina. Money came from Virginia. The Committees of Correspondence organized this relief effort, demonstrating that the coordination network could do more than spread information—it could coordinate relief efforts.

Colonists held meetings denouncing the Intolerable Acts. Colonial assemblies passed resolutions condemning Parliament's actions. The consensus was growing: Massachusetts today could be Virginia or Pennsylvania tomorrow. If Parliament could revoke Massachusetts's charter, it could revoke any charter. If Parliament could close Boston's port, it could close any port. If Parliament could ban town meetings, it could shut down any colonial assembly.

The question facing the colonies was what to do about it. Individual colonies couldn't stand against British power. But together, perhaps they could. The Committees of Correspondence began circulating a proposal: the colonies should send delegates to a general congress to coordinate their response. It would be similar to the Stamp Act Congress of 1765, but it would be larger and have a broader mandate.

Not everyone supported this idea. Loyalists warned that a continental congress would be treasonous and openly challenge British authority. Moderates worried it would escalate the crisis rather than resolve it. But the momentum was building. By the summer of 1774, twelve colonies had agreed to send delegates to Philadelphia. Only Georgia, the youngest and weakest colony, declined to participate.

The First Continental Congress would meet in September 1774. It would be the most significant gathering of colonial leaders in American history to that point. What they decided would determine whether the crisis could be resolved peacefully or whether the confrontation would escalate into something no one could control.

Britain had intended the Intolerable Acts to isolate Massachusetts and demonstrate the consequences of resistance. Instead, they had unified the colonies and pushed them toward coordinated action. The crackdown had backfired spectacularly. The point of no return was getting closer.

The First Continental Congress: A United Front

On September 5, 1774, fifty-six delegates from twelve colonies gathered in Philadelphia at Carpenters' Hall. They were lawyers, merchants, planters, and political leaders. Some were radicals who wanted strong action against Britain. Others were moderates hoping to find a path to reconciliation. A few were conservatives who worried the meeting itself was dangerously close to treason. However, they all recognized that something unprecedented was happening: the colonies were acting together in a way they never had before.

The delegates were an impressive group. Massachusetts sent Samuel Adams and his cousin John Adams. Virginia sent George Washington, Patrick Henry, and Richard Henry Lee. New York sent John Jay. Pennsylvania sent John Dickinson. South Carolina sent Christopher Gadsden. These men represented different regions, different economic interests, and different political philosophies. Getting them to agree on anything would be a challenge.

They didn't have the legal authority to meet. No king or Parliament had authorized this congress, and no governor had called them together. They were acting on their own initiative, claiming authority that came from the people they represented rather than from any higher power. This was radical in itself.

The first question was what to do. The delegates debated for weeks. Some wanted immediate military preparation. Others wanted to send another petition to the king. Some argued for cutting off all trade with Britain. Others worried that such drastic action would hurt the colonies more than it would hurt Britain.

One early proposal came from Joseph Galloway of Pennsylvania, a moderate who wanted to preserve the connection with Britain while addressing colonial grievances. Galloway proposed a Plan of Union that would create an American legislature with the power to veto parliamentary acts affecting the colonies. It would essentially create a new level of government between the colonies and Parliament, giving colonists a voice in imperial affairs while keeping them within the British Empire.

The radicals opposed the plan because it accepted Parliament's basic authority while just adding an American check on that power. To men like Samuel Adams, the fundamental principle was that Parliament had no right to legislate for the colonies at all. The plan was ultimately defeated.

Instead, the Continental Congress took a different approach. They passed a Declaration of Rights and Resolves that stated clearly what colonists believed their rights were. They had the right to life, liberty, and property. They had the right to participate in their own governance. They had the right to be free from taxation without representation. These weren't new arguments, but this was the first time representatives from twelve colonies had united behind them in such a formal way.

The declaration listed specific parliamentary acts that violated colonial rights: the Coercive Acts, the Quebec Act, various revenue acts, and the maintenance of a standing army in the colonies without consent. The document was carefully worded. It acknowledged the colonies' connection to Britain and their subordination to the king, but it rejected Parliament's authority to tax the colonies or legislate for their internal affairs.

The Congress also approved the Suffolk Resolves, a set of statements from Suffolk County, Massachusetts, that took a harder line. These resolves declared the Coercive Acts unconstitutional and called for Massachusetts to resist them. They recommended that the colony prepare defensive measures, including organizing militia units that would be ready to respond quickly. The Continental Congress's endorsement of these resolves was carefully worded to show solidarity with Massachusetts without issuing an explicit, continent-wide call to arms.

However, the Continental Congress's most powerful action was economic. The delegates created the Continental Association, an agreement to cut off trade with Britain. Starting December 1, 1774, the colonies would stop importing British goods. If Britain didn't repeal the Intolerable Acts by September 1775, the colonies would stop exporting goods to Britain as well.

This was non-importation on a scale that had never been attempted before. The Continental Association wasn't just a voluntary agreement among merchants. It created enforcement mechanisms. Each colony, county, and town would elect committees to monitor compliance. These committees would publish the names of violators, encouraging social pressure and economic boycotts against anyone who broke the agreement.

The Continental Congress also drafted petitions. They wrote to the king asking him to intervene and protect colonial rights from parliamentary overreach. They wrote to the British people explaining colonial grievances and hoping to find support among ordinary Britons who valued liberty. They wrote to the inhabitants of Quebec, trying to convince them to join the colonial cause. These petitions were respectful in tone but made it clear that colonists expected action, not just sympathy.

Before adjourning in late October, the delegates agreed to meet again in May 1775 if Britain hadn't addressed colonial grievances. This was significant. They weren't just gathering for one emergency meeting. They were establishing the Continental Congress as an ongoing institution, a permanent body representing colonial interests. Whether Britain recognized it or not, the colonies now had a central government.

The delegates returned home with mixed feelings. Some were energized by the unity they had achieved. Others worried they had gone too far. All of them knew that the next few months would be critical. Would Britain back down as it had with the Stamp Act and the Townshend Acts? Or would the conflict escalate?

The Continental Association went into effect as planned. Throughout the colonies, committees formed to enforce the boycott. Some operated fairly and focused on economic pressure. Others used intimidation and violence against suspected violators. Merchants who continued trading with Britain faced boycotts, public shaming, and sometimes attacks on their property. The committees became centers of patriot power, controlling local affairs and marginalizing those who disagreed with their policies.

The Continental Association worked remarkably well. Trade with Britain dropped dramatically. British merchants began losing money and pressuring Parliament to compromise. But this time, Parliament was in no mood to back down. They had tried backing down before, and it had only emboldened colonial resistance. This time, they would stand firm.

King George III and his ministers had concluded that the colonies needed to submit or be forced into submission. The king saw colonial resistance not as a legitimate defense of rights but as a rebellion against lawful authority. Parliament's credibility was at stake. If they backed down again, what authority would they have left? Better to face the crisis now than let it fester and grow worse.

In Britain, hardliners gained influence. They argued that the colonies had become spoiled and rebellious because Britain had been too lenient. What the colonies needed was firm discipline. Parliament should send more troops, enforce British law rigorously, and punish resistance harshly. Only then would order be restored.

In February 1775, Parliament declared that Massachusetts was in a state of rebellion. They authorized the use of military force to restore order. They began preparing to send more troops and to give British commanders broader authority to deal with resistance. The colonies would submit, or they would be conquered.

By the spring of 1775, both sides were locked into positions from which neither could easily retreat. The colonies had united behind a program of resistance and established mechanisms to coordinate their actions. Britain had committed to enforcing its authority by military force if necessary. The moderates who wanted compromise were losing ground on both sides.

All it would take was a spark to ignite the accumulated tensions into open warfare. That spark would come in Massachusetts, just as dawn broke on a spring morning in April 1775.

Chapter 5: The Shot Heard 'Round the World

The Midnight Ride

In April 1775, Massachusetts was a powder keg. British troops occupied Boston. Patriot militias drilled on town greens throughout the countryside. The Continental Association's enforcement committees controlled local affairs in most towns. Royal authority existed in Boston but barely extended beyond the city limits. Both sides were armed, watching each other, waiting.

Thomas Gage.[65]

General Thomas Gage commanded the British forces in Boston. He was also the royal governor of Massachusetts. Gage was in an impossible position. His superiors in London demanded that he enforce British authority and arrest the patriot leaders who were organizing resistance. However, he had only about three thousand troops, and Massachusetts had tens of thousands of militiamen. Any aggressive move might trigger an uprising he couldn't control.

Gage knew the patriots were stockpiling weapons and ammunition in towns outside Boston. Reports indicated that Concord, about twenty miles northwest of Boston, held a significant cache of military supplies, including cannons, muskets, gunpowder, and food. Gage decided to act. He would send a force to Concord to seize or destroy these supplies. The operation would be secret, conducted at night, and completed before the countryside could react. If done quickly, it might succeed without bloodshed.

But Boston was full of patriot spies. The British couldn't sneeze without someone reporting it to Samuel Adams and John Hancock, who were staying in Lexington, just outside Boston. When British officers began giving orders on April 18, patriot observers noticed unusual activity. Boats were being prepared. Officers were assembling. Troops were gathering. Something was happening.

The patriots had prepared for this moment. They had established a warning system. If British troops left Boston, riders would spread the alarm throughout the countryside, giving militiamen time to gather. The key question was which route the British would take—by land across the Boston Neck or by boat across the Charles River to Cambridge. The answer would determine which communities received the warning first.

Paul Revere, a Boston silversmith and member of the Sons of Liberty, was one of several riders prepared to carry the alarm. Revere arranged a signal system with patriots in Charlestown across the river. Lanterns would be hung in the steeple of Old North Church—one if the British went by land, two if by sea. This way, even if Revere couldn't get out of Boston himself, the signal would alert patriots on the other side.

On the night of April 18, around 10 p.m., British troops began moving. They were heading to boats at the water's edge. They would cross the Charles River and march inland. Two lanterns appeared in the Old North Church steeple. The British were going by sea.

Revere crossed the river in a small boat, rowing quietly past a British warship anchored in the harbor. He reached Charlestown and borrowed a horse. Around 11 p.m., he began riding west toward Lexington, where Samuel Adams and John Hancock were staying.

Revere wasn't alone. William Dawes, another patriot rider, took the land route out of Boston across the Boston Neck. A third rider, Dr. Samuel Prescott, would join them later. The famous image of a lone rider galloping through the night is romantic but inaccurate. This was an organized effort involving multiple people.

As Revere rode through the countryside, he stopped at houses to spread the alarm. The residents then alerted their neighbors. Church bells began ringing. Drums beat. Across the Massachusetts countryside, the alarm spread like wildfire.

Revere wasn't shouting "The British are coming!" as legend has it. The colonists still considered themselves British. He warned that "the regulars" were marching out. The distinction mattered. This wasn't an invasion by foreigners but a military action by their own government against its own people.

By midnight, Revere had reached Lexington and warned Adams and Hancock. Dawes arrived shortly after, having taken the longer route. The two men decided to continue on to Concord to warn patriots there and help move or hide the military supplies. Dr. Prescott, who happened to be out late courting a young woman, joined them.

About halfway to Concord, the three riders encountered a British patrol. The British had sent scouts ahead of their main force to cut off communications and capture messengers. The patrol stopped the riders. Prescott spurred his horse and jumped a fence, escaping into the countryside. He would complete the ride to Concord, warning the town.

Dawes also escaped, though he was thrown from his horse in the process and had to walk back to Lexington. Revere was captured. British officers questioned him roughly, threatening to shoot him if he didn't answer. Revere, thinking quickly, told them that hundreds of militia were gathering and that the British march was no longer secret. The officers kept Revere for a while and then released him, but took his horse. He walked back to Lexington, arriving in time to witness the confrontation that was about to unfold.

By dawn on April 19, the alarm had spread across the countryside. In dozens of towns, militiamen were grabbing their muskets and powder horns, kissing their families goodbye, and hurrying toward Lexington and Concord. Some were old men. Some were teenagers. They were farmers and craftsmen, not professional soldiers. But they had trained together. They knew how to handle their weapons. And they were angry.

The British force, about seven hundred men under Lieutenant Colonel Francis Smith, marched through the night toward their objectives. They moved slowly, burdened by their equipment and unfamiliar with the terrain. As dawn approached, they reached Lexington, expecting to find the town quiet and unaware.

Instead, they found armed men waiting for them on the town green.

The Skirmishes at Lexington and Concord

As the British column approached Lexington in the early morning light of April 19, 1775, they could see men gathered on the town green. These were members of the Lexington militia, commanded by Captain John Parker. Parker was a veteran of the French and Indian War, a farmer, and a man dying of tuberculosis. He knew his small force—perhaps seventy to eighty men—couldn't stop seven hundred British regulars. However, he also knew his duty was to show that the militiamen would stand their ground.

The exact words Parker spoke that morning are disputed by various accounts, but one version that has become famous captures the militia's intent: "Stand your ground. Don't fire unless fired upon. But if they mean to have a war, let it begin here."[i] The militia would stand as a statement of principle, but they wouldn't start a fight they couldn't win.

Major John Pitcairn commanded the British advance units. He was an experienced marine officer, professional, and by most accounts, decent. As his troops approached the green, he could see the armed colonists. This was exactly the kind of confrontation Gage had wanted to avoid. Pitcairn ordered his men to surround the militia but not to fire. He rode forward and shouted for the colonists to disperse and lay down their weapons.

What happened in the next few moments changed everything. Someone fired a shot. No one knows who. Both sides later claimed the other fired first. Witnesses gave contradictory testimony. In the confusion and tension of the moment, with dozens of nervous men holding loaded muskets in the dim light of dawn, someone's weapon discharged.

---

[i] "Stand Your Ground." https://www.nationalguard.mil/Resources/Image-Gallery/Historical-Paintings/Heritage-Series/Stand-Your-Ground/

The Battle of Lexington.[66]

That first shot—"the shot heard 'round the world," as it would later be called—broke whatever restraint existed. British soldiers, without orders from their officers, began firing. The volley was devastating at such close range. Militiamen fell. Some tried to return fire. Others ran. The whole confrontation lasted only a few minutes.

When the smoke cleared, eight militiamen lay dead on the Lexington Green. Ten more were wounded. The dead included Jonas Parker, a cousin of Captain John Parker, who stood his ground even after being shot and was killed while trying to reload. Jonathan Harrington was shot and crawled toward his house at the edge of the green, dying on his doorstep as his wife watched. Isaac Muzzy was a veteran, as were several others. These weren't radicals or troublemakers. They were respected members of their community who had turned out to defend their town.

Only one British soldier was slightly wounded, possibly by a ricocheting bullet. The disparity in casualties reflected the reality. This hadn't been a battle. It had been a brief, one-sided encounter. The militia had been outgunned and overwhelmed.

The British officers quickly restored order among their troops and reformed the column. They had fired without orders, which troubled officers like Pitcairn, but there was nothing to be done about it now. They had a mission to complete. The column marched on toward Concord, leaving behind the bodies on Lexington Green and a community in shock and rage.

The British reached Concord around 7 a.m. The town appeared quiet. Most of the militia had withdrawn to high ground north of town near the Old North Bridge, which crossed the Concord River. The British set about searching for military supplies. They found some—a few cannons, some wooden gun carriages, barrels of flour, and other provisions. They disabled the cannons by knocking off their trunnions. They burned the gun carriages. They smashed the barrels and dumped the flour.

But the patriots had been warned hours earlier. They had hidden or moved most of the supplies. What the British found and destroyed was a fraction of what Gage's intelligence had suggested was there. The mission was only partially successful, and the delay in searching gave more time for the militia to gather.

From the hills north of town, colonial militia watched smoke rising from the fires the British had set. They didn't know the British were just burning military supplies. They feared the British were burning the town itself. More militia companies arrived every few minutes, swelling the colonial force to several hundred men. The British had divided their force, with some companies in the town center and others stationed at the North Bridge.

The militia decided to advance toward the bridge. They weren't looking for a fight—they wanted to protect the town. As they approached, the British troops at the bridge grew nervous. They had about one hundred men facing a colonial force that now numbered four hundred or more and was still growing.

The British fired warning shots. The militia kept advancing. Then the British fired a volley directly at the approaching colonists. Two militia members fell dead—Isaac Davis and Abner Hosmer, both from Acton, Massachusetts. Davis had been at the head of his company, leading his men forward. He died instantly.

This time, the militia fired back. Major John Buttrick, commanding the colonial forces, shouted, "Fire, fellow soldiers, for God's sake, fire!" The militia delivered a devastating volley. Three British soldiers were killed. Several more were wounded, including four officers. The British soldiers, outnumbered and under fire, began to fall back in disorder.

This was different from Lexington. At the North Bridge, the colonial militia had stood their ground, fired back, and driven off British regulars. It was the first time in this conflict that colonists had successfully engaged

British troops in direct combat.

The British fell back to the center of Concord, leaving their wounded behind in their haste. The militia, uncertain what to do next, didn't press their advantage. They had driven off the British from the bridge, which was their objective. They weren't trying to destroy the British force. At least not yet.

Lieutenant Colonel Smith, who commanded the British expedition, realized he was in danger. His mission was complete—or as complete as it would get. More colonial militia were arriving every minute. He needed to get his men back to Boston before they were completely surrounded. Around noon, the British began their retreat.

The march back to Boston became a nightmare for the British troops. The colonial militia didn't line up in formations to fight European-style battles. They used tactics learned from decades of frontier warfare. They fired from behind stone walls, from inside buildings, and from behind trees. They moved through the countryside using their knowledge of every lane and path. More militia companies arrived from surrounding towns, joining the fight along the route.

The British column was under constant fire. Men fell wounded or dead. The troops were exhausted, having marched through the night and fought through the morning. Their ammunition was running low. Officers were shot down. The formation began to break down as soldiers stopped to fire back or simply tried to survive.

At Lexington, the British column met reinforcements—another one thousand troops under Lord Hugh Percy, complete with artillery. Percy's cannons drove back the surrounding militia and gave the battered column a chance to rest. But the respite was brief. As soon as the combined force began moving again, the militia resumed their attacks.

The retreat continued through the afternoon. The fighting was brutal and chaotic. Houses where militiamen had fired from were burned by angry British soldiers. Colonists who were captured or wounded were sometimes bayoneted. Any pretense of restraint began to disappear. This was no longer a police action to seize weapons. This was warfare.

British casualties mounted steadily. By the time the troops staggered back into Charlestown, across the river from Boston, they had suffered 73 killed, 174 wounded, and 26 missing. The colonial militia lost about 49 killed and 39 wounded. The British had started the day expecting a routine operation. They ended it as a defeated force, and they were lucky to have made it back to Boston at all.

The retreating British soldiers told stories of the day's fighting that emphasized the militia's tactics and ferocity. They had faced an enemy that didn't fight by European rules, that appeared and disappeared, and that seemed to be everywhere at once. For soldiers trained to fight formal battles with lines of infantry exchanging volleys, the experience was terrifying and confusing.

News of the Battles of Lexington and Concord spread rapidly through the colonies. Riders carried the story southward. Newspapers published accounts. The message was clear: British troops had fired on colonial militia. Men had died. This wasn't a riot or a protest that had gotten out of hand. This was the king's soldiers waging war on the king's subjects.

The colonial accounts emphasized that the British had fired first at Lexington. Paul Revere helped prepare a formal deposition describing the British as the aggressors. Whether that narrative was entirely accurate was less important than its effect. It unified the colonies in a way nothing else had.

Within days, thousands of militia from across New England were converging on Boston. They came from Massachusetts, Connecticut, New Hampshire, and Rhode Island. They brought their own weapons, supplies, and sense of duty. They set up camps around Boston, effectively trapping the British army in the city. The siege of Boston had begun.

What had started as a British march to seize weapons had turned into the first battle of a war. Neither side had planned for this to happen. The British officers just wanted to confiscate some military supplies. The militiamen just wanted to defend their town. But once the shooting started, there was no going back.

For years, both sides had been bluffing. Britain threatened to use force but usually backed down. The colonists protested loudly but rarely fought back. Each time, both sides stepped away from the edge. But on April 19, 1775, nobody blinked. Shots were fired, and men died. The bluffing was over.

The American Revolution had begun.

The Siege of Boston and the Battle of Bunker Hill

The days after Lexington and Concord saw Massachusetts transform into an armed camp. Militia from across New England poured toward Boston, setting up positions on the high ground surrounding the city.

Within a week, roughly 15,000 colonial troops encircled Boston. The British army, with about 6,500 soldiers, was trapped in the city with no easy way out.

This wasn't a formal siege with trenches and artillery bombardments. It was more of a standoff. The colonial militia controlled the countryside. British troops controlled Boston and the waters around it, thanks to the Royal Navy. Neither side had the capability to dislodge the other. But the British were contained—unable to move freely and dependent on supplies from the sea.

General Thomas Gage found himself in an increasingly uncomfortable position. He had more troops than the colonists, and they were professional soldiers rather than militiamen. But he was bottled up in a city, facing a hostile population in the surrounding countryside. Every foraging expedition risked another fight. His men were confined to an increasingly crowded city with limited supplies.

The colonial forces were disorganized. Militia from different colonies had different commanders, different traditions, and different levels of training. There was no unified command structure, no standardized procedures, and no clear chain of authority. What held them together was a common purpose and the determination to keep the British contained.

In early May, news arrived that changed the strategic situation. Ethan Allen and Benedict Arnold—yes, that Benedict Arnold, though he was still a patriot at this point—led a raid on Fort Ticonderoga in New York. The fort, on Lake Champlain, guarded the route between New York and Canada. It held a substantial number of cannons and other artillery. Allen's militia, the Green Mountain Boys, surprised the small British garrison and captured the fort without a fight. The artillery would eventually prove crucial to the siege of Boston.

On June 12, General Gage issued a proclamation. He offered pardons to all rebels who laid down their arms, with two exceptions: Samuel Adams and John Hancock. These two were considered the ringleaders, so they were too dangerous to pardon. The proclamation had little effect. The militiamen weren't interested in pardons. They wanted their grievances addressed.

By mid-June, the colonial forces decided to strengthen their position by occupying the high ground on the Charlestown Peninsula, north of Boston. The peninsula had two hills—Bunker Hill and Breed's Hill. Control of these heights would let the colonists threaten Boston with artillery. On the night of June 16, about 1,200 men under Colonel William Prescott marched onto the peninsula and began constructing fortifications.

Through the night, the men worked silently, digging trenches and throwing up earthwork walls on Breed's Hill, which was closer to Boston than Bunker Hill. The choice of Breed's Hill rather than Bunker Hill might have been a mistake; Bunker Hill was higher and farther from British guns. By dawn on June 17, the British in Boston awoke to see a fortification that hadn't existed the night before, positioned where it could threaten the city.

General Gage couldn't allow this. If the colonists mounted artillery on Breed's Hill, they could bombard Boston and the British ships in the harbor. He decided on a frontal assault. British troops would land on the peninsula and storm the colonial position. The attack would demonstrate British military superiority and break the siege.

Around 3 p.m., after hours of naval bombardment that did little damage to the earthwork fortifications, British troops began their assault. About 2,200 soldiers in red uniforms formed into lines and advanced up the hill. They carried packs weighing sixty to eighty pounds. The day was hot. The grass was high. The slope was steep.

The colonial militia waited behind their fortifications. They were short on ammunition; many had only a few rounds. Officers supposedly told them something like "Don't fire until you see the whites of their eyes," though the phrase may be apocryphal. The instruction was practical: conserve ammunition and wait until the enemy was close enough that every shot counted.

The British came within fifty yards. Then forty. The militia opened fire. The volley was devastating. British soldiers fell in rows. Officers were hit. The tight formations that made European armies so effective in open battle made them perfect targets for men firing from behind protective walls. The British line staggered and fell back.

The British reformed and attacked again. Again, the militia waited until the British were close. Again, the volley tore through the British ranks. And again, the attack failed.

General William Howe, commanding the British assault, ordered a third attack. This time, the British left their packs behind and fixed bayonets. They came faster and more determined. This time, many of the colonial defenders were out of ammunition. When the British reached the fortifications, the militia had to fight hand-to-hand or retreat. Most retreated, falling back across the peninsula to the mainland.

The British had won the battle. They controlled Breed's Hill and Bunker Hill. However, the victory had cost them dearly. British casualties were staggering: 226 killed and 828 wounded, out of about 2,200 engaged. Nearly half the attacking force was killed or wounded. Among the dead were many officers—the hardest casualties to replace. The colonial forces lost about 140 killed and 270 wounded.

General Howe was shaken by the casualties. The easy victory he had expected had turned into the bloodiest day British forces had experienced in years. The lessons of Bunker Hill would haunt him for the rest of the war, making him cautious about attacking entrenched positions.

The battle became known as Bunker Hill, even though most of the fighting occurred on Breed's Hill. The name stuck, perhaps because Bunker Hill was more prominent or because early reports confused the two. What mattered more than the name was what the battle demonstrated. The colonial militia had proven they could stand against British regulars. They had held their position through two assaults by professional soldiers and had only retreated when they ran out of ammunition. The British had won the field, but the moral victory belonged to the colonists.

The siege of Boston continued through the rest of 1775 and into early 1776. The standoff seemed permanent. The British couldn't break out, and the colonists couldn't force them out. Both sides waited, wondering what would come next. The war that had begun with shots on Lexington Green had become a stalemate around Boston.

But events were moving beyond Boston. The Continental Congress had reconvened in Philadelphia in May 1775, as planned. They now faced a very different situation than they had anticipated. War had begun. The question was no longer whether to resist British policy but how to organize and sustain that resistance. The colonies needed an army and a commander. They needed to decide whether they were still trying to reconcile with Britain or whether they were fighting for something more.

The war had begun. But what, exactly, were they fighting for?

Chapter 6: Declaring Independence: A New Nation is Born

Common Sense: A Pamphlet Changes Minds

In early 1776, colonial opinion on independence was deeply divided. While many colonists, particularly in the moderate Middle Colonies, still hoped for reconciliation with Britain, a growing movement for independence had taken firm root, especially in New England.

In May 1775, the Continental Congress reconvened. The delegates authorized the creation of the Continental Army and appointed George Washington as commander. They also sent the Olive Branch Petition to King George III, expressing loyalty to the Crown and begging him to protect the colonists from Parliament's oppression. The petition was respectful, even pleading. It blamed Parliament and the king's ministers for the crisis while affirming loyalty to the king himself.

The king rejected the petition. He didn't even formally receive it. In August 1775, George III issued a proclamation declaring the colonies to be in open rebellion. In his view, the colonists weren't loyal subjects defending their rights. They were rebels challenging lawful authority. The proclamation stated that all officials should suppress the rebellion and bring the traitors to justice. The colonists would submit or be defeated.

This rejection was a turning point. If the king wouldn't listen—if he saw colonial resistance as rebellion rather than a petition for redress—

what options remained? Could the colonies remain within the British Empire while fighting a war against British forces? The contradiction was becoming impossible to maintain.

Through the fall and winter of 1775, opinion began to shift. Fighting continued. The Continental Army laid siege to Boston, and colonial forces invaded Canada, hoping to bring Quebec into the rebellion, though the campaign ultimately failed. Each month of warfare made reconciliation seem less likely. However, most colonists still weren't ready to take the radical step of declaring independence.

Then, in January 1776, a pamphlet appeared that changed everything.

Common Sense, written by Thomas Paine, was published anonymously in Philadelphia on January 10, 1776. Paine was a recent immigrant from England who had struggled in various careers, including as a corset maker and customs official. While he lacked the formal education and high social standing of many colonial leaders, he was a gifted writer and orator. He arrived in America in 1774 with a letter of introduction from Benjamin Franklin, connecting him to influential circles in Philadelphia.

Common Sense was short—about fifty pages. It was written in plain language that anyone could understand. There was no fancy rhetoric and no classical allusions that only educated men would recognize. Paine wrote as though he were speaking to ordinary people in a tavern, using simple words and clear arguments. This accessibility was revolutionary in itself. Political debate had traditionally been the province of educated elites. Paine democratized it.

His argument was straightforward and radical. The problem wasn't just Parliament or the king's ministers. The problem was the monarchy itself. Kings were an absurdity—a violation of natural equality. Why should one man rule over millions simply because of his birth? There was no rational basis for a monarchy. It was a relic of ancient superstition, and it was time to be done with it.

Paine attacked King George III directly, calling him a "Royal Brute" and mocking the very idea of hereditary rule. He ridiculed the notion that Americans should feel loyalty to a distant island that had only brought them trouble. Britain wasn't the "mother country"—it was a tyrannical parent that abused its children. The time had come for America to grow up and leave home.

Paine believed America and Britain had fundamentally different interests. Britain wanted to exploit America for its own benefit. America's future lay in trade with the entire world, not in subordination to British commercial interests. Remaining tied to Britain would drag America into European wars that had nothing to do with American needs.

He also made a practical argument: America needed foreign allies to win the war. France and Spain—Britain's enemies—might support American independence, but they would never help colonists who claimed to be fighting merely to restore their rights within the British Empire. If America wanted French ships and French money, it needed to declare independence and offer something in return—the chance to weaken Britain by taking away its colonies.

However, *Common Sense* was more than just a list of arguments. It painted a vision of what America could become. An independent America would be a refuge for liberty, a place where people governed themselves through elected representatives. America would be a new kind of nation, founded not on conquest or hereditary right but on the principle of consent. It would be an example to the world, proof that people could rule themselves without kings or aristocrats.

"We have it in our power to begin the world over again," Paine wrote.[i] This wasn't just a political dispute or a constitutional argument. This was a chance to create something entirely new. The colonists could show the world that a government could be based on reason and equality rather than tradition and force.

The impact of *Common Sense* was extraordinary. Its circulation was unprecedented. Traditional estimates claim that as many as 150,000 copies were sold within months, though this figure may be exaggerated. Even conservative modern estimates place the number in the tens of thousands—a staggering figure for the time. The pamphlet was read aloud in taverns, at town meetings, and in military camps. It was discussed, debated, and passed around.

Common Sense thrust independence into the center of public debate, shifting it from a radical fringe idea to a plausible mainstream option. Not everyone was convinced. Loyalists remained loyal. Many moderates worried about the risks of independence. Would America survive

---

[i] "Common Sense." https://constitutioncenter.org/the-constitution/historic-document-library/detail/thomas-paine-common-sense-1776

without British protection? Could the colonies unite into a single nation? Would independence lead to chaos and mob rule? These were legitimate concerns.

But Paine had reframed the question. The issue wasn't whether independence was risky. The issue was whether staying tied to Britain was possible or desirable. The war was already happening. Men were already dying. The king had already declared them rebels. At what point did clinging to the hope of reconciliation become delusion?

Common Sense also gave people permission to think what they had been afraid to say out loud. Independence had seemed too radical and too dangerous. But Paine made it seem not only possible but necessary—and even inevitable. He gave people the arguments they needed to justify what their experience had already taught them. Britain would never treat the colonies fairly, and there was no going back to the way things were.

By the spring of 1776, the movement toward independence was gaining momentum. Colonial assemblies began instructing their delegates to vote for independence in the Continental Congress. However, the Continental Congress needed to make the decision official. They would also need to explain to the world why they were taking this unprecedented step. What they needed was a declaration.

The Second Continental Congress: The Great Debate

By May 1776, the Continental Congress faced a decision it could no longer avoid. The war was in its second year. Thousands of men were fighting and dying. The king had declared them rebels. Foreign assistance was essential, but no European power would openly support colonists who claimed to be loyal British subjects fighting their own government. The logic of the situation pointed toward independence, but taking that step was terrifying.

The Continental Congress that spring included some of the most talented political leaders in American history. John Adams of Massachusetts had been pushing for independence for months. Benjamin Franklin of Pennsylvania, the colonies' most famous citizen, had returned from London, convinced that reconciliation was impossible. Richard Henry Lee of Virginia was eloquent and passionate. Thomas Jefferson, also of Virginia, was young but already recognized as a skilled writer. Roger Sherman of Connecticut was methodical and practical. These men and others wrestled with a decision that would change history.

On June 7, 1776, Richard Henry Lee stood before Congress and introduced a resolution: "That these United Colonies are, and of right ought to be, free and independent States, that they are absolved from all allegiance to the British Crown, and that all political connection between them and the State of Great Britain is, and ought to be, totally dissolved."[i]

The debate that followed was fierce and impassioned. John Adams argued that independence was already a fact. America was fighting a war. Britain treated Americans as rebels. Pretending they were still part of the empire served no purpose. Independence would let America seek allies, establish a government, and act as a nation rather than as colonies in revolt.

John Dickinson answered with equal conviction. He believed independence was premature. The colonies hadn't yet formed a real union or secured an alliance with France. Declaring independence before these things were in place, he warned, would be reckless. America would be vulnerable, isolated, and committed to a path with no way back.

The exchanges revealed how deeply divided the delegates were. Some were ready to vote at once; others needed time to consult their assemblies and gauge public sentiment. The Middle Colonies remained cautious.

The Second Continental Congress postponed the final decision but moved to prepare for it. A committee was appointed to draft a declaration explaining the reasons for separation. The document would justify the decision before the world, rally Americans to the cause, and state the principles on which the new nation would stand.

The committee included five men—Thomas Jefferson, John Adams, Benjamin Franklin, Roger Sherman, and Robert Livingston of New York—chosen to represent different regions and perspectives. Jefferson was asked to write the draft. He was known for his skill with words, and he was from Virginia, the largest and most influential colony. Having Virginia take the lead on independence made political sense.

Jefferson spent about two weeks writing in his rented rooms in Philadelphia, working at a small portable desk. He drew on ideas familiar to educated colonists: natural rights, government by consent, and the right of the people to alter or abolish oppressive governments. These concepts came from Enlightenment thinkers such as John Locke, from

---

[i] "Lee Resolution." https://www.archives.gov/milestone-documents/lee-resolution

English constitutional tradition, and from decades of colonial debate.

While Jefferson wrote, the Second Continental Congress continued to deliberate. Pressure for independence mounted, and more colonial assemblies instructed their delegates to vote in favor. On June 28, the committee submitted Jefferson's draft. The delegates read it and prepared for the final decision.

On July 1, the Continental Congress reconvened to vote on Lee's resolution. John Dickinson spoke one last time against independence, warning that America was leaping into an uncertain future. John Adams followed, defending independence with all his strength. He insisted that independence was not a choice but a necessity. All that remained was to recognize the fact and act as a free nation.

When the speaking ended, Congress took a preliminary vote. Nine colonies voted yes. Pennsylvania and South Carolina voted no. Delaware was split, with only two delegates present. New York abstained, lacking instructions from home.

Congress wanted near unanimity. A divided declaration would weaken its impact. Delegates worked through the night, negotiating with and persuading each other. When they voted again on July 2, the result had changed. Delaware's third delegate, Caesar Rodney, arrived after riding eighty miles through the night and cast the deciding vote. South Carolina reversed its position. In Pennsylvania, John Dickinson and Robert Morris abstained, allowing the majority to vote yes. New York still abstained, but twelve of thirteen colonies now favored independence.

July 2, 1776, was the day the Second Continental Congress officially voted for independence. John Adams believed this would be the date Americans celebrated forever. He wrote to his wife Abigail that July 2 "will be celebrated by succeeding generations as the great anniversary festival."[i]

He was wrong about the date.

The Declaration of Independence: Words for the World

With independence voted on July 2, Congress turned to Jefferson's draft declaration. The document needed to explain to the world why the colonies were taking this extraordinary step. It had to be convincing,

---

[i] "Letter from John Adams to Abigail Adams."
https://www.masshist.org/digitaladams/archive/doc?id=L17760703jasecond

principled, and powerful. Over the next two days, the Second Continental Congress debated the text, making changes, cutting sections, and polishing the language.

Jefferson sat through these discussions uncomfortably. Every alteration felt like a rebuke. Benjamin Franklin, seated beside him, supposedly tried to console him with a story about a man ordering a sign for his hat shop. The man's original text was edited and shortened by well-meaning friends until it said almost nothing. Franklin's point was that writing by committee always produces changes, and a writer shouldn't take them personally. Jefferson was not entirely comforted.

Congress made about forty changes to Jefferson's draft. Most were minor—a word here, a phrase tightened there—but one section was removed entirely. Jefferson had included a long passage blaming King George III for the slave trade and for blocking colonial attempts to restrict slavery. This claim was hypocritical—many colonists, including Jefferson himself, profited from slavery—but it added another grievance to the list.

Congress deleted it. Delegates from South Carolina and Georgia, whose economies depended on enslaved labor, objected forcefully. Some Northern delegates, whose colonies also had ties to the slave trade, were uneasy with the passage's hypocrisy, given that slavery existed in all Thirteen Colonies.

The final version of the Declaration of Independence, approved on July 4, 1776, has three main sections. It opens with a preamble explaining the purpose of the document, lists specific grievances against King George III, and concludes with the formal declaration that the colonies are free and independent states.

The most quoted passage is "We hold these truths to be self-evident, that all men are created equal, that they are endowed by their Creator with certain unalienable Rights, that among these are Life, Liberty and the pursuit of Happiness." These words are so familiar now that it is easy to miss how radical they were. *All men are created equal.* Not some men, not men of certain classes or backgrounds—all men. This was a direct rejection of the hierarchical society that had existed for centuries, where kings and nobles ruled over common people by inherited right. Jefferson declared that no one had a natural claim to rule over another.

The rights Jefferson listed—life, liberty, and the pursuit of happiness— were natural rights. A government did not grant these rights; they belonged to people by virtue of being human. A government's only legitimate purpose was to protect those rights. "To secure these rights, Governments are instituted among Men, deriving their just powers from the consent of the governed."

This was the heart of the declaration's philosophy: government exists to serve the people and derives its authority from their consent. If a government fails to protect rights or becomes destructive of them, "it is the Right of the People to alter or to abolish it, and to institute new Government."

But who counted as "the people?" That's where the beautiful words met ugly reality. Women couldn't vote or own property. Enslaved Black people had no rights at all. Native Americans weren't even part of the conversation. The soaring language about equality applied only to White men—and often only to those who owned land.

It was a painful contradiction, but it was also the starting point of a longer story. Those words created a promise on paper, even if the Founders didn't extend it in practice. Ever since, people who were excluded have pointed to that promise and demanded that America live up to it. The fight for civil rights, women's suffrage, and equality has all been about holding the country to its own declared ideals.

The Declaration of Independence also listed twenty-seven grievances against King George III. The king had refused to approve beneficial laws, dissolved colonial assemblies, obstructed justice, kept standing armies without consent, imposed taxes without representation, restricted trade, and transported colonists overseas for trial. The list built a case that the king had violated their rights.

All the grievances were directed at the king, not Parliament. After years of arguing about the limits of parliamentary authority, focusing on the monarch allowed the colonists to sever their final political tie to Britain: allegiance to the Crown.

Some of the charges were exaggerated or misplaced. For example, the declaration blamed the king for the actions of Parliament or of colonial governments themselves. However, strict accuracy was not the point. The goal was to present a clear, moral, and legal case for revolution. The declaration was, in essence, a brief argument for independence.

The final paragraph contained the act itself: "We, therefore ... do, in the Name, and by Authority of the good People of these Colonies, solemnly publish and declare, That these United Colonies are, and of

Right ought to be Free and Independent States; that they are Absolved from all Allegiance to the British Crown, and that all political connection between them and the State of Great Britain, is and ought to be totally dissolved."[i]

These were not light words. By signing, the delegates were committing treason against the British Crown. If America lost, they would likely hang. Franklin supposedly quipped as they prepared to sign, "We must, indeed, all hang together, or most assuredly we shall all hang separately."

The declaration ended with a collective vow: "And for the support of this Declaration, with a firm reliance on the protection of divine Providence, we mutually pledge to each other our Lives, our Fortunes and our sacred Honor." They were pledging everything—their lives, property, and reputations—to the success of the cause.

Declaration of Independence by John Trumbull.[67]

Fifty-six men eventually signed the Declaration of Independence, though not all on July 4. John Hancock, as president of the Second Continental Congress, signed first, writing his name large and bold. Tradition holds that he said he wrote it large so that King George could read it without spectacles. Whether true or not, the story captures the spirit of defiance.

---

[i] "Declaration of Independence: A Transcription." https://www.archives.gov/founding-docs/declaration-transcript

Signing the document was no formality. These men were putting their names to treason. If captured, they could be executed. Many suffered for their decision. Some had homes and property destroyed. Others were captured and imprisoned. Thomas Heyward Jr., Arthur Middleton, and Edward Rutledge of South Carolina were taken prisoner. Richard Stockton of New Jersey was captured, mistreated, and never fully recovered his health.

In July 1776, copies of the Declaration of Independence were printed and distributed across the colonies. It was read aloud in town squares, to military units, and to crowds eager for news. In Philadelphia, the State House Bell—later known as the Liberty Bell—rang out. In New York, a crowd tore down a statue of King George III and melted it into bullets.

The toppling of the statue of King George III.[a]

The Declaration of Independence changed everything. Before July 4, 1776, Americans were British subjects in rebellion. After July 4, they were citizens of a new nation. The war was no longer about rights within the empire—it was about survival as an independent country. There was no going back.

The declaration's legacy went far beyond the immediate crisis. Its ideas—equality, natural rights, consent of the governed, and the right to revolution—would inspire movements around the world. The French Revolution drew on its principles, and Latin American independence leaders cited it. Over time, its words would be invoked to challenge slavery, demand women's rights, and advance civil rights.

In 1776, those future struggles were distant. What mattered then was that America had declared itself independent. Now it had to fight to make that independence real. The British army would not simply withdraw because Congress had written an eloquent document. The war was just beginning. And for George Washington and the Continental Army, the summer of 1776 would bring their darkest days.

Chapter 7: The Darkest Hours: Washington's Struggle for Survival

The Disaster in New York

The Declaration of Independence transformed the war. Americans were no longer fighting to restore their rights as British subjects. They were fighting for an independent nation. Britain's response was overwhelming. In the summer of 1776, the largest military force it had ever sent to North America sailed into New York Harbor. George Washington and his Continental Army were about to face the full might of the world's most powerful empire.

New York was the obvious target. The city sat at the mouth of the Hudson River, controlling access to the interior. If Britain held New York, it could use the city as a base to split New England from the other colonies. The Hudson River Valley provided a natural corridor from New York City north to Canada. The city also had one of the finest natural harbors in North America, making it ideal for the Royal Navy's operations. From New York, British forces could strike anywhere along the coast.

After Washington fortified Dorchester Heights with captured artillery in March 1776, the British position in Boston became untenable. Their ships sat exposed to American guns on the high ground above, so they evacuated the city. Washington marched his army south to defend New

---

York. However, defending the city posed many problems. It sat on the southern tip of Manhattan Island and was completely surrounded by water. The East River separated Manhattan from Long Island, the Hudson from New Jersey, and the Harlem River cut across its northern end. Defending New York meant defending an island against an enemy that controlled the surrounding waters.

Britain's navy was the most powerful in the world. Its ships could land troops anywhere along hundreds of miles of coastline, outflank any defensive position, and cut off retreat routes by sailing warships into the rivers. Washington faced a problem that might not have had a solution. Some of his officers, including General Charles Lee, argued that New York couldn't be defended and should be abandoned. But Congress insisted the city be held. Abandoning it without a fight would look like cowardice and damage morale. Washington had to try.

He spread his army across multiple positions. Some troops went to Long Island, others stayed on Manhattan, and still others were positioned in New Jersey and up the Hudson River. Washington had about nineteen thousand men, but many were poorly trained militiamen with short enlistments. They lacked discipline, equipment, and battle experience. He was about to face the British Empire's finest troops with an army that included many untested soldiers.

By late June, ships began appearing on the horizon. More arrived daily. By August, there were around four hundred warships, transports, and supply ships carrying thirty-two thousand soldiers, including eight thousand Hessian mercenaries. It was the largest expeditionary force Britain had ever sent overseas. It was larger than most colonial cities. The sight filled New York's loyalists with joy and American soldiers with dread.

The British commander, General William Howe, was a veteran who had distinguished himself in the French and Indian War and at Bunker Hill, where he'd watched British soldiers die by the hundreds in frontal assaults. That experience made him cautious. His brother, Admiral Richard Howe, commanded the fleet.

In September, the Howes met a congressional delegation—including Benjamin Franklin, John Adams, and Edward Rutledge—on Staten Island. The meeting was polite but fruitless. The Howes could only offer pardons to rebels willing to submit; they had no authority to recognize independence or offer meaningful reforms. The Americans, having just declared independence, weren't interested in pardons. The meeting ended without agreement. The time for talking was over.

The British chose to strike first at Long Island. The western end—now Brooklyn—faced Manhattan across the East River. If they controlled Long Island, they could bombard Manhattan and make it untenable. On August 22, British troops began landing at Gravesend Bay on Long Island's southwestern shore. Boat after boat came ashore as thousands of British and Hessian soldiers landed unopposed. The Americans watched but couldn't stop the landing.

Washington had placed about ten thousand men on Long Island under General Israel Putnam, a veteran of the French and Indian War. The main American defensive position was at Brooklyn Heights, overlooking the East River. In front of it ran a wooded ridge called the Heights of Guan. If the British got past that ridge, they could push the Americans back to Brooklyn Heights and trap them against the river.

Four roads crossed the ridge through various passes. The Americans fortified three of them—Gowanus Road on the west, Flatbush Road in the center, and Bedford Road to the east. However, this left Jamaica Pass lightly guarded, as they assumed it was too far east to be a threat. They were wrong.

British officers scouted the area carefully, aided by local loyalists. They identified the weakness at Jamaica Pass, and General Howe devised a sophisticated plan. He would pin the Americans with frontal attacks on the fortified passes while leading his main force on a night march through Jamaica Pass to flank the American position.

On the night of August 26, Howe personally led ten thousand troops on the flanking march. Moving silently through woods and fields, the column stretched for miles. Local loyalist guides led the way. The few American sentries at Jamaica Pass were captured before they could raise the alarm. By dawn on August 27, the British were behind the American lines.

The battle began at daybreak. British and Hessian forces attacked the American positions at Flatbush and Bedford passes, pressing hard against the defenders. The Americans fought back, unaware these were diversionary attacks. The real blow was about to fall from behind.

Around nine in the morning, the British forces that had marched through Jamaica Pass struck the American rear. Troops who had been facing south, fighting off attacks from the front, suddenly heard musket fire and cannons behind them. They were surrounded. Panic spread quickly as American units broke and tried to retreat toward Brooklyn Heights, but British forces were cutting off escape routes.

Some units fought with desperate courage. Lord Stirling—an American general named William Alexander—led about four hundred Maryland soldiers in counterattacks against the British to hold open an escape route. The Maryland men charged again and again against superior numbers, buying time at a terrible cost. Most were killed or captured. The survivors became known as the "Maryland 400," their stand becoming legend.

Other Americans scrambled through swamps and woods to reach Brooklyn Heights. Some made it, but many didn't. By afternoon, the battle was over. The Americans had lost more than one thousand men killed, wounded, or captured, while British and Hessian losses were under four hundred. It was a devastating defeat.

The survivors fell back to Brooklyn Heights. Washington crossed from Manhattan during the battle and took command. His army was now trapped on a small patch of ground with its back to the East River, surrounded by British forces on land. British warships could sail into the river to bombard the position or block a retreat. If Howe ordered an assault, Washington's army might be destroyed.

But Howe hesitated. Having won a complete victory, he hoped to end the campaign without more bloodshed. He began siege operations instead—digging trenches, moving artillery forward, and preparing a formal assault. After Bunker Hill, he no longer rushed fortified positions. His caution gave Washington a narrow chance to act.

On the night of August 29, Washington made one of his most daring decisions: to evacuate the entire army from Long Island. The operation required perfect coordination. He needed boats, darkness, silence, and discipline. Some troops had to remain in the fortifications to deceive the British into thinking the army was still there.

Washington gathered every available vessel—rowboats, sailboats, fishing craft, and barges. The Marblehead Regiment from Massachusetts, composed of experienced sailors, manned many of them. After dark, troops quietly withdrew from the lines, marched to the shore, and were ferried across to Manhattan. The process repeated throughout the night in total silence. No lights, no talking. Those left in the fortifications kept campfires burning to disguise the retreat. Washington stayed until the end, ensuring every soldier who could be saved went across the river.

At dawn, discovery seemed certain. Then, as the sky began to lighten, a thick fog rolled in from the river, shrouding both shores. Under its cover, the evacuation continued. The last boats pushed off just as British troops discovered the empty fortifications. The fog had saved the Continental Army from annihilation.

The escape preserved Washington's army but not his position. The Battle of Long Island was a decisive defeat. New York's outer defenses were gone, and the battle revealed the Continental Army's weakness in open combat. Courage was not enough.

Washington still held Manhattan, but his situation there was just as perilous. The British controlled the surrounding waters and could attack at will. The question was not if they would strike again but when.

The answer came on September 15. British warships sailed into the East River and bombarded American positions at Kip's Bay. The cannon fire shattered the earthworks, and militia units—many facing combat for the first time—broke and ran. Washington, rushing to the scene, was enraged to see his men fleeing. He rode among them, shouting orders and pleading for them to stand, but panic had taken over. The retreat became a rout, and Washington's aides had to drag him away before the advancing British could capture him.

The collapse at Kip's Bay forced the Americans to abandon New York City. The southern end of Manhattan was cut off, trapping some units, which were captured. The British occupied the city and would hold it for the rest of the war.

Washington regrouped at Harlem Heights in northern Manhattan. The next day, September 16, British troops probed the American position, and a skirmish followed. This time, the Americans stood their ground and drove the British back. Though minor, the victory restored some confidence. Yet one success could not offset the campaign's mounting disasters.

Washington knew he couldn't hold Manhattan. The British could easily land north of him and trap the army again. In mid-October, he began withdrawing into Westchester County, leaving a garrison at Fort Washington, a stronghold on the northern end of the island. His officers assured him it could be held; he wasn't convinced, but he left nearly three thousand men there.

On October 28, British forces attacked at White Plains and again drove the Americans from the field. Defeats were piling up. Morale collapsed as soldiers deserted and militia went home. Washington's army was disintegrating.

The worst blow came on November 16 when British and Hessian forces attacked Fort Washington. The fort, though strong, was overcrowded and short on supplies. British warships had already sailed past it, proving it couldn't control the Hudson as intended. Attacked from multiple directions, the garrison fought bravely but was overwhelmed. Colonel Robert Magaw, realizing further resistance was hopeless, surrendered. Thousands of American soldiers were captured—veterans Washington could ill afford to lose. The British seized vital weapons and supplies. It was the campaign's worst defeat, and Washington bore part of the blame for leaving the fort manned despite warnings.

The attack on Fort Washington.[69]

Four days later, British forces crossed the Hudson into New Jersey and attacked Fort Lee, Fort Washington's twin across the river. Washington and his army were there when the attack came. They escaped narrowly, abandoning tents, artillery, and supplies in their haste.

The army retreated across New Jersey with the British in pursuit. The campaign that had begun in August with determination and hope had turned into a disaster. Washington had lost every major engagement and been driven from Long Island, Manhattan, and New Jersey. His army had dwindled from nearly twenty thousand men to perhaps five thousand. Winter was approaching, enlistments were expiring (the fixed periods they had agreed to serve, often just a few months or a year), and the Continental Army—and the revolution itself—seemed on the verge of collapse.

Retreat Across the Delaware

The retreat across New Jersey was a nightmare. Washington had perhaps five thousand men left with him, and that number dropped every day. The soldiers were exhausted, hungry, and poorly supplied. The Continental Congress had no money to buy food or equipment, and supply lines had collapsed. The men ate whatever they could find or went hungry.

Many had no shoes. Their boots had worn out during the long marches, and there were no replacements. They wrapped their feet in rags or strips of blanket to protect them from the frozen ground. Officers later wrote about seeing blood in the snow. Their clothing was falling apart. Uniforms had become tattered rags, and men wore whatever they could find—civilian clothes, blankets, captured British coats. They didn't look like an army; they looked like beggars.

They also had little ammunition left. The supplies abandoned at Fort Lee had included most of the army's gunpowder and musket balls, so what remained had to be rationed carefully. They had lost most of their artillery in the New York campaign, and the few cannons they still had were difficult to move because of the lack of horses. The army's tents had been abandoned. Men slept in the open or in whatever shelter they could find.

Morale was at rock bottom. These men had joined the Continental Army believing in the cause of independence. They had cheered the Declaration of Independence in July, but since then, they had done nothing but lose and retreat. Why should they believe the cause could still win?

The British pursued Washington's retreating army, but they didn't push hard. General Howe believed the rebellion was essentially finished. Winter was coming, and European armies didn't campaign in winter. The custom was to go into winter quarters—to settle into towns, rest, resupply, and wait for spring. Howe saw no reason to risk British soldiers when the American army was falling apart on its own.

Howe's strategic decision would have serious consequences. Instead of concentrating his army, he spread his forces across New Jersey in a chain of outposts. His reasoning made sense on paper. He wanted to control as much territory as possible, show New Jersey residents that British authority had been restored, and encourage loyalists to come forward. Having British troops visible throughout the countryside would accomplish these goals.

The outposts stretched from New Brunswick down through Princeton, Trenton, and several smaller towns. Each garrison numbered several hundred to a few thousand troops. Howe believed they were strong enough to defend themselves against any attack from Washington's weakened army. The garrisons included many Hessian troops—professional German soldiers from various principalities whom Britain had hired to fight in America. They were career soldiers who had trained since childhood.

The garrison at Trenton numbered about 1,500 men. They were primarily Hessians from regiments with names Americans found hard to pronounce—the Rall, Lossberg, and Knyphausen regiments. They were under the command of Colonel Johann Rall, an experienced officer who had distinguished himself in several battles during the New York campaign. Rall was confident, perhaps overconfident, in his men's abilities and had little respect for American soldiers, whom he had seen retreat in previous battles.

Washington's army reached the Delaware River in early December. The crossing into Pennsylvania was chaotic and desperate. However, Washington made one decision that showed his strategic thinking, even in a crisis. He ordered every boat along the Delaware River for miles in either direction to be collected and brought to the western bank. His men scoured the area, taking every boat they could find—ferries, fishing boats, cargo vessels, anything that floated. This meant that when Washington's army crossed to the Pennsylvania side, the British couldn't immediately follow. It bought Washington time.

The army camped in Pennsylvania, scattered along the western bank of the Delaware. They were safe for the moment, but the situation remained desperate. Behind them, across the river, New Jersey was largely under British control. Ahead of them, only thirty miles away, sat Philadelphia—the American capital, where the Continental Congress met. If the British captured Philadelphia, it would be a devastating psychological blow. The rebellion might not survive it.

The Continental Congress understood the danger. In early December, as British forces drew closer, Congress panicked. They voted to adjourn and flee to Baltimore, which was farther south. Before leaving, they passed a resolution giving Washington extraordinary powers. For six months, he would have near-dictatorial authority to conduct the war as he saw fit. He could requisition supplies, appoint officers, and make strategic decisions without consulting Congress. The resolution showed how desperate the situation had become. The Continental Congress was essentially admitting it couldn't help.

The situation was almost beyond description in its bleakness. The army was dissolving, the capital was being evacuated, and British forces controlled most of the Middle Colonies. Loyalists were taking oaths to the king and providing information about rebel activities. Many colonists who had supported independence in the summer were now hedging their bets, trying to make peace with what seemed to be the inevitable return of British authority.

Thomas Paine was with the army during the retreat. Earlier in the year, he had written *Common Sense*, the pamphlet that had done so much to push public opinion toward independence. Now he watched that cause die. He saw the soldiers' suffering—their bleeding feet, their despair, and their quiet talk of defeat.

In December, Paine wrote again. The result was *The American Crisis*, a pamphlet addressed to the American people. It opened with words that would become famous: "These are the times that try men's souls. The summer soldier and the sunshine patriot will, in this crisis, shrink from the service of their country; but he that stands by it now, deserves the love and thanks of man and woman."[i]

Paine distinguished between those who supported independence when it was easy and those who would stand by it when it seemed lost. He admitted how bad things looked but argued that liberty was worth fighting for, especially in the darkest times. "Tyranny, like hell, is not easily conquered," he wrote, "yet we have this consolation with us, that the harder the conflict, the more glorious the triumph."

Washington had Paine's pamphlet read aloud to the troops. The words helped, but words alone wouldn't save the army. Washington needed a victory, something to prove the cause wasn't lost.

---

[i] "The Crisis." https://www.ushistory.org/paine/crisis/c-01.htm?srsltid=AfmBOorS0drTmTO0tVRXaYquO8VrAM_OfKDO73VXg23Oc3JknYeU-mk4

Time was running out. Winter had arrived, and most enlistments would expire on December 31. These men had signed up for one year, and many planned to go home. They had done their part. They had fought and suffered for months.

If Washington didn't act soon, he would lose most of his army. By mid-January, he might have only a few hundred men left. The revolution would be over.

Washington looked at his options, and they were all bad. He couldn't defend Philadelphia with five thousand men, couldn't retreat farther south without abandoning the Middle Colonies, and couldn't sit still and watch his army disappear. That left only one option: attack.

It was a desperate idea. His army was in terrible condition. But Washington had learned something during the long retreat across New Jersey: playing it safe didn't work. Every position he had tried to defend, the British had outflanked or overpowered. If he was going to lose anyway, he might as well lose while trying to win.

Washington began studying his maps and consulting his officers. He met with generals Nathanael Greene and John Sullivan, gathering intelligence about Hessian positions and debating options. The British and Hessian outposts across the river in New Jersey were tempting targets since they were isolated from one another. If Washington could strike one quickly, he might win before reinforcements arrived.

Trenton made the most sense. It was close, just across the river and nine miles inland. The garrison wasn't large, about 1,500 Hessians, and the town's position wasn't particularly defensible. If Washington could get his army across the Delaware, march to Trenton, and attack by surprise, he had a chance.

The timing mattered enormously. Washington decided to attack on Christmas night. Christmas was an important holiday for the German soldiers at Trenton. They would likely be drinking and celebrating. More importantly, no one would expect an attack—especially from a beaten, demoralized army.

Washington's plan was tactically complex. He would divide his forces into three columns, each crossing the Delaware at a different location. They would then converge on Trenton from multiple directions, surrounding the town and cutting off escape routes. The plan required precise timing and coordination. All three columns needed to cross successfully, march to their positions, and attack simultaneously at dawn.

It was an ambitious plan. Everything had to go right—the crossings, the marches, the timing, the surprise. If any part failed, the operation could end in disaster.

But Washington had reached the point where caution was more dangerous than boldness. The safe choice was to do nothing and watch his army dissolve; the risky one was to attack and perhaps lose everything. At least attacking gave him a chance. He chose the risk. He would attack Trenton on Christmas night.

Crossing the Delaware: The Battles of Trenton and Princeton

December 25, 1776, was brutally cold. Snow had been falling on and off for days, covering the Pennsylvania countryside in white. The temperature dropped as evening approached. The Delaware River was choked with chunks of ice that had broken free from the banks and were floating downstream. The wind came in gusts, driving the snow horizontally. It was miserable weather, the kind that made people want to stay inside by a fire. It was perfect weather for what Washington had planned.

As the afternoon faded, Washington's men gathered at McConkey's Ferry, about nine miles north of Trenton. They had been told to prepare for a march, though many didn't know their true destination. Officers kept the plan secret as long as possible. The soldiers assembled quietly, checking their equipment and wrapping themselves in whatever clothing they had against the cold. They brought their artillery—several cannons that would be crucial if the attack succeeded.

The crossing began around sunset, perhaps six o'clock. Washington's plan called for three separate crossings at different locations, with about 2,400 men crossing at McConkey's Ferry under his direct command. The other two forces were supposed to cross downstream near Trenton to attack from the south and cut off Hessian escape routes. However, only Washington's crossing would succeed. The others were stopped by ice and bad weather, never making it across. Washington didn't know this yet. His plan depended on coordination among the three forces, and two-thirds of it was already failing.

The boats at McConkey's Ferry were Durham boats—long, flat-bottomed cargo vessels used to transport iron ore and heavy goods. Each could carry fifteen to twenty men plus equipment. They were sturdy but vulnerable to the ice and currents. One collision with a large ice chunk could punch a hole in a hull or capsize a boat.

The men handling the boats were mostly from Colonel John Glover's regiment from Marblehead, Massachusetts. They were fishermen and sailors who had spent their lives on the water. Without their expertise, the crossing would have been impossible. They took the oars and poles, guiding the boats through the current.

The crossing was harder than anyone expected. The river was about three hundred yards wide, but the current was strong, and the ice made a straight passage impossible. The boats had to weave between ice chunks, sometimes pushing them aside with poles, sometimes rowing hard to avoid collision. Spray from the waves soaked everyone. The cold was savage. Hands went numb. Feet lost feeling. Men shivered violently but kept rowing.

The artillery presented special problems. The cannons were heavy and awkward to load. Each gun had to be positioned carefully to keep the boat balanced. The horses that pulled the guns crossed separately, frightened by the water and ice. Loading and unloading took time, and time was something Washington didn't have. He planned to have everyone across by midnight, giving his army several hours to march nine miles to Trenton and attack at dawn.

But the crossing took far longer. Ice slowed everything, and darkness made the work harder. Each trip took longer than the one before as men grew colder and more exhausted. Boats went back and forth for hours—loading soldiers, rowing across, unloading, and returning for more. The hours crawled by.

Washington himself crossed early, then stood on the New Jersey shore watching his army slowly accumulate. He paced in the snow, checking his pocket watch by lantern light, watching the minutes slip away. By midnight—when everyone was supposed to be across—only about half the force had made it.

Washington Crossing the Delaware by Emanuel Leutze.[70]

It was three o'clock in the morning before the last boat arrived. The entire force was finally across, but they were three hours behind schedule. Dawn would come around seven. The march to Trenton would take at least three hours, maybe longer in the dark and snow. Washington did the math. They would arrive in daylight, not darkness. The element of surprise would be gone.

Every calculation suggested calling off the attack. They were behind schedule, two of the three forces had failed to cross, and the men were exhausted. A cautious commander would have turned back.

But Washington had committed too much to retreat. Turning around meant failure after all the hardship they had endured. They had come this far through terrible conditions. They might never get another chance. Washington gave the order to advance.

The march to Trenton was a test of endurance. The storm had intensified. Snow mixed with sleet and freezing rain. The wind cut through their clothing. The road turned to mud and slush. Soldiers slipped and fell, hands too numb to grip muskets. Some wrapped their feet in rags because they had no shoes, and the rags quickly froze. Officers later wrote of seeing blood in the snow. Several soldiers collapsed and didn't rise again, but the column couldn't stop.

Washington rode up and down the line, encouraging his men. Officers struggled to keep units together in the darkness and storm. The army wasn't marching in neat formations; it was more like a mob stumbling through the night, driven by desperation and Washington's will.

About four miles from Trenton, Washington divided his force into two columns. General Nathanael Greene took one and approached from the north along Pennington Road. General John Sullivan took the other and approached from the west along River Road. The plan was to attack simultaneously, trapping the Hessians in the town. Coordinating in the dark through unfamiliar terrain was nearly impossible. They had to rely on timing and hope both columns arrived together.

As the gray morning light came through the storm, the two columns neared Trenton. The small town sat on flat ground near the Delaware River. It had about a hundred buildings, mostly houses and shops. The Hessians had quarters throughout the town, with pickets (small units of soldiers) on the roads, but the storm and holiday had made them careless. They had celebrated Christmas and were cold, tired, and likely hungover.

Around eight o'clock, both American columns reached their positions almost simultaneously. Despite the delays and hardships, Washington's army had arrived in the right place at nearly the right time. It was an organizational miracle.

The attack began when American advance parties encountered Hessian pickets. Musket shots rang out. The pickets fell back, firing as they retreated. The storm muffled the sound, and the Americans pressed forward, not giving the Hessians time to organize.

Sullivan's column struck from the west, pushing into town along King and Queen Streets. Greene's men attacked from the north along Pennington Road. American artillery—those same cannons that had been dragged through the snow—was set up at key intersections and fired down the streets. The thunder of cannon fire echoed through the town, waking Hessians who had been sleeping off their celebrations.

Colonel Johann Rall, the Hessian commander, had been warned several times about a possible American attack, but he dismissed the reports. He didn't believe Washington's beaten army could fight again. On Christmas night, Rall attended a party, where he drank heavily. When the alarm sounded on the morning of December 26, he was slow to respond.

The Hessians tried to form up, but chaos ruled. American forces were attacking from multiple directions. Cannon fire tore through their ranks.

The storm made it hard to see or hear orders. Units became separated, officers lost control, and confusion spread. The Hessians were professional soldiers, trained for orderly battle under clear commands. This was not that kind of fight. The Americans had the initiative.

Rall organized a counterattack and led his men forward, but American artillery fire was devastating. Cannonballs tore through the ranks, while musket fire came from houses and fences. Rall was struck by two musket balls and fell from his horse, mortally wounded. With their commander down, the Hessian resistance collapsed.

The battle lasted about ninety minutes. The Hessians tried to retreat but found escape routes blocked. Surrounded and disorganized, officers began surrendering their units. White flags appeared, and the firing ceased.

The Battle of Trenton was a complete American victory. Nearly nine hundred Hessian soldiers were captured, along with their weapons, ammunition, and supplies. Six cannons and thousands of muskets were taken. American casualties were astonishingly light—two men had frozen to death on the march, and only a few were wounded in combat, including Lieutenant James Monroe, the future president.

The Capture of the Hessians at Trenton *by John Trumbull. In the center of the painting is Washington and the mortally wounded Hessian Colonel Johann Rall. On the left, the wounded Lieutenant James Monroe is helped by Dr. John Riker. On the right is Major General Nathanael Greene on horseback.*[71]

The victory was everything Washington had hoped for. His battered army had beaten professional soldiers and captured an entire garrison. The supplies would help sustain them through the winter, but the psychological effect was even greater.

Word spread quickly through the colonies. People who had lost faith began to believe again. The British weren't invincible. The Continental Army could win. Soldiers who had planned to go home reconsidered. Militia units began reforming. The revolution had been saved—at least for the moment.

But Washington knew one victory wasn't enough. The British would retaliate. He persuaded many of his soldiers to extend their enlistments six more weeks with a small bounty and sent urgent appeals for militia reinforcements. By early January, his army numbered about five thousand men again.

Washington recrossed the Delaware into New Jersey. By January 2, 1777, he was back in Trenton. The British responded quickly. Lord Cornwallis, one of Britain's best generals, postponed his winter leave and marched south from New York with about eight thousand troops, determined to trap and destroy Washington's army.

On January 2, Cornwallis's forces pushed toward Trenton, skirmishing with the Americans throughout the day. Washington fought a delaying action, slowing their advance but falling back gradually. By evening, his army was positioned just south of Trenton along Assunpink Creek. The British were in front of them; the creek was behind them. Washington's army was pinned.

Cornwallis could have attacked immediately, but his officers persuaded him to wait until morning. The Americans were trapped, with no escape. Cornwallis reportedly said they had "the old fox" cornered and would catch him at dawn. It was the same mistake British commanders had made before.

Washington had no intention of being there in the morning. That night, he executed another daring escape. He left campfires burning and a small force that made noise to deceive the British sentries, while the main army slipped away on a back road. They circled around the British army, heading northeast toward Princeton, where another garrison was stationed.

The night march was another ordeal. The road had been muddy earlier, but it had frozen into deep ruts after dark. To move silently, the army wrapped artillery wheels with rags. Men marched through the freezing night, exhausted but driven by Washington's determination.

By dawn on January 3, Washington's army approached Princeton. He hadn't planned a major battle—only to raid the British supply depot and move north—but British troops leaving Princeton for Trenton collided with his force on Stony Brook Road.

The initial fighting went badly. General Hugh Mercer's brigade met two British regiments and was driven back. Mercer was bayoneted and mortally wounded. The situation looked dire.

Then Washington arrived. Seeing his troops retreating, he rode forward to rally them, even though he was an enormous target on his white horse. His aides begged him to fall back, but he refused.

Washington organized the retreating men, brought up reinforcements, and personally led a counterattack. He rode at the front, directly into British fire. Witnesses on both sides were astonished. Musket balls flew around him, but none struck. The Americans surged forward, inspired by his courage. The British line broke and retreated toward Princeton, pursued by the Americans.

Fighting continued in the town and around Nassau Hall, the main building of the College of New Jersey (later Princeton University). Some British troops barricaded themselves inside. American artillery fired at the building, and a cannonball reportedly decapitated a portrait of King George II. The remaining British soldiers surrendered.

The Battle of Princeton was another American victory. It was smaller than Trenton, but it was just as vital for morale. In eight days, Washington had won two battles.

Cornwallis, who had expected to capture Washington, now found himself threatened. Washington's army was behind him, between him and his supplies at New Brunswick. Cornwallis had to retreat to avoid being cut off. The British abandoned most of their positions in New Jersey, falling back to New York.

Washington took his exhausted army north to Morristown in the hills of northern New Jersey. The position was excellent. It was defensible, with good sight lines and close enough to threaten British outposts while remaining safe. The army went into winter quarters to rest and rebuild. The immediate crisis was over.

The Trenton-Princeton campaign didn't win the war, but it saved it. The British still had larger armies and greater resources, yet Washington had achieved something more important: he had kept the Continental Army alive and proven it could defeat British regulars. He had restored hope.

Most of all, Washington had shown the qualities that made him indispensable. He had courage—his ride at Princeton proved that—and the rare ability to persevere when reason said to give up. The cause had seemed doomed, yet Washington refused to accept defeat.

Chapter 8: The Turning of the Tide

The British Plan to Split the Colonies

Trenton and Princeton had saved the Continental Army from collapse, but they hadn't won the war. The British still controlled New York City and had vastly superior resources. As 1777 began, British commanders in London developed a new strategy to end the rebellion once and for all. The plan was elegant in its simplicity: cut the colonies in half.

The concept made perfect sense. New England was the heart of the rebellion. Massachusetts, Connecticut, Rhode Island, and New Hampshire had been the most radical colonies, the first to resist British authority, and the source of much of the revolutionary fervor. If New England could be isolated from the other colonies, cut off from supplies and support, the rebellion might collapse. The Southern and Middle Colonies were more moderate, with significant loyalist populations. Without New England's influence, they might make peace with Britain.

The geography practically invited this strategy. The Hudson River Valley provided a natural corridor running north-south through New York. Lake Champlain extended farther north into Canada. If British forces controlled this water route from Canada to New York City, they would effectively split the colonies. Communication and trade between them would become nearly impossible.

The plan called for a three-pronged attack converging on Albany, New York. General John Burgoyne would lead the main force south from Canada, moving down Lake Champlain and then overland to the Hudson River. A smaller force under Lieutenant Colonel Barry St.

Leger would move east from Lake Ontario through the Mohawk Valley. General William Howe's army in New York City would move north up the Hudson. The three forces would meet at Albany, securing the entire corridor and splitting the colonies.

On paper, the plan looked brilliant, even simple. However, it required perfect coordination among three separate armies operating across hundreds of miles of difficult terrain with no reliable way to communicate. Yes, Britain had the troops, the supplies, and the naval power to execute it. The Americans would be forced to defend multiple positions simultaneously, spreading their limited forces thin. Even if one British column failed, the others might succeed. But the plan underestimated how effectively American forces could respond when defending their home territory.

General John Burgoyne, who would lead the main invasion from Canada, was confident to the point of arrogance. He was a veteran officer, a member of Parliament, and a playwright who enjoyed society and entertainment. He believed the American rebellion was a temporary disturbance that would collapse under professional military pressure. He had spent the winter in London lobbying for command of the northern campaign and assuring officials that he could accomplish the mission's objectives.

Burgoyne assembled an army of about eight thousand men at Fort St. Johns on the northern end of Lake Champlain. The force included British regulars, German mercenaries, Canadian militia, and Native American allies. They were well equipped and well supplied. Burgoyne's army was slowed by an enormous baggage train of over one hundred carts carrying not only essential military supplies but also personal luggage and luxuries that reflected the commander's confidence in a swift, easy campaign. The army looked impressive.

In June 1777, Burgoyne's army moved south down Lake Champlain on boats and barges. The first objective was Fort Ticonderoga, the American stronghold guarding the southern end of the lake. The fort had symbolic importance—it was where Ethan Allen and Benedict Arnold had captured British cannons in 1775, the same cannons Washington had dragged to Boston to force the British evacuation.

The American garrison at Ticonderoga numbered about 2,500 men under General Arthur St. Clair. When Burgoyne's much larger force arrived and began surrounding the fort, St. Clair faced an impossible situation. The British positioned artillery on a high hill overlooking the fort, making the position untenable. On July 5, St. Clair evacuated the fort under cover of darkness, retreating south toward Albany. He saved his army from certain capture, but the loss of Ticonderoga without a major battle provoked outrage in Congress and among the public. St. Clair was widely condemned as a coward. It would take a court-martial the following year to officially clear his name and vindicate his decision.

Burgoyne occupied Ticonderoga and continued south, confident of success. The Americans were retreating before him. Albany was less than one hundred miles away. But despite the successful capture of the fort, Burgoyne's campaign was facing serious problems. The easy phase was already over.

The terrain between Ticonderoga and Albany was heavily forested, swampy in places, and crisscrossed with creeks and ravines. There were few good roads. Burgoyne's large baggage train became a massive liability. The army could move only a few miles per day as men cleared roads and built bridges. American forces under General Philip Schuyler made the going even slower by destroying bridges, felling trees across roads, and diverting streams to flood the path ahead.

Burgoyne's supply line stretched back to Canada, and it was growing longer and more vulnerable every day. His army needed enormous quantities of food, ammunition, and forage for the horses. The deeper into New York he went, the harder it became to keep the army supplied. Meanwhile, American militia forces were gathering, watching his movements, and harassing his foraging parties.

By late July, Burgoyne had reached Fort Edward on the Hudson River, but his advance had slowed to a crawl. He needed supplies, especially horses to haul his artillery and wagons. His scouts reported that the Americans had supplies and horses stockpiled at Bennington, in what's now Vermont. Burgoyne decided to send a detachment to raid Bennington and bring back what they needed.

The Bennington expedition turned into a disaster. On August 16, a force of about seven hundred men under Lieutenant Colonel Friedrich Baum encountered a much larger American militia force commanded by General John Stark. The militia, mostly New Hampshire men, attacked aggressively. After fierce fighting, the German troops were overwhelmed and captured. A relief column sent to help them was also defeated. Burgoyne lost nearly one thousand men—killed, wounded, or captured—along with artillery and supplies he desperately needed.

The defeat at Bennington was the first clear sign that Burgoyne's campaign was in trouble. Meanwhile, the other two prongs of the British strategy were failing. St. Leger's expedition from the west bogged down in a siege at Fort Stanwix in the Mohawk Valley. American forces under Benedict Arnold marched to relieve the fort, and St. Leger's Native American allies abandoned him. He was forced to retreat back to Canada; his part of the plan completely failed.

More critically, General Howe never moved north from New York to support Burgoyne. Instead, Howe had decided to pursue a different objective entirely. He loaded his army onto ships and sailed south to attack Philadelphia. Howe's decision has puzzled historians for centuries. He had received orders about the overall plan, but the orders were ambiguous enough that he felt free to pursue what he saw as a more important target. Capturing Philadelphia, the American capital, seemed more valuable than a slow march up the Hudson.

Howe's decision left Burgoyne on his own, pushing deeper into enemy territory without support. By early September, Burgoyne had crossed to the western side of the Hudson River near Saratoga, about thirty miles north of Albany. He was now committed. Crossing back would be difficult. His supplies were running low, and the supply lines stretched dangerously far back to Canada. His army was exhausted from months of difficult marching. And ahead of him, American forces were gathering in growing numbers. His situation was becoming more precarious every day.

The Americans had a new commander for the northern army. General Horatio Gates had replaced Philip Schuyler in August. Gates was a cautious, methodical officer who understood defensive warfare. He chose a strong position at Bemis Heights, overlooking the river road that Burgoyne would have to use. The American forces dug in, building fortifications designed by Polish engineer Thaddeus Kosciuszko. The position was naturally strong and made stronger by the earthworks. If Burgoyne wanted to reach Albany, he would have to go through the Americans at Bemis Heights.

The Battle of Saratoga: A Stunning American Victory

By mid-September 1777, Burgoyne's situation was growing desperate, but he refused to admit it. He had come too far to turn back. Retreating to Canada would mean abandoning the entire campaign, admitting failure, and leaving his army vulnerable during a long withdrawal through hostile territory. He decided to push forward and try to break through the American position at Bemis Heights. It was a gamble, but Burgoyne believed his professional troops could defeat the Americans in open battle.

The American position at Bemis Heights was formidable. General Horatio Gates had about nine thousand men, and more militia were arriving daily. The fortifications ran along high ground overlooking the river road. Any British attempt to advance along the road would expose them to devastating fire from above. Burgoyne would have to find another way.

Burgoyne decided to divide his force. He would send one column along the river road to pin the Americans' attention there, while his main force would swing west through the forests and try to flank the American position. It was a complicated maneuver through difficult terrain, but Burgoyne had confidence in his troops' discipline and training.

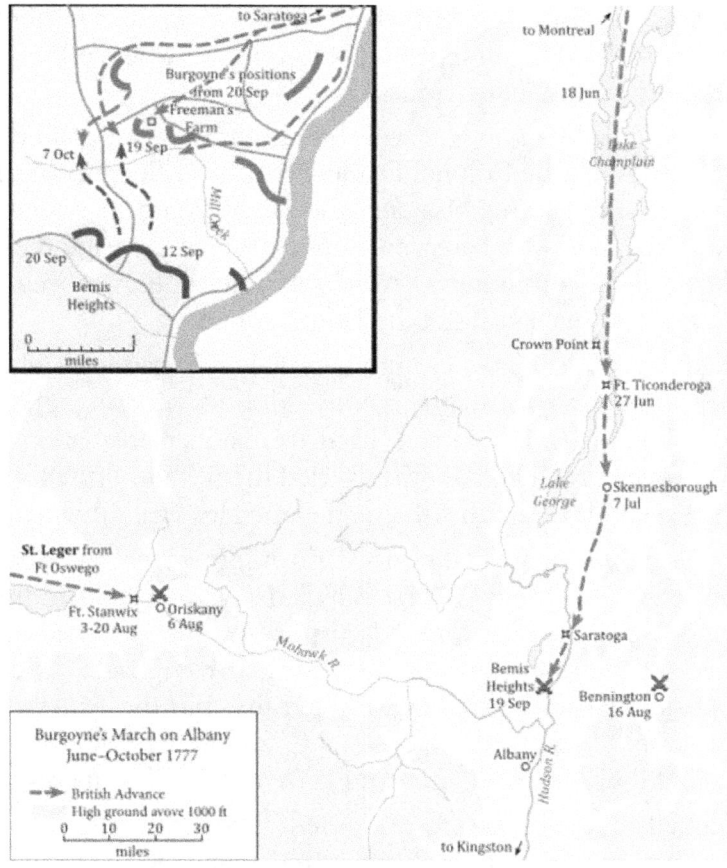

The movements of the Saratoga campaign.[73]

On September 19, Burgoyne's flanking column moved through the woods west of the American position. The column moved slowly, cutting through dense forest, trying to maintain formation in unfamiliar terrain. Around one o'clock in the afternoon, they emerged into a clearing—Freeman's Farm, a small homestead with open fields surrounded by woods.

American scouts had been tracking Burgoyne's movements. When word reached Gates that the British were moving through the forest, one of his subordinate officers demanded permission to attack. That officer was Benedict Arnold, one of the Continental Army's most aggressive and talented combat leaders. Arnold had played a crucial role in the American victory at Ticonderoga back in 1775 and had fought bravely in Canada. He was ambitious, proud, and hungry for glory.

Gates was cautious by nature and wanted to stay in the fortifications and let the British attack prepared positions. But Arnold argued that they should strike the British while they were strung out in the forest, disorganized by the difficult terrain. Gates reluctantly agreed to send out American units to engage the British.

The Battle of Freeman's Farm began in the early afternoon as American troops, led by Colonel Daniel Morgan's riflemen, attacked the British force in the clearing. Morgan's men were expert marksmen, many of them frontiersmen who had grown up hunting in the wilderness. They used turkey calls to communicate with each other as they moved through the forest, a sound that confused the British soldiers.

The fighting at Freeman's Farm was brutal and chaotic. Units fired at each other from the edge of the woods. Men took cover behind trees, fences, and buildings. The British tried to maintain formation and use disciplined volley fire. The Americans used the terrain, firing from cover and falling back before the British could come close with their bayonets.

The battle raged for several hours. British forces held the clearing but took heavy casualties. Arnold personally led several attacks, riding along the line and urging his men forward. His energy and aggression kept the Americans attacking even when they were driven back. The British artillery, positioned in the clearing, poured fire into the American lines. The Americans had lighter guns that couldn't match the British firepower, but they had more men and kept pressing the attack.

By nightfall, both sides were exhausted. The British held Freeman's Farm, but they had lost about six hundred men killed and wounded—

casualties they could not afford. The Americans had lost fewer men and could absorb their losses more easily since militia reinforcements continued arriving. More importantly, the Americans had stopped the British advance. Burgoyne had not broken through the American position.

Burgoyne now faced a critical decision. His advance had stalled, and casualties were mounting. However, he still believed he could succeed if he pressed forward. He decided to wait for the reinforcements and supplies he hoped were coming from New York, though no such help was actually on the way.

For the next two and a half weeks, the two armies faced each other. Burgoyne's situation grew worse daily. His supplies dwindled. Desertions increased, particularly among his Canadian militia and Native American allies, who saw that the campaign was failing and went home. American forces grew stronger as militia units from across New York and New England arrived. By early October, Gates commanded over fifteen thousand men, nearly twice Burgoyne's strength.

Meanwhile, Benedict Arnold and Horatio Gates quarreled bitterly. Arnold felt he deserved credit for the victory at Freeman's Farm, but Gates had written his official report without mentioning Arnold's role. Arnold was furious. The two men argued, and Gates stripped Arnold of his command, essentially confining him to camp. It was a petty move that reflected the tension between Gates's cautious defensive strategy and Arnold's aggressive battlefield instincts.

By October 7, Burgoyne could wait no longer. His supplies were nearly exhausted. No reinforcements had arrived. He had to either attack or retreat. He decided on one more attempt to break the American line. He formed a reconnaissance force of about 1,500 men—his best troops— and sent them to probe the American position, looking for a weakness they could exploit.

The Second Battle of Saratoga, also called the Battle of Bemis Heights, began in the early afternoon of October 7. Burgoyne's reconnaissance force advanced into open fields near the American position and immediately came under heavy fire. American forces under General Enoch Poor attacked the British left. Daniel Morgan's riflemen struck the British right. The British formation began to crumble under the concentrated attacks.

Benedict Arnold, though officially relieved of command, couldn't stay away from the fighting. When he heard the battle beginning, he mounted his horse and rode toward the sound of gunfire. Gates ordered him to stay in camp, but Arnold ignored the order. He rode onto the battlefield and began rallying American troops and leading charges.

Arnold's presence transformed the American attack. While Gates had established the formidable defensive position and overall strategy at Bemis Heights, it was Arnold's tactical brilliance and personal bravery on the battlefield that turned the engagement into a decisive victory. He rode along the American line, pointing out targets, urging men forward, and personally leading assaults on British positions. He was everywhere at once and fearless in his exposure to enemy fire. Soldiers who had been fighting cautiously suddenly pushed forward more aggressively with Arnold leading them.

The British line broke. Their troops fell back toward their fortifications in confusion. Arnold pursued them, riding directly at a fortified position called the Breymann Redoubt and urging the troops to follow him. American soldiers stormed the redoubt. In the chaos of close-quarters fighting, Arnold's horse was shot and fell on him, breaking his leg—the same leg that had been wounded at Quebec. As he lay pinned beneath his dead horse, an American soldier nearly shot him, not recognizing him in the confusion.

The Americans captured the Breymann Redoubt, a key position in the British defenses. The British fell back to their inner fortifications, having lost another six hundred men. Burgoyne's army was now completely trapped. His defenses had been breached. He had perhaps five thousand effective troops left, surrounded by over fifteen thousand Americans. His supplies were gone. There was no possibility of reinforcement. Retreat was no longer feasible.

For the next few days, Burgoyne tried to find a way out. He considered attempting to fight his way north back to Ticonderoga, but his officers convinced him it was impossible. The Americans surrounded his position and controlled all the roads. Rain poured down, making conditions miserable for his troops, who were camped in the open with inadequate supplies.

On October 13, Burgoyne called a council of war with his officers. He proposed several desperate options, but his subordinates told him the truth: the army was trapped and beaten. Further resistance would only lead to pointless casualties. Burgoyne finally accepted reality. On October 17, 1777, he surrendered his entire army to General Gates.

The surrender ceremony was carefully choreographed to preserve British dignity. Burgoyne, dressed in full uniform, met Gates and formally surrendered his sword. Gates immediately returned it—a gesture of respect between professional officers. The British troops marched out of their fortifications with their colors flying and drums beating and then laid down their arms. Nearly six thousand British and German soldiers became prisoners of war.

The terms of surrender were relatively generous. The captured troops were supposed to be allowed to return to Britain on the condition that they wouldn't fight again in America. They became known as the "Convention Army" after the convention that established the surrender terms. The Continental Congress later violated these terms, keeping most of the prisoners in America for years. Congress didn't trust that Britain would honor its end of the bargain, and they worried that experienced soldiers would simply be redeployed against them. So, they stalled, found technicalities, and kept the captured army on American soil.

The Battle of Saratoga was the most significant American victory of the war to that point. An entire British army had been forced to surrender. The grand British strategy to split the colonies had failed. Burgoyne had marched into New York with confidence and professional troops, but poor planning, difficult terrain, overstretched supply lines, and determined American resistance had destroyed his army.

The victory had immediate effects on American morale. After years of defeats and setbacks, the Continental Army had won a major, undeniable victory. They had beaten British regulars, not just in a small raid like Trenton but in a sustained campaign. The victory proved that American forces could win more than just tactical surprises—they could win strategic campaigns.

But Saratoga's most important effect wouldn't be felt in America. The news of the victory would travel across the Atlantic to Europe, where it would convince France that the Americans might actually win their war for independence. France's decision to support America would transform the entire conflict.

The French Alliance: The World Turned Upside Down

From the moment Americans declared independence, they knew they would need help from Europe. Fighting Britain alone would be nearly impossible. Britain had the world's most powerful navy, a professional army, vast financial resources, and a global empire to draw upon. The American colonies had none of these things. If America was going to win, it needed a powerful ally. And there was really only one option: France.

France and Britain were ancient enemies. They had fought each other for centuries in a long series of wars over territory, trade, and power. Most recently, they had fought the Seven Years' War—the same conflict Americans called the French and Indian War. Britain had won decisively, taking Canada and other French territories. The French defeat had been humiliating and expensive. Ever since 1763, France had been looking for an opportunity to weaken Britain and perhaps recover some of what it had lost.

The American rebellion offered France exactly that opportunity. If the American colonies broke away from Britain, the British Empire would be dramatically weakened. Britain would lose its most valuable colonies and the trade that came with them. For France, this wasn't primarily about ideology or sympathy for republican ideals. It was cold, strategic calculation. The rebellion offered a golden opportunity to weaken their greatest rival and restore the European balance of power that had been shattered by France's humiliating defeat in the Seven Years' War. France wouldn't need to fight a direct war or conquer territory. They could simply help the Americans and watch Britain defeat itself.

However, France faced a dilemma. If France entered the war and America was defeated anyway, France would have gained nothing and risked war with Britain for no reason. The French government wanted proof that Americans could actually win before committing to open support. Supporting a colonial rebellion against a monarchy was also ideologically awkward for an absolute monarchy, though this concern was secondary to the strategic opportunity.

The American diplomat in Paris was Benjamin Franklin, and he was perfectly suited for the task. Franklin was already famous in France as a scientist and philosopher. His experiments with electricity had made him a celebrity among French intellectuals. He was witty, charming, and shrewd. He understood how to navigate French politics and how to present America's case in terms that would appeal to French interests.

Franklin arrived in Paris in December 1776, just as Washington's army was retreating across New Jersey. The timing was terrible. The American cause looked like it was collapsing. Franklin had to convince the French to support what appeared to be a failing rebellion. He did so with patience, charm, and careful cultivation of French opinion. He presented himself as the embodiment of American virtue—simple, honest, and republican. Franklin wore a fur cap instead of the fashionable wigs of French aristocrats. He played the role of the American philosopher-patriot, and French society loved him.

But charm alone wouldn't secure an alliance. The French government, led by Foreign Minister Comte de Vergennes, wanted proof that Americans could actually win before committing France to open support. They were willing to provide secret aid—money, weapons, and supplies shipped through dummy companies—but they wouldn't openly ally with America until they saw evidence that the investment would pay off.

For most of 1777, Franklin worked to keep French interest alive while American military fortunes remained uncertain. Then, in December 1777, news reached Paris of the American victory at Saratoga. An entire British army had surrendered. The Americans had won a major campaign. Suddenly, American independence seemed possible rather than just a desperate dream.

The news of Saratoga transformed the diplomatic situation. Vergennes and King Louis XVI decided that America was worth supporting openly. If colonists could win victories like Saratoga, they might actually succeed in breaking away from Britain. And if France didn't act quickly, America might negotiate peace with Britain before France could benefit from British weakness.

In February 1778, France and America signed two treaties. The Treaty of Amity and Commerce established trade relations between the two nations, recognizing American independence. More importantly, the Treaty of Alliance was a military pact. France and America became formal allies. France committed to fighting until American independence was secured. Neither nation would make peace with Britain without the other's consent. France would provide military forces, naval support, and financial aid.

The French alliance changed everything about the war. America was no longer a collection of rebel colonies fighting alone against the British Empire. America now had a powerful ally with a professional army and, most critically, a navy that could challenge British naval superiority. The war transformed from a colonial rebellion into a global conflict between European powers, with America as one of the main battlegrounds.

The immediate practical benefits of the alliance were enormous. French money helped finance the Continental Army. French weapons, ammunition, and supplies flowed to America in much larger quantities than the secret aid that had come before. French military officers volunteered to serve with American forces, bringing European military expertise. Some, like the Marquis de Lafayette, became heroes of the American cause. Lafayette, who had arrived in America in 1777 at age nineteen, became like an adopted son to Washington and a symbol of French-American friendship.

However, the most important French contribution was its navy. The Royal Navy had given Britain unchallenged control of American waters. British forces could land anywhere on the coast. They could supply their armies by sea and blockade American ports. American forces had no way to counter British naval power. The French Navy changed that.

The entry of France into the war forced Britain to reconsider its entire strategy. Britain now had to worry about French attacks on its possessions in the Caribbean, in India, and in the Mediterranean. British forces had to be diverted from America to protect other parts of the empire. The British navy, which had dominated American waters, now had to worry about encountering French fleets. The comfortable assumption that Britain could win the war simply by applying superior force was no longer valid.

Spain joined the war against Britain in 1779, though not as a formal American ally. Spain had its own interests and grievances against Britain. The Spanish primarily fought to recover Gibraltar and other territories, not to support American independence. Still, Spanish entry into the war further stretched British resources and complicated British strategic planning.

Even the Netherlands would eventually be drawn into the conflict, further isolating Britain diplomatically and economically. What had started as Britain's attempt to suppress a colonial rebellion had mushroomed into a global war that Britain was fighting essentially alone against most of Europe.

The French alliance didn't guarantee American victory, and it didn't end the war quickly. Britain was still powerful and determined. British forces still controlled New York and would launch new campaigns in the South. Years of hard fighting remained. However, the alliance fundamentally changed the nature of the conflict and America's chances of winning.

Perhaps most importantly, the alliance legitimized American independence in European eyes. When France formally recognized American independence and allied with America, it signaled to the world that America was a real nation, not just rebellious colonists. Other European nations followed France's lead in recognizing America, opening diplomatic and commercial relationships. America entered the community of nations.

French involvement in the American Revolution would also have profound consequences for France itself. French officers and soldiers who fought in America saw republican government in action. They brought revolutionary ideas back to France. The enormous debt France accumulated supporting America would contribute to the financial crisis that would trigger the French Revolution in 1789. In helping America break free from the monarchy, France planted seeds that would eventually grow into its own revolution.

For now, though, in 1778, what mattered was that America had gained a powerful ally. The Battle of Saratoga had proven that Americans could win major victories. The revolution that had seemed on the verge of collapse just a year earlier now had a real chance of success. The tide was turning.

Chapter 9: The War in the South and the Final Showdown

A New Strategy: The Southern Campaign

After the Battle of Saratoga and the French alliance, the war in the North settled into a frustrating stalemate. The British held New York City. Washington's army camped in the countryside around the city, too weak to attack but strong enough to prevent the British from controlling much territory beyond their fortifications. Both armies watched each other and skirmished occasionally, but neither could gain a decisive advantage. The war had reached an impasse.

That stalemate might have been impossible just months earlier. During the brutal winter of 1777–1778, Washington's army nearly disintegrated at Valley Forge, Pennsylvania. The soldiers arrived exhausted after months of campaigning and defeats around Philadelphia. They had no proper shelter. Men built crude log huts that barely kept out the cold. There weren't enough blankets. Clothing wore out, and replacements never came. Soldiers marched barefoot in the snow, leaving bloody tracks. You could follow the army's movements by the trail of blood.

The food situation was desperate. Some days there was no food at all. Men boiled their shoes to make something they could swallow. They survived on "firecake"—flour and water mixed into a paste and cooked over flames. Disease spread through the crowded, filthy camp. Typhus, typhoid fever, dysentery, and pneumonia killed thousands. About one in six men died that winter. Others simply walked away. Desertions climbed steadily as soldiers decided anything was better than starving and freezing at Valley Forge.

Why was the supply system such a disaster? The Continental Congress had no money and limited authority. State governments were supposed to provide supplies, but they often didn't. The army's quartermaster department was disorganized; supplies that did exist often sat in warehouses while soldiers starved because no one could coordinate transportation. Farmers near Valley Forge sometimes had food but wouldn't sell it for the nearly worthless Continental currency. They'd rather sell to the British in Philadelphia for gold. Washington watched his army waste away and could do almost nothing about it.

But that winter also brought transformation. A Prussian officer named Baron Friedrich von Steuben arrived in February 1778 and revolutionized how the Continental Army fought. The men didn't know formal military drills or how to fight as coordinated units. They loaded muskets differently. They couldn't march in formation. In battle, they were brave but chaotic. Steuben, who spoke almost no English and had exaggerated his military credentials to get the job, created a training program from scratch. He cursed in German and French while translators shouted commands in English. He started with a model company of 120 men, training them personally, and then used those men to train others. He drilled them relentlessly on the basics: how to stand, how to march, how to load and fire in synchronized volleys, and how to move as a unit under fire.

Steuben also simplified everything. European armies had complicated drill manuals with dozens of movements. Steuben cut it down to what actually worked in American conditions. He wrote it all down in a manual called *Regulations for the Order and Discipline of the Troops of the United States*. It became the official drill book for the US Army and remained in use for decades.

By spring, the ragged survivors of Valley Forge had become a disciplined fighting force capable of standing toe-to-toe with British regulars. When they marched out to confront the British that June at the Battle of Monmouth, they fought with a cohesion and professionalism they'd never shown before. Valley Forge had nearly destroyed Washington's army. Instead, it forged it into something far more dangerous.

Meanwhile, British strategists in London looked for a way to break the deadlock. They needed a new approach—a different theater where they might have better success. Their attention turned south to the Carolinas and Georgia. These colonies seemed to offer unique opportunities that the northern colonies did not.

The South had substantial loyalist populations, or so the British believed. Many Southerners had remained loyal to the Crown throughout the conflict. If British forces moved into the South, these loyalists would rally to the king's standard, provide intelligence, join militia units, and help the British control the countryside. The Southern Colonies also produced valuable crops—tobacco, rice, and indigo—that Britain wanted to secure. Economically and strategically, the South seemed worth the effort.

The plan was to move south, capture the major port cities, and then expand control inland. Local loyalists would help maintain order. The Southern Colonies would be brought back under royal control. Once the South was secured, British forces could move north, squeezing the rebellion between armies advancing from both directions. The Continental Army would be forced to fight on multiple fronts and would eventually collapse. It was a sound strategic concept that addressed the failures of previous campaigns.

The southern strategy began in late 1778. A British force sailed from New York and captured Savannah, Georgia, in December. The city fell quickly. British forces then spread out across Georgia, establishing a network of outposts. By early 1779, Georgia was largely under British control. The first phase of the southern campaign had succeeded brilliantly.

Encouraged by this success, the British prepared for the next objective: Charleston, South Carolina. Charleston was the largest and wealthiest city in the South. It was a major port and the political center of South Carolina. If Charleston fell, South Carolina would likely follow. The campaign to take Charleston would be the largest British military operation in the South during the entire war.

In December 1779, a British fleet carrying about 8,500 troops under General Sir Henry Clinton sailed from New York toward Charleston. The fleet arrived in February 1780 and began landing troops south of the city. The Americans had about 5,500 Continental and militia troops defending Charleston, commanded by General Benjamin Lincoln.

Lincoln had orders from Congress to hold the city at all costs. Those orders would prove disastrous.

The siege of Charleston lasted from late March to early May 1780. British forces surrounded the city by land while British warships blockaded the harbor. They dug siege trenches, moving their artillery closer day by day in the methodical European style. The Americans were trapped. Their only hope was that relief forces might attack the British from behind and break the siege. But no relief came.

The siege of Charleston by Alonzo Chappel.[78]

By early May, the situation inside Charleston was hopeless. British artillery was pounding the city. Supplies were running low, and disease was spreading. There was no realistic possibility of escape or relief. On May 12, 1780, General Lincoln surrendered the entire garrison. Nearly 5,500 American soldiers became prisoners of war, along with ships, supplies, and ammunition. It was the largest single surrender of American troops in the entire war and a devastating blow to the American cause in the South.

British forces quickly moved to occupy the rest of the state, establishing a network of fortified posts throughout the backcountry. By June 1780, Georgia and South Carolina were under British control. The southern strategy seemed to be working perfectly.

General Clinton returned to his headquarters in New York, leaving Lord Charles Cornwallis with operational command of British forces in the South. Cornwallis was an aggressive, confident officer who believed he could crush what remained of American resistance in the Carolinas and then move north into Virginia and eventually link up with British forces in the North. Victory seemed within reach.

Congress desperately needed to send a new army south to contest British control. They chose General Horatio Gates—the victor of Saratoga—to command. Gates was given a small force of Continental troops and told to raise militia along the way. He marched south in the summer of 1780 to confront the British.

On August 16, 1780, Gates's army met Cornwallis's forces near Camden, South Carolina. The Battle of Camden was a complete disaster for the Americans. Gates's militia troops panicked almost immediately when the British attacked. They broke and ran, many throwing away their weapons as they fled. Gates himself fled the battlefield, riding nearly two hundred miles in three days to escape. His army was shattered, with losses estimated at nearly two thousand men killed, wounded, or captured. British losses were minimal.

The defeat at Camden, following so closely after the loss of Charleston, seemed to doom the American cause in the South. Two major American armies had been destroyed in less than four months. British forces controlled the entire region. Loyalists were coming forward in large numbers. The southern strategy was succeeding beyond British expectations.

But beneath the surface, the situation was more complicated than it appeared. British control of the South was shallow. They held the cities and major towns, but controlling the vast countryside was another matter entirely. The British had assumed that loyalists would help them control the territory. Some did, but many were intimidated by their patriot neighbors or simply wanted to stay out of the conflict. The British also made a crucial mistake: they treated the civilian population harshly, even those who claimed loyalty to the Crown.

British and loyalist forces in the South often engaged in brutal reprisals against anyone suspected of supporting the rebellion. Homes were burned, property was seized, and people were imprisoned or executed without trial.

One of the most notorious incidents occurred at Waxhaws in South Carolina on May 29, 1780. A British cavalry force under Lieutenant Colonel Banastre Tarleton caught up with a retreating Continental regiment commanded by Colonel Abraham Buford. The Americans were outnumbered and tried to surrender. Buford raised a white flag, but Tarleton's men didn't stop. They kept charging, slashing with sabers and bayoneting men who had already thrown down their weapons and raised their hands. Soldiers begging for mercy were cut down where they stood. The killing continued even after organized resistance had ended. Of Buford's 420 men, 113 were killed, and another 150 were so badly wounded they couldn't be moved. Only about fifty men escaped unharmed.

The brutality at Waxhaws shocked both sides. Patriots called it a massacre and accused Tarleton of ordering his men to give "no quarter"—to take no prisoners. "Tarleton's Quarter" became a rallying cry for American forces in the South, and some used it to justify their own refusal to take British prisoners.

These harsh tactics, intended to intimidate the population into submission, had the opposite effect. They created resentment and drove people into active resistance. Men who might have stayed neutral picked up weapons and joined patriot militia units. The British were creating the very resistance they sought to suppress.

The war in the South was about to enter a new and vicious phase. It would become a guerrilla war, fought not by organized armies in open battles but by irregular forces using hit-and-run tactics. The British would find that conquering territory and holding it were two very different challenges.

Guerrilla Warfare and a Grinding War of Attrition

After the disasters at Charleston and Camden, the American military presence in the South seemed finished. But war isn't just fought by regular armies on battlefields. In the Carolina backcountry, a different kind of war was beginning—one that the British were unprepared for and couldn't win.

Patriot militia leaders emerged throughout South Carolina and North Carolina, leading bands of fighters who knew the terrain intimately. These weren't professional soldiers. They were farmers, hunters, and frontiersmen who fought on their own terms. They would strike British outposts or supply trains, inflict casualties, and disappear back into the swamps and forests before the British could respond. They avoided pitched battles against superior British forces and instead wore down the enemy through constant harassment.

The most famous of these militia leaders was Francis Marion, known as the "Swamp Fox." Marion operated in the swamps and marshlands of eastern South Carolina with a force that rarely numbered more than a few dozen men. He would emerge from the swamps, attack a British post or supply convoy, and vanish back into terrain that British troops couldn't navigate. British officers sent forces to hunt him down, but Marion was always gone before they arrived. His raids disrupted British supply lines and forced the British to garrison more troops at defensive positions—troops that couldn't be used offensively.

Other partisan leaders operated similarly. Thomas Sumter, called the "Gamecock," led militia forces in central South Carolina. Andrew Pickens commanded patriot fighters along the Georgia border. These men and their bands kept resistance alive when the Continental Army had been driven from the region. They prevented the British from controlling the countryside and made it dangerous for loyalists to openly support the Crown.

British commanders found themselves in an impossible position. They controlled the major towns and cities, but they couldn't move supplies or communications through the countryside without heavy guards. Every road became dangerous. Every foraging expedition risked ambush. British soldiers were spread across dozens of isolated posts, each needing supplies and reinforcements, but the supply lines connecting them were under constant attack.

In October 1780, a significant patriot victory provided a boost to American morale. At Kings Mountain, near the border between the Carolinas, a force of about one thousand British loyalist militia was surrounded and destroyed by frontier militia forces. The loyalists took position on a hilltop, assuming the high ground would give them an advantage. But the patriot militia, many of them expert marksmen, used the trees for cover and picked off the defenders. The loyalist commander was killed, and his entire force was killed, wounded, or captured. The victory at Kings Mountain showed that American forces could still win significant engagements and intimidated loyalists who might have been considering active support for the British.

The Battle of Kings Mountain.[74]

Meanwhile, Congress had to replace Horatio Gates after his disgrace at Camden. They made one of the best decisions of the war: they appointed Nathanael Greene to command the southern army. Greene was one of Washington's most trusted generals, a self-taught military strategist who understood both conventional and irregular warfare. He had fought in nearly every major campaign in the North and had learned from both victories and defeats.

Greene took command in December 1780 and immediately assessed the situation. He had only about two thousand Continental troops that were poorly supplied and demoralized. Cornwallis commanded a larger, better-equipped British force. Greene couldn't win a direct confrontation, but he didn't need to. Greene understood that his goal wasn't to destroy the British army in a single battle—it was to make the British occupation of the South unsustainable.

Greene developed a strategy of exhaustion. He would avoid major battles unless the circumstances strongly favored the Americans. He would keep his army intact and mobile, forcing the British to chase him across the Carolinas. He would coordinate with the partisan militia leaders, supporting their raids and using them to gather intelligence. He would make the British wear themselves out trying to control territory they couldn't hold.

In January 1781, Greene made a bold decision. He split his already small army, sending half under General Daniel Morgan west toward the Appalachian frontier. Dividing one's force in the face of a superior enemy violated basic military doctrine, but Greene had a purpose. By splitting his army, he forced Cornwallis to make a choice: keep his army concentrated and watch the Americans operate in two places at once, or divide his own force to pursue both American columns.

Cornwallis divided his force. He sent a column under Lieutenant Colonel Banastre Tarleton to pursue Morgan. Tarleton was an aggressive cavalry commander known for his ruthless tactics and, among Americans, for brutal treatment of prisoners. His pursuit of Morgan would lead to one of the most tactically brilliant American victories of the war.

On January 17, 1781, Tarleton caught up with Morgan at a place called Cowpens in western South Carolina. Morgan had about one thousand men, a mix of Continental troops and militia. He chose his ground carefully and deployed his forces in an unconventional formation. He placed his militia in front, knowing they were likely to break and run when facing British regulars. However, instead of seeing this as a weakness, Morgan incorporated it into his plan. He told the militia to fire two volleys and then retreat behind the Continental line. The militia did exactly that.

When the militia fell back, Tarleton's forces charged forward, thinking the Americans were breaking. But they ran into Morgan's Continental troops, who stood firm and delivered devastating volleys. At the most crucial moment, American cavalry under Colonel William Washington charged into the British flank. The British force, which had been pursuing what it thought was a defeated enemy, suddenly found itself surrounded and outnumbered. Tarleton's force was destroyed. Over eight hundred British soldiers were captured, and Tarleton barely escaped with a remnant of his men.

The Battle of Cowpens by William Ranney.[75]

The Battle of Cowpens was a masterpiece of tactical planning. Morgan had used his militia's weaknesses as part of a deliberate plan and had perfectly executed a double envelopment—the same maneuver Hannibal had used at Cannae nearly two thousand years earlier. It was proof that American commanders had learned their craft and could beat British professionals through superior tactics.

Cornwallis was furious. He had lost a significant portion of his army, and his aggressive subordinate had been humiliated. He became obsessed with catching and destroying Greene's and Morgan's forces. To increase his army's speed, he made the drastic decision to destroy a significant portion of his baggage train, burning wagons, supplies, and equipment that would slow the pursuit. He would chase the Americans down and crush them.

What followed was one of the most famous pursuits in military history. Cornwallis chased Greene's army across North Carolina for weeks in the dead of winter. The armies raced toward the Dan River, the border between North Carolina and Virginia. If Greene could cross the river, he would be safe. If Cornwallis caught him first, Greene's army would be destroyed.

Greene reached the Dan River first, barely ahead of Cornwallis. He collected boats and ferried his army across to safety in Virginia. Cornwallis arrived at the river to find the Americans on the far shore and no boats to pursue them. The exhausting chase had accomplished nothing. Cornwallis's army was worn out, deep in North Carolina, far from its supply base in South Carolina, and no closer to destroying the American army.

Greene rested and resupplied in Virginia, then crossed back into North Carolina, gathering militia reinforcements. He was now ready to fight. On March 15, 1781, Greene's army met Cornwallis at Guilford Courthouse in North Carolina. Greene had about 4,400 men, more than half of them militia. Cornwallis had about 2,100 professional soldiers.

The Battle of Guilford Courthouse was fierce and bloody. Greene used a similar deployment to Morgan's at Cowpens, placing militia in front to absorb the first British assault, then falling back to Continental troops in stronger positions. The British attacked aggressively, pushing through the American lines in savage close-quarters fighting. At the end of the day, the British held the battlefield, but they had been devastated. Cornwallis lost over five hundred men—more than a quarter of his army. Greene's losses were lower, and his army remained intact.

Technically, Guilford Courthouse was a British victory because they held the field, but it was a Pyrrhic victory. Cornwallis couldn't afford to lose a quarter of his army in battles he "won." After the battle, he had to withdraw toward the coast to rest and resupply. Meanwhile, Greene's army, though defeated on the field, was still operational and still a threat.

This was Greene's strategy in action. He didn't need to win battles in the traditional sense. He just needed to make the British wear themselves down chasing him while the partisan militias controlled the countryside.

After the Battle of Guilford Courthouse, Cornwallis made a fateful decision. He marched his exhausted army east to Wilmington on the North Carolina coast and then decided to abandon the Carolinas entirely and march north into Virginia. He believed that Virginia was the key to controlling the South. If he could conquer Virginia, the Carolinas would eventually fall. It was a strategic gamble that reflected his frustration with the grinding war of attrition in the Carolinas.

Greene didn't follow Cornwallis into Virginia. Instead, he turned south back into South Carolina. With Cornwallis gone, Greene could attack the British outposts that Cornwallis had left behind. Over the following months, Greene and the partisan leaders systematically reduced British control in South Carolina. They attacked British posts one by one—some they captured, others they besieged until the British abandoned them. Greene fought several more battles at Hobkirk's Hill, Ninety-Six, and Eutaw Springs. He lost most of them in the tactical sense, but each battle cost the British dearly in casualties they couldn't replace.

By late 1781, British control of the South had collapsed everywhere except Charleston and Savannah. They held two port cities but had lost the interior. The southern strategy, which had seemed so successful after the capture of Savannah and Charleston, had failed. The British had conquered territory but couldn't hold it.

Meanwhile, Cornwallis's decision to march into Virginia would lead directly to the climactic conclusion of the war.

Yorktown: The World's End

In the spring of 1781, Lord Cornwallis marched his army into Virginia, convinced that this was where the war would be decided. Virginia was wealthy, populous, and strategically important. It was also Washington's home state and the political center of the Southern Colonies. If Cornwallis could control Virginia, he could threaten the other states from a position of strength.

Upon arriving in Virginia, Cornwallis took command of the British forces already operating there, which included a contingent led by the now-infamous traitor Benedict Arnold. Yes, that Benedict Arnold. The hero of Saratoga had turned traitor in 1780, selling military secrets to the British and attempting to surrender the strategic fortress at West Point. When his plot was discovered, Arnold fled to British lines and was given a command in the British army. His presence in Virginia, commanding loyalist forces, added a bitter note to the conflict.

Washington sent the Marquis de Lafayette south with a small force of Continentals to shadow the British in Virginia. Lafayette was outnumbered and couldn't risk a major battle, but he could harass British movements and prevent them from operating freely. Throughout the summer of 1781, Lafayette and Cornwallis maneuvered around Virginia, neither able to bring the other to decisive battle.

Cornwallis established his main base at Yorktown, a small tobacco port on the York River near the entrance to Chesapeake Bay. The location seemed strategically sound. Yorktown had a good harbor where British ships could resupply the army. It was on a peninsula, which limited the directions from which it could be attacked. Cornwallis fortified the position and settled in, confident that he could hold Yorktown indefinitely and use it as a base for operations throughout Virginia.

But Cornwallis had made a critical error in choosing Yorktown. The position was strong only if the British controlled the waters around it. If they lost control of the water, even temporarily, Cornwallis's army would be trapped on a peninsula with no escape route.

In the summer of 1781, an extraordinary opportunity emerged. The French Navy, which had been operating in the West Indies, was preparing to sail north to the American coast. Admiral Comte de Grasse commanded a powerful fleet of twenty-eight ships of the line—the largest warships of the era. If de Grasse brought his fleet to Chesapeake Bay at the right moment, the French Navy could temporarily control the waters around Yorktown.

Washington and the French commander in America, Comte de Rochambeau, began coordinating a complex plan. Washington commanded about four thousand Continentals near New York. Rochambeau had about four thousand French regulars with him. If they could march these forces to Virginia and arrive at the same time as the French fleet, they could trap Cornwallis at Yorktown. The plan required perfect timing and coordination across hundreds of miles. If any part of the plan failed, the opportunity would be lost.

Washington faced a difficult decision. His instinct was to attack New York, which was still held by the main British army under General Henry Clinton. Taking New York would be a more significant strategic victory than capturing a smaller British force in Virginia. However, attacking New York's strong fortifications would be enormously costly, even with French support. The opportunity at Yorktown might never come again.

Washington decided to go to Virginia. In mid-August 1781, the American and French armies began moving south. They marched through New Jersey and Pennsylvania, then by boat down Chesapeake Bay. The operation was a logistical marvel. Moving nearly eight thousand troops with artillery, supplies, and equipment over such distances required careful planning and execution.

Washington executed a masterful deception to keep the British in New York from discovering his true objective. He had his troops build ovens for baking bread, set up camps, and conduct reconnaissance that suggested an imminent attack on New York City. General Clinton, the commander in New York, was naturally cautious and received conflicting intelligence. The combination of Washington's feint and Clinton's hesitation kept the main British army immobilized in New York while the allied force marched south. Clinton didn't send reinforcements to Cornwallis until it was too late.

On August 30, Admiral de Grasse's French fleet arrived in Chesapeake Bay with twenty-eight ships of the line and several smaller vessels. The fleet also brought an additional three thousand French troops. The French Navy quickly established control of the bay, anchoring at the mouth of the York River and cutting off Cornwallis's water route to the ocean.

On September 5, a British fleet under Admiral Thomas Graves arrived from New York with nineteen ships of the line, hoping to relieve Cornwallis. The British fleet found that the entrance to Chesapeake Bay was held by the larger French fleet. The Battle of the Chesapeake—also called the Battle of the Virginia Capes—was fought that afternoon. The fleets engaged in a running artillery duel that lasted for hours. Neither side achieved a decisive tactical victory, but the strategic outcome favored the French. The British fleet was damaged and unable to force its way into the bay. After a few days of maneuvering, Graves withdrew and sailed back to New York for repairs.

The Battle of the Chesapeake.[76]

The French fleet remained in control of Chesapeake Bay. Cornwallis was now trapped, as French warships blocked his escape by sea. American and French armies were marching toward Yorktown to trap him by land. He sent urgent messages to General Clinton in New York requesting immediate reinforcements. Clinton promised to send help, but the help would arrive too late.

By late September, Washington's combined American and French force—nearly seventeen thousand troops—had surrounded Yorktown. Cornwallis had about eight thousand men inside the fortifications. He was outnumbered more than two to one, cut off from supply and reinforcement, and had no possibility of escape. But his position was still strong. Yorktown's fortifications were substantial. If Cornwallis could hold out long enough, perhaps Clinton's reinforcements would arrive, or perhaps the French fleet would be forced to leave.

Washington and Rochambeau began formal siege operations. They dug trenches approaching the British fortifications in the methodical European style, moving their artillery closer day by day. The siege progressed rapidly. The American and French forces had overwhelming numbers and plenty of artillery. They pounded the British positions relentlessly.

By mid-October, the situation inside Yorktown was desperate. British fortifications were being systematically destroyed by artillery fire. Supplies were running low. There was no sign of relief from New York. On the night of October 14, American and French forces stormed two key British redoubts in coordinated assaults. Alexander Hamilton, Washington's aide-de-camp, led one of the attacks, gaining glory in what would be one of the war's final battles. The redoubts were captured after brief but fierce fighting.

With the outer defenses breached, Cornwallis attempted one last desperate gamble. On the night of October 16, he tried to evacuate his army across the York River to Gloucester Point, hoping to break out and march north to link up with British forces in New York. But a sudden storm scattered the boats and made the crossing impossible. Cornwallis had to abandon the attempt.

On the morning of October 17—exactly four years after Burgoyne's surrender at Saratoga—Cornwallis requested a ceasefire to negotiate surrender terms. The fighting stopped. Negotiations took two days as officers worked out the details. On October 19, 1781, the formal surrender ceremony took place.

Surrender of Lord Cornwallis by John Trumbull.[77]

The surrender at Yorktown was carefully choreographed. British soldiers marched out of their fortifications with their flags cased and their bands playing. Tradition holds that the British band played a tune called "The World Turned Upside Down," though this detail may be apocryphal. The British soldiers marched between two lines of American and French troops stretching for nearly a mile. They laid down their weapons in surrender.

Cornwallis himself did not attend the ceremony, claiming illness. He sent his second-in-command, General Charles O'Hara, to surrender in his place. According to the traditional account, O'Hara first approached Rochambeau, perhaps thinking it less humiliating to surrender to a European professional than to colonial rebels. Rochambeau directed him to Washington. O'Hara then approached Washington, but Washington refused to accept the sword from anyone other than Cornwallis's equal in rank. Since Cornwallis had not come, Washington directed O'Hara to surrender to Washington's second-in-command, General Benjamin Lincoln—the same Lincoln who had been forced to surrender at Charleston.

Over eight thousand British soldiers became prisoners of war. The British lost all their artillery, weapons, and supplies. It was the most complete American victory of the war and the second time an entire British army had been forced to surrender.

When news of the surrender reached London in late November, the political impact was immediate and devastating. The British government's support for continuing the war collapsed. Lord North, the prime minister who had led Britain's war effort, reportedly exclaimed, "Oh God! It is all over!" The House of Commons began debating whether to continue fighting or seek peace. Within months, North's government fell, and new leadership came to power that was committed to ending the war.

Fighting continued sporadically for more than a year after Yorktown. The British still held New York, Charleston, and Savannah. Skirmishes occurred in various locations. However, Yorktown was the decisive military victory that broke the political will in London to continue the conflict. The question was no longer whether America would win independence, but what the terms of peace would be. The war would not officially end until the Treaty of Paris in 1783, but after Yorktown, American independence was a foregone conclusion.

On a peninsula in Virginia, the combined forces of America and France had trapped and captured a British army. The world's most powerful empire had been defeated by colonial rebels whom it had dismissed as rabble.

Chapter 10: An Unlikely Victory: How Did They Do It?

The American victory in the Revolutionary War was improbable. On paper, Britain should have won easily. Britain had the world's most powerful navy, a professional army with decades of combat experience, vast financial resources, and a global empire. The American colonies had none of these advantages. They had no navy to speak of and only a fledgling army, though over the course of the war, the Continental Army grew more professional and was supplemented by a small navy and thousands of privateers who harassed British shipping. They had chronic money problems and no experience managing a war effort. Yet America won. How?

There's no single answer. The American victory resulted from multiple factors working together. Understanding why America won requires looking at several different elements that combined to produce an unlikely outcome.

The Leadership of George Washington

If any single person was indispensable to an American victory, it was George Washington. His genius wasn't primarily in battlefield tactics—he lost more major battles than he won—but in his strategic vision, his ability to hold the army together, and his political skill. He understood what mattered most and focused on that rather than chasing tactical victories that wouldn't win the war.

A portrait of George Washington.[78]

Washington understood that he didn't need to destroy the British army to win the war. He just needed to keep the Continental Army alive and fighting. As long as an American army existed in the field, the revolution continued. Britain would have to keep spending money, deploying troops, and fighting a war that grew more expensive and less popular at home. Washington knew that time was on America's side.

This meant avoiding unnecessary risks. After the disasters in New York in 1776, Washington became much more cautious about fighting major battles unless circumstances favored him. He would retreat rather than risk his army's destruction. He would avoid battle rather than engage on unfavorable terms. This frustrated many people who wanted aggressive action, but Washington understood that preserving the army was more important than winning individual battles.

When Washington did fight, he chose his moments carefully. Trenton and Princeton came when the army desperately needed victories to survive. Those attacks were high-risk, but the alternative was watching the army dissolve. At Yorktown, Washington saw an opportunity created by French naval power and moved decisively to exploit it. He could be bold when the situation demanded it, but he was never reckless.

Washington also had personal qualities that inspired loyalty and kept the army together through terrible hardships. He shared his soldiers' suffering. During the brutal winter at Valley Forge in 1777–1778, Washington endured the same harsh conditions as his men. He didn't live in luxury while his troops suffered. This mattered enormously to the common soldiers.

His officers respected him because he listened to their advice and made sound decisions under pressure. He held councils of war where generals could debate strategy openly. Washington didn't pretend to have all the answers. When he made a decision, his officers trusted that he had considered all options and chosen the best path forward. This created a command structure based on mutual respect rather than just military hierarchy.

Washington also had the political skill to navigate the complicated relationship between the Continental Army and the Continental Congress. Congress controlled funding, supplies, and strategic policy. Washington commanded the army. These roles inevitably created tensions. Congress sometimes made unrealistic demands or failed to provide necessary support. Washington had to balance military needs with political realities, pushing Congress for what he needed while maintaining the principle of civilian control over the military.

Perhaps most importantly, Washington never tried to seize power for himself. This seems obvious now, but it wasn't obvious then. Throughout history, successful military commanders have often used their armies to take political power. The Roman Republic fell when generals like Julius Caesar refused to give up their commands. Washington commanded an army that was sometimes unpaid, poorly supplied, and frustrated with Congress. He could have attempted to use that army to impose his will on the civilian government. Many officers would have followed him.

Washington never did this. He demonstrated unwavering commitment to republican principles, most famously in 1782 when officers suggested the army should seize political power to force Congress to pay them. Washington rejected any such idea, insisting on civilian control of the military. When the war ended, he resigned his commission and went home to his farm, voluntarily giving up power. This act stunned Europe, where military commanders didn't just walk away from power. King George III reportedly said that if Washington did this, he would be "the greatest man in the world."

Washington's leadership held the Continental Army together through its darkest times. His strategic patience kept the army alive when aggressive action would have destroyed it. His personal character inspired loyalty from soldiers and officers who stayed with him through years of hardship. His political skill maintained the army's relationship with Congress. And his commitment to republican principles ensured that military success wouldn't lead to military dictatorship. These qualities were more valuable than tactical genius.

Fighting on Home Turf

Americans fought on their own ground, which gave them advantages that British forces struggled to match. American soldiers knew the terrain. They knew which roads were passable, where the rivers could be crossed, and where forests provided cover. British forces often operated in unfamiliar territory with unreliable maps, though they also employed skilled engineers and local loyalist guides to help navigate the challenges.

The psychological advantage of defending home territory was equally important. American soldiers were fighting for their own land, their own families, and their own communities. When the war came to their region, they had personal stakes in the outcome. British soldiers were fighting far from home for reasons that often seemed abstract. They followed orders and did their duty, but they weren't fighting for their own survival or their children's future.

The vast distances in America worked against the British. Britain was trying to control territory that stretched hundreds of miles along the coast and extended deep into the interior. Moving armies across these kinds of distances took weeks. Supply lines stretched for hundreds of miles and were vulnerable to attack. Communications were slow and unreliable. British commanders in different regions sometimes didn't know what their colleagues were doing until weeks after the fact.

Americans could disperse when threatened and regroup when opportunities arose. British armies could effectively occupy major cities and establish networks of fortified posts, but controlling the vast, hostile countryside proved far more difficult. When British forces marched through an area, Americans would fade into the forests and swamps. When the British moved on, Americans would return. This was especially true in the South, where partisan warfare made British control of the interior impossible despite their capture of major cities.

The decentralized nature of American society also worked in America's favor. Britain was trying to defeat not just an army but an entire society that was spread across a vast territory. There was no single vital point that, if captured, would end the war. The British took Philadelphia, the capital, and the war continued. They controlled New York for the entire war, and it didn't matter strategically. They couldn't strike a single decisive blow because there was no single point to strike.

The French Contribution

It's difficult to overstate the importance of French support to the American victory. While the alliance presented challenges of coordinating strategy between two very different powers with sometimes competing priorities, the infusion of French military, naval, and financial resources fundamentally altered the balance of power. The most obvious contribution was military. French troops fought alongside Americans at Yorktown and in other campaigns. French officers brought professional military expertise that the Continental Army lacked. Men like Lafayette, Rochambeau, and the engineers who designed American fortifications provided knowledge and experience that made the Continental Army more effective.

However, the French Navy was the truly decisive contribution. Britain's control of the seas had been a massive advantage throughout the war. British armies could move by ship, be supplied by ship, and be reinforced by ship. American forces couldn't counter this. The French Navy changed that. At Yorktown, French naval control of Chesapeake Bay trapped Cornwallis and made the decisive victory possible. Without that French fleet, Cornwallis could have been resupplied or evacuated by sea, and the siege would have failed.

French financial support kept the American war effort alive. The Continental Congress had no power to tax and struggled constantly to fund the army. French loans and subsidies provided essential money that paid for supplies, equipment, and ammunition. Spain and the Netherlands also provided financial support, but France was the primary source. Without this foreign money, the Continental Army might have collapsed from lack of resources long before Yorktown.

France's entry into the war also forced Britain to fight on multiple fronts. British forces had to be diverted to defend possessions in the Caribbean, India, Gibraltar, and other parts of the empire. The Royal Navy had to protect British interests worldwide rather than concentrate only on American waters. This dispersal of British resources eased the pressure on American forces and made Britain's strategic situation far more difficult.

France didn't support America out of ideological sympathy. This was a strategic move. France wanted to weaken Britain, and supporting American independence accomplished that goal. However, regardless of French motives, the support was essential. America won its independence with crucial help from a European power that provided the military, naval, and financial resources America lacked.

The Will of the People

Armies and strategies don't fight wars by themselves. Wars are fought by people, and the American Revolution was ultimately won by the determination of ordinary people who refused to give up despite overwhelming odds and terrible hardships.

The revolution was never universally popular, and support varied dramatically by region. A common estimate suggests that perhaps 30 to 40 percent of colonists actively supported independence, 15 to 20 percent remained loyalists, and a substantial remainder remained neutral or less active. These proportions shifted over time and differed greatly between areas. Revolutionary fervor ran much stronger in New England than in places like New York or the Carolina backcountry, where loyalist sentiment remained powerful. The revolution succeeded because enough people in enough places remained committed to independence despite the odds.

The soldiers of the Continental Army endured conditions that would have broken most armies. They served for years with irregular pay and sometimes no pay at all. They wore rags when proper uniforms weren't available. They went hungry because supply systems failed repeatedly. They suffered through brutal winters at Valley Forge, Morristown, and other winter encampments, where disease and cold killed more men than British bullets did. They watched friends die from wounds, disease, and exposure. And most of them stayed and kept fighting.

These weren't professional soldiers who had no choice. These were farmers, craftsmen, and laborers who could have gone home. Many did desert, especially when conditions became unbearable, but enough stayed to keep the army alive. They stayed because they believed in the cause. They believed that what they were fighting for—independence, self-government, liberty—was worth the sacrifice.

Militia forces played a crucial role that's often underappreciated. Militia weren't reliable in conventional battles against British regulars. They often broke and ran when faced with professional soldiers in open combat. However, militias could defend their local areas, gather intelligence, harass British supply lines, and make British control of occupied territory costly and difficult. In the South, partisan militia forces under leaders like Francis Marion, Thomas Sumter, and Andrew Pickens prevented the British from controlling anything beyond the major cities.

Women contributed in ways that don't fit neatly into traditional military narratives but were essential to the war effort. Women ran farms and businesses while men were away fighting, keeping the economy functioning. They nursed wounded soldiers and provided intelligence about British movements. Some, like Deborah Sampson, disguised themselves as men and fought in the army. Many more, like Martha Washington and other officers' wives, followed the army from camp to camp, washing clothes, cooking, and maintaining morale.

An engraved portrait of Deborah Sampson.[79]

The civilian population endured enormous hardships. Both British and American armies requisitioned supplies, sometimes with payment but often without it. Farms were destroyed, and towns were burned. Families were torn apart by divided loyalties. The war brought inflation that destroyed savings and made basic goods unaffordable. People went without necessities so the army could have what it needed.

Despite all this, enough Americans stayed committed to the cause. They didn't give up when Washington retreated across New Jersey in

1776. They didn't give up when Charleston fell in 1780. They didn't give up during the long years when victory seemed distant and uncertain. This resilience—the simple refusal to quit—was as important as any military strategy.

The ideals expressed in the Declaration of Independence mattered. The words about equality and natural rights gave people something to believe in beyond just resistance to British taxes. These ideas weren't perfectly realized—slavery continued, women had no political rights, and property qualifications limited voting. But the ideals themselves were powerful. They suggested that government should be based on consent, that people had rights that governments couldn't violate, and that ordinary people could govern themselves. These ideas inspired people to keep fighting even when the situation looked hopeless.

The revolution succeeded because enough Americans believed in it strongly enough to endure years of hardship and uncertainty. Washington's leadership mattered. French support mattered. Strategic factors mattered. But at its core, the revolution succeeded because ordinary people decided it was worth the cost and refused to give up. That stubborn determination to see it through, even when success seemed impossible, made the difference between victory and defeat.

Britain lost the war not because its army was consistently defeated on the battlefield—British forces actually won a majority of the major engagements—but because many of these victories came at an unsustainable cost in casualties and failed to achieve their strategic goals. Battles like Bunker Hill and Guilford Courthouse were tactical victories that weakened the British army without destroying American resistance. The war ended not with a decisive military defeat but with Britain's recognition that the cost of continuing wasn't worth the potential benefit of winning.

The American Revolution was won by an improbable combination of factors: Washington's leadership, the advantages of fighting on home ground, crucial French support, and the determination of people who believed that independence was worth any price. No single factor alone would have been sufficient. Together, they produced a victory that seemed impossible when the war began.

Chapter 11: Peace and Its Problems: A Fragile Union

The Treaty of Paris

Winning the war was one thing. Building a nation was something else entirely. The surrender at Yorktown in October 1781 effectively ended major fighting, but the war dragged on for nearly two more years while diplomats negotiated peace terms. When peace finally came, Americans faced a new challenge: how to govern themselves. They had declared independence and won it on the battlefield, but they had to figure out what kind of country they wanted to be. The process would prove almost as difficult as winning the war itself.

Peace negotiations began in Paris in 1782. The American delegation included some of the most talented diplomats the new nation could field. Benjamin Franklin was already in Paris, where he had been representing American interests since 1776. John Adams arrived from the Netherlands, where he had been securing loans and diplomatic recognition. John Jay came from Spain, where he had been trying unsuccessfully to get Spanish support. Together, these three men would negotiate the terms that would formally end the war and establish America's place among nations.

The negotiations were complicated by the web of alliances and interests involved. America was allied with France, and France was allied with Spain. Britain was at war with all three. Each nation had its own goals that sometimes conflicted with those of the others. France wanted to weaken Britain, but it didn't necessarily want America to become too strong. Spain wanted to limit American expansion westward to protect its own territories. Britain wanted to minimize its losses and perhaps drive a wedge between America and its allies.

The American diplomats had clear instructions from Congress: seek independence, secure the widest possible boundaries, obtain fishing rights off Newfoundland, and try to get the British to evacuate their military posts in the West. However, the American diplomats, particularly Franklin and Jay, suspected that France might try to limit American gains to serve French interests. They decided to negotiate directly with Britain, technically violating their instructions to coordinate with the French.

The decision to negotiate separately turned out to be shrewd. The British were willing to be generous with territorial concessions, partly to drive a wedge between America and France and partly because controlling distant western territories would be difficult anyway.

Britain recognized American independence, of course—that was the foundation of everything else. But the boundaries Britain accepted were remarkably generous. America's western boundary would be the Mississippi River. The northern boundary would roughly follow the Great Lakes. The southern boundary would be set at the 31st parallel, the northern edge of Spanish Florida. This gave America a vast territory stretching from the Atlantic to the Mississippi, more than doubling the land area of the original Thirteen Colonies.

Britain also agreed to American fishing rights off Newfoundland and in the Gulf of St. Lawrence. This was crucial for New England, where fishing was a major industry. British negotiators recognized that trying to exclude American fishermen from these waters would create endless conflicts.

The treaty had provisions that would prove more controversial. Britain agreed to withdraw its troops from American territory "with all convenient speed," but the phrase was vague enough to cause problems. British forces would remain in frontier posts in the Northwest Territory for more than a decade, claiming they were waiting for Americans to fulfill their treaty obligations.

Those obligations involved debts and loyalists. American citizens owed substantial debts to British merchants from before the war. The treaty stated that creditors on both sides should face no legal obstacles to collecting legitimate debts. Many Americans who had borrowed money before the war were unhappy about this provision, and many states would obstruct debt collection for years.

The treatment of loyalists was even more contentious. Thousands of Americans had remained loyal to Britain during the war. Many had fought for Britain or provided intelligence and support. With an American victory, these loyalists faced an uncertain future. Some had already fled to Canada, Britain, or other parts of the British Empire. Those who remained feared retribution.

The treaty tried to address this. It stated that Congress would "earnestly recommend" to the states that they restore confiscated loyalist property and allow loyalists to return safely. However, this language was weak—Congress could only recommend, not require—and most states ignored the recommendation. Loyalists who had fought against independence were not welcome. Their property remained confiscated, and many were forced into permanent exile. Britain considered this a violation of the treaty, and it became one justification for Britain's continued occupation of frontier posts.

Despite these problems, the Treaty of Paris was a diplomatic triumph for America. The new nation had secured recognition of its independence from the most powerful empire in the world. It had obtained territory far larger than anyone had expected. It had also gained fishing rights and access to the Mississippi River, though navigation rights would later be contested with Spain. The American diplomats had negotiated skillfully and achieved nearly everything they had hoped for.

The final treaty was signed on September 3, 1783, in Paris. After more than eight years of war, peace had finally come. British troops evacuated New York City in November 1783, and Washington made a triumphal entry into the city. On December 4, Washington said farewell to his officers at Fraunces Tavern in New York in an emotional ceremony. A few weeks later, he traveled to Annapolis, where Congress was meeting, and formally resigned his commission as commander in chief. He then returned to Mount Vernon, his plantation in Virginia, as a private citizen.

Washington's entry into New York.[80]

The war was over. America was independent. But the hard work of building a functioning nation was just beginning, and it would quickly become clear that winning independence was only the first challenge.

The Articles of Confederation: A Government Designed to Be Weak

America's first national government was established under the Articles of Confederation, which had been drafted by Congress in 1777 and finally ratified by all thirteen states in 1781. The Articles of Confederation created a loose association of independent states rather than a strong national government. This wasn't an accident or an oversight. It was deliberate. The founders had just fought a war against what they saw as a tyrannical central authority in Britain. They were deeply suspicious of concentrated power, so they wanted to ensure that no American government could become oppressive the way the British government had been.

The result was a national government with almost no power. Under the Articles of Confederation, Congress could declare war, make peace, conduct foreign relations, and manage relations with Native American tribes. It could coin money, establish post offices, and settle disputes between states. These powers looked significant on paper, but Congress had no way to enforce its decisions.

Congress had no power to tax, which was the most crippling limitation. Congress could request money from the states, but it couldn't require them to pay. Each state decided whether and how much to contribute. Most states contributed far less than requested, and some contributed nothing at all. Congress was perpetually broke, unable to pay its debts or fund basic government operations.

Congress also had no power to regulate trade between states or with foreign nations. Each state set its own trade policies. They imposed tariffs on goods from other states, treating each other almost like foreign countries. They negotiated their own agreements with foreign nations. This created economic chaos. Merchants couldn't predict what rules would apply as goods moved between states. Foreign nations had no single American government to negotiate with and played states off against each other.

Congress couldn't enforce its own laws or treaties. If Congress passed a resolution, it relied on the states to implement it. If a state chose to ignore Congress, there was nothing Congress could do about it. For instance, the Treaty of Paris said states should restore loyalist property, but most states ignored this provision. Congress had no way to force compliance.

Major decisions required the approval of nine of the thirteen states. This meant that five states could block any significant action. Amending the Articles of Confederation required the unanimous consent of all thirteen states, which made reform essentially impossible. Any single state could veto changes, and there was always at least one state opposed to any given reform.

There was no executive branch. Congress handled all of the administrative duties through committees. This was slow and inefficient. There was no president or prime minister to provide leadership or make quick decisions in emergencies. There was no standing national court system or supreme judiciary. Congress could establish temporary tribunals to resolve specific disputes between states, but there was no permanent, independent judiciary to interpret laws or settle conflicts.

The underlying philosophy was that sovereignty resided in the states, not in the nation. The states were the real governments with real power. The national government was merely a cooperative arrangement between independent states, similar to a modern international organization. States retained the right to govern themselves in virtually all matters.

This system had some advantages. It preserved state autonomy, which many people valued. It prevented the emergence of a tyrannical central government, which had been a major concern. Individual states could experiment with different policies and learn from each other. The diversity of approaches allowed states to find solutions that worked for their particular circumstances.

However, the disadvantages quickly became overwhelming. The national government couldn't pay its debts. It had borrowed huge sums from France, Spain, the Netherlands, and private creditors to finance the war. After the war ended, these debts came due. Congress had no money to pay them. American credit collapsed, and foreign nations refused to lend more money or extend existing loans. American diplomats were humiliated when they tried to negotiate with foreign powers while representing a government that couldn't pay its bills.

The government couldn't pay its own soldiers either. The Continental soldiers had been promised payment for their service. After the war ended, most of them were sent home with certificates promising future payment instead of actual money. These certificates quickly lost value as everyone realized the government couldn't redeem them. Soldiers who had fought for years received almost nothing. Some sold their pay certificates to speculators for pennies on the dollar just to get something. The treatment of veterans was a national disgrace.

Economic problems mounted. Trade between states became increasingly complex as states erected barriers against each other. The national economy suffered. Without the power to regulate commerce, Congress couldn't negotiate effective trade agreements with foreign nations. Britain refused to open its markets to American goods or allow Americans to trade with British colonies on favorable terms. Spain closed the Mississippi River to American navigation, cutting off trade routes for western settlers.

The government couldn't maintain order on the frontier. Settlers were moving west into territories that were technically under federal jurisdiction, but the government had no money to administer these lands, no troops to protect settlers from conflicts with Native Americans, and no courts to settle disputes. Frontier regions were essentially lawless.

States acted like independent countries. Some maintained their own navies. New York charged duties on goods from New Jersey. Virginia and Maryland disputed control of the Potomac River. New Hampshire and New York both claimed Vermont. Without a strong central authority to resolve these disputes, conflicts between states could potentially lead to interstate warfare.

By the mid-1780s, many American leaders were deeply worried. The experiment in self-government seemed to be failing. The nation had won independence, but it couldn't function as a nation. Something had to change. However, the Articles of Confederation were nearly impossible to amend, and any attempt to strengthen the national government faced opposition from those who feared concentrated power.

The crisis came to a head in Massachusetts in 1786, when economic hardship and government dysfunction led to an armed uprising that shocked the nation.

Shays' Rebellion: A Nation on the Brink

In the mid-1780s, Massachusetts farmers faced a crushing economic crisis. The state government had accumulated substantial debt during the war and needed money to pay it off. The legislature raised taxes dramatically, demanding payment in hard currency—gold or silver coin— rather than paper money or agricultural goods. This created an impossible situation for many farmers.

Farmers didn't have hard currency. They earned their living by growing crops and raising livestock, which they traded for other goods and services. The local economy ran on barter and credit, not cash. When tax collectors demanded payment in coin, farmers had to sell their crops and animals for whatever cash they could get, often at very low prices. Many couldn't raise enough money to pay their taxes, no matter what they sold.

The state government responded to nonpayment harshly. Courts began foreclosing on farms and ordering debtors imprisoned. In Massachusetts at the time, you could be jailed for debt even if you were simply too poor to pay. Farmers who had fought in the American Revolution and survived years of hardship were now losing their land and going to prison because they couldn't pay the high taxes the state had set.

The farmers tried working through the political system. They petitioned the legislature for lower taxes, the right to pay in goods rather than coin, and a delay in debt collection. The legislature, dominated by merchants and creditors from eastern Massachusetts, largely ignored these petitions. The divide between merchants and farmers grew wider. The farmers felt betrayed by a government that seemed to serve wealthy creditors while crushing ordinary people.

In August 1786, the crisis exploded into violence. Armed groups of farmers began forcing courts to close so they couldn't issue foreclosure orders or debt judgments. They weren't trying to overthrow the government; they were trying to prevent the courts from taking their farms. It was a desperate attempt to stop the legal machinery that was destroying their lives.

The leader who emerged was Daniel Shays, a former captain in the Continental Army. Shays had fought at Bunker Hill, Ticonderoga, Saratoga, and other major battles. He had been a good soldier and a respected officer. After the war, he returned to his farm in western Massachusetts and struggled, like his neighbors, to pay the crushing taxes. When the rebellion began, Shays became one of its prominent leaders, though the movement had no single commander and was more a spontaneous uprising than an organized rebellion.

The rebels called themselves "Regulators," and they saw themselves as defending the principles of the American Revolution. They had fought against British tyranny; now, they were fighting against what they saw as tyranny from their own state government—taxation without genuine representation since the government had ignored their petitions.

Through the fall of 1786, the Regulators forced courts to close across western Massachusetts. The state government tried to respond, but it had no real military force to deploy. Congress had no troops and no money to raise any. Massachusetts was on its own.

Governor James Bowdoin called out the militia, but many militiamen sympathized with the rebels and refused to serve. The state had no money to pay soldiers even if they were willing to fight. In desperation, wealthy merchants in Boston raised private funds to equip an army. In January 1787, General Benjamin Lincoln, who had surrendered Charleston and, in a symbolic act of restored honor, accepted Cornwallis's surrender at Yorktown, led about four thousand troops west to suppress the rebellion.

Shays led about 1,200 men in an attempt to capture the federal armory at Springfield, where weapons and ammunition were stored. If the rebels could arm themselves with weapons, they would be much harder to suppress. On January 25, 1787, Shays's forces approached the armory. The militia defending it fired artillery over the rebels' heads as a warning and then fired directly into their ranks when they continued to advance. Four rebels were killed, and twenty were wounded. Shays's force broke and retreated.

General Lincoln pursued the rebels through the winter. On February 4, Lincoln's forces surprised Shays's men at Petersham in a night march through a snowstorm. The rebels scattered without a fight. Shays fled to Vermont, and the rebellion collapsed. Over the following weeks, hundreds of rebels were captured. Many were tried for treason. Some were sentenced to death, though most were eventually pardoned. Shays himself was pardoned in 1788 and lived quietly in New York until his death in 1825.

Shays's Rebellion was put down, but its impact was profound. The rebellion terrified America's political leadership. These weren't radicals or criminals; they were farmers and war veterans—ordinary people who had been pushed beyond their limits. If such people could take up arms against their own government, what did that say about the republic's stability?

The rebellion exposed the weakness of the government under the Articles of Confederation. Massachusetts had almost lost control of its western counties. The national government had been completely unable to help. What would happen if a larger rebellion broke out? What if foreign powers intervened to support rebels? Congress couldn't raise an army, couldn't collect taxes to fund one, and couldn't enforce order. The nation seemed to be on the verge of anarchy.

George Washington, watching from Mount Vernon, was deeply disturbed. He had hoped to retire from public life, but the rebellion convinced him that the nation was in danger of collapse. He wrote to his correspondents that without a stronger national government, the nation would fall apart. The American Revolution would have been for nothing.

Many other leaders reached similar conclusions. The Articles of Confederation weren't working. The national government was too weak. Reform was essential, but reforming the Articles of Confederation seemed impossible because any single state could block changes.

This desperate situation led to a critical decision. If the Articles of Confederation couldn't be amended through the normal process, perhaps they needed to be replaced entirely. In May 1787, delegates from the states gathered in Philadelphia for a convention to revise the Articles of Confederation. However, many delegates arrived with a more radical plan: to write a completely new constitution that would create a fundamentally different and much stronger national government.

Shays's Rebellion had done what years of economic problems and diplomatic failures couldn't quite do. It had scared America's leaders enough to attempt something that would have seemed impossible just a few years earlier—the creation of a powerful central government. The rebellion showed that the choice wasn't between a weak government and a strong one; it was between a stronger government and chaos. That realization would shape the debates at the Constitutional Convention and ultimately lead to the creation of the government Americans live under today.

Chapter 12: "We the People": Crafting the Constitution

The Constitutional Convention: A Secret Meeting in Philadelphia

In May 1787, delegates from twelve of the thirteen states gathered in Philadelphia. Rhode Island refused to send representatives, suspicious of any attempt to strengthen the national government. The other states sent their most experienced political leaders. Most delegates were established figures—lawyers, merchants, planters—in their thirties and forties. They had significant experience in state and national government.

George Washington was there, reluctantly. He had wanted to remain in retirement at Mount Vernon, but his friends convinced him that the nation needed him. His presence gave the convention legitimacy. If Washington thought constitutional reform was necessary, people would take it seriously. The delegates unanimously elected him president of the convention, and he presided over the meetings with his characteristic dignity.

Benjamin Franklin attended at age eighty-one, the oldest delegate by far. His health was failing, and he couldn't stand for long periods, but his reputation and wisdom made him an influential voice. James Madison of Virginia, just thirty-six years old, was perhaps the best-prepared delegate. He had spent months studying ancient and modern governments, analyzing their strengths and weaknesses. He arrived in Philadelphia with detailed plans for a new government structure.

Alexander Hamilton represented New York, though his fellow New York delegates opposed major reform and often outvoted him. Gouverneur Morris of Pennsylvania was one of the convention's most eloquent speakers. Roger Sherman of Connecticut was practical and experienced. These men and dozens of others would spend the summer of 1787 in Philadelphia debating the fundamental questions of how to structure a government.

The convention met in the Pennsylvania State House, the same building where the Declaration of Independence had been signed eleven years earlier. The delegates immediately made a crucial decision: their deliberations would be secret. No reporters were allowed. Delegates were forbidden from discussing the debates with outsiders. Guards were posted at the doors. Windows were kept closed despite the summer heat to prevent eavesdropping, making the sessions sweltering.

The secrecy rule was controversial but essential. It allowed delegates to speak freely, change their minds, and compromise without worrying about public reaction. If every statement had been reported to newspapers, delegates would have felt pressure to maintain rigid positions to satisfy their constituents. The secrecy allowed them to negotiate honestly and find a middle ground. Of course, some delegates kept private notes. James Madison's detailed records of the debates would eventually provide history with a thorough account of what happened, but these notes weren't published until decades later.

The convention's official purpose was to revise the Articles of Confederation. But within days, it became clear that many delegates wanted to do something far more radical. On May 29, Edmund Randolph of Virginia presented the Virginia Plan, largely written by Madison. This wasn't a revision of the Articles of Confederation—it was a blueprint for an entirely new government.

The Virginia Plan proposed a national government with three branches: legislative, executive, and judicial. The legislative branch would have two houses. Representation in both houses would be based on population. Larger states would have more representatives than smaller states. This legislature would have broad powers, including the ability to disallow state laws that conflicted with national interests. The executive branch would enforce national laws. The judicial branch would have a supreme court and lower federal courts. This was a complete departure from the weak national government under the Articles of Confederation.

The Virginia Plan sparked intense debate. Large states generally supported it because population-based representation would give them more power. Small states were horrified. Under the Articles of Confederation, each state had one vote regardless of size. The Virginia Plan would make small states like Delaware or New Jersey almost irrelevant compared to large states like Virginia or Pennsylvania. Small-state delegates argued this was unacceptable and threatened to walk out.

William Paterson of New Jersey presented an alternative called the New Jersey Plan. This plan kept the basic structure of the Articles of Confederation but strengthened Congress's powers. Each state would continue to have one vote. The national government would gain the power to tax and regulate commerce, but states would remain the primary centers of political power.

The convention faced a fundamental question. Would America be a nation of states or a nation of people? The Virginia Plan suggested a nation of people, where individuals were directly represented in a national government. The New Jersey Plan suggested a nation of states, where states remained the primary political units.

Debates grew heated, and at times, the convention seemed on the brink of collapse. Delegates from small states insisted on equal representation. Delegates from large states insisted on proportional representation. Neither side would compromise. Some delegates threatened to leave. If the convention failed, the nation might fall apart. The sense of crisis was real.

The breakthrough came from Connecticut. Roger Sherman and Oliver Ellsworth proposed what became known as the Connecticut Compromise, or the Great Compromise. The national legislature would have two houses, as the Virginia Plan suggested, but with different rules for each. In the House of Representatives, representation would be based on population, as large states wanted. In the Senate, each state would have two senators regardless of size, as small states wanted. Laws would need approval from both houses, meaning neither large states nor small states could dominate. Neither side got everything they wanted, but both got enough to accept the plan.

The Great Compromise passed on July 16 by a single vote. It was the turning point of the convention. With this fundamental issue resolved, delegates could move forward on other questions. However, many difficult issues remained, and the convention would spend the rest of the summer working through them.

The Three-Fifths Compromise

The Great Compromise solved the question of representation in Congress, but it immediately raised another contentious issue: how would population be counted? This question forced the convention to confront the most divisive and morally troubling issue in American society—slavery.

Slavery existed in nearly all the states, though it had been abolished in Massachusetts and Vermont. Slavery was largely concentrated in the South. Northern states were beginning to phase it out through gradual emancipation laws, but the process was slow. Southern states had no intention of ending slavery; their economies depended on it. Enslaved people made up a large portion of the Southern population. In South Carolina and Georgia, they were nearly half the total population.

If representation in the House was going to be based on population, the question became whether enslaved people would be counted. Southern states wanted them counted. This would give Southern states more representatives in Congress, even though enslaved people couldn't vote and had no rights. Northern states objected. Why should Southern states get extra representation based on people who were treated as property and had no political voice?

The debate over counting enslaved people was fundamentally about power. If enslaved people were counted fully, Southern states would have significantly more influence in the House of Representatives. If they weren't counted at all, Northern states would dominate. Each side pushed for whatever counting method would maximize its own political power.

The Three-Fifths Compromise resolved this issue through a morally repugnant calculation. For purposes of representation and taxation, an enslaved person would count as three-fifths of a free person. Five enslaved people would count the same as three free people. This formula wasn't new; it had been proposed years earlier for tax purposes under the Articles of Confederation. Now it was being applied to representation as well.

The compromise satisfied no one's principles but gave both sides something. Southern states got increased representation based on their enslaved populations, though not as much as if enslaved people were counted fully. Northern states prevented Southern states from gaining full representation for people who had no rights. The compromise enshrined slavery in the Constitution by treating enslaved people as fractional human beings for political purposes.

The Three-Fifths Compromise wasn't the only way the Constitution protected slavery. The convention included other provisions that Southern states demanded for their participation. The Constitution prohibited Congress from banning the international slave trade for twenty years, until 1808. This guaranteed that Southern states could continue importing enslaved people from Africa for at least two more decades. The Constitution also included a fugitive slave clause requiring that people who escaped from slavery be returned to their enslavers, even if they reached states where slavery was illegal.

The convention's treatment of slavery was a moral failure. Some delegates condemned slavery as immoral during the debates. Gouverneur Morris called slavery "a nefarious institution" and "the curse of heaven." George Mason of Virginia, himself a slaveholder, warned that slavery would bring "the judgment of heaven" on the nation. Yet despite these objections, the convention chose to protect slavery rather than challenge it.

The delegates made this choice for practical political reasons. Southern states, particularly South Carolina and Georgia, made it clear that they would not join a union that threatened slavery. If the convention tried to restrict slavery, the Southern states would walk out, and the union would fail. The delegates from the Northern states faced an agonizing choice: accept slavery's continuation and create a union, or oppose slavery and watch the nation fall apart.

They prioritized preserving the union over confronting slavery directly. They told themselves that slavery might fade away naturally over time, that the new government could address the issue later, and that preserving the union was more important than resolving slavery immediately. These rationalizations would prove tragically wrong. Slavery didn't fade away—it grew stronger and more entrenched. The Constitution's protections for slavery would help sustain the institution for another seventy years. It took a civil war to end it.

The delegates also made compromises on other divisive issues. Later in the convention, they debated how the president should be chosen. Some wanted direct election by the people, while others wanted Congress to choose the president. The convention created the Electoral College, a complicated system in which each state would choose electors who would then vote for the president. The number of electors each state had would equal its total number of senators and representatives, combining elements of both state equality and population-based representation.

They debated what powers the president should have. Some feared a strong executive would become a monarch. Others argued that a weak executive couldn't govern effectively. The convention gave the president substantial powers—commanding the military, conducting foreign policy, appointing federal officials, and vetoing legislation—but balanced these with checks from Congress and the courts.

The convention debated how federal judges should be chosen and how long they should serve. It was decided that the president would nominate judges and that the Senate would confirm them. This would make the judiciary branch independent of political pressure.

The delegates debated whether to include a bill of rights listing specific freedoms the government couldn't violate. George Mason argued strongly for this, but most delegates thought it was unnecessary. The Constitution only granted the federal government specific, limited powers, they reasoned, so there was no need to list things it couldn't do. This decision would later prove controversial and almost prevented the Constitution's ratification.

Throughout these debates, the convention struggled with tensions. They wanted a government strong enough to function effectively but not so strong that it could become tyrannical. They wanted to protect both majority rule and minority rights. They wanted to balance federal power with state sovereignty. They wanted to create a government that could adapt to changing circumstances but couldn't be changed too easily.

By early September, the convention had worked out most of the major issues. A Committee on Style, led by Gouverneur Morris, wrote the final text. Morris contributed the Constitution's famous opening words: "We the People of the United States." The original draft had begun with a list of states, but Morris changed it to emphasize that the Constitution derived its authority from the people themselves, not from the states.

On September 17, 1787, the delegates gathered for the final time to sign the document they had created. Not everyone was satisfied. Some delegates had left in protest during the summer. Three delegates present refused to sign: Edmund Randolph and George Mason of Virginia and

Elbridge Gerry of Massachusetts. They had various objections, including the lack of a bill of rights and concerns about the power of the new government.

Benjamin Franklin gave a closing speech that captured the convention's spirit of compromise. He admitted the Constitution wasn't perfect: "I confess that there are several parts of this Constitution which I do not at present approve," he said, "but I am not sure I shall never approve them."[i] He noted that he had changed his mind many times during the debates as he learned from others. He urged the remaining delegates to sign despite their reservations because the Constitution was the best they could do under the circumstances.

Thirty-nine delegates signed the Constitution. It was then sent to Congress, which forwarded it to the states for ratification. The convention had exceeded its authority—it was supposed to revise the Articles of Confederation, not write a completely new constitution—but it had created a document that would structure American government for centuries to come.

The signing of the US Constitution.[ii]

---

[i] "Benjamin Franklin to the Federal Convention." https://press-pubs.uchicago.edu/founders/documents/a7s3.html

A New Blueprint for a Nation

The Constitution created a fundamentally different government than what had existed under the Articles of Confederation. Instead of a loose association of sovereign states, it created a true federal system in which power was divided between national and state governments. This federal structure was the Constitution's most innovative feature—and its most difficult to explain and defend.

The Constitution established three branches of the national government, each with distinct powers and the ability to check the others. This separation of powers, with checks and balances, was designed to prevent any part of the government from becoming too powerful.

The legislative branch, Congress, would make the laws. Congress consisted of two houses. The House of Representatives would be elected directly by the people every two years. The number of representatives each state had would be based on population, though the Three-Fifths Compromise meant enslaved people would be counted partially. The House would have special powers, including the sole power to originate bills for raising revenue. The Senate would consist of two senators from each state, chosen by state legislatures for six-year terms. The Senate would have special powers, including approving treaties and confirming presidential appointments.

Congress received new powers that the national government had never had under the Articles of Confederation. It could levy taxes and collect revenue, regulate trade between the states and with foreign nations, and coin money and set its value. Congress could also create post offices, build roads, raise armies, maintain a navy, and declare war. These powers gave the national government the strength and authority it had always lacked under the old system.

But Congress's powers weren't unlimited. The Constitution named specific powers Congress had and implicitly reserved all other powers to the states or the people. Congress couldn't pass laws on any subject it chose; it could act only within its constitutional authority. This was meant to reassure people who feared an all-powerful national government.

The executive branch, headed by the president, would enforce the laws. The president would be elected through the Electoral College for four-year terms. The Constitution didn't actually limit how many terms a president could serve, though Washington would set a precedent of serving only two two-year terms—a tradition not broken until the 1940s.

The president had significant powers. He was commander in chief of the armed forces. He could make treaties with foreign nations and appoint ambassadors, federal judges, and other officials, subject to Senate approval. He could veto legislation, though Congress could override his veto with a two-thirds vote. He had a duty to "take care that the laws be faithfully executed."

The president's powers were substantial but limited. He couldn't make laws himself. He couldn't spend money without congressional appropriation or declare war. He could be impeached by the House and tried by the Senate for "treason, bribery, or other high crimes and misdemeanors." The presidency was powerful but not a monarchy. The president was an elected official, not a hereditary ruler, and he was subject to the law like everyone else.

The judicial branch, headed by the Supreme Court, would interpret the laws and the Constitution. Federal judges would be appointed by the president with Senate confirmation and would serve for life with good behavior. This lifetime tenure was meant to insulate judges from political pressure, allowing them to make decisions based on law rather than popular opinion.

The Constitution created the Supreme Court but left it to Congress to determine how many justices it would have and to create lower federal courts. The Constitution gave federal courts jurisdiction over certain types of cases, including disputes between states, cases involving foreign diplomats, and cases arising under federal law. The Constitution didn't explicitly grant the courts the power of judicial review—the ability to declare laws unconstitutional—which the Supreme Court would assert in the early 1800s.

The three branches had the power to check each other, creating a balanced government. Congress could make laws, but the president could veto them. The president could veto laws, but Congress could override his veto. The president could appoint judges and officials, but the Senate had to confirm them. Congress could pass laws, but courts could interpret them and potentially rule them unconstitutional. The president and judges could be impeached and removed by Congress. No branch could dominate the others permanently.

The Constitution also created a federal system that divided power between the national government and the state governments. The national government had certain powers; the states retained all powers not specifically granted to the federal government. This federal structure meant that Americans would be citizens of both their state and the nation, subject to both state and federal laws.

The Constitution could be amended, but not easily. Amendments required approval by two-thirds of both houses of Congress and ratification by three-fourths of the states. This high bar meant the Constitution wouldn't be changed by temporary popular passions, but it could be amended when there was a broad consensus that change was needed.

The Constitution included the supremacy clause, stating that the Constitution and federal laws made under it were "the supreme law of the land." If state laws conflicted with federal laws, federal laws prevailed. This was crucial to making the federal government functional. Under the Articles of Confederation, states could ignore national laws; under the Constitution, they couldn't.

What the Constitution didn't include was as notable as what it did. There was no bill of rights listing specific freedoms the government couldn't violate. Many people saw this as a dangerous omission. How could citizens trust a powerful government without explicit protections for freedom of speech, religion, the press, and assembly? Without protection against unreasonable searches and seizures? Without guarantees of trial by jury and other legal rights?

The absence of a bill of rights would become the primary objection to ratification. It would nearly cause the Constitution to fail. The Federalists who supported the Constitution would eventually have to promise that a bill of rights would be added through amendments as soon as the new government was established. That promise would be kept with the addition of the first ten amendments in 1791.

The document the delegates created wasn't perfect. It indirectly protected slavery through provisions like the Three-Fifths Compromise, the slave trade clause, and the fugitive slave clause. The Constitution left voting qualifications to the states, most of which limited voting to property-owning White men. It created a complicated system that would sometimes lead to deadlock and inefficiency. However, it established principles—popular sovereignty, limited government, separation of powers, checks and balances, and federalism—that would define American government. And it created a framework that could be amended when those principles required it.

Conclusion: The Echoes of 1776

The American Revolution didn't end with the signing of the Constitution in 1787. In many ways, it was just beginning. The document still had to be ratified, and that fight proved almost as contentious as writing it. Federalists, who supported the Constitution, clashed with Anti-Federalists, who feared it created a government too powerful and too distant from the people.

The debate raged in newspapers, town meetings, and state conventions throughout 1787 and 1788. Alexander Hamilton, James Madison, and John Jay wrote a series of essays published in New York newspapers under the pseudonym "Publius," explaining and defending the Constitution. These essays, later collected as *The Federalist Papers*, became the most important commentary on the Constitution and what its framers intended. They argued that the Constitution's checks and balances would prevent tyranny while creating a government strong enough to function effectively.

During those debates, it became clear that adding a bill of rights was necessary to win ratification. James Madison, who had first thought such a measure unnecessary, came to see it as essential. When the new Congress met in 1789, Madison drafted twelve amendments protecting individual liberties. Ten were ratified by the states in 1791, becoming the Bill of Rights. It guaranteed freedom of speech, religion, the press, and assembly. People had the right to bear arms and had protections against unreasonable searches and seizures. They were entitled to a trial by jury, due process, and freedom from cruel and unusual punishment.

George Washington became the first president under the new Constitution. He was inaugurated in April 1789 in New York City. He served two terms and then voluntarily stepped down, establishing a precedent that would last until the 1940s. His peaceful transfer of power was as important as any wartime act. It proved that American leaders would respect both law and the will of the people.

The new government immediately faced challenges. Treasury Secretary Alexander Hamilton proposed controversial plans to pay back war debts and create a national bank. Thomas Jefferson and James Madison opposed his vision of a strong federal government and industrial economy, favoring a republic of independent farmers with power centered in the states. Their conflict led to the formation of America's first political parties—Federalists and Democratic-Republicans—and demonstrated that disagreement was a normal feature of democratic life, not a threat to it.

The American Revolution's influence extended far beyond America's borders. The Declaration of Independence's assertion that all men are created equal and possess natural rights helped inspire the Age of Revolutions that swept the Atlantic world. The French Revolution of 1789 drew on Enlightenment ideals and the American example, though it followed a far more violent path. In the early 1800s, Latin American revolutionaries likewise cited the American struggle as they fought for independence from Spain and Portugal.

Yet the American Revolution left unfinished business. The Constitution's compromises over slavery postponed the issue rather than solving it. With the invention of the cotton gin in the 1790s, slavery expanded and became more profitable, entrenching it in Southern society. The contradiction between America's founding ideals of liberty and the reality of slavery grew more painful until the Civil War finally abolished it—without ending the struggle for equality.

Native Americans were also left in a precarious position. The new government coveted lands in the West. Although the Constitution empowered Congress to regulate commerce with Native tribes, expansion meant displacement and broken treaties. The American Revolution's ideals of liberty and self-government were not extended to Native peoples, whose lands and cultures were steadily eroded.

Women who had contributed so much to the revolutionary cause found that independence brought no political equality. Abigail Adams's plea to her husband to "remember the ladies" went unheeded. Women couldn't vote or hold office, and married women, under coverture, couldn't own property in their own names. The American Revolution's ideals would eventually inspire the women's rights movement, but that struggle would take generations.

Despite its failures to fulfill its promises, the American Revolution established principles that proved transformative. The idea that all people are created equal was radical in the 1770s. Once declared, it could not be contained. The abolitionists would quote it, women's rights advocates would invoke it, and civil rights leaders would demand that the nation live up to it. Each generation used the founders' own words to push America closer to its ideals.

The American Revolution also established the principle that people have the right to change their government. For most of history, rulers claimed divine authority or conquest. The American Revolution asserted that government exists to serve the people, and when it destroys the people's rights, they can alter or abolish it. That idea remains powerful today.

The Constitution's checks and balances, separation of powers, and federalism created a framework for managing political conflict without violence. Americans would disagree—sometimes bitterly—about their government, but they had institutions to resolve those disputes: elections, legislatures, courts, a free press, and the right to petition and protest. The system sometimes failed, as in the Civil War, but it provided mechanisms for peaceful change that have sustained American democracy for more than two centuries.

The American Revolution showed that ordinary people could govern themselves—a notion that was radical in the 1770s. Most contemporaries believed democracy led inevitably to chaos and tyranny and that only elites could rule wisely. The American Revolution rejected that. Farmers, merchants, and craftsmen could debate issues, choose leaders, and govern responsibly. This faith in the political capacity of ordinary citizens was among the American Revolution's most radical legacies.

The cost was enormous. Roughly twenty-five thousand Americans died in the war—about 1 percent of the population. Many more were wounded, imprisoned, or ruined financially. The war divided families and communities, and its bitterness lingered for years.

Was it worth it? America won independence and built a government on revolutionary principles, though those principles applied fully only to a portion of the population. The ideals of 1776 took generations to realize, and the work of fulfilling them continues.

Still, the American Revolution was a pivotal event in world history. It laid the foundation for what became the United States, inspired democratic movements abroad, and established enduring principles of equality, natural rights, and government by consent. It proved that colonies could break free from empires and create new governments based on reason rather than tradition or force.

The revolution that began in 1775 on a village green in Massachusetts didn't end in 1783 with peace or in 1787 with a Constitution. It continues as each generation strives to live up to the ideals declared in Philadelphia in 1776. Its greatest legacy is not only the independence it achieved, but the enduring challenge to live by the principles it proclaimed.

Part 3: The Civil War for Beginners

The Story of the War Between the States Simplified for People Who Slept Through History Class

Introduction:
A War in Your Own Backyard

Imagine waking up one morning to discover that your country has split in half. Some of your friends and family now live in a different nation. The flag you've known your entire life no longer flies over your home. Brothers choose opposite sides and prepare to shoot at each other across battlefield lines. This isn't the plot of a movie or the premise of a novel. This actually happened in the United States of America.

The American Civil War lasted from 1861 to 1865. It was the bloodiest conflict in American history, with historians estimating between 650,000 and 750,000 total deaths from combat, disease, and war-related causes. This exceeded American military deaths in World War I and World War II combined. Civilians also suffered greatly from disease, displacement, and economic hardship. Major cities like Atlanta and Columbia saw widespread destruction. Families were torn apart forever.

However, this war was about much more than the staggering death toll. The Civil War decided what kind of nation America would become. Would it remain a collection of independent states that could leave whenever they wanted? Or would it become a single, unified country with a strong national government? Would it continue to allow human beings to be bought and sold as property? Or would it live up to the words in the Declaration of Independence that "all men are created equal?"

These questions had been simmering beneath the surface of American politics for decades. By 1861, they boiled over into the most devastating war the nation had ever seen.

Why This War Matters

You might wonder why you should care about a war that ended more than 150 years ago. The answer is simple: the Civil War created the America we know today.

Before the war, the concept of federal versus state identity was more complex than sometimes portrayed, but many Americans felt stronger loyalty to their state. The federal government in Washington was relatively weak and had less direct impact on people's daily lives. Most Americans had little contact with it.

The war changed all of that. It established once and for all that states could not leave the Union. It created a much stronger federal government. It ended slavery, freeing four million African Americans from bondage. It launched the United States on the path to becoming a modern industrial power.

The Civil War also established principles that still guide America today: the idea that the federal government can step in to protect individual rights when state governments won't; the belief that America should be a land of opportunity for everyone, regardless of race; and the conviction that the Union must be preserved, even at tremendous cost.

You can't understand modern America without understanding the Civil War. The debates about federal versus state power that raged in the 1860s continue today. The struggle for racial equality that began with emancipation is still ongoing. The question of what it means to be American—a question the war tried to answer—remains relevant in our diverse, complex society.

A Quick Glance at the Two Sides: The Union and the Confederacy

When the war began, the United States split into two opposing nations. The Union consisted of the Northern and Western states that remained loyal to the federal government in Washington. Twenty-three states stayed in the Union, including California, which had just joined the country in 1850. The Union had about 18.5 million people, plus roughly 3.1 million more in the border states that allowed slavery but didn't secede.

The Union had several major advantages. It contained most of America's factories, railroads, and banks. It controlled the U.S. Navy, which could blockade Southern ports. It had more than twice as many people as the Confederacy, which meant it had more soldiers and more workers to support the war effort.

Abraham Lincoln led the Union as president. A Republican from Illinois who had been elected in 1860, Lincoln had promised to prevent slavery from expanding into new territories. He insisted throughout the war that his primary goal was preserving the Union, though he eventually made ending slavery a war aim as well.

The Confederacy was formed by eleven Southern states that left the Union between December 1860 and June 1861. These states had a combined population of about 9 million people, but roughly 3.5 million of them were enslaved African Americans who were generally barred from fighting for the Confederate cause (except in very limited non-combat roles).

The Confederate states were South Carolina, Mississippi, Florida, Alabama, Georgia, Louisiana, Texas, Virginia, Arkansas, North Carolina, and Tennessee. They elected Jefferson Davis, a former U.S. senator from Mississippi, as their president.

The Confederacy's main advantage was that it didn't need to conquer the Union—it only needed to defend itself long enough for the North to give up. Confederate soldiers were fighting for their homes and their way of life. Many were excellent horsemen and marksmen who had grown up hunting and riding. They also had some of the best military officers in America, including Robert E. Lee, who had been offered command of the Union forces but chose to fight for his home state of Virginia instead.

The fundamental difference between the two sides came down to slavery. By 1860, slavery had been abolished in all the Northern states, though it remained legal in the border states of Delaware, Maryland, Kentucky, and Missouri. The Confederacy, on the other hand, was built on slavery.

What to Expect on This Journey

This book will take you through the entire Civil War from beginning to end. You'll learn why the war started, how it was fought, and what happened when it ended. Along the way, you'll meet the key people who shaped this dramatic period of American history.

We'll start with the roots of the conflict. Slavery had been a source of tension since America's founding. By the 1850s, that tension was tearing the country apart. You'll see how a series of political crises and compromises failed to resolve the fundamental disagreement over slavery's future.

Then we'll follow the war itself, year by year and battle by battle. You'll experience the shock of the first major battle at Bull Run, when both sides realized this wouldn't be the short, easy war they had expected. You'll witness the carnage at Antietam, the bloodiest single day in American history. You'll see how Ulysses S. Grant rose from obscurity to become the Union's most successful general. You'll follow Robert E. Lee as he won stunning victories against larger Union armies before finally meeting defeat.

You'll also learn how the war changed as it progressed. What started as a fight to preserve the Union became a war to end slavery. What began as a conflict between armies became a total war that targeted civilian property and morale. The America that emerged from the war was fundamentally different from the America that entered it.

Finally, we'll examine what happened after the fighting stopped. The assassination of Abraham Lincoln shocked the nation and complicated the process of rebuilding the South. The period called Reconstruction saw remarkable achievements in expanding civil rights, but it also witnessed a violent backlash that undermined many of those gains.

Throughout this journey, we'll focus on the human side of these momentous events. History isn't just about dates and battles—it's about real people making difficult choices under extraordinary circumstances. You'll meet enslaved people who risked everything for freedom, soldiers who fought bravely for causes they believed in, and ordinary civilians whose lives were turned upside down by forces beyond their control.

By the end of this book, you'll understand not just what happened during the Civil War but also why it happened and what it meant for America. You'll see connections between the issues that divided Americans in the 1860s and the challenges we still face today. Most importantly, you'll appreciate the courage and sacrifice of the generation that preserved the Union and ended slavery at an almost unimaginable cost.

The Civil War was one of America's defining moments. It tested whether a nation founded on the principle that all people are created equal could survive. The fact that you're reading this book in a united America where slavery has been abolished for more than a century tells you how that test turned out. But the story of how we got there—that's a tale worth telling.

Chapter 1: A House Dividing

Picture this: It's 1858, and a tall, lanky lawyer from Illinois stands before a crowd in Springfield. Abraham Lincoln looks out at the faces staring back at him and delivers a line that will echo through history: "A house divided against itself cannot stand." He was quoting Jesus from the Bible, but he was talking about America. And he was right—the country was tearing itself apart over one issue that just wouldn't go away: slavery.

It's hard to imagine today, but by 1860, people in America had been buying and selling other human beings for more than two centuries. What started as just another way to get work done had become the backbone of how the South lived and made money. In the North, people were building factories and cities, paying workers wages, and increasingly saying that owning people was wrong.

These two worlds were heading for a massive collision. To understand why neighbors ended up shooting at each other, you need to understand what slavery really looked like, how it made some people incredibly wealthy, and why it split America right down the middle.

The "Peculiar Institution": What Was Slavery in America?

Here's something that might surprise you: Southerners called slavery their "peculiar institution." Not peculiar like "weird"—peculiar like "special to us." They thought it made the South unique. However, slavery in America wasn't unique at all. It was part of a horrific system that had enslaved millions of Africans across the Americas for centuries.

Let's be clear about what slavery in America actually meant. When you owned a slave, you owned a person the same way you owned a horse or a piece of furniture. You could sell them. You could rent them out to someone else. You could give them away as a wedding present. When you died, your slaves were passed down to your children along with the rest of your possessions.

Think about that for a moment. Imagine if someone could legally own you—decide where you lived, what work you did, whether you could get married, even whether your children could stay with you. That was the reality for nearly four million Americans in 1860.

Southern law stated that slaves had no rights. They couldn't vote, own anything, make contracts, or travel without a pass. If a slave tried to testify against a White person in court, their word meant nothing. And while some Southern states technically made killing a slave a crime by the 1800s, the reality was different. White juries almost never convicted other White people for killing enslaved people, making the legal protection essentially meaningless.

Most slaves spent their lives growing crops—tobacco in Virginia, rice in South Carolina, sugar in Louisiana, and cotton across the Deep South. Picture working from sunrise to sunset, six days a week, picking cotton bolls under the blazing sun. Your hands would be cut and bleeding from the sharp cotton plants. During harvest time, you'd work even longer hours.

But slaves weren't just on plantations. Walk through Charleston or New Orleans in 1860, and you'd see slaves everywhere—cooking in kitchens, building houses, loading ships, and even working in the few factories the South had. Some became skilled craftsmen. A few were allowed to hire themselves out and keep part of their earnings. But skilled or unskilled, they were still someone else's property.

Slavery also existed beyond the traditional Southern states. In Indian Territory (present-day Oklahoma), some Cherokee, Creek, Choctaw, and other Native American nations had adopted slavery during the early 1800s as part of their efforts to assimilate into White Southern society and avoid forced removal from their ancestral lands. The Cherokee Nation, in particular, developed a plantation economy similar to that of Georgia and Alabama, complete with enslaved African Americans working cotton and tobacco fields.

By 1860, wealthy Cherokee families owned about four thousand enslaved people out of a total Cherokee population of roughly twenty-one thousand. The Cherokee Nation's constitution, adopted in 1827, explicitly protected slavery and prohibited the emancipation of enslaved people without the owner's consent—language that mirrored Southern state constitutions.

This adoption of slavery would have devastating consequences during the Civil War. The Cherokee Nation split apart, with some Cherokee fighting for the Union and others joining the Confederacy. Stand Watie, a wealthy Cherokee slaveholder, became a Confederate general and would be the last Confederate commander to surrender in June 1865.

Slave owners weren't all the same. Some were brutal monsters who whipped people for the smallest infractions. Others were more paternalistic, convincing themselves they were taking care of their "family" of slaves. But here's the thing—even the "kindest" master still owned human beings. Even under the best conditions, you lived your entire life at someone else's mercy.

Don't think slaves just accepted this quietly. They fought back in countless ways. Some ran away, though the odds of making it to freedom were not great. Others worked slowly, broke tools "accidentally," or pretended to be sick. Many learned to read and write in secret, even though it was illegal. They created their own communities and kept their families together as much as they could, even when the law said their marriages didn't count and their children weren't really theirs.

Every once in a while, slaves rebelled violently. These uprisings scared White Southerners to death, and they crushed them with overwhelming force. Still, the threat was always there, a constant reminder that you can't keep millions of people in chains forever without consequences.

By 1860, about 3.9 million people lived in slavery in the United States. Most of them were in the Deep South, where cotton was king and fortunes were built on their backs.

King Cotton: How an Invention Fueled a Crisis

Here's a story that shows how one small invention can change the course of history. In 1793, a recent Yale graduate named Eli Whitney was visiting a plantation in Georgia. He watched slaves struggling to clean cotton—separating the useful cotton fibers from the sticky green seeds of short-staple cotton. Cotton was incredibly difficult to process by hand. One person might clean about a pound in a whole day of tedious work.

Whitney was the kind of man who liked to figure out how things worked. Watching this slow process, he had an idea. What if you could build a machine to do this work? In just ten days, he cobbled together a simple device with wire brushes and rollers. He called it the cotton gin (short for engine). His machine could clean cotton much faster than anyone could by hand—some say fifty times faster, though the exact speed varied.

Whitney probably had no idea he was about to transform America and make slavery more profitable than it had ever been.

Before the cotton gin, slavery was actually dying out in some places. The tobacco farms of Virginia and Maryland weren't making as much money as they used to. Many of the Founding Fathers, some of whom owned slaves, thought slavery would gradually disappear. Thomas Jefferson wrote that holding slaves was like "holding a wolf by the ear"—it was dangerous, but you didn't know how to let go safely.

The cotton gin changed everything overnight. Suddenly, cotton was incredibly profitable to grow. Production exploded from about 3,000 bales in 1790 to over 4 million bales by 1860. The South became the world's cotton supplier, providing three-quarters of the cotton that fed British textile mills and four-fifths of what American factories used.

And cotton needed slaves. Lots of them. The cotton gin could clean cotton fast, but someone still had to plant it, tend it, and pick it by hand. Cotton picking was brutal work. You had to bend over in the hot sun for hours, your fingers bleeding from the sharp bolls, racing to fill your quota before dark.

This cotton boom made slaves incredibly valuable as capital investments. A healthy young man might sell for $1,200 to $1,500—we're talking about hundreds of thousands of dollars in today's money. By 1860, the total value of all slaves in America was about $3 billion, representing the single largest financial asset in the entire U.S. economy. It was more than all the railroads and factories combined.

Cotton fever spread across the Deep South like wildfire. Planters bought up land in Alabama, Mississippi, Louisiana, Arkansas, and Texas. They brought their slaves with them or bought new ones at slave markets in cities like New Orleans and Charleston. Families were torn apart as the cotton economy pulled people westward.

The cotton boom created a class of incredibly wealthy planters who owned hundreds of slaves each. These planters built mansions, sent their children to fancy colleges, and controlled Southern politics. They had millions of dollars invested in slaves, and they weren't about to let that investment disappear.

However, cotton didn't just make rich planters richer. It made the entire South dependent on slavery. Small farmers who owned just a few slaves still benefited from high cotton prices. Poor White farmers who owned no slaves at all still supported the system since it guaranteed they wouldn't be at the bottom of society.

Cotton also made Southerners think they were invincible. They sold their cotton to buyers in New York and Liverpool, making huge profits. They used that money to buy manufactured goods from the North and Europe. "Cotton is king!" they proclaimed. Surely no one would dare mess with slavery when so much money was at stake.

They were wrong. By 1860, cotton had made slavery more entrenched and profitable than ever. However, it had also made the South a one-crop economy dependent on forced labor. When the crisis came, all that wealth tied up in slaves and cotton couldn't save them.

Two Different Worlds: Life in the North vs. the South

By 1860, the North and South had developed into two very different societies. A visitor traveling from Boston to Charleston would feel like they were entering a different country.

The North was becoming an industrial, urban society. Factories sprouted up in cities like Lowell, Massachusetts, and Pittsburgh, Pennsylvania. These factories produced textiles, iron goods, shoes, and other manufactured products. The North had about 85 percent of the country's factories and produced more than 90 percent of its manufactured goods.

Northern cities were growing rapidly. Immigrants poured in from Ireland, Germany, and other European countries. They provided cheap labor for the factories and helped build the canals and railroads that connected Northern markets. By 1860, about a quarter of Northerners lived in cities or towns.

The typical Northern worker was a free wage laborer. He could quit his job, move to a new city, or start his own business if he saved enough money. This system wasn't perfect—factory workers often faced dangerous conditions and low pay. But they had rights that enslaved people didn't have. They could marry whom they chose, keep their families together, and hope for a better future.

Northern society valued education, hard work, and self-improvement. Public schools became common. Newspapers and books were widely available. Northern churches often preached that slavery was a sin. Many

Northerners believed in "free soil, free labor, free men"—the idea that free wage labor was morally superior to slave labor.

The South remained largely agricultural and rural. About 80 percent of Southerners lived on farms or in small towns. The region had few factories, fewer railroads, and almost no public schools. Wealthy planters sent their children to private schools or hired tutors, but most poor Whites received little or no formal education.

Southern society was hierarchical and based on race. At the top were the large planters who owned fifty or more enslaved people. These "planter aristocrats" made up less than 1 percent of the population but controlled most of the wealth and political power. Below them were smaller planters and farmers who owned a few enslaved people. The majority of White Southerners owned no enslaved people at all, but they still supported the system because it guaranteed them a higher social status than Black people.

At the bottom of Southern society were enslaved African Americans, who made up about 40 percent of the population in the slave states. Free Black people, who numbered about 250,000 in the South, faced severe restrictions on their movements and rights.

The economic differences between North and South were striking. The North had more railroads, more banks, more factories, and more schools. Its economy was diversified and growing rapidly. The South remained dependent on agriculture, especially cotton. It imported most of its manufactured goods from the North or Europe.

These economic differences led to political conflicts. The North wanted high tariffs to protect its industries from foreign competition. The South wanted low tariffs so it could buy cheap manufactured goods and sell cotton freely to foreign buyers. The North supported government spending on roads, canals, and railroads. The South opposed such spending because it would mainly benefit Northern businesses.

But the deepest difference was over slavery itself. Many Northerners had come to see slavery as morally wrong and economically backward. They believed free wage labor was more efficient and more in keeping with American values of liberty and equality. Most White Southerners saw slavery as natural, beneficial, and essential to their way of life. They believed God had made Black people inferior to White people and intended them to be slaves.

These weren't just economic disagreements—they were different visions of what America should be. The North was becoming a modern, industrial, democratic society. The South remained a hierarchical, agricultural society built on racial slavery. By 1860, it was becoming clear that these two systems couldn't coexist peacefully in one nation.

Voices for Freedom: The Abolitionist Movement

While most White Americans accepted slavery as a fact of life, a growing number of people in the North began demanding its immediate end. These abolitionists, as they were called, played a crucial role in turning slavery into a national political issue.

The abolitionist movement had deep roots in Christian faith. Many abolitionists were evangelical Protestants who believed slavery was a sin against God. If America continued to allow human bondage, they argued, God would punish the entire nation. The Bible taught that all people were created in God's image. How could Christians support a system that treated human beings as property?

One of the most famous abolitionists was William Lloyd Garrison, a Boston newspaper publisher who founded *The Liberator* in 1831. For thirty-five years, Garrison's newspaper attacked slavery in the harshest terms. He called the Constitution "a covenant with death and an agreement with hell" because it protected slavery. He demanded immediate emancipation and full equality for Black Americans. Garrison shocked many people by insisting that women should have equal rights in the abolitionist movement.

The most powerful abolitionist voices belonged to people who had experienced slavery firsthand. Frederick Douglass escaped from slavery in Maryland in 1838 and became one of the most effective speakers and writers in American history. His autobiography, *Narrative of the Life of Frederick Douglass, an American Slave*, sold thousands of copies and opened Northern eyes to the brutal reality of slavery.

Douglass was a brilliant orator who could hold audiences spellbound for hours. He spoke from personal experience about the whippings, family separations, and daily humiliations of slavery. When pro-slavery speakers claimed that enslaved people were happy and treated well, Douglass could counter with the truth. "No man can put a chain about the ankle of his fellow man without at last finding the other end fastened about his own neck," he declared.[i]

---

[i] https://teachingamericanhistory.org/document/the-civil-rights-case/

Sojourner Truth, who was born into slavery in New York, became another powerful abolitionist speaker. Standing nearly six feet tall, she had a commanding presence and a gift for memorable phrases. When White feminists complained about their lack of rights, Truth reminded them of the double burden faced by Black women. "Ain't I a woman?" she asked in her most famous speech.

Harriet Beecher Stowe wasn't an abolitionist speaker, but her novel *Uncle Tom's Cabin* might have done more to turn Northern opinion against slavery than all the speeches combined. Published in 1852, the novel told the story of Uncle Tom, an enslaved man whose Christian faith sustained him through terrible suffering. Stowe wrote the book to show Northerners what slavery really looked like.

Uncle Tom's Cabin became a publishing sensation. It sold 300,000 copies in its first year and eventually sold over 2 million copies in the United States. It was translated into dozens of languages and even adapted for the stage. For many Northerners, it was their first real look at the horrors of slavery. When Abraham Lincoln met Stowe during the Civil War, he supposedly said, "So you're the little woman who wrote the book that made this great war!"

The abolitionists used every tool available to spread their message. They published newspapers and books. They organized lecture tours and petition campaigns. They smuggled enslaved people to freedom through the Underground Railroad, a secret network of safe houses and guides. Harriet Tubman, herself an escaped slave, made nineteen dangerous trips to the South and helped about seventy enslaved people reach freedom.

Not all abolitionists agreed on tactics. Some, like Garrison, believed in "moral suasion"—convincing Americans through speeches and writing that slavery was wrong. Others, like Frederick Douglass, thought political action was necessary. Still others, like John Brown, believed violence was the only way to end slavery.

Most White Northerners weren't abolitionists. Many disliked slavery, but they didn't want immediate emancipation. Some feared that freed slaves would move north and compete for jobs. Others worried that abolition would break up the Union. And even though many opposed slavery, many Northerners still held racist beliefs and did not support full equality for Black Americans. Even Abraham Lincoln, who hated slavery, wasn't an abolitionist until the Civil War began.

But the abolitionists kept slavery in the public eye. They made it impossible for Americans to ignore the moral questions raised by human bondage. They forced politicians to take stands on slavery's expansion. They helped create the Republican Party, which opposed the spread of slavery into new territories. Most importantly, they kept alive the idea that slavery was incompatible with American values of liberty and equality.

Southern leaders understood the threat abolitionists represented. They banned abolitionist literature from the mails and offered rewards for the capture of prominent abolitionists. They argued that Northern attacks on slavery threatened the South's entire way of life.

By 1860, the abolitionists had succeeded in making slavery a national issue that could no longer be ignored or compromised away. They hadn't convinced most Americans to support immediate emancipation, but they had planted seeds of doubt about slavery that would grow during the war. When the fighting began, their decades of moral argument would help transform a war to save the Union into a war to free the slaves.

The house was indeed dividing, just as Lincoln had predicted. The question was whether it could be put back together and at what cost.

Chapter 2: The Cracks Begin to Show

By the 1820s, America had a problem that wouldn't go away. Every time the country wanted to add a new state, the same question came up: would it allow slavery or not? This wasn't just about drawing lines on a map. It was about political power, economic interests, and the future of the nation itself.

For forty years, politicians tried to solve this problem with compromises. They drew lines across the continent, made deals about which states could have slaves, and hoped the issue would somehow resolve itself. But each compromise just made the tensions worse. By 1860, the political system had completely broken down, and Americans were ready to fight a war rather than accept another deal.

Here's how it all fell apart.

The Balancing Act: The Missouri Compromise of 1820

In 1819, Missouri wanted to join the Union as a slave state. Sounds simple enough, right? Wrong. If Missouri came in as a slave state, the South would have more senators than the North. That would give slaveholders control of the U.S. Senate.

Northern politicians weren't about to let that happen. They had their own plan: Missouri could join, but only if it banned slavery. Southern politicians went ballistic. Missouri was south of the Ohio River, in territory where slavery had always been expected. If the North could ban slavery in Missouri, where would it end?

The debate got nasty fast. One Georgia congressman warned that forcing Missouri to ban slavery would kindle "a fire which all the waters of the ocean cannot put out." A New York congressman shot back that slavery was a sin that should weigh on everyone's soul. These weren't dry policy discussions—they were angry fights about the nation's future.[i]

For months, Congress was deadlocked. Some people started talking about the Union breaking apart. Then Henry Clay, a congressman from Kentucky, stepped in with a compromise. Clay was known as the "Great Compromiser" because he had a talent for finding middle ground that nobody really liked but everybody could live with.

Clay's deal actually consisted of three separate agreements bundled together. First, Missouri would join as a slave state. Second, Maine (which had been part of Massachusetts) would join as a free state, keeping the balance in the Senate. Third, and most importantly, Congress would draw a line across the rest of the Louisiana Territory at latitude 36°30'. North of that line, slavery would be banned. South of it, slavery would be allowed.

The Missouri Compromise passed in 1820, and most Americans breathed a sigh of relief. The crisis was over. The Union was saved. However, not everyone was happy. Thomas Jefferson, the elderly ex-president, said the compromise filled him with terror. He compared it to "a fire bell in the night" that woke him up to the danger facing the country. "This momentous question, like a fire bell in the night, awakened and filled me with terror," he wrote. "I considered it at once as the knell of the Union."[ii]

Jefferson understood something that many politicians missed. The Missouri Compromise didn't solve the slavery problem—it just postponed it. Someday, Americans would have to decide whether slavery would expand or die out. When that day came, no amount of congressional dealmaking would be enough.

For thirty years, though, the Missouri Compromise helped keep the slavery question from completely dominating national politics. It didn't make the issue disappear; tensions over slavery flared up during the annexation of Texas, the Mexican-American War, and the Compromise

[i] https://www.senate.gov/artandhistory/history/minute/Missouri_Compromise.htm

[ii] https://www.monticello.org/research-education/thomas-jefferson-encyclopedia/fire-bell-night-quotation/

of 1850. The annexation of Texas in 1845 brought a huge new slave state into the Union, upsetting the careful balance between free and slave states. The Mexican-American War (1846-1848) raised explosive questions about whether slavery would be allowed in the vast territories won from Mexico. When Congressman David Wilmot proposed banning slavery from these new territories, his "Wilmot Proviso" passed the House but failed in the Senate, revealing how the slavery issue divided the country along sectional lines.

The Compromise of 1850 temporarily defused this crisis by admitting California as a free state while allowing other territories to decide the slavery question for themselves. However, the compromise also included the Fugitive Slave Act, which required Northerners to help capture runaway slaves. This law turned many previously moderate Northerners against slavery by forcing them to participate in the system they disliked.

Still, the 36°30' line from the Missouri Compromise provided a framework that both sides could work with. New states came into the Union in pairs—one free, one slave—maintaining the delicate balance. Americans could focus on other things, like building railroads, expanding westward, and making money.

But in the 1850s, everything changed. New territories wanted to become states. Gold was discovered in California. Americans were talking about building a railroad to the Pacific. Suddenly, that line drawn across the map in 1820 wasn't enough anymore. The slavery question was back, and this time, it wouldn't go away.

Bleeding Kansas: A Preview of the War to Come

In 1854, Senator Stephen Douglas of Illinois had what he thought was a brilliant idea. Douglas wanted to organize the territories of Kansas and Nebraska so that a transcontinental railroad could be built through them. But there was a problem: both territories were north of the line drawn in the Missouri Compromise, which meant slavery would be banned there.

Southern senators wouldn't vote for Douglas's bill unless he gave them something in return. So Douglas came up with a new concept: "popular sovereignty." Instead of Congress deciding whether territories could have slavery, the people living there would vote on it themselves. It sounded democratic and fair. It was a disaster.

Douglas's Kansas-Nebraska Act repealed the Missouri Compromise and opened both territories to slavery if the residents wanted it. The bill barely passed Congress, but it passed. President Franklin Pierce signed it into law in May 1854.

Northern politicians were furious. They had considered the Missouri Compromise a sacred agreement. Now it was dead, killed by what they saw as Southern greed for more slave territory.

The Kansas-Nebraska Act changed American politics. The old Whig Party finally collapsed. Northerners who hated slavery were left with nowhere to go. So, they built something new.

In 1854, they came together and created the Republican Party. Its members weren't all abolitionists. Most didn't call for ending slavery where it already existed. However, they agreed on one thing: slavery must not spread into the new territories.

Trouble started when people actually tried to settle Kansas. Pro-slavery settlers poured in from Missouri, determined to make Kansas a slave state. Anti-slavery settlers came from New England and other free states, equally determined to keep Kansas free. Both sides were armed and angry.

The pro-slavery settlers got there first and set up a territorial government in the town of Lecompton. They passed laws making it illegal to speak against slavery. The penalty for helping a slave escape was death. Even questioning whether someone had a right to own slaves could land you in prison.

The anti-slavery settlers refused to recognize this government. They set up their own capital in the town of Lawrence and elected their own legislature. Kansas now had two governments, each claiming to be legitimate.

Violence was inevitable. In May 1856, a pro-slavery mob attacked Lawrence, burning buildings and destroying the offices of anti-slavery newspapers. Three days later, a fierce abolitionist named John Brown decided to get revenge. Brown and his sons murdered five pro-slavery settlers along Pottawatomie Creek, hacking them to death with swords.

The killings triggered a low-intensity guerrilla conflict that simmered for years. Pro-slavery "Border Ruffians" from Missouri crossed into Kansas to vote illegally and intimidate free-state settlers. Anti-slavery "Jayhawkers" raided pro-slavery settlements and freed slaves. The violence wasn't universal—most settlers tried to live peacefully—but the fighting was brutal enough to earn the territory the nickname "Bleeding Kansas." Over the course of four years, the political violence claimed around fifty to sixty lives.

The violence wasn't limited to Kansas. In May 1856, Senator Charles Sumner of Massachusetts gave a speech in the U.S. Senate attacking slavery and personally insulting Senator Andrew Butler of South Carolina. Two days later, Butler's cousin, Congressman Preston Brooks, walked into the Senate chamber and beat Sumner unconscious with a walking stick.

Southern congressmen thought Brooks was a hero for defending his family's honor. They sent him dozens of new walking sticks to replace the one he broke on Sumner's head. Northern congressmen were horrified that political disagreement had turned to physical violence.

The Sumner-Brooks incident showed how completely the two sides had stopped listening to each other. What looked like justified revenge to one side looked like savage brutality to the other. There was no common ground left.

Kansas became a symbol of the national crisis. Here was democracy in action, and it had produced chaos and bloodshed. Popular sovereignty couldn't work if the two sides hated each other so much that they were willing to kill rather than accept defeat.

By 1858, Kansas had become a free territory, but the damage was done. Americans had seen that the slavery question couldn't be settled peacefully through voting. They had watched their political system break down into violence. They had gotten a preview of the civil war that was coming.

A Supreme Betrayal: The Dred Scott Decision

Just when it seemed like things couldn't get worse, the Supreme Court stepped into the slavery debate with one of the most infamous decisions in American legal history. The case involved a slave named Dred Scott who had sued for his freedom.

Dred Scott had been the property of an Army surgeon named Dr. John Emerson. In the 1830s, Emerson took Scott to live in Illinois (a free state) and later to Wisconsin Territory (where slavery was banned by the Missouri Compromise). After several years, they returned to Missouri, where Emerson died in 1843.

Scott might have lived out his life in slavery, but abolitionists encouraged him to sue for his freedom. Their argument seemed logical: Scott had lived for years in places where slavery was illegal. Didn't that make him a free man? The case worked its way through the courts for over a decade, finally reaching the Supreme Court in 1856.

Chief Justice Roger Taney, a Maryland slaveholder, saw the case as a chance to settle the slavery question once and for all. He wanted to rule that Congress had no power to ban slavery in the territories. But to do that, he first had to decide whether Scott had the right to sue in federal court at all.

In March 1857, Taney announced the Supreme Court's decision. It was a bombshell. First, he ruled that Black people could never be American citizens, whether they were enslaved or free. The Founding Fathers, Taney claimed, had viewed Black people as "beings of an inferior order" with "no rights which the White man was bound to respect."[i]

Since Scott wasn't a citizen, he couldn't sue in federal court. The case should have ended there. But Taney kept going. He ruled that Congress never had the power to ban slavery in the territories. The Missouri Compromise had been unconstitutional all along. Slavery was legal in every territory until that territory became a state and chose to ban it.

The decision was everything Southern slaveholders had hoped for. The federal government couldn't stop slavery's expansion. Even territories that had banned slavery would have to allow it again.

Northern reactions ranged from shock to rage. The *New-York Tribune* called it "wicked," "atrocious," and "abominable." Abraham Lincoln said the decision was based on "assumed historical facts which are not really true."[ii] Frederick Douglass was even blunter: "This very attempt to blot out forever the hopes of an enslaved people may be one necessary link in the chain of events preparatory to the downfall and complete overthrow of the whole slave system."[iii]

The Dred Scott decision made compromise almost impossible. If slavery was legal in every territory, as the Supreme Court had ruled, then Stephen Douglas's "popular sovereignty" was meaningless. Territorial residents couldn't vote to ban something that was constitutionally protected.

The decision also made the new Republican Party's main issue—stopping slavery's expansion—seem hopeless. Republicans would need to amend the Constitution to stop slavery from spreading. That would

---

[i] https://www.acslaw.org/expertforum/no-rights-which-the-white-man-was-bound-to-respect/

[ii] https://billofrightsinstitute.org/primary-sources/speech-on-dred-scott-decision

[iii] https://frederickdouglasspapersproject.com/item/8829

require two-thirds of both houses of Congress and three-fourths of the states. With the South controlling a third of the states, it would never happen.

Many Northerners began to suspect a vast conspiracy. First, the Kansas-Nebraska Act repealed the Missouri Compromise. Then the Supreme Court said that the Missouri Compromise had been illegal all along. It looked like Southern slaveholders and their Northern allies (called "doughfaces") were working together to spread slavery everywhere.

Republicans started warning that slavery wouldn't stop with the territories. What would stop slavery from spreading to free states? Illinois and Ohio might be forced to accept slavery just like Kansas and Nebraska.

The Dred Scott decision didn't settle the slavery question; it actually made the crisis worse. By claiming that Black people could never be citizens and that slavery was constitutionally protected everywhere, the Supreme Court had made peaceful compromise almost impossible. The two sides weren't just disagreeing about policy anymore. They were operating under completely different understandings of what America was supposed to be.

John Brown's Raid: Hero or Terrorist?

By 1859, most Americans were trying to find peaceful solutions to the slavery crisis. But one man had run out of patience with talk. John Brown believed God had called him to destroy slavery by force. His raid on a federal weapons arsenal would terrify the South, electrify the North, and push the nation to the brink of war.

Brown was a strange, intense man who saw himself as God's instrument of justice. He had failed at everything he tried—farming, business, land speculation—but he had succeeded in one thing: killing people he considered enemies of God. In Kansas, Brown and his followers had murdered five pro-slavery settlers. And he still wasn't satisfied.

Brown had a plan that was either brilliant or insane, depending on one's point of view. He wanted to capture the federal arsenal at Harpers Ferry, Virginia, and distribute weapons to enslaved people throughout the region. They would rise up and fight for their freedom. The rebellion would spread across the South until slavery collapsed under the weight of its own violence.

It was a fantasy, but Brown believed in it completely. He spent months raising money from wealthy abolitionists in New England, telling them he planned to create "fortifications" in the Virginia mountains where escaped slaves could defend themselves. He didn't mention that he planned to start a war.

On the night of October 16, 1859, Brown and twenty-one followers cut telegraph wires and seized the arsenal at Harpers Ferry. His force included five Black men, both free and formerly enslaved. They took several hostages, including Lewis Washington, the great-grandnephew of George Washington. Then they waited for enslaved people to join their rebellion.

The massive uprising Brown expected never materialized. Local enslaved people had no idea what was happening, and even if they had known, joining would have meant almost certain death. A few enslaved men were briefly forced to join Brown's party, but no spontaneous rebellion occurred. Instead of the slave revolt he had fantasized about, Brown got a few curious onlookers and a lot of angry locals.

By morning, militia companies were surrounding the arsenal. Brown and his men were trapped in the engine house of the Baltimore and Ohio Railroad. President James Buchanan sent federal troops under Colonel Robert E. Lee (yes, the future Confederate general) to end the crisis.

The siege lasted thirty-six hours. On October 18, Lee's Marines stormed the engine house. Brown was wounded and captured. Ten of his followers were dead, including two of his sons. The raid was over almost before it began.

However, the raid's impact was enormous. Southern newspapers screamed that Brown was part of a vast Northern conspiracy to murder White Southerners in their beds. They pointed out that wealthy abolitionists had funded his activities. If this was what the anti-slavery movement really wanted, then the South could never be safe in the Union.

Northern reactions were more complicated. Most Northern politicians condemned Brown's violence. Abraham Lincoln said that it violated the law and could never succeed. But many Northerners also admired Brown's willingness to die for his beliefs, even if they disagreed with his methods.

Brown's trial became a sensation. Instead of pleading insanity, which might have saved his life, Brown used the courtroom as a stage to explain his actions. "I believe that to have interfered as I have done...in behalf of His despised poor, was not wrong, but right," he declared. "Now, if it is deemed necessary that I should forfeit my life for the furtherance of the ends of justice, and mingle my blood further with the blood of my children and with the blood of millions in this slave country whose rights are disregarded by wicked, cruel, and unjust enactments, I submit; so let it be done."[i]

Brown was sentenced to death and hanged on December 2, 1859. Brown's execution made him a martyr in the North. Ralph Waldo Emerson compared him to Jesus Christ. Henry David Thoreau called him "an angel of light." Church bells tolled across New England on the day he died. At his funeral, someone sang what would become the Civil War's most famous song: "John Brown's body lies a-mouldering in the grave, but his truth goes marching on."

The South was horrified by this sympathy for Brown. Here was a man who had tried to start a race war, and Northerners were treating him like a hero. If this was what the North really thought, then the two parts of the country could never coexist peacefully.

Brown's raid didn't start the Civil War, but it convinced many Southerners that war was inevitable. They began forming militia companies and stockpiling weapons. When Abraham Lincoln was elected president a year later, they were ready to act.

The Election of 1860: The Final Straw

The presidential election of 1860 should have been democracy in action—Americans choosing their leader through peaceful voting. Instead, it became the final act in the breakdown of American politics. By election day, the country was so divided that no single candidate could win support from both the North and the South.

The trouble started with the Democratic Party, which had held the country together for decades by including both pro-slavery and anti-slavery members. In April 1860, Democrats met in Charleston to choose their presidential candidate. The obvious choice was Stephen Douglas of Illinois, the author of the Kansas-Nebraska Act and the most prominent Northern Democrat.

---

[i] https://www.zinnedproject.org/materials/john-brown-last-speech

But Southern Democrats had had enough of Douglas. His "popular sovereignty" doctrine had failed in Kansas, where anti-slavery settlers had won. Even worse, Douglas had opposed the Lecompton Constitution, which would have made Kansas a slave state. Southern Democrats wanted a candidate who would actively promote slavery, not just allow it.

When Northern Democrats nominated Douglas anyway, delegates from eight Southern states walked out of the convention. They held their own convention and nominated Vice President John Breckinridge of Kentucky on a platform demanding federal protection for slavery in all territories.

Meanwhile, remnants of the old Whig Party and other moderates formed the Constitutional Union Party. They nominated John Bell of Tennessee and tried to avoid the slavery issue entirely, focusing instead on preserving the Union.

This left the field open for the Republicans, who nominated Abraham Lincoln of Illinois. Lincoln wasn't the most radical Republican—that would have been William Seward of New York—but he wasn't the most moderate either. His position was clear: slavery could continue where it already existed, but it must not be allowed to expand into new territories.

The campaign was really four separate regional elections. In the North, it was Lincoln versus Douglas. In the South, it was Breckinridge versus Bell, with Douglas getting some support in border areas. Lincoln's name didn't even appear on the ballot in most Southern states.

Lincoln won the election without getting a single vote from the Deep South. He received less than 40 percent of the total popular vote but won a majority of electoral votes by sweeping the North. Douglas came in second in popular votes but won only Missouri and part of New Jersey. Breckinridge carried most of the South, while Bell won three border states.

The results showed how completely the country had split along sectional lines. To many Southerners, the election proved that the North no longer cared about Southern interests. If Northerners could elect a president without a single Southern vote, what would stop them from using federal power to destroy slavery?

Southern newspapers were already talking about secession before the election results were official. Lincoln tried to reassure the South. In his first message after the election, he promised he had no intention of interfering with slavery where it already existed. "I have no purpose, directly or indirectly, to interfere with the institution of slavery in the States where it exists," he said. "I believe I have no lawful right to do so, and I have no inclination to do so."[i]

But Southern leaders weren't listening anymore. They had spent forty years watching the North grow stronger and richer while the South remained dependent on cotton and slaves. They had seen anti-slavery sentiment grow in the North while the federal government offered more protection to slavery. Now, a "Black Republican" (as they called Lincoln) was president, elected by Northern votes alone.

The election of 1860 was the final proof that the American political system couldn't handle the slavery question. For eighty years, the country had been held together through compromises that satisfied nobody completely but gave everybody something. Now there was nothing left to compromise about. Lincoln wouldn't allow slavery to expand. Southern leaders wouldn't accept restrictions on expansion. One side had to win, and the other had to lose.

The house that Lincoln had warned about was finally falling down. The question was whether it could be rebuilt and what it would look like if it could.

---

[i] https://avalon.law.yale.edu/19th_century/lincoln1.asp

Chapter 3: The South Leaves the Union

Abraham Lincoln's election hit the South like a thunderbolt. Here was a man who had received minimal support from the slave states—in part because he wasn't on the ballot in some states—and had been elected president primarily by Northern voters. To many White Southerners, this proved what they had feared for decades: the North no longer cared about Southern interests. If Northerners could control the presidency without them, what would stop them from using federal power to destroy slavery?

Secession: The Great Divorce

South Carolina had been threatening to leave the Union since the 1830s. It had nearly seceded over federal tariffs that Southerners called the "Tariff of Abominations." The state's leaders developed a theory called "nullification"—the idea that states could declare federal laws unconstitutional and refuse to enforce them. When that crisis was resolved through compromise, South Carolina's radical politicians, known as "Fire-Eaters," didn't give up. They just waited for a better opportunity.

Now, with Lincoln's election, the state's leaders saw their chance. On November 10, 1860, just four days after the election, the South Carolina Legislature called for a state convention to consider secession. Governor William Henry Gist had already been secretly corresponding with other Southern governors about coordinating their states' departures from the Union.

On December 17, 1860, delegates from across South Carolina gathered in Columbia for the secession convention. These weren't hotheaded radicals acting in the heat of passion; they were the state's most prominent lawyers, planters, and politicians. Many had been planning this moment for years. They had one question to decide: Should South Carolina remain in the United States?

The debate didn't last long because there really wasn't much debate. The delegates had been elected specifically to take South Carolina out of the Union, and they knew their constituents expected them to do it. On December 20, 1860, the convention voted unanimously—169 to 0—to secede from the Union.

The formal announcement came at 1:30 that afternoon. A messenger rushed from the convention hall to the crowd waiting outside and shouted, "The Union is dissolved!" Church bells rang throughout Charleston. Crowds filled the streets, cheering and singing "Dixie" and "The Marseillaise." Cannons fired in celebration. Women threw flowers from balconies. Men lit bonfires and shot off fireworks. South Carolina was no longer part of the United States.

The state's "Declaration of the Immediate Causes" explained exactly why it was leaving. It wasn't just about states' rights in general or tariffs or constitutional theory. It was mainly about slavery. The declaration complained that Northern states had "assumed the right of deciding upon the propriety of our domestic institutions" and had "encouraged and assisted thousands of our slaves to leave their homes."

Most importantly, South Carolina's leaders were terrified of what Lincoln might do as president. They pointed out that Republicans had declared that slavery was morally wrong and must not be allowed to expand. If slavery couldn't expand, it would eventually die out. "A geographical line has been drawn across the Union," the declaration stated, "and all the States north of that line have united in the election of a man to the high office of President of the United States whose opinions and purposes are hostile to slavery."[i]

Other Southern states weren't far behind, but the process wasn't identical everywhere. Mississippi seceded on January 9, 1861, with its convention voting 84 to 15 to leave the Union. Florida followed on

[i] https://constitutioncenter.org/the-constitution/historic-document-library/detail/south-carolina-declaration-of-secession-1860

January 10 (62 to 7), then Alabama on January 11 (61 to 39). Georgia's convention was more divided, passing secession by 208 to 89 on January 19. Louisiana left on January 26 (113 to 17), and Texas completed the first wave on February 1 (its convention vote was 166 to 8).

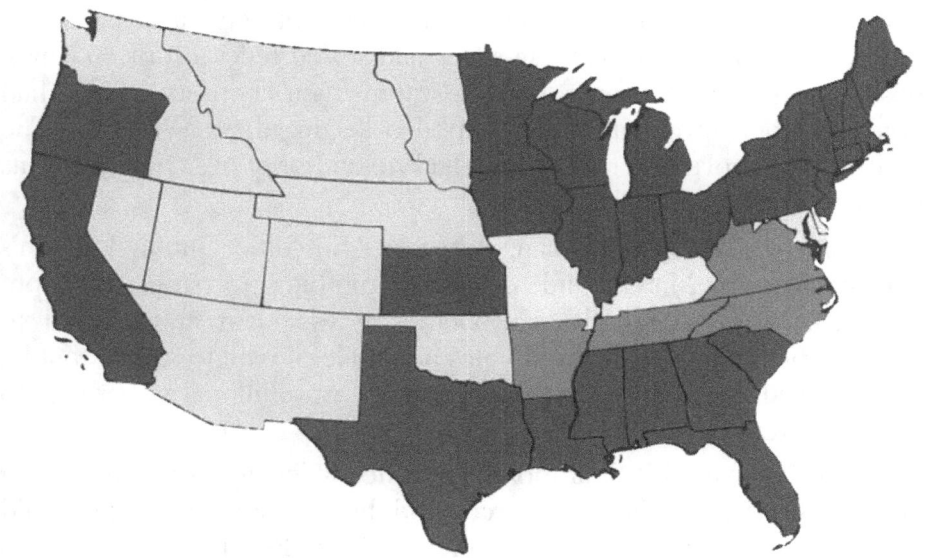

What the United States looked like in 1861. The dark red are states that seceded before April 15, 1861. The orange states seceded after April 15, 1861. The yellow states permitted slavery but did not secede. The blue states are where slavery was banned. The grey areas were U.S. territories under Union Army control.[82]

Each state held a convention rather than a direct popular vote, which meant that wealthy planters and lawyers had disproportionate influence. In most cases, these conventions had been elected before Lincoln's victory, when secession seemed less likely. But once South Carolina acted, the momentum became unstoppable.

Not everyone in these states supported secession. The votes in the conventions often reflected deep divisions within Southern society. The opposition came from different groups for different reasons. Some were Whigs who had always supported the Union and believed compromise was still possible. Others were small farmers who worried that secession would lead to a war that would be fought with their blood for the benefit of wealthy planters. Still others were businessmen who feared that leaving the Union would hurt trade and commerce.

But the wealthy planters who dominated Southern politics were determined to protect their enormous investment in enslaved people. They owned most of the land, controlled most of the newspapers, and held most of the political offices. When they decided that Lincoln's election was unacceptable, they had the power to drag their states out of the Union regardless of what poorer White people wanted.

The speed of secession caught many Americans off guard. In just six weeks, six states had left the Union, and a seventh (Texas) was about to follow. By February 1861, these states had seized federal forts, arsenals, post offices, and customs houses within their borders. They had organized their own armies and started collecting their own taxes. The United States government suddenly had no authority over millions of its former citizens.

President James Buchanan, who was in office until Lincoln's inauguration in March, did essentially nothing to stop secession. Buchanan was a Pennsylvanian Democrat who had always tried to appease the South. He believed states had no legal right to secede, but he also believed the federal government had no constitutional power to stop them by force.

Buchanan spent his final months in office wringing his hands, issuing proclamations that nobody obeyed, and hoping someone else would solve the problem. His secretary of war, John Floyd of Virginia, was secretly transferring weapons and supplies to Southern arsenals. His treasury secretary, Howell Cobb of Georgia, resigned to help organize the Confederacy. By the time Buchanan left office, much of his Cabinet had either resigned or was actively working against the federal government.

Some Northern politicians tried to find a compromise that would bring the seceded states back. Senator John Crittenden of Kentucky proposed a series of constitutional amendments that would have permanently protected slavery where it existed and allowed it to expand into territories south of the old Missouri Compromise line. But Lincoln refused to accept any compromise that allowed slavery to expand.

By March 1861, when Lincoln finally took office, seven states were out of the Union and four more were considering secession. The United States was facing the greatest crisis in its history, and nobody knew how to solve it.

Creating the Confederacy: A New Government Is Born

The seceded states didn't want to be independent forever. They wanted to create a new nation that would protect slavery and Southern interests. In February 1861, delegates from the seven seceded states met in Montgomery, Alabama, to form the Confederate States of America.

The delegates worked with remarkable speed and efficiency. They had been planning this moment for months, and many had brought draft documents with them. In just four days, they wrote a new constitution, elected a president and vice president, and began organizing a government. They borrowed heavily from the U.S. Constitution—after all, they liked most of it—but with some crucial changes that revealed what they really cared about.

The Confederate Constitution explicitly protected slavery in language that the U.S. Constitution had avoided. Article I, Section 9 stated clearly: "No bill of attainder, ex post facto law, or law denying or impairing the right of property in negro slaves shall be passed." Article IV, Section 3 guaranteed that Confederate citizens could travel to any territory with their slave property and that "the institution of negro slavery, as it now exists in the Confederate States, shall be recognized and protected by Congress and by the Territorial government."

Unlike the U.S. Constitution, which never used the word "slavery" (referring instead to "persons held to service or labor"), the Confederate Constitution mentioned slavery and enslaved people repeatedly. There was no ambiguity about what this new nation was founded to protect.

Interestingly, the Confederate Constitution also banned the international slave trade. Article I, Section 9 prohibited "the importation of negroes of the African race from any foreign country other than the slaveholding States or Territories of the United States of America." This wasn't because Confederate leaders opposed slavery; they were trying to reassure the Upper South states that they weren't radical extremists who wanted to reopen the African slave trade. The U.S. had ended the slave trade back in 1808.

Many people in Virginia, North Carolina, and Tennessee supported slavery but opposed importing more enslaved people from Africa. Some worried it would drive down the value of the slaves they already owned. Others feared that newly imported Africans would be harder to control than American-born slaves.

The Confederate Constitution also made several changes designed to prevent the kind of federal activism that Southerners had come to hate. The president would serve a single six-year term instead of being eligible for re-election, which theoretically would make him less dependent on political parties and special interests. Congress couldn't fund internal improvements like roads and canals unless they were directly related to navigation or defense. The government couldn't impose protective tariffs that would benefit Northern manufacturers at the expense of Southern consumers.

These changes reflected decades of Southern complaints about federal policies. Southerners had long argued that tariffs were unconstitutional taxes that forced them to pay higher prices for manufactured goods to protect Northern industries. They had opposed federal spending on internal improvements as unconstitutional and unfair since they didn't benefit from the projects. The Confederate Constitution was designed to prevent these abuses of federal power.

For their president, the delegates chose Jefferson Davis of Mississippi. Davis was a logical choice for several reasons. He was a West Point graduate who had served with distinction as a U.S. senator, secretary of war under Franklin Pierce, and colonel in the Mexican-American War. He was known as a moderate who had opposed immediate secession and tried to find compromises to keep the Union together right up until Mississippi left. The delegates hoped his reputation for reasonableness would help convince the wavering Upper South states to join the Confederacy.

Davis wasn't their first choice—that distinction probably belongs to Robert Toombs of Georgia, a fiery orator who had been pushing for Southern independence for years. However, Toombs had some personal problems (he drank too much) and political problems (he was seen as too radical). Davis was a safer choice since he could appeal to moderates both in the South and in Europe, where the Confederacy would need diplomatic recognition.

Davis was also from Mississippi, one of the newer cotton states, which balanced

Jefferson Davis.[88]

the ticket geographically against candidates from the older states like South Carolina and Georgia. His military experience would be valuable if the crisis led to war, which seemed increasingly likely. Also, his ownership of a large plantation called Brierfield, with more than a hundred enslaved workers, proved his commitment to the institution that the Confederacy was created to protect.

For vice president, they chose Alexander Stephens of Georgia, a brilliant but peculiar man who had actually opposed secession until his state voted to leave. Stephens was small and sickly—he weighed less than ninety pounds and looked like he might blow away in a strong wind—but he had one of the sharpest minds in American politics. He was known for his constitutional expertise and his ability to debate complex legal questions.

Like Davis, Stephens was chosen partly to reassure moderates that the Confederacy wasn't controlled by the radical Fire-Eaters. He had served in Congress for sixteen years and had many friends in the North who respected his intelligence and integrity. His opposition to immediate secession actually made him more valuable as a symbol of Confederate moderation.

The choice of Davis and Stephens sent a clear message: the Confederacy wanted to be seen as a respectable constitutional government led by experienced, moderate politicians. They weren't wild-eyed revolutionaries trying to destroy American institutions. They were conservative defenders of what they saw as the original American principles, which they believed the North had abandoned.

In his inaugural address delivered on February 18, 1861, on the steps of the Alabama State Capitol, Davis tried to sound reasonable and defensive. He claimed the Confederate states were simply exercising their fundamental right to form a new government when the old one no longer served their interests, just as the American colonies had done in 1776.

Davis insisted that the Confederacy had no aggressive intentions toward the United States. "All we ask is to be let alone," he said, a phrase that would become a Confederate rallying cry. The new nation didn't want to conquer the North or interfere with Northern institutions. It just wanted to protect its own way of life from what Davis called "the tyranny of an unbridled majority."

Alexander Stephens was more honest about what the Confederacy really stood for. Three weeks after Davis's inaugural speech, Stephens gave a speech in Savannah that became known as the "Cornerstone Speech." In it, he explained that the new Confederate nation was built on fundamentally different principles than the United States.

Stephens argued that the American Founding Fathers had been wrong to include the idea that "all men are created equal" in the Declaration of Independence. That was "an error" that had caused decades of political trouble. "Our new government is founded upon exactly the opposite idea," Stephens declared. "Its foundations are laid, its cornerstone rests, upon the great truth that the negro is not equal to the white man; that slavery subordination to the superior race is his natural and normal condition."[i]

Stephens went on to explain that this wasn't just a political arrangement but a scientific and moral truth. He proclaimed that the Confederate States of America was humanity's first government explicitly founded on the principle of racial inequality.

The Confederate government set up shop in Montgomery, but it was clearly temporary. If Virginia joined the Confederacy, the capital would probably move to Richmond, which was larger, more industrial, and closer to where the battlefields would likely be. For now, though, Montgomery would have to do.

By March 1861, the Confederate States of America was a functioning government with its own president, congress, Cabinet, and army. It controlled seven states with a population of about 5 million people (including 3.5 million enslaved African Americans). It had seized most federal property within its borders and was negotiating with European countries for recognition as an independent nation.

All it needed now was for the rest of the world—especially the United States—to accept that it really was an independent country. That was going to be much harder to arrange.

Meet the Presidents: Abraham Lincoln vs. Jefferson Davis

As the United States faced the greatest crisis in its history, two very different men prepared to lead the opposing sides. Abraham Lincoln and Jefferson Davis had surprisingly similar backgrounds, but they would

---

[i] https://www.battlefields.org/learn/primary-sources/cornerstone-speech

prove to have very different ideas about how to run a country and fight a war.

Both men were born in Kentucky within a year and about a hundred miles of each other. Both served in Congress and became skilled public speakers. However, their paths diverged as they aged, and by 1861, they represented two completely different visions of what America should be.

Abraham Lincoln was fifty-two years old when he became president in March 1861. He had grown up in a one-room log cabin in Kentucky and then moved with his family to Indiana and later to Illinois. His family was poor; his father was an unsuccessful farmer who could barely sign his own name. Lincoln was largely self-educated, reading every book he could get his hands on, including the Bible, *Aesop's Fables*, and *Pilgrim's Progress*.

Lincoln in 1860."

Lincoln was awkward and ungainly, standing six feet four inches tall at a time when most men were much shorter. His clothes never seemed to fit right, and his hair was always messy. He had large hands and feet, prominent cheekbones, and deep-set eyes that gave him a gaunt, almost haunted appearance. His voice was high and nasal, with a Kentucky accent that sounded strange to sophisticated Easterners. But when he spoke, people listened. He had a gift for explaining complex ideas in simple terms and for using humor and folksy stories to make his points stick.

Lincoln's humor was legendary. He could defuse tension with a funny story or devastate an opponent with a perfectly timed joke. When Stephen Douglas accused him of being two-faced during one of their famous debates, Lincoln replied, "If I had two faces, would I be wearing this one?" His law partner, William Herndon, said Lincoln could "story it" out of any difficult situation.

But beneath the folksy exterior was a sharp, ambitious politician with a first-rate mind. Lincoln could quote long passages from the Bible, Shakespeare, and Robert Burns from memory. He had trained himself to think logically and argue persuasively. As one contemporary observed, "His mind was like a piece of steel—very hard to scratch anything on it, and almost impossible to rub it out."

Politically, Lincoln was a moderate Republican who hated slavery but wasn't an abolitionist when he entered the presidency. He believed slavery was morally wrong—"If slavery is not wrong, nothing is wrong," he once wrote—but he also believed the Constitution protected it where it already existed.[i] His goal was to stop slavery from expanding into new territories, hoping that containment would put it "in the course of ultimate extinction."

Lincoln's political experience was limited but impressive. He had served four terms in the Illinois Legislature and one term in Congress, where he had opposed the Mexican-American War and introduced a bill to abolish slavery in Washington, D.C. He lost a Senate race to Stephen Douglas in 1858, but their debates made him a national figure. Still, when Republicans nominated him for president in 1860, many people thought he was unqualified for the job. The *New York Herald* called his nomination "a slaughter of the innocents."

Jefferson Davis was fifty-three when he became president of the Confederacy, just one year older than Lincoln. But the similarities ended there. While Lincoln grew up in poverty, Davis was raised in comfortable circumstances on his family's plantation in Mississippi. His father, Samuel Davis, owned ten slaves and had enough money to send Jefferson to good schools, including Transylvania University in Kentucky and the U.S. Military Academy at West Point.

Davis looked every inch the Southern gentleman. He was tall and lean, with sharp, aristocratic features, piercing gray eyes, and carefully groomed hair and beard. Unlike the rumpled Lincoln, Davis dressed impeccably and carried himself with military bearing. He could be charming when he chose to be, but he often seemed cold and distant. He took himself very seriously and didn't appreciate jokes at his expense.

Davis's military experience was extensive and distinguished. After

---

[i] https://www.abrahamlincolnonline.org/lincoln/speeches/hodges.htm

graduating from West Point in 1828 (23rd in a class of 33), he served seven years as an Army officer on the western frontier. He fought in the Black Hawk War in 1832, a war that Lincoln also fought in. Davis resigned from the Army in 1835 to marry Sarah Knox Taylor, daughter of future president Zachary Taylor, but she died of malaria just three months after their wedding.

Devastated by his wife's death, Davis became a recluse for eight years, rarely leaving his plantation. But when the Mexican-American War broke out in 1846, he volunteered to command a regiment of Mississippi volunteers. His regiment fought heroically at the Battle of Buena Vista, where Davis was wounded in the foot but continued to lead his men. He became a genuine war hero and was offered a promotion to brigadier general, which he declined because he believed the federal government had no constitutional authority to appoint general officers for state volunteer units.

After the war, Davis served in the U.S. Senate, where he became known as one of the South's most effective defenders of slavery and states' rights. He served as secretary of war under President Franklin Pierce from 1853 to 1857 and was widely considered one of the most effective war secretaries in American history. He modernized the Army's weapons and equipment, expanded the system of western forts, and oversaw the surveys for a transcontinental railroad.

When Mississippi seceded in January 1861, Davis was serving his second term in the Senate. He gave a farewell speech that brought tears to the eyes of his colleagues, then returned home expecting to become a Confederate general. According to his wife, he was plowing a field at his plantation when a messenger arrived with news that he had been chosen as the Confederacy's provisional president.

The two men had fundamentally different ideas about presidential power and how to run a government. Lincoln believed the Constitution gave the president broad emergency powers during times of crisis. He was willing to suspend the writ of habeas corpus, spend money without congressional authorization, and expand federal authority to unprecedented levels.

Davis, by contrast, was a strict constitutionalist who believed in limited government even during wartime. He insisted on following proper legal procedures and respecting states' rights, even when doing so made it harder to coordinate the Confederate war effort. When Georgia and

North Carolina refused to cooperate with Confederate conscription laws, Davis argued with them rather than simply overriding their objections.

Lincoln was a masterful politician who understood that democracy required compromise, persuasion, and coalition-building. He knew how to work with difficult people, manage competing egos, and keep fractious coalitions together. He was willing to fire subordinates who didn't perform, but he preferred to win people over rather than force them to comply. His Cabinet included former political rivals who had competed with him for the presidential nomination, but he gradually won their respect and loyalty.

Davis was less skilled at the political arts. He had strong opinions and wasn't good at accepting criticism or working with people who disagreed with him. Throughout the war, he feuded with Confederate generals like Joseph E. Johnston and P. G. T. Beauregard, governors like Joseph Brown of Georgia and Zebulon Vance of North Carolina, and congressmen who questioned his policies. His rigid personality and inability to compromise made it difficult for him to build the kind of political consensus the Confederacy needed to survive.

Perhaps most importantly, the two men had different relationships with slavery. Lincoln saw slavery as morally wrong and inconsistent with American principles, even though he was willing to tolerate it temporarily for political reasons. As the war progressed, he became increasingly committed to ending slavery entirely.

Davis, by contrast, saw slavery as a positive good that benefited both White and Black people. He believed enslaved people were better off than free wage workers in the North and that slavery was sanctioned by the Bible and the Constitution. He never wavered in his belief that the South was fighting for a just cause.

As the crisis deepened in early 1861, both men hoped to avoid war. Lincoln was willing to avoid confrontation so long as federal property and authority were respected, but he did not accept the legality of secession or the permanent loss of Southern states. Davis believed the North wouldn't fight to keep the South in the Union. Both were wrong. Within two months, they would be leading their countries into the bloodiest war in American history.

Chapter 4: The First Shots and the First Battle

By March 1861, America was balanced on a knife's edge. Seven states had left the Union, but nobody had fired a shot yet. Maybe, just maybe, this crisis could be resolved without bloodshed. Both sides still hoped the other would back down.

Abraham Lincoln took the oath of office on March 4, 1861, promising he had no intention of attacking the South. But he also made it clear that the Union would defend itself and its property. The question was: what would happen when these two promises collided?

The collision came at a small fort on an island in Charleston Harbor. Fort Sumter wasn't strategically important. It wasn't even finished. However, it became the symbol of whether the United States government still had any authority in the seceded states. When Confederate forces opened fire on the fort on April 12, 1861, they started the bloodiest war in American history.

The Standoff at Fort Sumter: The War Begins

Fort Sumter sat on a manmade island in Charleston Harbor, about three miles from the city. The fort was supposed to protect Charleston from naval attack, but by 1861, it had become something else entirely. It was a test of wills between two governments that both claimed to be legitimate.

The fort's commander was Major Robert Anderson, a career Army officer from Kentucky who had actually owned slaves. Anderson was no abolitionist, but he was a loyal U.S. officer who took his oath seriously. When South Carolina seceded in December 1860, Anderson found himself in an impossible position. He commanded about eighty soldiers in a state that no longer considered itself part of the United States.

Anderson had originally been stationed at Fort Moultrie, an older fort on the mainland that was impossible to defend. On December 26, 1860, he secretly moved his garrison to Fort Sumter, which was surrounded by water and much easier to hold. South Carolina officials were furious. They saw the move as an act of war.

President Buchanan, who was in his final weeks in office, didn't know what to do. He sent a merchant ship, the *Star of the West*, to resupply Fort Sumter in January 1861. But when the ship approached Charleston Harbor, South Carolina, artillery opened fire and forced it to turn back. Anderson could have fired his own cannons to defend the supply ship, but he chose not to. Nobody wanted to be the one who started a war.

By the time Lincoln took office, the situation was desperate. Anderson's supplies were running low. He had maybe six weeks of food left. Lincoln faced a terrible choice: abandon the fort and look weak, or try to resupply it and probably start a war.

Lincoln tried to find a middle path. He announced that he would send supplies to Fort Sumter, but only food and medicine—no weapons or additional soldiers. He even sent advance notice to South Carolina officials, explaining that this was a humanitarian mission, not a military reinforcement.

Confederate leaders weren't buying it. They saw any attempt to resupply the fort as an act of aggression. Jefferson Davis and his Cabinet met in Montgomery and decided they couldn't allow Lincoln to succeed. If the federal government could hold Fort Sumter indefinitely, it would prove that secession was meaningless.

Davis ordered General P. G. T. Beauregard, the Confederate commander in Charleston, to demand Anderson's surrender. If Anderson refused, Beauregard was to take the fort by force. On April 11, 1861, Beauregard sent three Confederate officers across the harbor to Fort Sumter with a formal demand: surrender immediately or face bombardment.

P. G. T. Beauregard.[85]

Anderson received the ultimatum at 3:20 p.m. He was a professional soldier caught between two impossible loyalties. He had been born in Kentucky, had served in the U.S. Army for thirty-five years, and had taught artillery at West Point, where he had actually taught Beauregard. But Anderson was also a Southerner who understood why his neighbors wanted to leave the Union.

After consulting with his officers, Anderson sent back his reply: he would not surrender. But he added something that gave the Confederates hope. His supplies would run out in a few days anyway, and he would be forced to evacuate unless he was resupplied.

The Confederate officers returned to the mainland and reported Anderson's answer to Beauregard. The general telegraphed the news to Montgomery. Davis and his Cabinet met through the night, debating what to do. Some wanted to wait and let Anderson starve. Others argued that any delay would make the Confederacy look weak.

At 3:20 a.m. on April 12, Beauregard sent his final ultimatum. Anderson had one hour to surrender, or the bombardment would begin. Anderson again refused. At 4:30 a.m., Confederate artillery opened fire.

The first shot came from Fort Johnson, across the harbor from Sumter. The shell arced through the predawn darkness and exploded over the fort. Within minutes, Confederate batteries all around Charleston Harbor were firing at Anderson's garrison. The Civil War had begun.

The bombardment lasted thirty-four hours. Confederate gunners fired more than three thousand shells at Fort Sumter. Anderson's men fired back when they could, but they were hopelessly outnumbered. The Confederates had forty-three guns firing at them from multiple directions. Anderson had only twenty-one guns that could reach the Confederate positions.

Attack on Fort Sumter by Currier & Ives.[86]

Amazingly, nobody was killed during the bombardment. The Confederate gunners were trying to force a surrender, not massacre the garrison. Anderson's men stayed in the fort's lower levels, protected by thick masonry walls. The worst moment came when Confederate shells set fire to the fort's wooden buildings, filling the interior with smoke and threatening to reach the powder magazine.

By the afternoon of April 13, Anderson realized his situation was hopeless. His food was nearly gone, his ammunition was running low, and the fort was on fire. At 2:30 p.m., he raised a white flag. After thirty-four hours of bombardment, Fort Sumter had surrendered.

Beauregard allowed Anderson to surrender with full military honors. The next day, April 14, Anderson's men marched out of the fort with their flags flying and drums beating. They were even allowed to fire a fifty-gun salute to the American flag before lowering it for the last time. During this ceremony, one of the cannons exploded accidentally, killing Private Daniel Hough and mortally wounding Private Edward Galloway. They were the first casualties of the Civil War.

The news of Fort Sumter's fall electrified the nation. In the South, crowds celebrated in the streets. The Confederacy had stood up to the federal government and won. In the North, the attack on Fort Sumter was seen as an unprovoked assault on the American flag. Lincoln immediately called for seventy-five thousand volunteers to put down the rebellion.

The Upper South states, which had been reluctant to secede, now had to choose sides. Virginia, North Carolina, Tennessee, and Arkansas couldn't accept Lincoln's call for troops to invade the Lower South. Within six weeks, all four had joined the Confederacy. The war that both sides had hoped to avoid was now inevitable.

"A 90-Day War": The Naïve Rush to Enlist

After Fort Sumter, Americans on both sides rushed to volunteer for what they were sure would be a short and glorious war. Nobody imagined that the conflict would last four years and kill more than 600,000 people. Everyone thought their side would win quickly and easily.

In the North, Lincoln's call for thousands of volunteers brought an overwhelming response. Young men lined up outside recruiting stations. Militia units that had existed mainly for parades and social events suddenly found themselves preparing for real war. The problem wasn't finding volunteers—it was handling all the men who wanted to join.

Northern newspapers were confident that the rebellion would collapse quickly. *The New York Times* predicted the war would last thirty to sixty days. Horace Greeley's influential *New-York Tribune* declared that the rebels would give up as soon as they faced serious opposition.

The logic seemed sound. The North had twice as many people as the South, ten times as many factories, and most of the country's railroads and ships. How could a bunch of agricultural states hope to defeat the industrial might of the Union? It would be like David fighting Goliath, except this time, Goliath would win.

Southern confidence was just as high. White Southerners believed they were fighting for their homes and their way of life, while Northerners were fighting for abstract political principles. One Southerner could whip five Yankees, they said, because Southern men were natural fighters while Yankees were just money-grubbing shopkeepers.

The South also expected help from Europe. Britain and France needed Southern cotton for their textile mills. Surely they would intervene to keep the cotton flowing. "Cotton is king," Southerners had been saying for decades. Now they would find out if the rest of the world agreed.

Both sides had good reasons for optimism, but both sides were wrong about what kind of war they were getting into.

The volunteers who enlisted in 1861 were mostly young, enthusiastic, and completely unprepared for what was coming. Many had never been more than twenty miles from home. They had romantic ideas about war based on stories from the Mexican-American War and the Revolutionary War. They expected to march off to one big battle, defeat the enemy, and return home as heroes.

Military leaders shared this optimism. General Winfield Scott, the aging commander of the U.S. Army, thought he could end the rebellion without a major battle. His plan was to blockade Southern ports and control the Mississippi River. He argued the economic pressure would force the South to give up without much bloodshed.

Southern military leaders were equally confident. General Beauregard, the hero of Fort Sumter, claimed he could capture Washington with five thousand men. All the South had to do was win one major battle near the federal capital, he believed, and Northern morale would collapse.

The volunteer regiments that formed in 1861 reflected this casual attitude toward war. Many units elected their own officers, choosing popular men rather than experienced soldiers. Some regiments brought their own uniforms, leading to confusion on battlefields where nobody could tell friend from enemy. The 79th New York wore Scottish kilts. Zouave units dressed in colorful uniforms copied from French colonial troops, complete with baggy pants and fezzes. (The original Zouaves were French light infantry regiments raised in Algeria in the 1830s.)

Training was minimal and often ineffective. Most volunteers knew how to shoot—hunting was common in rural America—but they didn't know how to fight as units. They didn't understand military discipline or the importance of following orders without question. Many regiments spent more time drilling in parade formations than learning battlefield tactics.

The three-month enlistments that Congress had authorized reflected everyone's expectation of a short war. Why would anyone need to serve longer? The rebellion would be crushed by summer, and the boys would be home in time for harvest.

This casual attitude extended to military supplies and organization. The U.S. Army had only about sixteen thousand men in 1861, scattered in small posts across the western frontier. It had no experience handling hundreds of thousands of volunteers. The Quartermaster Corps, responsible for feeding and equipping the army, was overwhelmed almost immediately.

Soldiers arrived at training camps to find there weren't enough tents, uniforms, or rifles to go around. Some regiments were issued muskets from the War of 1812. Others got rifles but no ammunition. Food was often spoiled or insufficient, and medical care was primitive. More soldiers would die from disease than from enemy bullets.

But in the spring of 1861, these problems seemed minor. Both sides were confident that superior courage and fighting spirit would overcome any logistical difficulties. The war would be decided by one or two big battles, and the better side would win quickly and decisively.

They were about to learn how wrong they were.

The First Battle of Bull Run (Manassas): A Rude Awakening

By July 1861, both sides were ready for the big battle that would end the war. A Confederate force under General Beauregard was camped near Manassas Junction, Virginia, about thirty miles from Washington. A Union force under General Irvin McDowell was preparing to march south and crush the rebellion once and for all.

The pressure for action was intense. Northern newspapers demanded immediate movement. "Forward to Richmond!" declared the *New-York Tribune*. Politicians and citizens alike wanted to see the rebel army destroyed before the ninety-day volunteers went home.

McDowell wasn't eager to fight. He knew his men weren't ready. They had been drilling for only a few weeks, and many had never been in combat. But Lincoln and the politicians insisted. The rebels had to be defeated quickly before they grew stronger.

McDowell's plan was simple. He would march his army south, attack Beauregard's forces near Manassas, and drive them back toward Richmond. If everything went well, the war might be over in a few days.

The Union force that marched out of Washington on July 16 was an impressive sight. About thirty-five thousand men in blue uniforms filled the roads heading south. They were accompanied by supply wagons, artillery pieces, and even some members of Congress and newspaper reporters who had come along to watch the battle. Some brought picnic lunches, expecting to enjoy the show.

The march took longer than expected. The soldiers weren't used to long hikes in hot weather while carrying heavy packs. They broke ranks to pick berries, fill their canteens, and rest in the shade. What should have been a one-day march took two and a half days.

Beauregard wasn't surprised. Confederate spies in Washington had told him about McDowell's plans. He had about twenty-two thousand men positioned behind a small stream called Bull Run. The stream wasn't much of an obstacle, but it would force the Yankees to attack uphill while under fire.

Beauregard also had help coming. Another Confederate force under General Joseph E. Johnston was stationed in the Shenandoah Valley, about sixty miles away. If Johnston could bring his twelve thousand men to Manassas, the Confederates would have nearly equal numbers.

Joseph Johnston.[87]

The question was whether Johnston could get there in time. He was supposed to be watched by a Union force under General Robert Patterson, but Patterson was old and cautious. Instead of attacking Johnston or even keeping close track of him, Patterson let the Confederate general slip away.

Johnston's men made a fast march to Manassas and arrived just in time. Some of his troops reached the battlefield on the morning of July 21, the day of the battle. Others arrived during the fighting itself, tipping the balance at crucial moments.

The battle began before dawn on July 21, 1861. McDowell's plan was to attack across Bull Run at several points, with the main assault coming against the Confederate left flank. If it worked, he would roll up Beauregard's line and send the rebels running toward Richmond.

For most of the morning, the plan seemed to be working. Union forces crossed Bull Run and pushed back the Confederate defenders. Southern troops retreated up Henry House Hill, one of the key positions on the battlefield. It looked like the war might indeed be over in a single day.

But the Confederate line held. At the center of the resistance was a Virginia brigade commanded by General Thomas J. Jackson. As Confederate troops streamed past his position, Jackson's men stood firm like a stone wall. General Barnard Bee, trying to rally his own retreating troops, pointed to Jackson's brigade and shouted, "There stands Jackson like a stone wall!" The nickname stuck. From that day forward, Thomas Jackson was known as "Stonewall" Jackson.

Stonewall Jackson in 1863."

The arrival of Johnston's reinforcements began to turn the tide. Fresh Confederate troops poured into the battle just as the Union forces were becoming disorganized and tired. Some of Johnston's men still wore blue uniforms, causing confusion on both sides about who was friend and who was enemy.

By mid-afternoon, the Confederate counterattack was gaining momentum. Union troops that had been advancing all morning suddenly found themselves being pushed back. What had started as an orderly retreat began to turn into panic.

The collapse came suddenly. One minute, the Union Army was fighting hard and giving ground slowly. The next minute, soldiers were throwing down their weapons and running for the rear. Nobody could say exactly what triggered the rout, but once it started, it spread like wildfire.

Union soldiers streamed back across Bull Run in complete disorder. Officers lost control of their men. Artillery crews abandoned their cannons. Supply wagons clogged the roads leading back to Washington. The congressmen and reporters who had come to watch a victory found themselves caught up in a chaotic retreat.

The Confederate forces were too disorganized to pursue effectively. They had won the battle, but they were almost as confused as the Yankees. Many Southern soldiers were busy celebrating their victory or looting abandoned Union equipment. By the time Confederate officers restored order, the chance for a devastating pursuit had passed.

The casualties at Bull Run seemed enormous to people who had expected a bloodless war. The Union lost about 460 killed, 1,124 wounded, and 1,312 missing or captured. Confederate losses were 387 killed, 1,582 wounded, and 13 missing. By the standards of later battles, these were light casualties. But in July 1861, they shocked both sides.

More shocking than the casualties was the realization that the war wouldn't be over quickly. The Confederates had proved they could fight. The Union Army had proved it could be defeated. Both sides began to understand that they were in for a long, hard struggle.

Lincoln's response was immediate and decisive. Instead of seeking peace negotiations, he called for more volunteers—this time for three years instead of three months. If the rebellion couldn't be crushed quickly, it would have to be ground down slowly.

Jefferson Davis also understood the battle's meaning. The Confederacy had won its first major victory, but the Yankees hadn't given up. They would be back with more men and better preparation. The South would need to mobilize all its resources for a war of survival.

The age of innocence was over. Bull Run had taught both sides that this would be a real war and that it would be longer, bloodier, and more destructive than anyone had imagined.

The Anaconda Plan: The North's Grand Strategy

While everyone else was thinking about quick victories and short wars, one old general was developing a strategy for the long haul. Winfield Scott had been fighting in campaigns since the War of 1812. He knew that wars weren't always decided by single battles.

Scott's plan was simple in concept but massive in scope. Instead of trying to conquer the entire South by force, the Union would slowly strangle the Confederacy economically. Like an anaconda snake crushing its prey, the North would squeeze tighter and tighter until the South gave up.

The plan had three main parts. First, the Union Navy would blockade all Southern ports, cutting off trade with Europe. Second, Union forces would capture the Mississippi River, splitting the Confederacy in half and blocking trade through New Orleans. Third, Union forces would apply pressure along the border, forcing the Confederates to spread their forces thin.

The beauty of the plan was that it played to Union strengths. The North had most of the country's ships and could build more quickly than the South. It had the industrial capacity to supply and equip large armies for extended campaigns. Most importantly, it could afford to fight a long war of attrition.

However, Scott's plan had two major problems. First, it would take time—maybe years—to work. Second, it wasn't exciting. Northern politicians and newspapers wanted dramatic action, not a slow economic squeeze. They mockingly called it the "Anaconda Plan" and demanded immediate attacks on Richmond.

A cartoonish illustration of the Anaconda Plan.[89]

After Bull Run, though, Scott's ideas started looking better. Maybe the war couldn't be won with one grand battle. Maybe a patient, methodical approach made more sense than headlong assaults.

The blockade began almost immediately after Fort Sumter. Lincoln declared that Southern ports were closed to international trade. At first, the blockade was more of a legal fiction than a military reality. The Union Navy had only forty-two ships in commission, and most were scattered around the world. Blocking 3,500 miles of the South's coastline with fewer than 50 ships was impossible.

But the Union built ships faster than anyone had thought possible. Northern shipyards worked around the clock, turning out gunboats, cruisers, and monitors. By 1865, the Union Navy had grown to more than 670 ships. The blockade gradually tightened until almost no ships could get through.

The economic effects were devastating for the South. Before the war, the Confederacy had exported millions of bales of cotton and imported most of its manufactured goods. By 1863, cotton exports had fallen by more than 95 percent. Prices for imported goods skyrocketed. Items that had been common before the war, such as coffee, sugar, cloth, and medicine, became luxury items that only the wealthy could afford.

The Mississippi River part of the plan would take longer to implement, but it would prove equally effective. Control of the river would cut the Confederacy in half, preventing Confederate forces in Texas, Louisiana, and Arkansas from helping defend Virginia and the Carolinas. It would also give the Union control of New Orleans, the South's largest port and most important city.

Scott's plan wasn't glamorous, but it was effective. The Confederacy would find itself fighting on multiple fronts while its economy slowly collapsed. Union forces wouldn't have to win every battle—they just had to avoid losing the war while the blockade and economic pressure did their work.

Of course, the plan required patience, and patience was in short supply in 1861. Politicians wanted quick results. Generals wanted glorious victories. Soldiers wanted to go home. However, as the war dragged on, Scott's strategy would prove to be the foundation of the Union's victory.

The old general retired in November 1861, too old and sick to continue active duty. But his anaconda was already beginning to coil around the Confederacy. By the time the war ended, it would have squeezed the life out of the Southern economy and war effort.

Chapter 5: The War in the East: Chasing Richmond

After the Battle of Bull Run, it became clear that this war would be nothing like what anyone had expected. The Union needed a new plan and new leadership. Lincoln turned to a young general who promised to build a real army and march it to Richmond. For the next year and a half, that general would come tantalizingly close to ending the war, only to be stopped again and again by one of the most brilliant military minds in American history.

The story of the war in the East from 1862 to late 1862 is really the story of two men: George McClellan, the Union general who could organize and train an army better than almost anyone, and Robert E. Lee, the Confederate general who could outfight armies twice the size of his own. Their cat-and-mouse game around Richmond would produce some of the bloodiest battles in U.S. history and turn the Civil War into the grinding war of attrition that Winfield Scott had predicted.

Meet the Generals: McClellan vs. Lee

George Brinton McClellan, a thirty-four-year-old West Pointer, had already won some small victories in western Virginia. McClellan was everything the Union seemed to need. He was young, energetic, professionally trained, and brimming with confidence.

McClellan looked like a general straight out of a painting. He was short but powerfully built, with a carefully waxed mustache and piercing eyes. He rode his horse with perfect military bearing and always looked immaculate, even in the field. His soldiers adored him. They called him "Little Mac" and cheered wildly whenever he rode past their camps.

George McClellan.[90]

More importantly, McClellan could organize. He took the demoralized troops around Washington and turned them into what he called the Army of the Potomac. He drilled them relentlessly, taught them to march in formation, and made sure they had proper equipment and supplies. By the spring of 1862, he had built an army of more than 100,000 well-trained, well-equipped soldiers.

However, McClellan had a complex problem that would plague him throughout the war: he was overly cautious in a way that prevented decisive action. Part of this came from faulty intelligence. His spy chief, Allan Pinkerton, consistently told him that Confederate forces were two or three times larger than they actually were. Part came from his role as an organizer who understood how difficult it was to supply large armies and how catastrophic a major defeat would be for Union morale. And part came from enormous political pressure. Everyone knew that if the Army of the Potomac was destroyed, Washington might fall, and the war could be lost.

The result was a general who always needed more men, more supplies, and more time to prepare. He spent months planning elaborate campaigns that never seemed quite ready to launch. Despite all his advantages, he could never quite bring himself to take the risks that decisive victories required.

Lincoln grew increasingly frustrated with McClellan's delays. "If General McClellan does not want to use the army, I would like to borrow it for a time," the president said sarcastically.[i] But McClellan kept insisting he wasn't ready, that one more week of preparation would make all the difference.

On the Confederate side, the situation was more complicated. After Bull Run, the main Confederate army defending Virginia—which would become known as the Army of Northern Virginia—was commanded by General Joseph E. Johnston, a cautious, defensive-minded officer who preferred to avoid battle unless he had clear advantages. Johnston was competent, but he wasn't the aggressive leader that Jefferson Davis wanted.

The change came in June 1862, when Johnston was wounded during fighting outside Richmond. Davis replaced him with his military advisor, Robert E. Lee. At first, many people thought this was a mistake. Lee had graduated from West Point and served with distinction in the Mexican-American War, but his Civil War record so far wasn't impressive. He had failed to stop Union advances in western Virginia and had spent months digging defensive positions around Richmond that soldiers mockingly called him the "King of Spades."

Robert Edward Lee was fifty-five years old. He was a Virginia aristocrat whose family had been prominent since colonial times. His father was "Light-Horse Harry" Lee, a Revolutionary War hero. Robert's wife was Mary Custis Lee, whose family owned Arlington House overlooking Washington (now Arlington National Cemetery).

---

[i] https://www.thenmusa.org/biographies/george-b-mcclellan/

Robert E. Lee looked every inch the Southern gentleman. He was tall and dignified, with graying hair and beard and kind eyes that could turn steely when he was angry. He was soft-spoken and unfailingly polite, even to his enemies. His soldiers called him "Marse Robert" and would have followed him anywhere.

But Lee was also one of the most aggressive generals in American history. Unlike Johnston, who waited for perfect opportunities, Lee was willing to take enormous risks to achieve decisive results. He understood

Robert E. Lee in 1864.[21]

that the Confederacy couldn't win a long war of attrition. The South had to win quickly, and that meant attacking whenever possible, even when outnumbered.

Lee also had an intuitive understanding of his opponents. He could read McClellan like a book, predicting exactly how the Union general would react in any given situation. McClellan was methodical and cautious. He would always take the safe option, even when boldness might win the war. Lee exploited this weakness again and again.

The contrast between the two generals couldn't have been sharper. McClellan had everything—more men, better equipment, superior supplies—but lacked the killer instinct needed to win battles. Lee had almost nothing except his own tactical genius and an army that trusted him completely. For the next year, though, that would be enough.

The Peninsula Campaign: So Close, Yet So Far

By March 1862, McClellan finally had his plan ready. Instead of marching overland toward Richmond, which would mean fighting through heavily defended Confederate positions, he would transport his army by ship to the Virginia Peninsula. From there, he could march up the peninsula toward Richmond, forcing the Confederates to fight on ground of his choosing.

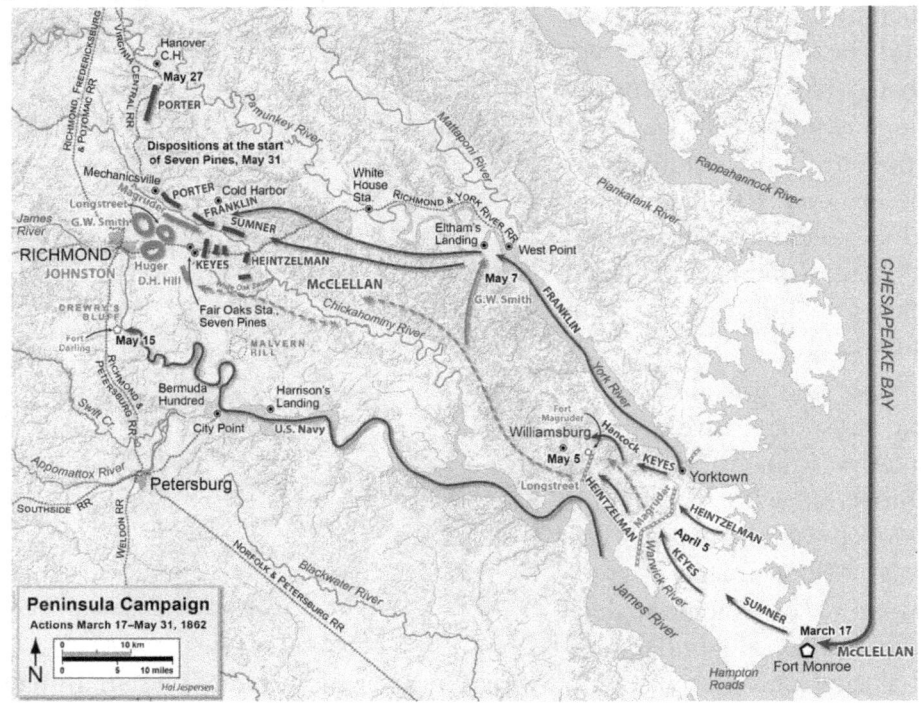

A map of the Peninsula Campaign.[93]

The plan was actually quite clever. The peninsula was the narrow strip of land between the York and James Rivers, southeast of Richmond. By approaching from this direction, McClellan could use Union naval power to support his advance and supply his army. He would also be much closer to Richmond than any Confederate force could get to Washington, giving him a significant strategic advantage.

Lincoln approved the plan reluctantly. He was worried about leaving Washington undefended, but McClellan promised to end the war quickly once he got his army moving. In March 1862, Union transports began ferrying more than 100,000 soldiers from Washington to Fort Monroe at the tip of the peninsula.

The movement was an impressive logistical achievement. More than four hundred ships carried McClellan's army, along with their horses, artillery, wagons, and supplies. It was the largest amphibious operation in American history up to that point. By early April, McClellan had landed his entire force and was ready to begin his march on Richmond.

Then the delays started. McClellan's first obstacle was Yorktown, the same place where British forces had surrendered to George Washington in 1781. The Confederate commander there was John B. Magruder, a theatrical officer who specialized in making small forces look larger than they were. Magruder had only about seventeen thousand men, but he marched them around constantly, making noise and showing themselves at multiple points to create the illusion of a much larger army.

McClellan took one look at the Yorktown defenses and decided he needed to conduct a formal siege. Instead of attacking immediately with overwhelming numbers, he brought up heavy artillery and began a methodical bombardment that lasted a month. By the time he was ready to assault the Confederate positions, Magruder had slipped away in the night.

This became the pattern for the entire Peninsula Campaign. McClellan would approach a Confederate position, overestimate its strength, and spend days or weeks preparing for an attack. By the time he was ready, the Confederates would have moved to the next defensive line. McClellan crept up the peninsula like a cautious cat stalking a mouse that was always one step ahead.

Meanwhile, Robert E. Lee was planning something much bolder. He had taken command of Confederate forces around Richmond just as McClellan's army was approaching the outskirts of the city. Lee could hear Union artillery firing at Confederate positions. He could see Union observation balloons floating over the enemy lines. (The Civil War was the first time in U.S. history that balloons were used for wartime purposes.) Richmond seemed to be doomed.

But Lee had noticed something that gave him hope. McClellan had divided his army on both sides of the Chickahominy River, a small stream that ran north of Richmond. If Lee could attack one wing of McClellan's army before the other wing could cross the river to help, he might be able to defeat McClellan.

Lee's plan was risky and complicated. He would leave only twenty-five thousand men to defend Richmond against seventy-five thousand Union troops south of the Chickahominy. Meanwhile, he would take sixty-five thousand Confederate soldiers to attack the thirty thousand Union troops north of the river. If everything went perfectly, he could destroy one-third of McClellan's army before the Union general knew what was happening.

The Seven Days' Battles began on June 26, 1862. For a week, Lee attacked McClellan's forces again and again, trying to destroy the Army of the Potomac before it could escape. The fighting was savage and confused, with attacks and counterattacks swirling through the Virginia woods and swamps.

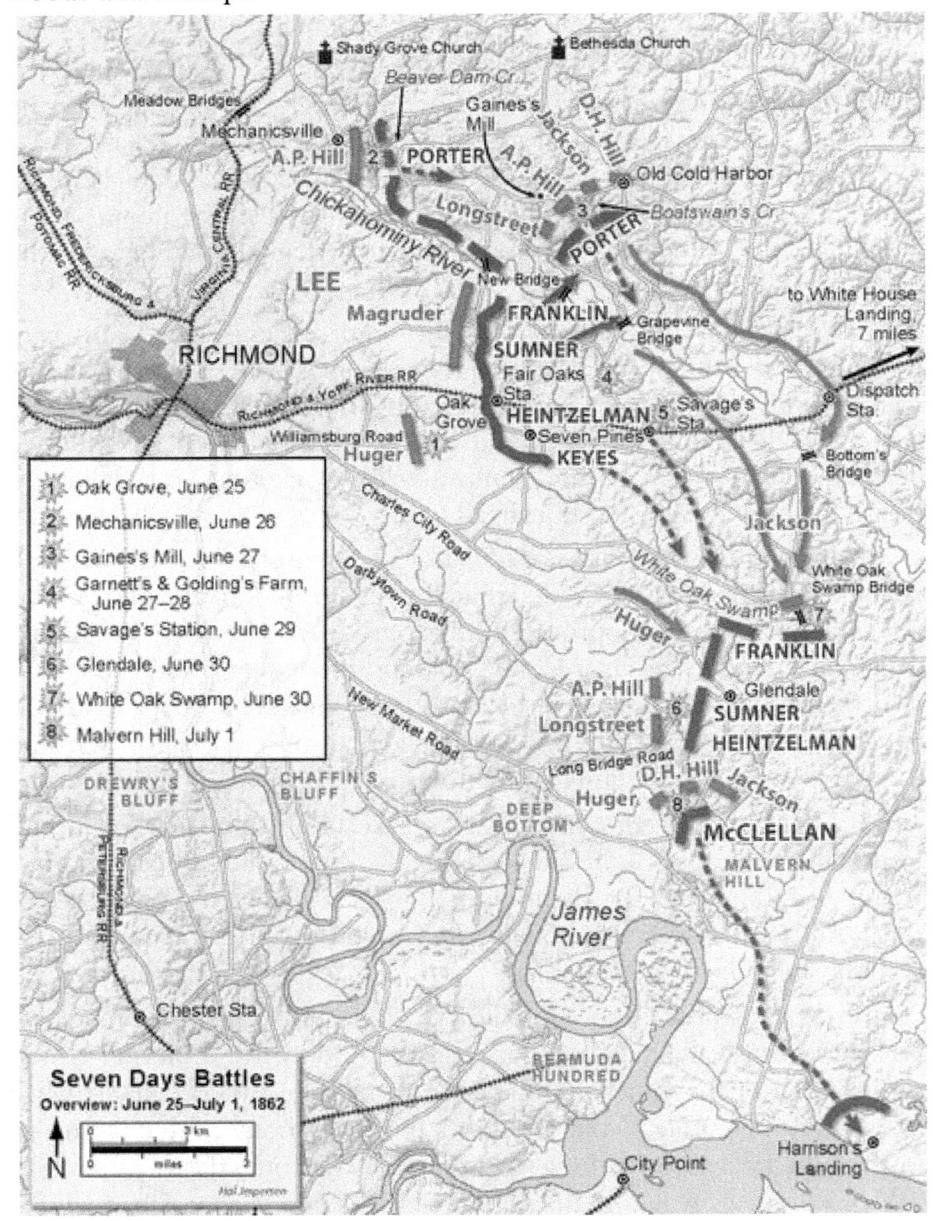

A map of the Seven Days' Battles.[98]

Lee's plan didn't work perfectly. His subordinates made mistakes, attacks went astray, and opportunities were missed. But the psychological effect on McClellan was devastating. Convinced that he was facing an army twice the size of his own, McClellan abandoned his advance on Richmond and began retreating toward the James River.

The retreat became known as McClellan's "change of base," but it was really a defeat. All spring, he had fretted about leaving Washington exposed. Now, after three months of campaigning, he was still thirty miles from Richmond with nothing to show for it.. His army was still intact, but his confidence was shattered.

The Peninsula Campaign was a perfect example of McClellan's strengths and weaknesses. He had planned and executed a brilliant strategic movement that put him in a position to capture the Confederate capital. His army was superbly organized and equipped. However, when the moment came to strike the decisive blow, he hesitated. Lee seized the initiative and never gave it back.

By August 1862, Lincoln had seen enough. He ordered McClellan to bring his army back to Washington and gave primary command in the field to a new general, John Pope, who promised to be more aggressive. Pope formed a new Army of Virginia from various forces around Washington, while McClellan was left in a diminished role. McClellan had come closer to ending the war than any Union general would come for another two years, but close wasn't good enough.

Pope's aggressive approach backfired spectacularly at the Second Battle of Bull Run in late August, where Lee handed him a crushing defeat. With Confederate forces advancing toward Washington and Pope's army in retreat, Lincoln reluctantly restored McClellan to command of the combined Union forces. Nobody liked McClellan's caution, but he was the only general who could organize a defense of the capital quickly enough to matter.

Antietam: The Bloodiest Single Day in American History

After driving McClellan away from Richmond, Robert E. Lee decided it was time to take the war to the enemy. In September 1862, he led his army across the Potomac River into Maryland, hoping to win a decisive victory on Union soil that might convince European nations to recognize Confederate independence.

Lee's invasion was a huge gamble. His army was tired from the fighting around Richmond and reduced by straggling and desertion to only about fifty-five thousand men. Many soldiers were barefoot and in rags. Some were so weak from hunger that they could barely march. However, Lee believed he had to act while Union forces were still disorganized after their defeat on the peninsula.

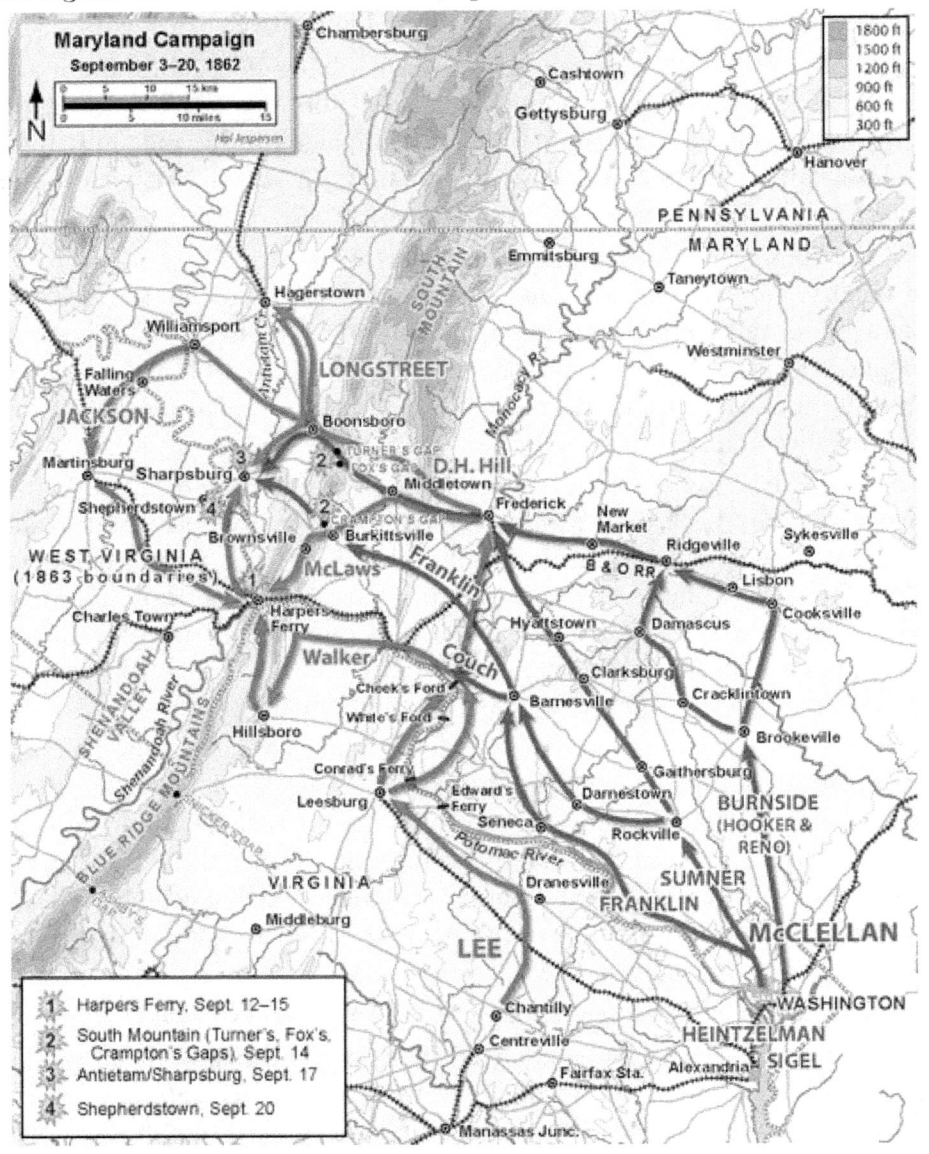

The Maryland Campaign.[94]

The invasion started well. Confederate forces crossed into Maryland and occupied the town of Frederick. Lee hoped that Marylanders would rally to the Confederate cause. After all, Maryland was a slave state that had been kept in the Union only by federal force. But the hoped-for uprising never materialized. Most Marylanders were content to watch from the sidelines.

Lee's next move was to divide his army, sending Stonewall Jackson to capture the Union garrison at Harpers Ferry while the rest of the army moved north toward Pennsylvania. It was a dangerous decision—dividing one's army in enemy territory violated every rule of military strategy—but Lee was confident that Union forces were too scattered to threaten him.

Then Lee suffered the worst luck imaginable. A copy of his detailed battle plans, wrapped around three cigars, was found by Union soldiers in an abandoned Confederate campsite. The plans showed exactly where every Confederate division was supposed to be and what it was supposed to do. When the plans reached McClellan (who had been restored to command after Pope's defeat at Second Bull Run), he was ecstatic.

McClellan had been given the chance of a lifetime. Lee's army was divided, with Jackson's corps twenty miles away at Harpers Ferry. If McClellan moved quickly, he could destroy Lee's forces before they could reunite. For once, the cautious Union general seemed ready to act decisively.

But even with Lee's plans in his hands, McClellan moved slowly. He spent precious hours verifying the intelligence and preparing his attack. This delay gave Lee time to realize his plans had been compromised. He began concentrating his scattered forces behind Antietam Creek, near the town of Sharpsburg, Maryland.

The Battle of Antietam was fought on September 17, 1862. McClellan had about eighty-seven thousand men available for the attack, while Lee could muster only about forty thousand. The odds were more than two to one in favor of the Union, the best advantage McClellan would ever hold in the war.

The battle began at dawn with a Union attack on Lee's left flank. Fighting raged around a small white church called Dunker Church, with casualties mounting on both sides. The Confederates gave ground slowly, but their line held. By mid-morning, the attack had stalled.

Battle of Antietam by Thure de Thulstrup. Note Dunker Church in the background.[95]

The focus then shifted to the center of the Confederate line, where Union forces tried to cross Antietam Creek at a narrow stone bridge. The bridge became a death trap, as Confederate sharpshooters on the heights above picked off Union soldiers trying to cross. After hours of fighting, Union forces finally took the bridge (now called Burnside's Bridge), but at enormous cost.

The most horrific fighting came in the center of the battlefield, around a farm lane that the Confederates had turned into a defensive position. Union attacks drove back the defenders, and the lane filled with Confederate dead. Soldiers started calling it the "Bloody Lane," and by the end of the day, more than seven hundred Confederate soldiers lay dead or dying there.

By afternoon, Lee's army was on the verge of collapse. His center had been broken, his flanks were under pressure, and he had no reserves left to plug the gaps in his line. One more Union attack might have destroyed the Army of Northern Virginia and ended the war.

But McClellan, true to form, hesitated. He had used less than three-quarters of his army and still had twenty thousand fresh troops in reserve. However, he was convinced that Lee had hidden reserves somewhere and was planning a counterattack. Instead of delivering the knockout blow, McClellan ordered his men to hold their positions and wait.

Lee spent the night of September 17 deciding whether to continue the fight or retreat back to Virginia. His army had suffered terrible casualties—about 13,700 killed, wounded, and missing out of 40,000 engaged. But McClellan's army had suffered even more—about 12,400 casualties out of 87,000 engaged. Still, Lee knew he couldn't afford another day of fighting with so few men left.

On the night of September 18, Lee's army slipped back across the Potomac into Virginia. McClellan didn't pursue. The great invasion of the North was over, and it had failed. But Lee's army had survived to fight another day.

The Battle of Antietam was the bloodiest single day in American history. Combined casualties totaled more than twenty-six thousand men killed, wounded, and missing—more than how many fell during the D-Day landings in World War II. The photographs of dead soldiers scattered across the battlefield shocked the Northern public, who had never seen such graphic evidence of the reality of war.

Politically, the Battle of Antietam was a Union victory. Lee's invasion had failed, and the Confederate Army had retreated. This gave Lincoln the political cover he needed to issue the preliminary Emancipation Proclamation five days later. European nations, which had been considering recognizing Confederate independence, decided to wait and see what happened next.

However, militarily, Antietam was a missed opportunity. McClellan had been given every advantage, but he had failed to destroy Lee's army when he had the chance. The war would continue for another two and a half years largely because McClellan lacked the killer instinct to finish what he had started.

Lincoln's patience with McClellan finally ran out in November 1862. After Antietam, McClellan spent weeks making excuses for not pursuing Lee's retreating army, claiming he needed more supplies and equipment. Lincoln had restored McClellan to command specifically to deal with the crisis of Lee's invasion, but once that crisis passed, the general's old habits returned. On November 7, 1862, Lincoln fired him for the final time. The Union would have to find yet another general to lead the Army of the Potomac against Robert E. Lee.

Lincoln on the field of Antietam.[96]

Chancellorsville: Lee's Masterpiece and Jackson's Last Battle

After Antietam, both armies settled into winter quarters and tried to recover from the bloodiest year of fighting in American history. Lincoln replaced McClellan with General Ambrose Burnside, a well-meaning but unimaginative commander who had distinguished himself in earlier battles but was unprepared for army-level command.

Burnside was under enormous pressure from Lincoln and Congress to attack before winter set in completely. His plan was straightforward but flawed: he would cross the Rappahannock

Ambrose Burnside.[97]

River at Fredericksburg and attack Lee's army directly. The problem was that Lee saw him coming and had weeks to prepare strong defensive positions on the heights overlooking the town.

The Battle of Fredericksburg on December 13, 1862, became one of the most lopsided disasters in Union military history. Burnside ordered wave after wave of frontal assaults against Confederate positions that were virtually impregnable. Union soldiers advanced across open ground into artillery and rifle fire from Confederate troops protected by stone walls and earthworks. The attacks continued for hours, with each assault ending in bloody failure.

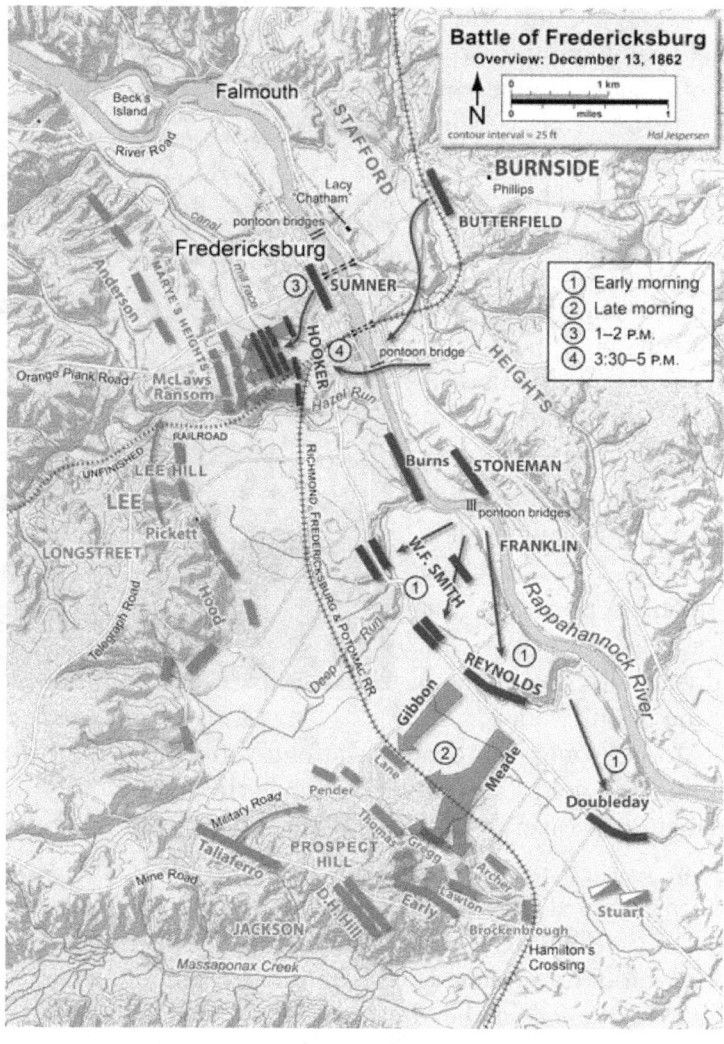

A map of the Battle of Fredericksburg.[98]

By the end of the day, Burnside had lost about 12,600 men compared to only 5,300 Confederate casualties. The Army of the Potomac limped back across the river, demoralized and decimated. Burnside was so distraught that he wanted to lead a final suicidal charge himself, but his subordinates talked him out of it.

After that debacle, Lincoln turned to General Joseph "Fighting Joe" Hooker, a hard-drinking, aggressive commander who promised to finally defeat Lee. Hooker spent the winter of 1862-63 rebuilding the Army of the Potomac's morale and preparing for a spring campaign. He had good reason for confidence. His army numbered about 130,000 men compared to Lee's 60,000. The Union forces were well supplied, well equipped, and eager to redeem themselves after the humiliation at Fredericksburg.

Hooker's plan for the spring campaign was actually quite clever. Instead of attacking Lee's strong positions at Fredericksburg directly, he would divide his army and outflank the Confederate line.

"Fighting Joe" Hooker."

Part of his force would demonstrate—a feint simulating an attack—against Fredericksburg to hold Lee's attention, while the main body would cross the Rappahannock River upstream and attack Lee from behind.

The plan worked perfectly—at first. By April 30, 1863, Hooker had managed to get most of his army across the river and into Lee's rear without being detected. However, instead of pushing forward aggressively, Hooker hesitated. When his advance units encountered Confederate resistance in the thick woods around Chancellorsville, he ordered them to pull back and take defensive positions. The area was known locally as "the Wilderness"—a tangled mass of dense woods and undergrowth that made it nearly impossible to coordinate large troop movements or use artillery effectively. The difficult terrain favored Lee's smaller, more maneuverable army over Hooker's larger force.

Lee recognized the threat immediately and made one of the boldest decisions of his career. Leaving a small force to watch the Union troops at Fredericksburg, he marched most of his army west to face Hooker's main force. Despite being outnumbered more than two to one, Lee decided to attack.

But Lee had an even more audacious plan in mind. On the evening of May 1, he met with Stonewall Jackson around a campfire to plan their next move. Jackson's scouts had discovered that the Union right flank was "in the air"—unprotected and vulnerable to attack. Lee decided to divide his already smaller army, sending Jackson with twenty-eight thousand men on a flanking march while Lee held Hooker's attention with just seventeen thousand troops.

Jackson's flanking march on May 2 was one of the most daring maneuvers in military history. His men marched twelve miles through dense woods, following obscure trails and back roads to reach Hooker's exposed right flank. The march took most of the day, and Union observers spotted Confederate troops moving through the forest. However, Hooker and his generals convinced themselves that Lee was retreating.

At 6:00 p.m. on May 2, Jackson's men burst out of the woods and smashed into the unprepared Union right flank. The XI Corps, composed largely of German immigrants, was caught completely by surprise. Some soldiers were cooking dinner when the screaming Confederate soldiers came charging out of the forest. The entire Union line collapsed in panic.

Jackson's attack might have destroyed Hooker's entire army, but darkness ended the assault before it could be completed. As night fell, Jackson rode forward with a small group of staff officers to scout the Union positions and plan a night attack. As they returned to Confederate lines, nervous Confederate sentries fired into the darkness, not realizing they were shooting at their own general.

Jackson was hit by three bullets—two in the left arm and one in the right hand. His left arm was so badly shattered that it had to be amputated. At first, doctors thought he would recover from his wounds.

But Jackson developed pneumonia and died on May 10, 1863.

Jackson's death was a devastating blow to the Confederate cause. He had been Lee's most trusted lieutenant and most aggressive corps commander. Jackson had an intuitive understanding of Lee's intentions and could execute complex maneuvers that other generals couldn't handle. His loss would be felt most keenly during Lee's upcoming invasion of Pennsylvania, when Lee would need subordinates who could act independently and aggressively.

A painting of the Battle of Chancellorsville.[100]

The immediate result of Chancellorsville was another stunning Confederate victory. Despite being outnumbered more than two to one, Lee had outmaneuvered and defeated another Union force. Hooker withdrew his forces across the Rappahannock, and the Army of the Potomac once again went back to camp to lick its wounds and wait for a new commander.

The victory at Chancellorsville convinced Lee that his army was invincible and that Northern morale was cracking. If he could win such a decisive victory while badly outnumbered, what might he accomplish if he took the war to Northern soil? The success at Chancellorsville planted the seeds for Lee's decision to invade Pennsylvania—a decision that would lead to the decisive battle at Gettysburg just two months later.

Chapter 6: The War in the West: Rivers of Blood

While McClellan and Lee fought their careful chess game in Virginia, a very different kind of war was being waged west of the Appalachian Mountains. Here, battles were fought for control of rivers and railroads, not capital cities. The distances were vast, the armies were smaller, and the fighting was often more brutal and decisive than anything happening in the East.

The Western theater would produce the generals who would eventually win the war for the Union. But first, both sides would learn just how deadly this conflict could become.

Meet the Western Generals: Grant, Sherman, and Forrest

The war in the West was dominated by three men who were as different from the Eastern generals as they were from each other. Ulysses S. Grant was a quiet, determined man who had failed at almost everything before the war started. William Tecumseh Sherman was a nervous, brilliant officer who understood that modern war was about destroying the enemy's will to fight. Nathan Bedford Forrest was a Confederate cavalry commander who had never read a military manual but had an instinctive genius for warfare.

Ulysses S. Grant didn't look like the man who would save the Union. He was short and rumpled, with a scraggly beard and clothes that never seemed to fit right. He had graduated from West Point but hated military life and resigned from the Army after serving in the Mexican-American

War. He had failed as a farmer, failed as a businessman, and was working as a clerk in his father's leather goods store when Fort Sumter was fired upon.

Grant in 1861.[101]

However, Grant had one quality that was rarer than gold in the Union Army: he was willing to fight. While Eastern generals spent months preparing for battles that never happened, Grant moved quickly and struck hard. He understood that the Union's advantages in men and material meant nothing unless they were used aggressively.

Grant also had a simple, clear understanding of what needed to be done. The Confederacy was a rebellion that had to be crushed. The Confederate forces were the rebellion's strength, so they had to be destroyed. Everything else—capturing cities, gaining territory, and winning public support—was secondary to the main job of defeating Confederate forces in battle.

Grant's drinking was already becoming legendary, though the stories were often exaggerated. He did drink, especially when he was bored or separated from his family, but he was not the hopeless drunk that his enemies portrayed. When he was actively campaigning, he stayed sober and focused. What some people mistook for alcoholism was actually Grant's intense concentration on the task at hand.

William Tecumseh Sherman was Grant's most trusted lieutenant and closest friend. Where Grant was calm and methodical, Sherman was high-strung and talkative. He chain-smoked cigars, paced constantly, and had a nervous energy that made everyone around him feel exhausted. His red hair and beard were always unkempt, and his uniform looked like he had slept in it.

Sherman came from a prominent Ohio family and had graduated from West Point, but he had left the Army to become a banker and lawyer. When the war started, he was superintendent of a military academy in Louisiana. Unlike many Northerners, Sherman understood the South well enough to know that this would be a long and hard war.

Sherman also understood something that most Civil War generals missed. In a democracy, wars were won as much by destroying the enemy's morale as by defeating their armies. If you could make Southern civilians tired of fighting, they would pressure their government to make peace. This insight would make Sherman one of the war's most effective and most controversial generals.

On the Confederate side, Nathan Bedford Forrest was unlike any other general in the war. He had no formal military education, no West Point training, and no experience commanding large units. Before the war, he had been a plantation owner and slave trader in Memphis. However, Forrest had an intuitive understanding of cavalry warfare, which made him one of the most feared Confederate commanders.

Forrest was tall and powerful, with dark hair and intense eyes that seemed to look right through a person. He had a violent temper and a vocabulary that could make hardened soldiers blush. He led from the front, often charging into battle with his saber drawn. During the war, he had twenty-nine horses shot out from under him and personally killed more than thirty Union soldiers in hand-to-hand combat.

Forrest's tactical philosophy was simple: "Get there first with the most men." He moved his cavalry faster than anyone thought possible, struck where the enemy least expected it, and disappeared before reinforcements could arrive. His raids disrupted Union supply lines, captured thousands of prisoners, and tied down Union forces that could have been used elsewhere.

Forrest was also involved in some of the war's most controversial incidents. His treatment of Black soldiers and civilians was brutal, even by Civil War standards. After the war, he would become the first grand wizard of the Ku Klux Klan. He represented both the tactical brilliance and the moral darkness of the Confederate cause.

These three men—Grant, Sherman, and Forrest—would dominate the war in the West. Their battles would be fought in places most Americans had never heard of, such as Fort Henry, Fort Donelson, Shiloh, and Vicksburg. But these obscure battlefields would prove more important to the war's outcome than the famous fights in Virginia.

The Battle of Shiloh: A Horrific Lesson in Carnage

By early 1862, Grant had won the Union's first significant victories of the war by capturing Fort Henry and Fort Donelson in Tennessee. These successes opened the Tennessee and Cumberland Rivers to Union gunboats and forced Confederate forces to abandon much of Kentucky and middle Tennessee. Grant was suddenly the most famous general in the Union Army.

However, Grant's success had made him overconfident. In April 1862, his army was camped near a small Methodist church called Shiloh, waiting for reinforcements under General Don Carlos Buell. Grant was so sure the Confederates wouldn't attack that he didn't even bother to have his men dig defensive trenches. The soldiers spent their time drilling and writing letters home, not preparing for battle.

Confederate General Albert Sidney Johnston had other plans. Johnston was one of the most respected soldiers in America before the war, and Jefferson Davis considered him the Confederacy's best general. Johnston had been gathering Confederate forces from across the region for one massive attack that would drive Grant's army into the Tennessee River and reverse all the Union gains in the West.

Johnston's plan was risky but potentially decisive. He would concentrate about forty thousand Confederate troops near Corinth, Mississippi, then march north and attack Grant's thirty-five thousand men before Buell's twenty-five thousand reinforcements could arrive. If the attack succeeded, Johnston might destroy Grant's entire army and regain control of Tennessee.

The Confederate attack began at dawn on April 6, 1862. Thousands of rebel soldiers came screaming out of the woods, catching the Union forces completely by surprise. Many Union soldiers were still in their tents or cooking breakfast when the firing started. Some barely had time to grab their rifles before the Confederate forces overran their camps.

The fighting was unlike anything Americans had seen before. This wasn't the confusion of Bull Run or the careful maneuvering of the Peninsula Campaign. This was a savage, close-quarters battle where men fought with rifles, bayonets, and fists. Units on both sides lost all organization, with the battle breaking down into dozens of individual fights scattered across miles of wooded terrain.

Grant himself was caught off guard. He was having breakfast at his headquarters nine miles away when he heard the gunfire. He immediately rode toward the battle, but by the time he reached his army, much of it was in full retreat. Union soldiers streamed toward the Tennessee River, some throwing away their weapons in panic.

However, Grant didn't panic. Instead of ordering a general retreat, he began organizing a defensive line near the river. He positioned artillery to cover the landing where Buell's reinforcements would arrive and sent staff officers to rally scattered units. Gradually, the Union retreat slowed and then stopped.

The key moment came when Confederate forces attacked a strong Union position that became known as the "Hornet's Nest." Union troops under General Benjamin Prentiss held this position for hours, even though they were surrounded and under attack from three sides. Confederate forces attacked again and again, with casualties mounting on both sides. Finally, after more than six hours of fighting, Prentiss surrendered what was left of his division. Their resistance gave Grant time to organize his defenses. They probably saved his army from complete destruction.

The day's heaviest loss came when Albert Sidney Johnston was mortally wounded while leading a Confederate attack. Johnston bled to death after being shot in the leg, probably because he didn't realize how serious his wound was until it was too late. His death was a devastating blow to Confederate morale and left General P. G. T. Beauregard in command of the attacking forces.

By evening, it looked like the Confederates had won a complete victory. They had driven Grant's army back to the river and captured thousands of prisoners. Some Union officers were already talking about surrender. But Grant refused to consider retreat.

Grant's confidence was based on two factors. First, Buell's reinforcements had begun arriving during the night, giving the Union Army fresh troops for the next day's fighting. Second, Grant understood that the Confederate attack had been as costly for them as it had been for the Union. Johnston's army was exhausted and disorganized after a day of heavy fighting.

The second day of Shiloh proved Grant right. Union forces counterattacked at dawn on April 7, gradually pushing back the tired Confederate troops. Beauregard, who lacked Johnston's aggressive instincts, ordered a retreat toward Corinth rather than continue the fight. By afternoon, Grant's army had recaptured most of the ground lost the day before.

The Battle of Shiloh was over, but its impact was just beginning to be felt. Union casualties totaled about thirteen thousand killed, wounded, and missing. Confederate losses were similar—about eleven thousand casualties, including the irreplaceable Albert Sidney Johnston. Combined, the two armies had suffered more casualties in two days than the United States had lost in all its previous wars combined.

The photographs and newspaper reports from Shiloh shocked both the North and South. Americans saw images of battlefield hospitals overflowing with wounded soldiers and burial details trying to deal with thousands of corpses. The romantic notion of war as a glorious adventure died in the mud and blood around Shiloh Church.

Grant came under severe criticism for being surprised by the Confederate attack. Northern newspapers called for his removal, claiming he had been drunk or incompetent. But Lincoln refused to fire his most successful general. "I can't spare this man," Lincoln reportedly said. "He fights."

The Fight for the Rivers: Capturing New Orleans

While Grant was learning hard lessons at Shiloh, the Union Navy was proving that Winfield Scott's Anaconda Plan could work. The key was controlling the Mississippi River, which would split the Confederacy in half and give the Union access to the heart of the South. The first step was capturing New Orleans, the largest city in the Confederacy and the mouth of the great river.

In 1862, New Orleans was one of America's most important and largest cities. It was the South's main port for international trade and the gateway for goods flowing down the Mississippi from the American heartland. If the Union could capture New Orleans, it would deal a devastating blow to the Confederate economy.

The city seemed almost impossible to attack. It was protected by two massive forts—Fort Jackson and Fort St. Philip—that guarded the approaches to the river. These forts had thick masonry walls and dozens of heavy cannons that could sink any ship trying to pass. The Confederates also had a small fleet of ironclad warships and fire rafts that could be sent downstream to attack Union vessels.

However, the Union Navy had advantages that Confederate planners hadn't considered. Most importantly, they had David Glasgow Farragut, a sixty-year-old naval officer who combined careful planning with aggressive tactics. Farragut had served in the Navy for about fifty years (he became a midshipman when he was nine years old). He understood both the technical details of naval warfare and the psychology of command.

Farragut's plan was audacious. Instead of trying to reduce the forts by bombardment, he would run his fleet past them at night and attack New Orleans directly. Once he controlled the city, the forts would be cut off and forced to surrender. It was risky—Confederate gunners would have point-blank shots at his ships as they passed—but it was also unexpected.

The Union fleet that gathered below New Orleans was impressive. Farragut had seventeen warships, including four powerful steam sloops that carried heavy guns. He also had a flotilla of mortar boats that would bombard the forts before the main attack. Most importantly, he had crews that trusted his leadership and were willing to follow him into what looked like a suicide mission.

The bombardment began on April 18, 1862. For six days, Union mortar boats fired thousands of shells at Fort Jackson and Fort St. Philip. The constant explosions damaged the forts' buildings and demoralized their garrisons, but they didn't knock out enough guns to make the passage safe. Farragut decided he couldn't wait any longer.

At 2:00 a.m. on April 24, Farragut's fleet began moving upriver. The ships moved in single file, with their engines muffled and their lights covered. For a few minutes, it looked like they might pass the forts undetected. Then, Confederate lookouts spotted the approaching vessels and opened fire.

The next two hours were like a scene from hell. Confederate guns fired as fast as they could load, sending shot and shell crashing into the Union ships. Farragut's vessels fired back, their guns lighting up the night with orange flashes. Fire rafts sent downstream by the Confederates added to the chaos, forcing Union ships to dodge floating infernos while under constant bombardment.

Farragut's flagship, the USS *Hartford*, was hit by a fire raft and burst into flames. The admiral himself helped fight the fire, calmly directing damage control while Confederate shells exploded around him.

By dawn, thirteen of Farragut's seventeen ships had made it past the forts. Three had been too damaged to continue, and one had been sunk. But the core of the Union fleet was now above the forts and racing toward New Orleans. The Confederate river defenses had been breached.

The capture of New Orleans itself was almost anticlimactic. The Confederate fleet was quickly defeated or scattered. The city's mayor tried to organize a resistance, but with no army to defend it and Union warships pointing their guns at the waterfront, New Orleans had no choice but to surrender. On May 1, 1862, Union forces occupied the largest city in the Confederacy.

The fall of New Orleans was a devastating blow to Confederate morale and a huge boost for Union spirits. The South had lost its most important port and the mouth of the Mississippi River. European merchants could no longer trade freely with the Confederacy, making the Union blockade much more effective.

The capture also proved that the Union Navy could accomplish what Union land forces had struggled to do: win decisive victories that actually ended Confederate resistance in important areas. While Eastern armies moved back and forth across the same ground in Virginia, the Navy was making permanent gains that couldn't be reversed.

Most importantly, the fall of New Orleans was another step in the implementation of Scott's Anaconda Plan. The Union now controlled both ends of the Mississippi River—St. Louis in the north and New Orleans in the south. All that remained was to capture the Confederate strongholds in between, particularly Vicksburg, Mississippi. Once that was accomplished, the Confederacy would be split in half, and its defeat would be inevitable.

Chattanooga: Grant's Gateway to Command

After the twin Union victories at Gettysburg and Vicksburg in July 1863, it looked like the momentum had shifted decisively toward the North. But in September, Confederate General Braxton Bragg reminded everyone that the war was far from over. At Chickamauga Creek in northern Georgia, Bragg's Army of Tennessee dealt the Union forces one of their worst defeats of the entire war.

Union General William Rosecrans had been maneuvering his Army of the Cumberland through Tennessee, trying to capture the vital railroad junction at Chattanooga. Bragg decided to make a stand at Chickamauga. From September 19 to September 20, 1863, the two armies clashed in some of the war's most confused and brutal fighting. The battle took place in thick woods where units got lost, communications broke down, and soldiers sometimes fired on their own men by mistake.

The decisive moment came on the second day when a Confederate breakthrough shattered the Union right flank. Rosecrans and much of his army fled in a panic back toward Chattanooga. Only General George Thomas, who earned the nickname "the Rock of Chickamauga," held his ground long enough for the army to escape complete destruction. However, it was still a devastating Confederate victory. The Union suffered about sixteen thousand casualties compared to eighteen thousand for the Confederates. Rosecrans's army was thoroughly demoralized.

BATTLE OF CHICKAMAUGA

A painting of the Battle of Chickamauga.[109]

The defeated Union Army retreated into Chattanooga and found itself trapped. Bragg's forces occupied the high ground surrounding the city—Lookout Mountain to the southwest and Missionary Ridge to the east. They controlled the roads and the river, cutting off Union supply lines. Rosecrans's army was slowly starving, with soldiers reduced to quarter rations and horses dying by the hundreds from lack of feed.

This was where Ulysses S. Grant entered the picture. In October 1863, Lincoln gave Grant command of the newly created Military Division of the Mississippi, which put him in charge of all Union forces between the Appalachian Mountains and the Mississippi River. Grant's first job was to save the Army of the Cumberland before it starved to death in Chattanooga.

Grant arrived at Chattanooga and immediately started fixing problems. He replaced Rosecrans with George Thomas and opened a new supply line—the "Cracker Line"—that brought food and ammunition to the trapped army. Within weeks, the starving soldiers were eating regular rations again. Grant also called for reinforcements, including Sherman's troops from Mississippi and "Fighting Joe" Hooker's forces from Virginia.

By late November, Grant was ready to break the siege. His plan was to attack Bragg's forces on both flanks while Thomas's men fought against the center. The attacks began on November 23, and over the next three days, the Union forces won one of their most dramatic victories of the war.

The most memorable moment came on November 24 when Hooker's men fought the "Battle Above the Clouds" on the slopes of Lookout Mountain. Fog and mist shrouded the mountain, giving the battle its romantic name, but the fighting was real. By evening, the Confederate forces had been driven off the mountain. Union soldiers planted their flag on the summit for all of Chattanooga to see.

The decisive action came on November 25 at Missionary Ridge. Grant's plan called for Thomas's Army of the Cumberland to make a limited attack on the Confederate rifle pits at the base of the ridge and then wait for Sherman's flank attack to develop. But something remarkable happened—something that military historians still debate today.

Thomas's men, many of them still smarting from their defeat at Chickamauga, stormed the rifle pits as ordered. Then, without orders and against all military logic, they kept going. They charged straight up the steep ridge toward the Confederate main line, climbing over rocks and fallen logs while Confederate artillery and rifle fire poured down on them. Officers tried to stop them, but the soldiers kept going, determined to redeem themselves.

Against all odds, the charge succeeded. Confederate defenders, amazed to see Union soldiers climbing the ridge under fire, began to panic and flee. Within an hour, Bragg's entire center had collapsed, and his army was retreating in disorder toward Georgia. It was one of the most spectacular battlefield victories of the entire war—and it happened almost by accident.

The victory at Chattanooga was decisive in multiple ways. It secured Tennessee for the Union and opened the door for Sherman's advance into Georgia. It restored the reputation of the Army of the Cumberland after its humiliation at Chickamauga. It also convinced Lincoln and Congress that Grant was the general they had been searching for—someone who could win battles and keep winning them. Within four months, Lincoln would promote Grant to general-in-chief of all Union forces and bring him east to finally deal with Robert E. Lee.

The Confederacy had won its last major victory in the West at Chickamauga, but the follow-up disaster at Chattanooga showed that tactical victories meant nothing without the resources to exploit them. The South was slowly running out of men, supplies, and options, while the North was finally finding the leadership it needed to win the war.

A War on a New Scale: Technology and Tactics

The battles in the West revealed how much warfare was changing during the Civil War. New technologies were making battles more deadly, and traditional tactics were becoming obsolete. The result was a dramatic increase in casualties and a fundamental shift in how wars were fought.

The most obvious change was in weapons technology. The Civil War was the first major conflict fought with rifled muskets as the standard infantry weapon. These rifles were accurate at much longer ranges than the smoothbore muskets used in previous wars. A good marksman could hit targets at three hundred or four hundred yards compared to eighty or one hundred yards for older weapons.

The increased range and accuracy of rifles made traditional tactics suicidal. For centuries, armies had won battles by marching in tight formations toward enemy positions and then charging with bayonets for the final assault. These tactics worked when muskets were inaccurate and slow to reload. However, rifles could cut down attacking troops long before they reached enemy lines.

Yet, Civil War generals continued to use the old tactics because they didn't understand how much weapons had improved. They ordered frontal assaults against prepared positions, sending their men across open ground into withering rifle fire. The results were predictable: enormous casualties for minimal gains.

Artillery was also becoming more deadly. Rifled cannons could hit targets accurately at distances of more than a mile. New types of ammunition—explosive shells, canister shot, and grapeshot—could devastate infantry formations. Artillery commanders learned to coordinate their fire with infantry attacks, softening up enemy positions before assaults began.

The Civil War also saw the first use of many technologies that would become standard in later conflicts. Railroads allowed armies to move troops and supplies faster than ever before. Telegraph lines provided instant communication between commanders and their governments. Photography brought images of the war to people who had never even seen a battlefield.

A Harvest of Death by Timothy H. O'Sullivan.[108]

Ironclad warships revolutionized naval warfare. The famous battle between the USS *Monitor* and the CSS *Virginia* (formerly the *Merrimack*) in March 1862 proved that wooden warships were obsolete. Within two years, both navies were building fleets of armored vessels that could withstand hits from the heaviest guns.

Medical technology, unfortunately, lagged behind weapons technology. Doctors in 1862 didn't understand that germs caused infection, so they didn't sterilize their instruments or wash their hands between patients. Field hospitals were often more dangerous than battlefields. More soldiers died from disease and infected wounds than from enemy bullets.

The combination of improved weapons and primitive medicine created casualty rates that shocked everyone. At Shiloh, nearly 25 percent of the soldiers who saw combat became casualties. At Antietam, the casualty rate was even higher. These numbers were far beyond anything Americans had experienced in previous wars.

The scale of the armies was also unprecedented. The Battle of Shiloh involved more than 100,000 men, which was larger than entire wars in previous centuries. Supplying these massive armies required new levels of organization and logistical planning. Armies needed hundreds of wagons to carry food, ammunition, and medical supplies. They needed thousands of horses and mules to pull the wagons and artillery pieces.

Communication became a critical factor in controlling these large armies. Commanders used signal flags, bugles, and drum calls to coordinate movements during battles. But in the smoke and noise of combat, these methods often failed. Units got separated from their commanders and fought on their own initiative. Battles became chaotic affairs where nobody had complete control.

The Civil War was becoming a total war in which entire societies, not just armies, were targeted. Sherman understood this better than most generals. "We are not only fighting hostile armies," he wrote, "but a hostile people, and must make old and young, rich and poor, feel the hard hand of war."[i]

This shift toward total war would become more apparent as the conflict continued. By 1864, Union forces would be deliberately destroying civilian property, not just military targets. Confederate

---

[i] https://cwnc.omeka.chass.ncsu.edu/items/show/144

guerrillas would be targeting Union supply lines and civilian officials. The distinction between soldiers and civilians, which had been clear in earlier wars, was beginning to blur.

As the war progressed, both sides learned that modern war was not a gentleman's game played by professional soldiers. It was a savage struggle that would consume entire generations and reshape the nation forever.

Chapter 7: The Emancipation Proclamation

By the summer of 1862, Abraham Lincoln faced a terrible choice. The war was going badly for the Union. McClellan had failed to capture Richmond. Lee had invaded Maryland. Thousands of young men were dying in battles that seemed to accomplish nothing. Meanwhile, Europe was considering recognizing Confederate independence. Something had to change, or the United States might not survive.

Lincoln had always hated slavery, but he had promised not to interfere with it where it already existed. He had been elected as a president who would preserve the Union, not free the slaves. However, by 1862, it was becoming clear that these two goals might be the same thing. If freeing the slaves would help win the war, then Lincoln was ready to do it.

The Emancipation Proclamation is one of the most important documents in American history, but it wasn't what most people think it was. It didn't free all the slaves. It didn't end slavery forever. What it did was transform the Civil War from a fight to preserve the Union into a war for human freedom. And once that transformation happened, there was no going back.

From Preserving the Union to Freeing the Slaves

When Lincoln took office in March 1861, his position on slavery was clear. He would not allow slavery to expand into new territories, but he would not interfere with slavery where it already existed. Politically,

Lincoln needed to keep the border states—Delaware, Maryland, Kentucky, and Missouri—in the Union. These states allowed slavery but had not seceded. If Lincoln moved too quickly against slavery, they might join the Confederacy, giving the South additional manpower and resources it desperately needed.

Constitutionally, Lincoln believed the federal government had no power to abolish slavery in the states where it existed. The Constitution protected property rights, and slaves were considered property under the law. Even if Lincoln wanted to free all the slaves, he wasn't sure he had the legal authority to do it.

However, Lincoln's thinking began to change as the war dragged on. By the summer of 1862, it was clear that this would be a long, costly conflict. The Union needed every advantage it could get. Freeing the slaves would deprive the Confederacy of crucial labor. It would allow Black men to join the Union Army, and it would make it much harder for European nations to support the Confederacy.

Lincoln also came under increasing pressure from abolitionists in his own party. Radical Republicans like Charles Sumner and Thaddeus Stevens argued that the war should be about ending slavery, not just preserving the Union. They pointed out that slavery was the cause of the war, so slavery had to be destroyed to prevent future conflicts.

Frederick Douglass, the famous escaped slave and abolitionist speaker, met with Lincoln several times to argue for emancipation. Pressure came from ordinary soldiers too. Union troops in the South encountered enslaved people every day. Many ran away from their masters and sought protection from Union forces. What should the army do with these "contraband," as they came to be called? Send them back to their masters? Put them to work for the Union? Free them?

Some Union generals took matters into their own hands. In August 1861, General John C. Frémont declared that all slaves owned by Confederate supporters in Missouri were free. Lincoln quickly overruled him, fearing it would drive Missouri out of the Union. But other generals continued to wrestle with the slavery question.

Lincoln gradually began to see emancipation as a military necessity. In July 1862, Congress passed the Second Confiscation Act, which authorized the president to seize rebel property, including slaves. The act also allowed enslaved people who escaped to Union lines to be declared free. Lincoln signed the bill, taking his first step toward emancipation.

By late summer 1862, Lincoln had decided to act, but he wanted to time his announcement carefully. If he issued an emancipation proclamation after a string of military defeats, it might look like a desperate act by a losing government. He needed a Union victory to give the proclamation credibility and force.

The victory came at Antietam in September 1862. Lee's invasion of Maryland had been stopped, and his army had retreated to Virginia. It wasn't the decisive victory Lincoln had hoped for, but it was enough. On September 22, 1862, five days after the battle, Lincoln issued the preliminary Emancipation Proclamation.

The preliminary proclamation was actually an ultimatum. Lincoln announced that on January 1, 1863, all slaves in areas still in rebellion would be declared free. The Confederate states had one hundred days to return to the Union and keep their slaves, or else they would lose them forever. It was Lincoln's final attempt to end the war through negotiation rather than force.

No Confederate state took Lincoln's offer. On January 1, 1863, Lincoln signed the final Emancipation Proclamation. The war for the Union had become a war for freedom.

"A Fit and Necessary War Measure": What the Proclamation Actually Did

The Emancipation Proclamation has become one of the most misunderstood documents in American history. Many people think it freed all the slaves in the United States. It didn't. Many think it ended slavery forever. It didn't do that either.

The proclamation was limited in scope. It applied only to slaves in areas "in rebellion against the United States." This meant it freed slaves in most of the Confederacy but not in the border states that remained in the Union. It also didn't apply to Confederate territory already under Union control, such as New Orleans and parts of Virginia and Tennessee.

This selective approach frustrated abolitionists, who wanted Lincoln to free all slaves everywhere. But Lincoln had good reasons for his caution. He still needed to keep the border states loyal to the Union. If he freed slaves in Kentucky or Missouri, those states might join the Confederacy.

He also worried about the legal basis for his action. Lincoln justified the Emancipation Proclamation as a war measure authorized by his powers as commander in chief. During wartime, the president could seize enemy property being used to support the rebellion. Since slaves were legally considered property and were clearly helping the Confederate war effort, Lincoln argued he had the authority to free them.

This legal justification was important because it meant the proclamation might not survive the end of the war. If Lincoln was freeing slaves only as a military measure, what would happen when the military emergency ended? Would the freed slaves go back to being enslaved? Lincoln and other Republican leaders realized they would need a constitutional amendment to make emancipation permanent.

The proclamation also did something that surprised many people: it authorized the enlistment of Black men in the Union Army and Navy. This was potentially the most important part of the entire document. If Black men could serve as soldiers, they would help the Union win the war. They would also prove their worthiness for citizenship and equal treatment. Frederick Douglass understood this immediately. "Once let the black man get upon his person the brass letters U.S.," he said, "let him get an eagle on his button, and a musket on his shoulder, and bullets in his pocket, and there is no power on earth which can deny that he has earned the right of citizenship in the United States."[i]

The proclamation had immediate effects in the areas where it applied. As Union armies advanced into Confederate territory, slaves learned they were legally free. Many left their plantations and headed for Union lines. Some joined the army, and others worked as laborers, cooks, and teamsters for the Union forces. The Confederate labor system began to collapse from within.

The psychological impact was enormous. Enslaved people who had been told Lincoln was their enemy now heard that he had declared them free. White Southerners who claimed they were fighting for states' rights could no longer hide the truth; the war was about slavery. With the Emancipation Proclamation, the meaning of the war had changed forever.

International reaction was also important. European nations that had been considering recognizing Confederate independence found it much harder to support a country explicitly fighting to preserve slavery. Britain

---

[i] https://www.archives.gov/education/lessons/blacks-civil-war

and France, which had abolished slavery in their own empires, couldn't publicly side with the Confederacy without appearing to endorse human bondage.

However, the proclamation created new problems for the Union. Many White soldiers, especially from the Midwest, had enlisted to preserve the Union, not to free slaves. Some expressed anger in letters they sent home and threatened to desert rather than fight for the freedom of Blacks, though actual large-scale desertions didn't occur. Most soldiers remained loyal to the Union cause despite their reservations. Democratic politicians accused Lincoln of changing the war's purpose without congressional approval.

Lincoln addressed these concerns in his typical way, with careful explanation and appeals to higher principles. The proclamation was necessary to win the war, he argued. And winning the war was necessary to preserve the Union.

The Emancipation Proclamation didn't end slavery immediately, but it marked the beginning of the end. On January 1, 1863, every Union victory would mean freedom for more enslaved people. The war had become a revolution.

Black Soldiers in Blue: Fighting for Freedom

The most immediate and dramatic result of the Emancipation Proclamation was the enlistment of Black men in the Union Army. Within two years, nearly 200,000 Black soldiers and sailors were serving in Union forces. They would prove to be some of the war's most effective and motivated fighters. These men understood they were fighting not just for the Union but also for their own freedom and that of their families.

The idea of arming Black men was controversial, even in the North. Many White Americans believed Black men wouldn't fight effectively and that they lacked the courage and discipline to be good soldiers. Others worried that giving weapons to Black men might lead to a race war or revenge killings. Some Union officers refused to command Black troops.

However, military necessity overcame racial prejudice. The Union needed soldiers, and Black men were eager to fight. Frederick Douglass had three sons who enlisted in the Union Army. The first official Black regiment was the 54th Massachusetts Infantry, which was organized in early 1863. The regiment was commanded by Robert Gould Shaw, a young White officer from a prominent abolitionist family. Shaw had initially been reluctant to take the assignment, but he came to believe deeply in his men's abilities and their cause.

The men of the 54th Massachusetts proved their courage at Fort Wagner, South Carolina, in July 1863. Shaw led his men in a desperate assault on the Confederate fort, knowing it was probably a suicide mission. Shaw was killed leading the charge, and nearly half his regiment became casualties, but they had shown that Black soldiers would fight and die as bravely as any White troops.

Black soldiers still had to fight discrimination within the Union Army. They were paid less than White soldiers—$10 per month compared to $13 for White troops. They were often given inferior weapons and equipment. Many were assigned to garrison duty or labor details rather than combat roles. Some White officers treated them as second-class soldiers.

The 54th Massachusetts again led the way in protesting unequal pay. The entire regiment refused to accept any pay rather than accept lower wages than White soldiers. Their protest, supported by Massachusetts Governor John Andrew and other abolitionists, eventually forced the War Department to equalize pay for all soldiers.

Black and White soldiers who volunteered to fight in the war.[104]

The performance of Black soldiers exceeded everyone's expectations except their own. They fought with particular determination because they knew what defeat meant. White soldiers who were captured became prisoners of war. Black soldiers who were captured faced enslavement or execution. The Confederacy refused to treat Black soldiers as legitimate prisoners of war, claiming they were rebellious slaves who should be returned to their masters or shot.

Some of the war's most dramatic moments involved Black soldiers fighting their former masters. In South Carolina and Georgia, regiments of former slaves raided the plantations where they had been enslaved. They freed their families and friends, burned the big houses where they had been whipped and humiliated, and recruited new soldiers from among the newly freed slaves.

Harriet Tubman, the famous conductor on the Underground Railroad, led one such raid in South Carolina. Working with the Union Navy, she guided gunboats up the Combahee River, destroying Confederate supplies and freeing more than seven hundred enslaved people. Many of the freed men immediately enlisted in Black regiments.

The impact of Black military service extended far beyond the battlefield. When White Americans saw Black men in uniform, carrying rifles and fighting for the flag, it challenged fundamental assumptions about race and citizenship. How could the nation deny equal rights to men who had bled and died for it?

By the end of the war, Black soldiers made up about 10 percent of the Union Army and 20 percent of the Union Navy. They had participated in more than four hundred battles and skirmishes. Sixteen Black soldiers and four Black sailors won the Medal of Honor. Their service was crucial to the Union victory and established their claim to full citizenship in the United States.

The Emancipation Proclamation had transformed the Civil War from a conflict about preserving the Union into a war for freedom. Black soldiers made that transformation real by putting their lives on the line for the cause of liberty. They proved that freedom was worth fighting for and that they were worthy of the freedom they were fighting to achieve.

Chapter 8: The High Water Mark of the Confederacy

The summer of 1863 would decide the fate of the Confederate States of America. Two massive campaigns were about to reach their climax, one along the Mississippi River, the other in the rolling hills of Pennsylvania. If the Confederacy could win both campaigns, European recognition and Northern war weariness might force Lincoln to negotiate for peace. If the Confederacy lost both, the rebellion might never recover.

The stakes couldn't have been higher. At Vicksburg, Mississippi, Ulysses S. Grant was trying to capture the last Confederate stronghold on the Mississippi River. If he succeeded, the Confederacy would be split in half. Meanwhile, Robert E. Lee was leading his army into Pennsylvania, hoping to win a decisive victory on Northern soil that would shock the North into making peace.

Both campaigns would peak within days of each other in early July 1863. When the smoke cleared, the Confederacy would still be fighting, but it would never again have such a good chance to win its independence. July 1863 would mark the beginning of the end for the Confederate dream.

The Vicksburg Campaign: Grant's Masterpiece

Vicksburg, Mississippi, was the key to everything. Perched on high bluffs overlooking the Mississippi River, the city controlled the last stretch of the great river still held by the Confederacy. As long as Confederate artillery could fire on Union shipping from Vicksburg's heights, the Union couldn't fully control the Mississippi. And as long as the Confederacy held Vicksburg, it could move supplies and reinforcements between the eastern and western parts of the country.

Lincoln understood Vicksburg's importance perfectly. "Vicksburg is the key," he said. "The war can never be brought to a close until that key is in our pocket."[i] But getting that key would prove to be one of the most difficult challenges of the entire war.

The problem was geography. The city had earned the nickname "Gibraltar of the West" because of its seemingly impregnable position. The Mississippi River curved around Vicksburg in a horseshoe bend, with the city sitting on bluffs that rose two hundred feet above the water. Confederate engineers had spent months fortifying these natural advantages, building a network of trenches, artillery positions, and obstacles that stretched for miles around the city. The land approaches were protected by swamps, bayous, and more Confederate fortifications. The Yazoo River Delta north of the city was a maze of waterways and swamps.

Grant had been trying to capture Vicksburg since late 1862, and every attempt had failed spectacularly. He had tried attacking from the north but had been stopped by swampy terrain that turned his soldiers into sitting ducks. He had tried to bypass the city by digging canals to change the course of the Mississippi River. The canals didn't work; the river refused to cooperate with human engineering. He had tried landing north of the city and marching overland, but Confederate cavalry kept cutting his supply lines and forcing him to retreat.

Each failure had cost Grant politically. Newspapers criticized his repeated defeats and called for his removal. Some politicians whispered that he was drinking again and couldn't handle the responsibility of high command. However, Lincoln continued to support his most aggressive general, even as the pressure mounted to try someone else.

By the spring of 1863, Grant was ready to try something completely different. Instead of attacking Vicksburg directly, he would march his army down the west side of the Mississippi River, cross below the city, and attack from the south and east. It was a risky plan that would require him to cut loose from his supply lines and live off the land in enemy territory.

---

[i] https://www.battlefields.org/learn/articles/long-gruesome-fight-capture-vicksburg

Most military experts thought Grant's plan was insane. Even Sherman, Grant's most trusted subordinate, thought it was too dangerous. "I tremble for the result," Sherman wrote. But Grant was convinced it was the only way to capture Vicksburg.

The campaign began in April 1863 when Union gunboats ran past Vicksburg's batteries under cover of darkness. Confederate artillery pounded the ships as they steamed past the city, but most made it through safely. The gunboats then waited south of Vicksburg to ferry Grant's army across the river.

Grant's army began crossing the Mississippi at Bruinsburg on April 30, 1863. Within three days, he had twenty thousand men on the east side of the river, with more arriving every hour. Instead of heading directly toward Vicksburg, Grant turned east toward Jackson, the capital of Mississippi. His plan was to defeat Confederate forces in the area before they could unite to defend Vicksburg.

What followed was one of the most brilliant campaigns in American military history. In eighteen days, Grant's army marched two hundred miles, won five battles, captured Jackson, and drove the Confederate forces back into Vicksburg's defenses. Grant kept his army moving so fast that Confederate commanders never had time to coordinate their responses.

The speed of Grant's advance was unprecedented. His soldiers marched up to twenty miles a day in the Mississippi heat, fighting battles and then continuing their advance without rest. Confederate General Joseph E. Johnston, who was trying to organize resistance, complained that he couldn't keep track of where Grant's army was or where it was going next.

The key to Grant's success was his willingness to abandon his supply lines and live off the countryside. Grant's men lived like locusts, consuming everything edible in their path. They raided smokehouses, cornfields, and chicken coops. They captured Confederate supply trains and distributed the contents to their own troops. When they couldn't eat something immediately, they destroyed it to prevent it from falling back into Confederate hands. It was a preview of the "total war" tactics that would later be used by Sherman and other Union generals.

The campaign also showed Grant's remarkable tactical flexibility. When he learned that Confederate General Joseph E. Johnston was trying to gather reinforcements at Jackson, Grant immediately changed direction and attacked the state capital. This wasn't part of his original plan, but Grant understood that flexibility was more important than rigid adherence to predetermined objectives.

After capturing Jackson and scattering Johnston's forces, Grant turned west toward Vicksburg, knowing that the city's garrison was now isolated and couldn't receive help. He had cut the last railroad line connecting Vicksburg to the rest of the Confederacy. The city was completely on its own.

The final approach to Vicksburg required Grant to fight two more battles against Confederate forces trying to prevent his army from reaching the city. At Champion Hill on May 16, Grant's army defeated a Confederate force trying to escape from Vicksburg. At Big Black River Bridge on May 17, they scattered the last Confederate field force between them and their objective.

By mid-May, Grant had driven Confederate forces into Vicksburg's inner defenses. The city was under siege. Grant tried two direct assaults on the Confederate trenches on May 19 and May 22, but both failed with heavy casualties. Vicksburg's defenses were simply too strong to be taken by storm. The Confederate trenches were protected by sharpened stakes, wire entanglements, and carefully positioned artillery that could sweep any attacking force with devastating fire. Grant settled in for a siege, surrounding the city and waiting for starvation to do what bullets couldn't. The siege would become a battle of endurance between Grant's determination and Vicksburg's will to resist.

The siege of Vicksburg lasted forty-seven days and became one of the most grueling ordeals of the entire war. Inside the city, Confederate soldiers and civilians gradually ran out of food. They ate horses, mules, dogs, cats, and rats. Children who had never known hunger learned what it meant to go to bed with empty stomachs.

As food became scarce, people became increasingly desperate. The wealthy, who had started the siege with well-stocked pantries, gradually joined the poor in the daily struggle to find something, anything, to eat. While most people managed to survive on reduced rations of whatever was available, some resorted to extreme measures. A few desperate individuals tried grinding up wallpaper to make a flour substitute or boiling leather items.

The constant artillery bombardment made life even more miserable. Union gunboats on the river and artillery positions on land fired into the city twenty-four hours a day. Residents dug caves in the hillsides to escape the shelling, creating an underground city of tunnels and chambers. Some caves were elaborately furnished with carpets and furniture salvaged from damaged homes. Others were simple holes in the ground where families huddled together, listening to the shells explode overhead. Children stopped playing in the streets because of the constant danger. Schools closed. Churches held services in cave shelters.

Outside the city, Grant tightened the noose methodically and relentlessly. He brought up heavy artillery to bombard Confederate positions around the clock. The constant noise of cannon fire could be heard for miles. He dug trenches that gradually crept closer to Confederate lines, using techniques borrowed from European siege warfare. Most importantly, he made sure no supplies could reach the besieged garrison.

Grant's siege lines eventually stretched for fifteen miles around the city. Union soldiers dug a maze of trenches, artillery positions, and supply depots that looked like a small city. They brought up enormous siege guns that could throw 200-pound shells into Vicksburg's defenses. They even began digging tunnels under Confederate fortifications, planning to blow them up with explosives.

The Union army outside Vicksburg grew larger and more comfortable as the siege continued. Fresh supplies arrived daily from the North. The soldiers ate well, received regular mail from home, and enjoyed entertainment provided by visiting performers. The contrast with the suffering inside the city couldn't have been starker.

The Confederate commander in Vicksburg was General John C. Pemberton, a Pennsylvania-born officer who had chosen to fight for the South because his wife was from Virginia. Pemberton was competent but cautious. He was exactly the wrong kind of general to face someone like Grant. He had allowed himself to be trapped in Vicksburg instead of fighting his way out when he still had the chance.

By early July, Pemberton knew the situation was hopeless. His men were starving, and his ammunition was running low. On July 3, 1863, he sent a message to Grant asking about surrender terms. Grant's reply was blunt: "The useless effusion of blood you propose stopping by this course can be ended at any time you may choose, by the unconditional surrender of the city and garrison."[i]

---

[i] https://www.battlefields.org/learn/primary-sources/grant-remembers-surrender-and-victory-vicksburg

Pemberton tried to negotiate better terms, but Grant held firm. On July 4, 1863–Independence Day–Vicksburg surrendered. Grant had captured an entire Confederate force of nearly thirty thousand men, along with the city's massive artillery and supply stocks. The Mississippi River was now completely under Union control from its source in Minnesota to its mouth in Louisiana.

The fall of Vicksburg was a devastating blow to the Confederacy. The western states of Texas, Louisiana, and Arkansas were now cut off from the rest of the country. Confederate forces could no longer move troops or supplies easily between the eastern and western theaters. Most importantly, the Union had achieved one of its key strategic objectives.

Grant's Vicksburg campaign established him as the Union's best general. He had shown that he could plan and execute complex operations, adapt to changing circumstances, and win decisive victories. Within a year, Lincoln would bring him east to take command of all Union forces. The man who had been working in his father's leather store three years earlier was now the North's greatest military asset.

The Gettysburg Campaign: Lee's Great Gamble

While Grant was tightening his grip on Vicksburg, Robert E. Lee was planning his own campaign that he hoped would end the war. Lee had spent the spring of 1863 reorganizing his army after Stonewall Jackson's death at the Battle of Chancellorsville in May. He was ready for his boldest gamble yet: a full-scale invasion of Pennsylvania that might force the North to sue for peace.

Lee had several compelling reasons for wanting to invade the North again. His army desperately needed supplies that were becoming harder to find in war-ravaged Virginia. Two years of campaigning had stripped the state bare of food, fodder, and equipment. An invasion of Pennsylvania would allow his army to live off the rich farmlands of the North while giving Virginia a chance to recover from the devastation of war.

A successful invasion might also convince European nations to recognize Confederate independence. Britain and France were still watching the war carefully, waiting to see which side would prove stronger. A major Confederate victory on Northern soil, especially one that threatened Washington or Baltimore, might finally tip European opinion in favor of the South.

Also, a major Confederate victory on Northern soil might turn Northern public opinion against the war and help Democrats win control of Congress in the 1864 elections. Lee understood that the Confederacy was fighting a war of endurance. If he could make the war costly enough for the North, Northern voters might decide that preserving the Union wasn't worth the price in blood and money.

Lee understood that time was working against the Confederacy. The Union blockade was slowly strangling the South's economy. Union forces were growing stronger while Confederate forces were being worn down by constant fighting and desertion. The Confederacy's window of opportunity was closing. If the South was going to win its independence, it had to win soon, before the North's advantages became overwhelming.

The strategic situation in Virginia also favored an invasion. Union forces around Washington were scattered and demoralized after their defeat at Chancellorsville. Lee's army, despite Jackson's loss, was at its peak strength and confidence. If Lee moved quickly, he might be able to get deep into Pennsylvania before Union forces could concentrate to stop him.

In early June 1863, Lee began moving his Army of Northern Virginia north through the Shenandoah Valley toward Pennsylvania. It was a risky move that would take his army far from its supply bases and put it deep in enemy territory. However, Lee was confident that his veterans could handle whatever the Union Army threw at them.

Lee's army was organized into three corps commanded by Lieutenant General James Longstreet, Lieutenant General Richard Ewell, and Lieutenant General A. P. Hill. Longstreet was Lee's "Old War Horse," a methodical fighter who preferred defensive tactics. Ewell had replaced Stonewall Jackson and was still learning how to handle independent command. Hill was aggressive but sometimes unreliable. These were experienced, battle-tested units that had fought together for two years. They were also tired from constant campaigning and reduced in numbers by casualties and stragglers. The Confederate force that marched into Pennsylvania in June 1863 was different from the army that had invaded Maryland the previous year. It was smaller, about seventy-five thousand men compared to nearly ninety thousand in 1862.

James Longstreet.[105]

But the army's morale remained high. These men had followed Lee through victory after victory. They believed he was invincible and that they were the finest soldiers in the world. They were eager to carry the war to Northern soil and show the Yankees what Confederate fighting men could do on their own territory.

The Union Army of the Potomac was now commanded by General George Gordon Meade, who had replaced Joseph Hooker just three days before the Battle of Gettysburg began. Meade was a competent but cautious general who had been thrust into command at the worst possible moment. He had no time to prepare for a major battle and little experience commanding such a large army.

Meade was known as "Old Snapping Turtle" because of his bad temper and aggressive appearance. He had a prominent nose and eyes that seemed to bore through whoever he was talking to. Unlike the gregarious McClellan or the flamboyant Hooker, Meade was all business, a professional soldier who had earned his position through competent service rather than political connections.

General George Meade.[106]

The change in command came at a critical moment. Hooker had lost Lincoln's confidence after his defeat at Chancellorsville and his disputes with the War Department. With Lee's army already deep in Pennsylvania, Lincoln needed a general who would fight aggressively. Meade had a reputation as a solid, reliable commander who wouldn't panic under pressure.

The two armies stumbled into each other near the small Pennsylvania town of Gettysburg on July 1, 1863. Neither Lee nor Meade had planned to fight there, but once the battle began, both sides kept feeding more troops into the fighting.

Confederate troops under General Henry Heth marched toward Gettysburg looking for supplies, particularly shoes for their barefoot soldiers. They ran into Union cavalry under General John Buford, who had occupied the town the previous evening. Buford immediately recognized the strategic importance of the high ground around Gettysburg and decided to hold it until infantry reinforcements could arrive.

The town of Gettysburg was a transportation hub where ten major roads converged like spokes on a wheel. It had no particular strategic value beyond its road network, but those roads made it easy for both armies to concentrate their forces there quickly. The surrounding countryside was rolling farmland broken by ridges, hills, and stone walls that would provide natural defensive positions for whoever got there first.

Buford's cavalry fought desperately to hold their positions west of town until Union infantry could arrive. They were armed with breech-loading carbines that could fire much faster than traditional muskets, giving them firepower that compensated somewhat for their smaller numbers. However, cavalry couldn't hold out indefinitely against determined infantry attacks.

The first Union infantry to reach the battlefield was the Iron Brigade, veteran troops from Wisconsin and Indiana who wore distinctive black hats and had a reputation as hard fighters. They arrived just as Buford's cavalry was being overwhelmed and immediately launched a counterattack that drove back the Confederate advance. For a few hours, it looked like the Union might be able to hold Gettysburg.

However, more Confederate troops kept arriving, and by afternoon, the Union forces were badly outnumbered. General John Reynolds, one of the Union Army's best corps commanders, was killed while directing his troops into position. His death was a severe blow to Union morale and left the field commanders without clear leadership during the crucial first hours of battle.

The first day of fighting went well for the Confederates. They drove Union forces through the town, capturing thousands of prisoners and seizing the streets of Gettysburg. Confederate soldiers celebrated what looked like another easy victory over the Yankees. However, Union troops managed to retreat to strong defensive positions on Cemetery Hill and Cemetery Ridge south of town, where they could make a stand.

The retreat through Gettysburg was chaotic but not panicked. Union soldiers fell back through the streets in reasonably good order, helped by the confusion caused by fighting in a built-up area. The pursuit of the Confederates was slowed by the need to secure prisoners and reorganize units that had become scattered during the street fighting.

By the evening of July 1, the Union Army held a fishhook-shaped line that would prove very difficult to break. Cemetery Hill formed the "eye" of the fishhook, with Cemetery Ridge extending south like the shaft and Culp's Hill curving around to the east like the barb. This position gave Union forces interior lines. They could move troops from one threatened point to another much faster than the Confederate forces attacking from the outside.

Lee arrived on the battlefield late in the afternoon and immediately saw both the opportunity and the danger. His army had won a tactical victory and driven the enemy from the field, but the Union Army was concentrating on strong defensive ground. Every hour that passed would make the Union position stronger as more troops arrived and defensive works were improved.

Lee considered calling off the attack and moving around the Union Army to find better ground, a maneuver that had worked for him many times before. But his blood was up from the day's success, and he was reluctant to give up the momentum his army had gained. He also worried that retreating might demoralize his troops and convince them that he lacked confidence in their abilities.

Lee had built his reputation on taking calculated risks, but this risk was greater than most. He was attacking an enemy that outnumbered him, held strong defensive positions, and was fighting on its own soil. His army was tired from weeks of marching and had just fought a hard battle. However, Lee believed his veterans could accomplish anything if properly led.

The second day of fighting at Gettysburg was even bloodier than the first. Lee attacked both flanks of the Union line, trying to break through at Little Round Top on the left and Culp's Hill on the right. The fighting was savage and desperate, with units on both sides suffering enormous casualties.

The Battle of Gettysburg by Thure de Thulstrup.[107]

The day began with confusion and missed opportunities. Lee had ordered General Richard Ewell to attack Culp's Hill "if practicable," but Ewell decided the position was too strong. This was exactly the kind of situation where Stonewall Jackson would have found a way to attack, but Ewell was more cautious than his predecessor. The delay gave Union forces time to strengthen their positions and bring up reinforcements.

Meanwhile, Lee planned his main attack against the Union left flank, where Little Round Top anchored the southern end of the Union line. If Confederate forces could capture this rocky hill, they could place artillery there that would make the entire Union position untenable. Lee assigned this crucial mission to General James Longstreet's corps, but Longstreet was reluctant to attack.

Longstreet had argued against the Battle of Gettysburg, preferring to move around the Union Army and force it to attack Confederate positions. But Lee was determined to attack, and Longstreet had no choice but to obey orders. The attack finally began in the late afternoon, hours later than Lee had intended. The delay had given Union forces time to strengthen their defenses and position troops to meet the Confederate assault.

The fighting around Little Round Top became the stuff of legend. The hill was defended by the 20th Maine Infantry under Colonel Joshua

Lawrence Chamberlain, a college professor who had volunteered for military service when the war began. Chamberlain's men were positioned at the extreme left of the Union line, which meant that if they broke, the Confederate forces could roll up the entire Union Army. The fighting was desperate, with Confederate troops from Alabama and Texas charging up the rocky slopes again and again. Chamberlain's men fought back with rifles, bayonets, rocks, and anything they could use as a weapon.

Running low on ammunition and facing another Confederate charge, Chamberlain made a decision that would make him famous. Instead of retreating or surrendering, he ordered his men to fix their bayonets and counterattack. His entire regiment charged down the hill into the surprised Confederate troops. The desperate charge broke the Confederate attack and saved Little Round Top. It probably saved the entire Union Army.

Elsewhere on the battlefield, the fighting was equally intense. At Devil's Den, a jumble of massive boulders south of Little Round Top, Union and Confederate troops fought at close quarters among the rocks. At the Wheatfield, attacks and counterattacks surged back and forth across a farmer's field, leaving it carpeted with bodies. At the Peach Orchard, Union General Daniel Sickles advanced his corps beyond the main Union line and was nearly destroyed before other units could rescue the survivors.

The second day's fighting cost both armies terribly, but it didn't break the Union line. Lee's attacks had come close to success at several points, but the Union Army held on through desperate fighting and last-minute reinforcements. As night fell, both armies prepared for what everyone knew would be the decisive day of battle.

Lee spent the night of July 2 planning his final assault. Against the advice of General Longstreet, he decided to attack the center of the Union line on Cemetery Ridge. Longstreet argued that the position was too strong and that Lee should move around the Union Army instead of attacking it directly. Lee was convinced that one more push would break Union resistance. He had seen his army perform miracles before. At Chancellorsville just two months earlier, they had defeated a Union force twice their size. Lee was also running out of options. Every day his army stayed in Pennsylvania made it weaker and more vulnerable to Union counterattacks.

Lee's plan for July 3 was based on the principle of concentration. Instead of attacking multiple points as he had done the previous day, he would mass his strength against a single point and try to break through. If he could rupture the Union center, he could then roll up both flanks and destroy Meade's army completely.

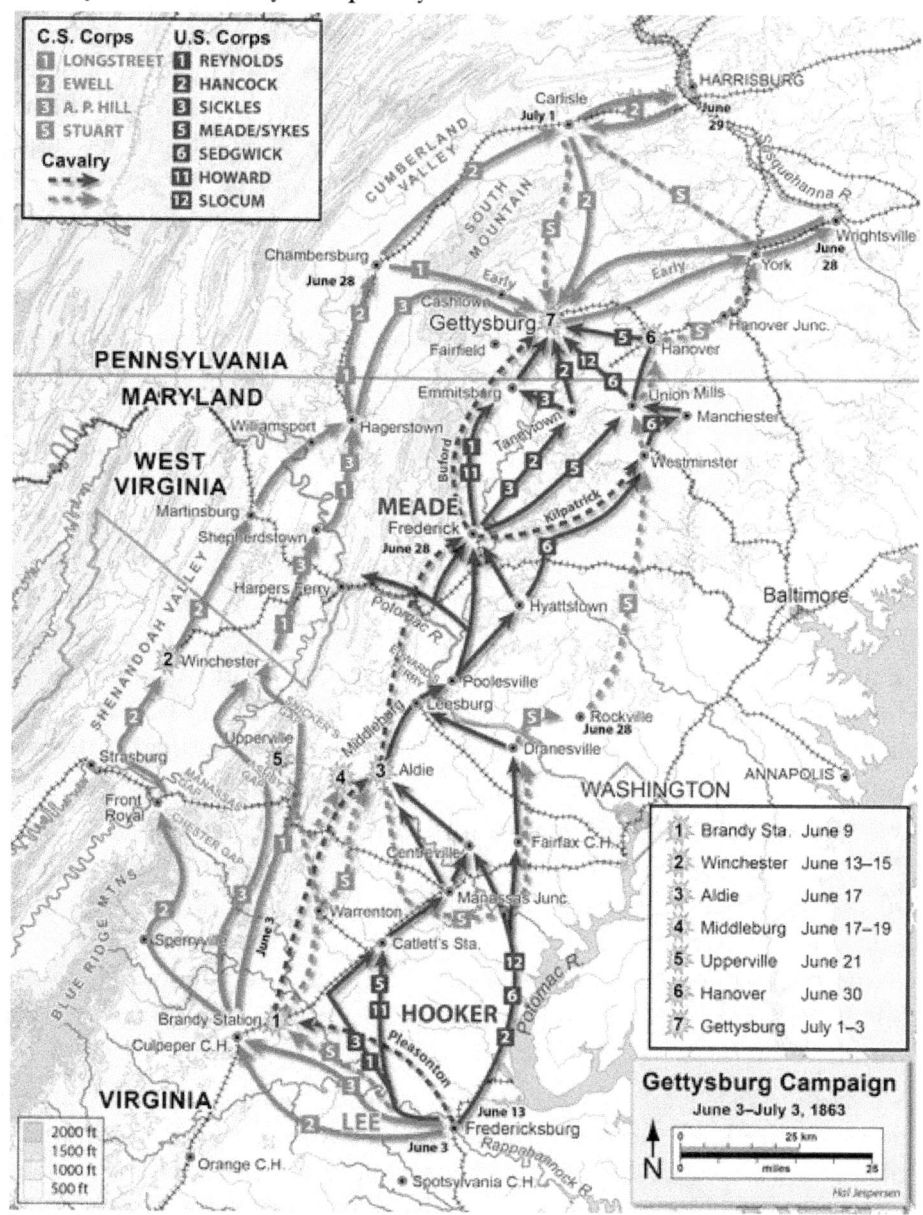

A map of the Gettysburg campaign through July 3, 1863. Cavalry movements are shown with dashed lines.[106]

The attack that would become known as Pickett's Charge began with the largest artillery bombardment in the history of the Western Hemisphere. Lee massed 150 cannons for a massive barrage that was supposed to weaken the Union center and demoralize Union troops. The bombardment began at 1:00 p.m. and continued for two hours. The noise was so loud that it could be heard in Pittsburgh, 150 miles away.

Confederate artillery chief General E. Porter Alexander supervised the bombardment from a position where he could observe its effects. Alexander was one of the most competent artillery officers in either army, and he understood that everything depended on his guns. If the artillery bombardment failed to break up the Union defenses, the infantry assault would be suicide.

But the Confederate bombardment was less effective than it appeared. Most of the shells passed over the Union line and landed in the rear areas, doing little damage to the troops who would have to repel the infantry attack. Union artillery chief General Henry Hunt had ordered his guns to stop firing after a while, creating the impression that they had been silenced when they were actually being saved for the infantry assault.

When the artillery barrage ended, about 12,500 Confederate soldiers began their advance across nearly a mile of open ground toward the Union center. It was a magnificent sight—long lines of Confederate infantry advancing in perfect order with flags flying and bands playing. The attack was led by General George Pickett's division of Virginians, which gave the assault its name, though Pickett's men made up only about a third of the attacking force.

It was a tactical disaster waiting to happen. The Confederate infantry had to cross nearly a mile of open ground under fire from Union artillery and infantry. The Union position on Cemetery Ridge was protected by stone walls that provided perfect cover for defending troops. Worst of all, the Confederate attack was being made in broad daylight, giving Union defenders plenty of time to see it coming and prepare their response.

Union artillery and rifle fire cut down the advancing Confederates by the hundreds. The Union guns had been loaded with canister shot, metal cans filled with iron balls that turned cannons into giant shotguns. When these rounds exploded among the advancing Confederate ranks, they created gaps that could be seen from miles away.

Despite the devastating fire, some Confederate troops managed to reach the Union line. About 150 men under General Lewis Armistead actually broke through the Union defenses and engaged in hand-to-hand combat around Union artillery positions. Armistead himself was mortally wounded while trying to turn a captured Union cannon against its former owners.

The men who reached the Union line fought with desperate courage, but they were too few to exploit their breakthrough. Within an hour, the attack had failed completely. More than half the attacking force had become casualties, with about 6,500 men killed, wounded, or missing. Lee's great gamble had failed catastrophically.

The failure of Pickett's Charge marked the end of Lee's invasion of Pennsylvania. His army was too badly damaged to continue fighting, and he had no choice but to retreat to Virginia. The three-day Battle of Gettysburg had cost Lee about twenty-eight thousand casualties out of seventy-five thousand men engaged. The Union army had suffered about twenty-three thousand casualties out of eighty-five thousand engaged.

An illustration of Pickett's Charge.[109]

Lee's retreat was agonizing. A wagon train of wounded soldiers, seventeen miles long, struggled through the rain back toward Virginia. Lee rode among his broken units, telling his men that the failure was his fault, not theirs.

The Battle of Gettysburg was the largest battle ever fought in North America and probably the most important battle of the Civil War. Lee's defeat ended the last serious Confederate threat to Northern territory. The Army of Northern Virginia would never again have the strength to launch a major invasion. From Gettysburg onward, the Confederacy would be fighting a defensive war for survival.

The Gettysburg Address: Four Score and Seven Years Ago

Four months after the Battle of Gettysburg, Abraham Lincoln traveled to the battlefield to help dedicate a national cemetery for the soldiers who had died there. The ceremony was organized by the states whose troops had fought at Gettysburg, and Lincoln was invited almost as an afterthought. The main speaker was Edward Everett, a famous orator and former Harvard president, who was expected to give a two-hour speech about the battle's significance.

Lincoln was asked to make "a few appropriate remarks" after Everett finished his oration. Nobody expected the president's brief comments to be particularly memorable. He worked on his speech during the train ride to Gettysburg. He faced a difficult challenge. How could he honor the dead without seeming to exploit their sacrifice for political purposes? How could he explain why the war had to continue when so many people were already exhausted by the carnage?

The ceremony took place on November 19, 1863, before a crowd of about fifteen thousand people. Everett spoke for two hours, giving a detailed account of the battle and comparing it to ancient Greek and Roman conflicts. It was exactly the kind of flowery, erudite oration that Americans expected at important public events.

Then Lincoln stood up. He spoke for less than three minutes, delivering only 272 words. Many people in the crowd weren't even sure he had finished when he sat down. However, Lincoln's brief address would become one of the most famous speeches in American history, redefining the war's purpose in just ten sentences.

Lincoln began with the famous phrase "Four score and seven years ago," placing the current conflict in the context of American founding principles. He was dating the nation's birth not to the Constitution of 1787 but to the Declaration of Independence of 1776, with its promise that "all men are created equal."

He then acknowledged that he and the other speakers couldn't truly consecrate the battlefield where they stood. "But, in a larger sense, we can not dedicate—we can not consecrate—we can not hallow—this ground," he said. "The brave men, living and dead, who struggled here, have consecrated it, far above our poor power to add or detract."

The speech's most important passage came at the end, where Lincoln called for "a new birth of freedom" and defined American government as "government of the people, by the people, for the people." This wasn't just a war to preserve the Union as it had been—it was a war to create a better Union based on the principle of human equality, with the abolition of slavery and liberty extended to all Americans.

Edward Everett immediately recognized the power of Lincoln's remarks. In a letter to the president the next day, Everett wrote, "I should be glad if I could flatter myself that I came as near to the central idea of the occasion in two hours as you did in two minutes."[i]

The Gettysburg Address transformed how Americans thought about their nation and their war. Lincoln had taken a battlefield dedication and turned it into a redefinition of American democracy. The soldiers who died at Gettysburg hadn't just died to preserve the Union; they had died to ensure that "government of the people, by the people, for the people, shall not perish from the earth."

The speech also marked Lincoln's growth as a leader and communicator. The prairie lawyer who had once seemed out of place in sophisticated Washington now spoke with the voice of a prophet. He had found the words to explain why the war's enormous sacrifices were necessary and what kind of nation might emerge from the conflict.

The summer of 1863 marked a turning point in the Civil War. Grant's victory at Vicksburg and Lee's defeat at Gettysburg had shifted the military balance decisively in favor of the Union. But Lincoln's address had done something equally important. It had given the war a moral purpose that would sustain the North through the long, bloody campaigns still to come.

The Confederacy was still fighting, but it was no longer fighting to win. It was fighting to survive. And as Lincoln made clear at Gettysburg, the Union was now fighting for something larger than mere survival. It was fighting for a new birth of freedom that would make America worthy of the sacrifices made on its behalf.

---

[i] https://www.abrahamlincolnonline.org/lincoln/speeches/gettysburg.htm

Chapter 9: Grant Takes Command

By early 1864, Lincoln had a problem that was keeping him awake at night. The war was entering its fourth year, and Northern patience was wearing dangerously thin. Despite spectacular victories at Gettysburg and Vicksburg, the Confederacy was still fighting with stubborn determination. Robert E. Lee's Army of Northern Virginia remained dangerous and defiant on the battlefield, seemingly as strong as ever. The 1864 presidential election was approaching like a storm cloud, and Lincoln needed decisive military progress to convince war-weary voters that the Union could actually win this thing.

The political situation was becoming desperate. Democrats were calling for peace negotiations, and even some Republicans were losing faith in the war effort. Newspapers that had once supported the war were now questioning whether the enormous cost was worth it. Mothers were hiding their sons to keep them from being drafted. Draft riots had torn apart New York City the previous summer.

Lincoln had tried general after general in the East, but none had been able to finish off Lee. McClellan was too cautious, always needing more men and more time. Burnside had been a disaster at Fredericksburg. Hooker had been outmaneuvered at Chancellorsville despite having twice as many men as Lee. Meade was competent but unimaginative, content to avoid defeat rather than seek decisive victory.

What Lincoln needed was someone who understood that this war wouldn't end with clever maneuvers or single decisive battles. It would end only when the Confederate forces were destroyed and the South's will to fight was completely broken. The Union needed a general who was willing to accept enormous casualties to achieve final victory.

The president had been watching Ulysses S. Grant's performance in the West with growing interest. Grant had captured Forts Henry and Donelson when everyone else was failing. He had held his ground at Shiloh when lesser generals might have retreated. Most importantly, he had captured Vicksburg through sheer determination and brilliant strategy. Grant seemed to understand something that Eastern generals missed: wars were won by destroying enemy armies, not by occupying territory.

In March 1864, Lincoln decided he had finally found his man. He promoted Ulysses S. Grant to general-in-chief of all Union forces and gave him a simple mission: end this war. Grant would bring to the Eastern theater the same relentless, aggressive approach that had won victories in the West. However, he also discovered that fighting Robert E. Lee was very different from fighting anyone else.

"The Butcher": Grant's Overland Campaign

Grant's plan for 1864 was elegantly simple in concept but revolutionary in execution. Instead of trying to capture Richmond or maneuver Lee into unfavorable positions, Grant would attack Lee's army directly and keep attacking until it was destroyed.

This was a fundamental shift in Union strategy. Previous commanders had focused on geographic objectives, such as capturing Richmond or seizing railroad junctions. Grant understood that the Confederacy's strength lay in its armies, not its cities. As long as Lee's army remained intact, the war would continue. But if that army could be destroyed, the Confederacy would collapse regardless of what territory it still controlled.

Grant understood something that previous Eastern commanders had missed: the Union could afford heavy casualties in a way that the Confederacy could not. The North had a much larger population and could replace its losses through immigration, conscription, and voluntary enlistment. The South could not. Its manpower was finite and shrinking. If Grant could force Lee into a series of bloody battles, the Confederate army would eventually be worn down to nothing.

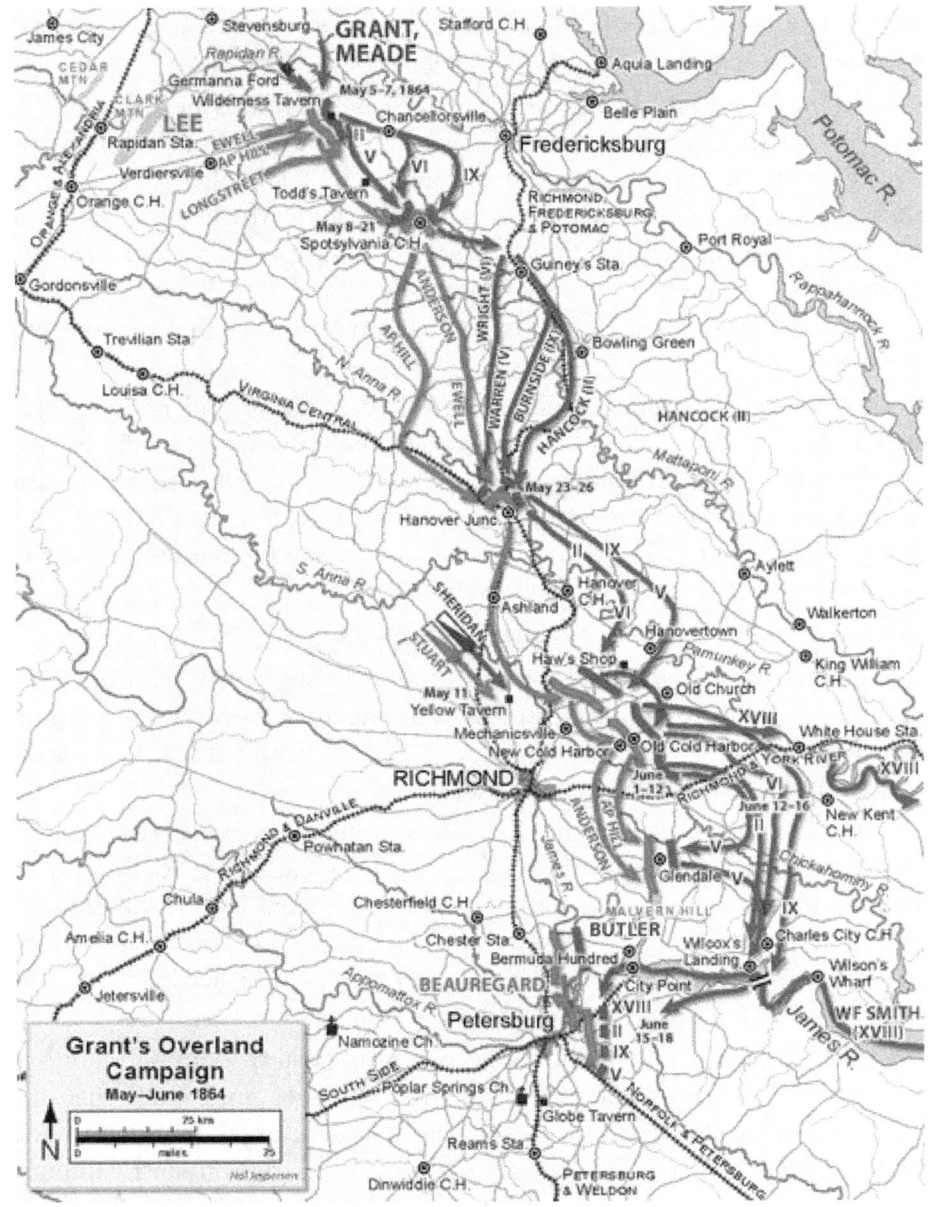

A map of the Overland Campaign.[110]

This strategy would earn Grant the nickname "the Butcher" from critics who were horrified by the casualties his campaigns produced. Northern newspapers accused him of treating soldiers like disposable pawns. Families who lost sons in Grant's campaigns called him a heartless killer. But Grant saw it as the only way to end the war quickly and permanently.

Grant also planned to coordinate Union forces across multiple theaters for the first time in the war. While he focused on destroying Lee's army in Virginia, General William T. Sherman would advance through Georgia toward Atlanta. General Benjamin Butler would threaten Richmond from the south. General Franz Sigel would advance up the Shenandoah Valley. The idea was to stretch Confederate resources so thin that they couldn't concentrate enough force to stop any single Union advance.

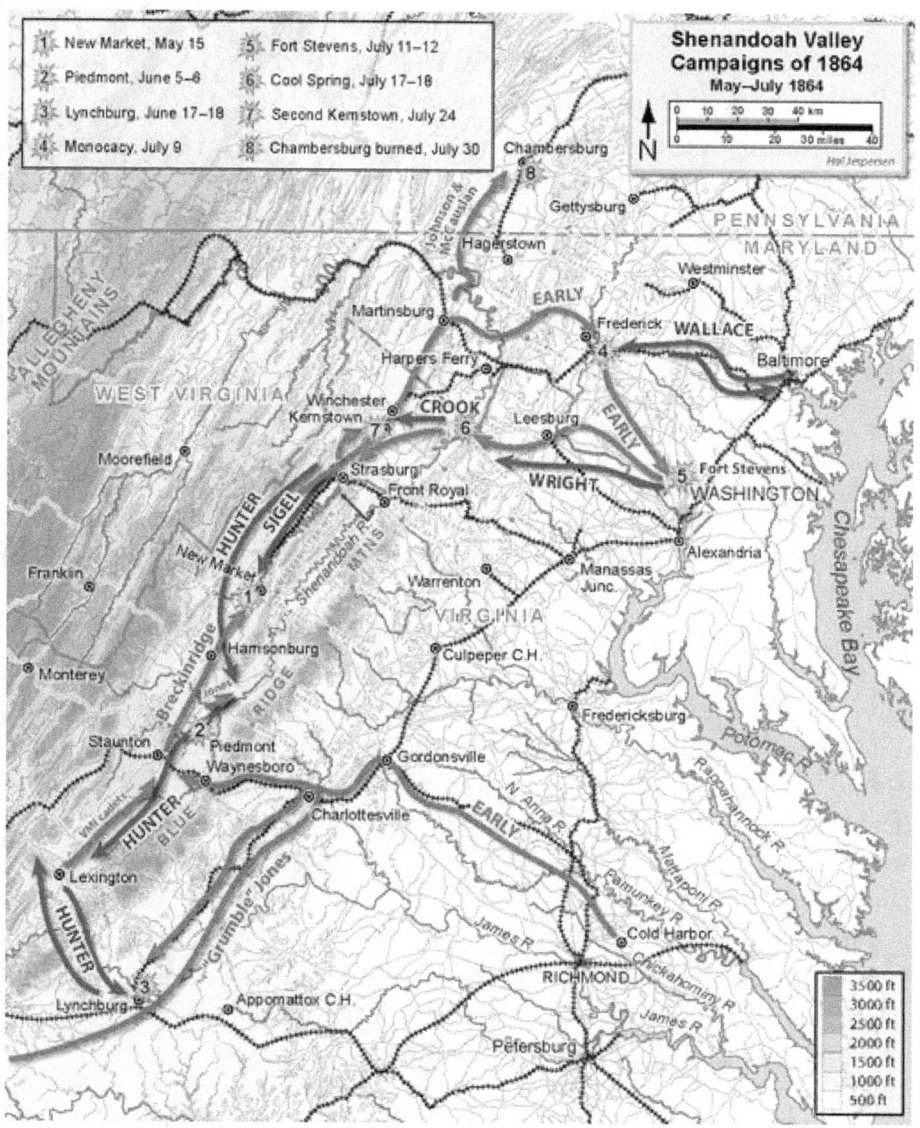

Shenandoah Valley operations from May to June 1864.[111]

The coordinated strategy had mixed results. Sherman's advance in Georgia proceeded successfully, but the other supporting campaigns faced setbacks. Butler's army became bottled up at Bermuda Hundred, a peninsula south of Richmond, and failed to threaten Richmond effectively. Sigel's advance up the Shenandoah Valley ended in an embarrassing defeat at the Battle of New Market on May 15, where his 6,500 Union troops were routed by a smaller Confederate force that included cadets from Virginia Military Institute. The sight of teenage boys charging Union lines became one of the war's most famous episodes, but it also meant that Confederate forces in the Shenandoah Valley remained free to potentially reinforce Lee.

The Overland Campaign began on May 4, 1864, when Grant crossed the Rapidan River with about 120,000 men—the largest army ever assembled on the North American continent. His plan was to move quickly through an area called the Wilderness, a tangled mass of woods and undergrowth where Lee had defeated Hooker the previous year. Grant hoped to get through the Wilderness before Lee could attack and then fight on open ground where Union advantages in numbers and artillery would be decisive.

The Army of the Potomac that crossed the Rapidan was different from previous Union armies in the East. Grant brought experienced Western officers with him, men who understood his aggressive style of warfare. The army was also better supplied and equipped than any previous Union force. Wagon trains stretched for miles, carrying everything from ammunition to medical supplies to pontoon bridges.

But Lee had other ideas. As soon as he learned that Grant was crossing the river, Lee moved his sixty-five thousand men into the Wilderness to attack. If he had to fight Grant, Lee wanted to do it on ground that would neutralize Union advantages. In the thick woods of the Wilderness, Union artillery would be useless, and superior numbers would mean less. Lee had used this same strategy to defeat Hooker at Chancellorsville.

The Battle of the Wilderness began on May 5 and lasted two days. The fighting took place in dense woods where soldiers often couldn't see more than a few yards in any direction. Units got lost in the undergrowth and sometimes fired on their own men. The sound of rifle fire was constant. The dry undergrowth caught fire from muzzle flashes, and wounded soldiers were burned alive in the spreading flames. The smell of smoke mixed with the stench of gunpowder and blood. Soldiers reported hearing wounded men screaming as the fires approached, but they couldn't reach them through the enemy fire. It was warfare at its most nightmarish.

General James Longstreet, Lee's most trusted corps commander, was wounded by friendly fire during the battle; he was shot by his own men in the confusion of fighting in thick woods. Though Longstreet survived his wounds, his temporary absence from the battlefield was a severe blow to Confederate morale and effectiveness. Lee was forced to take personal command of Longstreet's corps during the crisis, exposing himself to enemy fire until his soldiers begged him to get back to safety.

The battle was a tactical draw, with both armies suffering heavy casualties but neither gaining a decisive advantage. Union losses were about eighteen thousand killed, wounded, and missing. Confederate losses were smaller—about eleven thousand—but Lee could afford them less. For the Confederacy, every casualty was irreplaceable.

The Battle of the Wilderness marked the beginning of a new kind of war. Previous Union commanders would have retreated after such a bloody fight, declaring the battle too costly to continue. Grant pushed forward. When his staff officers suggested falling back to regroup, Grant reportedly exploded in anger. "I am heartily tired of hearing about what Lee is going to do," he said. "Some of you always seem to think he is suddenly going to turn a double somersault, and land in our rear and on both of our flanks at the same time. Go back to your command, and try to think what we are going to do ourselves, instead of what Lee is going to do."[i]

After the Battle of the Wilderness, Grant continued south, trying to get between Lee's army and Richmond. Lee matched him move for move, and the two armies clashed again at Spotsylvania Court House. The fighting at Spotsylvania was even bloodier than the Wilderness, with Union forces launching repeated attacks against Confederate entrenchments that grew stronger every day. Lee's engineers had learned from previous battles and constructed elaborate defensive works almost overnight. The Confederate lines featured multiple rows of trenches, earthworks reinforced with logs, and carefully positioned artillery that could sweep approaching attackers with devastating fire.

---

[i] https://npshistory.com/publications/civil_war_series/25/sec6.htm

Grant's attacks at Spotsylvania showed both his determination and his learning curve. On May 10, he ordered a frontal assault against the Confederate center, which failed. Instead of giving up, Grant studied the results and planned a more sophisticated attack. He noticed that the Confederate line bulged outward in one area, creating a salient, a position that jutted out and could be attacked from multiple directions.

At dawn on May 12, Grant launched a massive surprise attack against this salient with twenty thousand men. The assault initially succeeded, breaking through Confederate lines and capturing thousands of prisoners, including an entire division. However, Lee quickly counterattacked. The battle's climax came at a place soldiers called the "Bloody Angle," where Union troops had broken through Confederate lines and engaged in twenty hours of continuous hand-to-hand combat. Men fought with rifles until their ammunition ran out. Then they continued with bayonets, swords, rocks, and fists. Soldiers stood on piles of dead bodies to get high enough to fire over the earthworks. The carnage was so intense that an oak tree twenty-two inches in diameter was cut down by rifle fire from the thousands of bullets hitting the same spot hour after hour.

Rain turned the battlefield into a quagmire of mud and blood. Wounded men drowned in shell holes filled with rainwater. The constant firing created so much smoke that soldiers fought by muzzle flashes, often shooting at targets they couldn't see.

At one point during the fighting, Confederate General John B. Gordon tried to lead a counterattack personally, but his men refused to let him. "General, you must not go!" they shouted, grabbing his horse's bridle and forcing him back. They had already lost too many officers and couldn't afford to lose Gordon too.

The fighting at the Bloody Angle finally ended when Confederate engineers built a new line of trenches behind the salient during the night. Lee's army withdrew to these new positions, abandoning the bloody ground they had fought so hard to hold. Both sides were exhausted, but Grant had proven he could break Confederate lines when he concentrated enough force at the right point.

Grant kept pushing south, but Lee kept blocking his path. They fought at the North Anna River, where Lee tried to trap part of Grant's army by positioning his forces in an inverted V that would allow him to defeat Grant's separated wings one at a time. The plan was brilliant, but

Lee became sick during the battle and couldn't coordinate the complex maneuvers needed to make it work.

They fought again at Cold Harbor, where Grant launched his most disastrous frontal assault of the entire campaign. On June 3, Grant ordered a direct attack against Confederate trenches that had been strengthened for days. The attack lasted less than an hour and cost seven thousand Union casualties, many of them killed in the first few minutes. Confederate losses were fewer than 1,500.

Grant had underestimated how strong Confederate defenses had become and overestimated his army's ability to break through prepared positions. After Cold Harbor, Grant wrote in his memoirs, "I have always regretted that the last assault at Cold Harbor was ever made."[i]

However, Cold Harbor served Grant's strategic purpose. Lee's army was still intact, but it was steadily weakening. Confederate casualties during the Overland Campaign were proportionally much higher than Union losses. Lee had started the campaign with about sixty-five thousand men. By early June, he had fewer than fifty thousand effectives left. The Overland Campaign, which lasted six weeks, cost the Union army about sixty-five thousand casualties—about the size of the entire Confederate Army at the start of the campaign.

The psychological impact on Confederate soldiers was devastating. They had grown accustomed to Union forces retreating after major battles. Now they faced an enemy that kept coming no matter how many casualties it suffered. Confederate morale began to crack under the relentless pressure.

By mid-June, Grant had pushed Lee back to the outskirts of Richmond and Petersburg. Lee's army was still dangerous, but it was trapped in defensive positions, and its numbers were fewer. The war had become a siege, and sieges favored the side with more men and supplies. Grant had accomplished his strategic objective: Lee's army was pinned down and slowly being destroyed.

Stalemate at Petersburg: The Misery of Trench Warfare

When Grant realized he couldn't break Lee's defenses around Richmond through direct assault, he changed tactics with characteristic flexibility. In mid-June 1864, he executed one of the war's most

---

[i] https://emergingcivilwar.com/2025/05/09/a-thousand-words-a-battle-cold-harbor/

successful strategic movements, secretly moving his army south of the James River to attack Petersburg, a crucial railroad junction that supplied Richmond. If Grant could capture Petersburg, he could cut off supplies to both Lee's army and the Confederate capital, forcing them to surrender or starve.

The move to Petersburg was a masterpiece of military logistics. Grant had to transport 115,000 men, as well as their equipment, artillery, and supply trains, across the James River without Lee detecting their movement. Union engineers built a pontoon bridge more than 2,100 feet long—one of the longest military bridges ever constructed. The entire operation took place under the cover of darkness, and elaborate deception measures were designed to convince Lee that Grant was still threatening Richmond directly.

The city was defended by General P. G. T. Beauregard with only about 2,500 Confederate troops. It was a pitifully small force to hold such an important position. For three crucial days (June 15-18), Beauregard's men held off Union attacks that should have overwhelmed them easily. The Confederate defense was heroic, but it succeeded mainly because Union commanders were cautious, remembering the bloody repulses they had suffered during the Overland Campaign.

General William F. "Baldy" Smith commanded the first Union assault on Petersburg. He had a clear opportunity to capture the city on June 15. His eighteen thousand men faced fewer than three thousand Confederate defenders behind hastily built earthworks. But Smith hesitated, convinced that the light resistance was a trap. He spent hours reconnoitering and planning instead of attacking immediately.

The delay was fatal to Union hopes for a quick victory. By the time Smith finally attacked on the evening of June 15, he had wasted precious daylight hours. His men did capture some Confederate positions, but darkness ended the assault before they could exploit their success. Beauregard used the night to strengthen his defenses and call for reinforcements.

This pattern repeated over the next two days. Union forces would attack, make some progress, and then halt to reorganize. Each delay gave Beauregard more time to prepare. Confederate reinforcements began arriving from Richmond as Lee realized the threat to Petersburg. By June 18, when Grant was ready to launch a coordinated assault with his entire army, Lee had rushed enough troops to Petersburg to make the defenses impregnable.

The failed assault on June 18 cost Grant about ten thousand casualties and ended his hopes of taking Petersburg by storm. Union soldiers, exhausted from weeks of continuous fighting during the Overland Campaign, attacked halfheartedly against positions they could see were too strong to carry. Many regiments refused to advance when ordered, and officers reported widespread demoralization in the ranks.

What followed was a nine-month siege that became a preview of World War I. Both armies dug elaborate networks of trenches, underground shelters, and communication tunnels that stretched for miles around Petersburg. The opposing lines were sometimes less than one hundred yards apart, close enough for soldiers to talk to each other across no man's land. Snipers made it deadly to show one's head above the trenches during daylight.

The trench systems that developed around Petersburg were far more sophisticated than anything seen in previous American wars. Confederate engineers, led by Captain Hugh Douglas, created multiple defensive lines with bombproofs (fortified shelters designed to protect soldiers or supplies from artillery fire), traverses, and carefully planned fields of fire. Union engineers responded by digging approach trenches, saps, and covered ways that allowed them to move closer to Confederate positions.

Life in the trenches was miserable for both sides, but the experience was different for each army. Union soldiers were generally better supplied, with regular deliveries of food, ammunition, and mail from the North. They had access to newspapers, books, and even some luxuries like coffee and tobacco. However, they also faced the psychological burden of being the attackers, knowing they would eventually have to leave their trenches and assault Confederate positions.

Confederate soldiers in the Petersburg trenches faced constant hunger and hardship. Supply trains from the South became less frequent and less reliable as Union cavalry and guerrilla warfare disrupted the railroads. Rations were reduced again and again until soldiers were receiving less than half the food they needed to maintain their strength.

Soldiers on both sides lived like moles, spending most of their time underground. Rain turned the trenches into muddy rivers that bred disease and made movement almost impossible. Summer heat made the confined spaces unbearable. Disease spread rapidly in the unsanitary conditions, with dysentery and typhoid claiming more victims than enemy bullets.

Soldiers never knew when an enemy sniper might pick them off or when artillery shells might explode in their positions. The constant threat of sudden death created a level of stress that many men couldn't handle. Many developed what we would now recognize as post-traumatic stress disorder, though Civil War doctors called it "nostalgia" or "soldier's heart."

Soldiers developed various ways of coping with trench warfare. They wrote letters home, played cards, read whatever books they could find, and told stories to pass the time. Some carved elaborate decorations in the walls of their dugouts. Others kept pets—dogs, cats, and even raccoons—to provide companionship and distraction from the war.

Informal truces sometimes developed between the opposing lines. Soldiers would agree not to shoot during certain hours so that both sides could perform necessary tasks like gathering wood or burying the dead. Some areas became neutral zones where soldiers from both armies would meet to trade tobacco for coffee or newspapers for food.

But the siege was also marked by increasing savagery as the war dragged on. Both sides used sharpshooters to target officers and artillery crews. Explosive devices called "torpedoes" (primitive land mines) were buried in no man's land to kill unwary soldiers. Psychological warfare became common, with each side trying to demoralize the other through taunts, false rumors, and propaganda.

Union forces gradually extended their lines westward, trying to cut the railroads that supplied Petersburg. Each extension forced Lee to stretch his own lines thinner. Lee's army was slowly being strangled, but the process was taking much longer than Grant had hoped.

The siege featured several dramatic incidents that broke the monotony of trench warfare. In July 1864, Union engineers dug a tunnel under Confederate lines and packed it with eight thousand pounds of gunpowder. The explosion created a crater 170 feet long and 30 feet deep, but the follow-up attack was botched and turned into a massacre of Union troops trapped in the crater.

As winter approached, conditions in both armies deteriorated. Confederate soldiers were on half-rations, and many lacked adequate clothing and blankets. Desertion rates soared as soldiers left to check on their families or simply gave up hope. Lee's army was melting away through casualties, disease, and desertion.

Grant, meanwhile, was under enormous political pressure. The 1864 presidential election was approaching, and many Northerners were tired of the endless casualties with no apparent progress. Democratic candidate George McClellan was running on a platform that called for negotiations with the Confederacy. If Lincoln lost the election, the war might end in a compromise that left slavery intact.

However, Grant understood that time was on his side. Every day the siege continued, Lee's army got weaker while Grant's got stronger. Fresh troops and supplies flowed to the Union Army while the Confederates gradually starved. It was only a matter of time before Lee's lines collapsed.

The siege of Petersburg lasted 292 days and cost both armies enormous casualties, but it accomplished Grant's strategic objective. Lee's army was pinned in place and slowly being destroyed. When the end came in April 1865, it would come quickly because Grant had spent nine months systematically wearing down Confederate resistance.

The Army of Northern Virginia, which had seemed invincible for three years, was finally beaten, not in a single dramatic battle but through the slow, grinding process of attrition that Grant had imposed. Critics called Grant a butcher, and the casualties his campaigns produced were indeed horrific. However, Grant's relentless pressure on Confederate forces shortened the war and probably saved lives in the long run. A war of maneuver might have lasted years longer and cost even more in human suffering.

Lee's men were still brave and still dangerous, but they no longer had the strength to win the war. Grant had turned the conflict into a mathematical equation: more Union soldiers plus more Union supplies plus time equals Confederate defeat.

All that remained was for the equation to reach its inevitable conclusion.

Chapter 10: Total War

By late 1864, the Civil War had evolved into something that would have been unrecognizable to the soldiers who fought at Bull Run three years earlier. What had started as a conflict between armies had become a war against entire societies. The Union was no longer content to simply defeat Confederate forces in battle; it was determined to destroy the South's ability and will to continue fighting.

This transformation was most clearly embodied in General William Tecumseh Sherman, Grant's most trusted lieutenant and closest friend. While Grant pinned down Lee's army in the trenches around Petersburg, Sherman was preparing to march through the heart of the Confederacy, bringing the war directly to Southern civilians who had supported the rebellion. His campaign would redefine the very nature of warfare and hasten the Confederacy's collapse.

Sherman understood something that many of his contemporaries missed: in a democracy, wars were won as much by destroying the enemy's morale as by defeating their armies. If you could convince Southern civilians that continued resistance was hopeless, they would pressure their government to make peace. This insight would make Sherman one of the war's most effective and most controversial generals.

Sherman's March to the Sea: "War is Hell"

After capturing Atlanta in September 1864, Sherman faced a strategic dilemma. Confederate General John Bell Hood had retreated with his army intact and was threatening Sherman's long supply line back to Tennessee. Sherman could spend months chasing Hood around the

Southern countryside, or he could try something completely different.

Sherman's solution was audacious and unprecedented. He would abandon his supply lines entirely, cut loose from his base, and march his army three hundred miles across Georgia to the sea. Along the way, his soldiers would live off the land and systematically destroy everything that could support the Confederate war effort.

The plan violated every conventional rule of military strategy. Armies were supposed to protect their supply lines, not abandon them. They were supposed to concentrate their forces, not spread them across hundreds of miles of enemy territory. But Sherman understood that conventional rules didn't apply to this situation. His army was composed of veteran soldiers who had proven themselves in dozens of battles. Georgia's defensive forces were weak and scattered. Most importantly, the psychological impact of such a march would be devastating to Confederate morale.

"I can make the march, and make Georgia howl," Sherman telegraphed to Grant. The phrase captured Sherman's understanding that this would be psychological warfare as much as military strategy. The goal wasn't just to destroy Confederate resources—it was to break the South's will to fight by demonstrating that the Confederate government couldn't protect its own people.

Sherman's March to the Sea.[119]

Sherman had been thinking about this kind of warfare for years. He believed that the Southern people had to be made to feel the full weight of war before they would give up their rebellion. "We are not only fighting hostile armies," he wrote, "but a hostile people, and must make old and young, rich and poor, feel the hard hand of war."[i]

Lincoln and Grant approved Sherman's plan, though both understood its risks. If Sherman's army was destroyed or trapped deep in Confederate territory, the political consequences could be devastating. The 1864 presidential election was just weeks away, and a military disaster could hand the presidency to Democrat George McClellan, who was running on a platform of peace.

On November 16, 1864, Sherman began his march with sixty-two thousand veteran soldiers organized into two wings. Before leaving Atlanta, he ordered the destruction of the city's military facilities—depots, arsenals, factories, and railroad infrastructure that could support the Confederate war effort. The destruction was extensive but not indiscriminate. Sherman's official orders targeted military and industrial facilities, not civilian homes. However, fires set to destroy military targets spread beyond their intended bounds. Confederate General John Bell Hood's own destruction of ammunition trains before evacuating added to the devastation.

Sherman's army moved across Georgia in a broad front, spreading destruction across a wide swath of the state. The soldiers had been given explicit orders about what they could and couldn't destroy, but the line between legitimate military targets and civilian property quickly blurred. Official policy allowed foraging for food and the destruction of infrastructure, but many soldiers interpreted these orders broadly.

The destruction was systematic and thorough. Sherman's engineers tore up railroad tracks using specialized tools called "Sherman's neckties"—heated rails that were twisted around trees to make them unusable. They burned bridges, destroyed telegraph lines, and demolished anything that could move supplies or information. Cotton gins, gristmills, and warehouses went up in smoke. Livestock was either consumed by the army or driven off to prevent Confederate use.

But the march also revealed the war's impact on individual families. Soldiers found abandoned plantations where owners had fled, leaving

---

[i] https://cwnc.omeka.chass.ncsu.edu/items/show/144

behind enslaved people who didn't know whether to stay or go. They encountered wealthy families reduced to hiding their valuables and begging for food. They saw poor White farmers who had lost sons in the war and now watched their remaining livestock and grain disappear into Union supply wagons.

The march revealed both the best and worst of Sherman's army. Many soldiers stuck to the rules, taking only what they needed to survive and treating civilians with respect. However, others used the march as an excuse for looting, vandalism, and worse. Sherman later admitted as much, though he argued that such excesses were inevitable in war.

Sherman's "bummers," as the foraging parties were called, became legendary figures who inspired both fear and folklore. These soldiers ranged far from the main columns, sometimes traveling twenty or thirty miles from the army to find supplies. Some bummers were disciplined soldiers following orders; others were little better than armed bandits who took whatever they wanted.

The bummers learned to read the landscape like a book. They knew that freshly turned earth meant buried valuables, that nervous livestock indicated nearby grain supplies, and that well-maintained outbuildings suggested prosperous farms worth searching. They became experts at interrogating slaves and poor Whites, who often revealed information about hidden Confederate supplies or the movements of enemy troops.

Georgia civilians experienced the march differently depending on their social class and location. Wealthy plantation owners, who had been the most enthusiastic supporters of secession, suffered the heaviest losses. Their grand houses were often burned, their livestock confiscated, and their enslaved laborers liberated. Poor White farmers, who had been reluctant participants in the Confederate cause, sometimes received better treatment from Union soldiers who saw them as fellow common people.

Women bore much of the burden of dealing with Sherman's army. With most men away fighting, women had to face the foragers alone, trying to protect their families and property as best they could. Some hid food and valuables in wells, slave cabins, or remote locations. Others tried to appeal to the soldiers' sympathy by emphasizing their poverty or their opposition to the war.

The psychological impact of Sherman's march was enormous. For three years, most Georgians had been largely untouched by the war.

They had sent their sons to fight in Virginia and Tennessee, but their own homes and farms had remained safe. Now the war had come to them with a vengeance, and there was nothing the Confederate government could do to stop it.

The march shattered the myth of Confederate invincibility that had sustained Southern morale for years. If Union armies could march unopposed through the heart of Georgia, what did that say about the Confederacy's ability to defend itself? If Jefferson Davis's government couldn't protect Georgia, how could it protect any Confederate state?

Confederate General Joseph Wheeler's cavalry tried desperately to slow Sherman's advance, but they were hopelessly outnumbered and outmaneuvered. Wheeler's cavalry corps was spread thin trying to monitor Sherman's movements across the state. His troopers could harass Sherman's foragers and occasionally attack isolated units, but they couldn't seriously threaten an army of sixty-two thousand veterans.

And as Sherman's army moved deeper into Georgia, it was joined by thousands of enslaved people who saw the Union soldiers as liberators. These refugees, known as "contrabands," created both opportunities and problems for Sherman. They provided valuable intelligence about Confederate movements and local conditions, but they also slowed the army's movement and consumed supplies.

The contraband column that followed Sherman's army became a migration of biblical proportions. Families carried their possessions in wagons, carts, or on their backs. Children who had never been more than a few miles from their birthplace walked hundreds of miles toward an uncertain freedom. Old people who had spent their entire lives in bondage struggled to keep up with the army that represented their only hope of liberation.

Sherman's attitude toward the Black refugees was complex and often contradictory. He understood that their liberation was one of the war's key objectives, but he also worried that too many refugees would interfere with his military mission. He was not an abolitionist by conviction; he had supported slavery before the war and remained skeptical about Black equality. However, he understood that freeing slaves was essential to destroying the Confederate war effort.

The treatment of contraband refugees became one of the most controversial aspects of Sherman's march. At Ebenezer Creek in Georgia, Union General Jefferson C. Davis (not the Confederate president) ordered his engineers to remove pontoon bridges before all the refugees could cross, leaving hundreds stranded on the Confederate side of the swollen stream. Many drowned trying to swim across or were recaptured by Confederate cavalry. The incident became a symbol of the Union Army's ambivalent attitude toward the people it was supposed to be liberating.

The March to the Sea took 32 days and covered 285 miles. Sherman's army reached Savannah on December 21, 1864, having encountered almost no serious resistance along the way. The city surrendered without a fight, giving Sherman control of Georgia's most important port and completing one of the most successful campaigns in American military history.

Sherman sent a telegram to Lincoln offering Savannah as a Christmas present to the nation. Lincoln was delighted, both with the military success and its timing just after his reelection.

The March to the Sea had accomplished everything Sherman hoped. It had destroyed vast amounts of Confederate property, disrupted the Southern economy, and demonstrated that the Confederate government couldn't protect its own territory. Most importantly, it had convinced many Southerners that continued resistance was hopeless.

But Sherman wasn't finished. From Savannah, he planned to march north through South Carolina, the state that had started the war. If Georgia had been made to "howl," South Carolina would be made to pay an even heavier price for its role in the rebellion.

The 1864 Election: Lincoln's Last Battle

While Sherman was marching through Georgia, Abraham Lincoln was fighting for his political life in the most important election in American history. The 1864 presidential race would determine not just who led the country but also whether the United States would continue fighting to preserve the Union or seek a negotiated peace that might leave the Confederacy independent.

By the summer of 1864, Lincoln's political situation looked desperate. The war was in its fourth year, casualties were mounting, and many Northerners were exhausted by the conflict. Grant's Overland Campaign had cost sixty-five thousand Union casualties with no apparent progress. Sherman was besieging Atlanta, but the city hadn't fallen. The economy was struggling under the burden of war debt and inflation that had driven prices up by more than 75 percent since 1861.

Public opinion polls, though primitive by modern standards, showed Lincoln trailing badly. Republican leaders in key states like Pennsylvania and Indiana warned that the party faced disaster in November. Even Lincoln's friends worried that he had become too associated with an unpopular war to win reelection.

The casualty lists published in newspapers every day told the story of the North's suffering. Families in small towns across the Midwest and Northeast had lost sons, fathers, and brothers. The 1863 draft riots in New York had shown how explosive opposition to the war could become. The New York City draft riots erupted in July 1863 and became one of the largest civil disturbances in American history. They revealed deep cracks in Northern support for the war.

The trouble began with the first federal draft lottery, which was implemented through the Enrollment Act of March 1863. Working-class immigrants, especially the Irish, were furious about a provision that allowed wealthy men to pay $300 to avoid service or hire a substitute. This meant the draft fell heavily on poor families who couldn't afford the exemption, leading to bitter complaints that this was "a rich man's war but a poor man's fight."

On July 13, angry crowds attacked draft offices and government buildings, but the violence quickly spiraled out of control and turned viciously racial. Many White working-class New Yorkers feared that freed slaves would migrate north and compete for their jobs, and they resented fighting in a war that might flood the labor market with Black workers willing to work for lower wages. Mobs burned the Colored Orphan Asylum, lynched Black men they found on the streets, and terrorized Black neighborhoods throughout the city.

An illustration of the draft riots.[118]

For four days, New York City was in chaos until federal troops—ironically, units returning from the victory at Gettysburg—restored order. At least 120 people died, though the actual toll might have been much higher, and property damage exceeded $1 million. The riots showed how the war's burdens fell unequally on different social classes and exposed the ugly racial tensions that complicated Northern support for emancipation, demonstrating that Lincoln's war was creating as much division in the North as unity. By 1864, draft resistance was widespread, with thousands of men fleeing to Canada or hiding in remote areas to avoid military service.

Lincoln faced opposition from multiple directions. Radical Republicans thought he was too soft on slavery and too willing to readmit Southern states without adequate guarantees of Black rights. Senator Benjamin Wade of Ohio and Representative Thaddeus Stevens of Pennsylvania led a faction that wanted to replace Lincoln with someone more committed to racial equality and harsher treatment of a defeated South.

Conservative Republicans worried that the Emancipation Proclamation had changed the war's purpose in ways that made victory impossible. They argued that the war had started as a fight to preserve the Union, not to free slaves, and that Lincoln had exceeded his authority by adding abolition to the war's objectives. Some conservative Republicans secretly hoped for a negotiated peace that would restore the Union without ending slavery.

Democrats denounced the war as an unconstitutional tyranny and called for immediate peace negotiations. The Democratic Party was divided between "War Democrats," who supported the Union cause, and "Peace Democrats" (called "Copperheads" by their enemies), who wanted to end the fighting immediately. The Peace Democrats were strongest in the Midwest, where many people had family and economic ties to the South.

The Democratic Party nominated George B. McClellan, Lincoln's former general, on a platform that called the war a "failure" and demanded "immediate efforts" for peace. McClellan himself didn't fully embrace the peace platform—he still believed the Union should be preserved—but his running mate, George Pendleton of Ohio, was a vocal opponent of the war. The Democratic campaign argued that Lincoln had transformed the war to preserve the Union into an abolition crusade that could never succeed.

Lincoln's own party was deeply divided. Some Republicans tried to dump Lincoln in favor of Treasury Secretary Salmon P. Chase, who had been maneuvering for the nomination for months. Others supported General John C. Frémont, who ran as the candidate of the Radical Democracy Party on a platform calling for more aggressive war and harsher treatment of the South.

The Republican Party convention in Baltimore was contentious, with delegates arguing bitterly about war policy and reconstruction plans. Lincoln won renomination on the first ballot but without enthusiasm from many party leaders. To balance the ticket and appeal to War Democrats, the Republicans nominated Andrew Johnson of Tennessee, a Democrat who had remained loyal to the Union, as Lincoln's running mate.

Through the summer of 1864, Lincoln's chances looked increasingly bleak. Horace Greeley, the influential editor of the *New-York Tribune*, wrote that Lincoln's reelection was "an impossibility." Even Lincoln himself was pessimistic. In August, he wrote a sealed memorandum predicting his own defeat: "This morning, as for some days past, it seems exceedingly probable that this Administration will not be re-elected."[i]

However, Lincoln refused to consider changing his war aims to improve his chances. When Democrats suggested that he could win easily by abandoning emancipation, Lincoln rejected the idea. He understood that backing down on slavery would betray the thousands of Black soldiers fighting for the Union and make a mockery of everything the war had accomplished.

The turning point came in early September when Sherman captured Atlanta. The news electrified the North and gave Lincoln's campaign new momentum. Here was proof that the Union could win decisive victories, that the sacrifices of four years of war were leading somewhere. Sherman's success was followed by Admiral David Farragut's capture of Mobile Bay, which closed a major Confederate port, and General Philip Sheridan's devastating campaign in the Shenandoah Valley, which destroyed the "breadbasket of the Confederacy" and eliminated a key invasion route.

These military successes transformed the political landscape. Voters who had been ready to give up on the war suddenly saw hope for Union victory. The Democratic argument that the war was a "failure" became much harder to sustain when the Union forces were clearly winning. McClellan found himself in the awkward position of criticizing a war effort that was finally succeeding.

Lincoln also benefited from the soldier vote. Most Union soldiers remained loyal to the president who had led them through four years of war. They understood better than civilians how close the Union was to victory and how disastrous it would be to quit now.

The election campaign revealed deep divisions in American society about the war's purpose and conduct. Republicans argued that only total victory could justify the enormous sacrifices already made. Democrats claimed that Lincoln had exceeded his constitutional authority and transformed a limited war into a revolutionary crusade. The debate

---

[i] https://www.battlefields.org/learn/primary-sources/lincolns-blind-memo

would continue long after the election ended.

Lincoln also had to manage the complex politics of emancipation. The president had issued the Emancipation Proclamation as a war measure, but its permanence depended on Union victory and a constitutional amendment. Lincoln made the passage of the Thirteenth Amendment, which would abolish slavery permanently, a key part of his campaign platform.

On election day, November 8, 1864, Lincoln won a decisive victory. He received 55 percent of the popular vote and 212 electoral votes to McClellan's 21. The soldier vote was even more lopsided—Lincoln received about 80 percent of the votes cast by Union troops.

The election results devastated Confederate morale. Many Southerners had convinced themselves that Northern war weariness would lead to Lincoln's defeat and a negotiated peace. When Lincoln won reelection decisively, it became clear that the North would fight until the Confederacy was completely defeated. Jefferson Davis and other Confederate leaders began preparing for the bitter end.

The End at Appomattox: "The War is Over. The Rebels Are Our Countrymen Again."

By the spring of 1865, the Confederacy was collapsing on all fronts. Sherman had marched through South Carolina with even greater destruction than he had inflicted on Georgia and then advanced into North Carolina, where he was approaching a junction with Union forces moving inland from the coast. Union forces controlled most of the Mississippi River and were pushing into Alabama and Mississippi. General Philip Sheridan had devastated the Shenandoah Valley so thoroughly that "a crow flying over it would have to carry its own provisions."

Most devastating of all, Lee's Army of Northern Virginia was trapped in the trenches around Petersburg, slowly starving and melting away through desertion. What had once been the South's finest army was now a shadow of its former self. Soldiers were receiving quarter-rations and many lacked shoes, blankets, and adequate weapons. Desertion rates had reached crisis levels as men left to check on their families or simply gave up hope of Confederate victory.

Confederate records show that by March 1865, Lee had fewer than fifty-five thousand effective troops. Every day brought new reports of soldiers slipping away in the night. Some left notes for their officers explaining that they could no longer fight while their families starved at home.

Lee knew his situation was hopeless, but he wasn't ready to give up. In late March 1865, he launched a desperate attack against Fort Stedman, trying to break through Union lines and force Grant to shorten his own lines. The plan was to create a gap in Union defenses that would allow Lee to escape or at least improve his negotiating position.

The attack on Fort Stedman began before dawn on March 25, with Confederate troops temporarily capturing the fort and adjacent trenches. For a few hours, it looked like Lee's gamble might succeed. However, Union reinforcements quickly sealed the breach, and Confederate troops found themselves trapped in the captured positions. The attack failed catastrophically, costing Lee five thousand casualties he couldn't afford to lose—it was nearly 10 percent of his remaining army. It was the last offensive operation the Army of Northern Virginia would ever attempt.

Grant responded to Lee's desperate attack by extending his lines even farther west, trying to cut the last railroads supplying Petersburg. The South Side Railroad and the Richmond and Danville Railroad were Lee's lifelines, bringing what little food and supplies still reached his army. If Grant could cut these railroads, Petersburg would become completely untenable.

On April 1, Union forces under General Philip Sheridan crushed Confederate troops at Five Forks, a crossroads about ten miles southwest of Petersburg. The battle was a complete Union victory, with Sheridan's cavalry and infantry capturing thousands of Confederate prisoners and cutting the South Side Railroad. Lee's last major supply line was severed.

The disaster at Five Forks made Petersburg's position impossible to maintain. Lee sent a telegram to Jefferson Davis warning that Richmond and Petersburg would have to be evacuated immediately.

Lee's army began a desperate retreat westward on the night of April 2-3, hoping to reach the Richmond and Danville Railroad and then move south to join forces with General Joseph E. Johnston's army in North Carolina. But the Confederate troops were exhausted, hungry, and demoralized. Many simply laid down their weapons and walked home rather than continue a hopeless fight. Lee started the retreat with about thirty-five thousand men, but hundreds deserted every day.

The fall of Richmond on April 3, 1865, marked the effective end of the Confederate government. Union troops marched into the Confederate capital to find much of the business district in flames. Confederate authorities had ordered the burning of tobacco warehouses and other supplies to prevent their capture, but the fires had spread out of control. Jefferson Davis and other officials fled south in a special train, hoping to continue the war from Georgia or the Trans-Mississippi region. But without Richmond and without Lee's army, the Confederacy was just a government in exile with no real power.

Abraham Lincoln visited the fallen Confederate capital on April 4, walking through the streets where he had been denounced as a tyrant for four years. Black residents of Richmond greeted him as a liberator, and Lincoln spoke briefly about the need for reconciliation and healing.

Grant pursued the Confederates relentlessly, using his superior numbers and mobility to stay ahead of Lee's retreat. Union cavalry under Sheridan moved parallel to Lee, constantly threatening to cut off the Confederate escape route. Union infantry followed close behind, ready to attack if Lee tried to make a stand.

The end came at a small Virginia town called Appomattox Court House. On April 8, Lee found his retreat blocked by Union cavalry and infantry. He was surrounded, outnumbered four to one, and almost out of supplies. Some of his officers urged him to disperse the army and continue fighting as guerrillas, but Lee rejected the idea.

On the morning of April 9, 1865, Lee sent a message to Grant asking for a meeting to discuss surrender terms. Grant agreed immediately, understanding that this was the moment he had been working toward for eleven months of continuous campaigning.

The two generals met in the parlor of Wilmer McLean's house in Appomattox Court House. Ironically, McLean had moved to this quiet village to escape the war after a Confederate cannonball crashed through his kitchen during the First Battle of Bull Run in 1861. "The war began in my front yard and ended in my front parlor," McLean later said, capturing the strange coincidence that bookended America's bloodiest conflict.

The scene in McLean's home was heavy with symbolism. Lee arrived in his finest uniform with his ceremonial sword, while Grant appeared in a simple field uniform covered with mud from the road. Lee represented the old aristocratic South, while Grant embodied the democratic North.

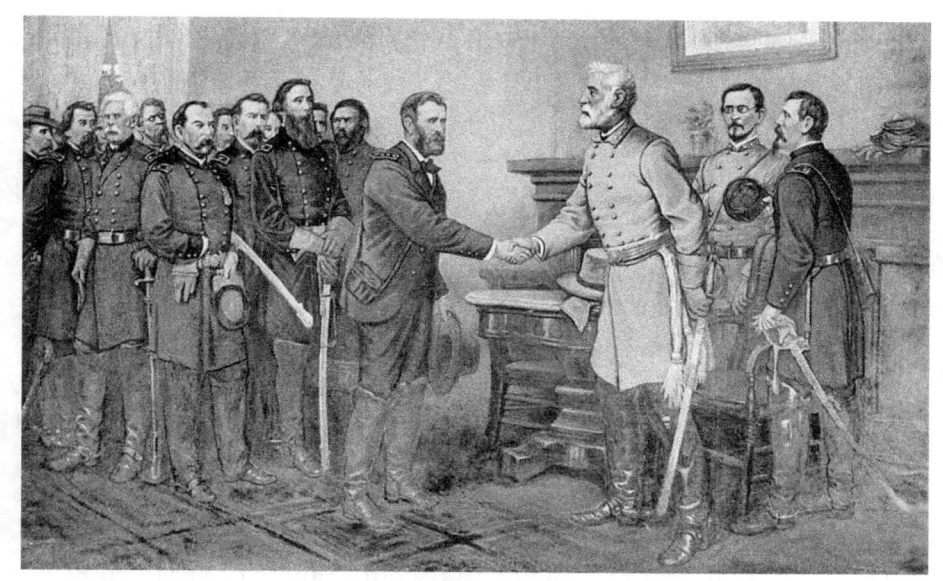
Lee surrenders to Grant.[114]

Grant's surrender terms were generous, reflecting Lincoln's desire for reconciliation rather than revenge. Confederate officers could keep their sidearms and personal property. Soldiers who owned horses could take them home for spring plowing. All Confederate soldiers would be "paroled and disqualified from taking up arms again ... until properly exchanged." There would be no mass executions or imprisonment.

Lee accepted the terms with quiet dignity. As he prepared to leave, Grant did something that surprised everyone present: he ordered his men not to celebrate. "The war is over," Grant told his staff. "The rebels are our countrymen again." It was a gesture of respect for Lee and a signal that the Union wanted to heal the nation's wounds rather than deepen them.

The formal surrender ceremony took place on April 12, with Union General Joshua Lawrence Chamberlain—the hero of Little Round Top—receiving the Confederate surrender. As Confederate units marched past to stack their weapons and surrender their battle flags, Chamberlain ordered his men to present arms in salute. It was a final gesture of respect between soldiers who had fought each other with such determination.

Lee's surrender effectively ended the Civil War, though some Confederate forces remained in the field. General Johnston surrendered to Sherman in North Carolina on April 26. The last Confederate force east of the Mississippi surrendered in Alabama on May 4. The final Confederate general to surrender was Stand Watie, a Cherokee leader who didn't give up until June 23, 1865.

The war was over, but its consequences were just beginning. Four years of fighting had killed more than 600,000 Americans and wounded hundreds of thousands more. The South was devastated, its economy destroyed, and its social system overturned. Four million enslaved people were now free, but their future remained uncertain.

Most tragically, Abraham Lincoln would not live to guide the nation through the difficult process of reconstruction. Just five days after Lee's surrender, Lincoln was assassinated by actor John Wilkes Booth at Ford's Theatre in Washington. The man who had preserved the Union and freed the slaves would not see the peace he had fought so hard to achieve.

The Civil War had ended not with compromise or negotiation but with total Union victory and Confederate defeat. The United States had been preserved, slavery had been abolished, and the federal government had demonstrated that secession was impossible. However, the work of rebuilding the nation and securing the rights of freed slaves was just beginning.

Chapter 11: The Assassination of a President

The war was over. Lee had surrendered at Appomattox, and the remaining Confederate forces were laying down their weapons one by one. After four years of unimaginable bloodshed, Americans could finally start to heal. Abraham Lincoln, the man who had held the nation together through its darkest hour, was already thinking about how to rebuild the country and bring the South back into the Union.

But one man wasn't ready for peace. John Wilkes Booth, a prominent actor and Confederate sympathizer, saw Lincoln's victory as a catastrophe that had to be reversed. On the evening of April 14, 1865—just five days after Lee's surrender—Booth would commit one of the most shocking political crimes in American history.

The Plot to Kill a President

John Wilkes Booth was one of the most famous actors in America, a member of a theatrical family that was to the 1860s what Hollywood dynasties are today. His father, Junius Brutus Booth, had been a legendary Shakespearean actor. His brother Edwin was considered the finest actor of his generation. John Wilkes was handsome, charismatic, and successful enough to earn a substantial income that made him wealthy by the standards of the time.

Booth was also a passionate Confederate sympathizer who saw Lincoln as a tyrant who had destroyed the South and freed the slaves. Unlike his brother Edwin, who supported the Union, John Wilkes Booth had spent the war years raging against Lincoln's policies and dreaming of a Confederate victory. When Lee surrendered at Appomattox, Booth's dreams turned to thoughts of revenge.

Booth's hatred for Lincoln was personal and intense. He couldn't stand the thought of the president celebrating victory while the South lay in ruins. In his diary, Booth expressed his belief that he was justified in his actions, writing: "I am here in despair. And why? For doing what Brutus was honored for ... And yet I for striking down a greater tyrant than they ever knew am looked upon as a common cutthroat."[i] In Booth's twisted mind, killing Lincoln would be an act of justice, not murder.

The assassination plot actually began as something quite different. For months, Booth had been planning to kidnap Lincoln and trade him for Confederate prisoners or concessions. He recruited a small group of conspirators, including Lewis Powell (also known as Lewis Paine), a former Confederate soldier; David Herold, a young pharmacy clerk; and George Atzerodt, a German immigrant who repaired boats. The plan was to grab Lincoln during one of his frequent trips to the theater and spirit him away to the South.

Lee's surrender changed everything. There was no longer any point in kidnapping Lincoln—the Confederacy was finished. Booth's desperation led him to a much darker plan. If he couldn't save the Confederacy, he could at least avenge its defeat by killing the man responsible for its destruction.

Booth's new plan was ambitious and deadly. He would kill not just Lincoln but also Vice President Andrew Johnson and Secretary of State William Seward. With the top three officials in the line of succession dead, the federal government would be thrown into chaos. Maybe, just maybe, this would give the South a chance to rise again.

On the morning of April 14, 1865, Booth learned that Lincoln would be attending a performance of *Our American Cousin* at Ford's Theatre that evening. Booth knew the theater well. He had performed there many times and could move around the building without attracting attention. Here was his chance.

Booth spent the day making final preparations. He assigned Powell to kill Secretary Seward, who was recovering from a carriage accident at his home. Atzerodt was supposed to murder Vice President Johnson at his

---

[i] https://law2.umkc.edu/faculty/projects/ftrials/lincolnconspiracy/boothdiary.html

hotel. Herold would help Powell escape after the Seward attack. Booth himself would handle Lincoln.

The plan called for precise timing, with all three attacks meant to happen simultaneously around 10:15 p.m. to prevent any of the targets from being warned. If the coordinated assault succeeded, the Union government would be decapitated in a single night. The timing of the Lincoln and Seward attacks was remarkably close to the planned schedule, though Atzerodt would fail to carry out his part of the conspiracy.

What Booth didn't fully understand was that killing Lincoln wouldn't bring back the Confederacy. The war was over, not because of Lincoln's personal leadership but because the Union had completely defeated the Confederate forces. Even if the assassination plot succeeded, it would only create a temporary crisis, not reverse the outcome of the war.

But Booth wasn't thinking clearly anymore. He was consumed by rage and desperate for some way to strike back at the victorious North. The assassination plot was less a rational plan than an act of theatrical revenge by a man who had spent his life playing dramatic roles on stage.

"Now He Belongs to the Ages": A Nation in Mourning

On the evening of April 14, 1865, Abraham and Mary Lincoln attended the theater as planned, accompanied by Major Henry Rathbone and his fiancée, Clara Harris. The party sat in a decorated box overlooking the stage, enjoying a light comedy that was supposed to provide relief from the stresses of war.

The play was in its third act when Booth made his move. He had timed his attack for a moment when he knew the audience would be laughing loudly. The laughter would cover the sound of his pistol shot.

At approximately 10:15 p.m., Booth slipped into the presidential box. Lincoln was leaning forward in his rocking chair, watching the play and probably thinking about the peace that was finally coming to America. Mary Lincoln was sitting beside him, holding his hand. Booth pulled out a single-shot derringer pistol and fired one bullet into the back of Lincoln's head. The president slumped forward, mortally wounded but still breathing. Major Rathbone lunged at Booth, who pulled out a hunting knife and slashed Rathbone's arm to the bone. Then Booth leaped from the box to the stage, breaking his leg in the fall but managing to shout "Sic semper tyrannis!"—"Thus always to tyrants!"—before limping away.

The assassination of Abraham Lincoln.[115]

The theater erupted in chaos. Some people thought the attack was part of the play. Others screamed and rushed for the exits. A young Army doctor named Charles Leale reached Lincoln first and immediately saw that the wound was fatal. The bullet had entered behind Lincoln's left ear and lodged behind his right eye, causing massive brain damage.

Lincoln was carried across the street to a boarding house owned by William Petersen. He was placed in a small back bedroom on a bed that was too short for his tall frame. Through the long night, government officials, family members, and doctors kept vigil as Lincoln slowly died. Mary Lincoln sat beside the bed, sometimes talking to her unconscious husband, sometimes breaking down in tears.

The other parts of Booth's conspiracy fell apart. Powell did attack Secretary Seward, fighting his way into Seward's house and slashing the secretary's face with a knife before escaping. Seward survived, though he was badly wounded. Atzerodt lost his nerve and never attempted to kill Vice President Johnson. He spent the evening drinking in hotel bars instead of committing murder.

As word of the attack spread through Washington, the city filled with angry, frightened crowds. Secretary of War Edwin Stanton took control of the manhunt for Booth and ordered martial law in the capital.

Lincoln died at 7:22 a.m. on April 15, 1865. Secretary Stanton, who had often clashed with Lincoln during the war but had come to respect his leadership, spoke the words that captured the nation's grief: "Now he belongs to the ages."

The news of Lincoln's death spread across the country by telegraph, stunning a nation that had been celebrating the war's end just days earlier. In New York, crowds gathered in the streets, some weeping openly. In Chicago, businesses closed, and flags flew at half-mast. Even in the defeated South, many people were shocked by the assassination. General Joseph E. Johnston, who had just surrendered to Sherman, called it "a disgrace to the age."

The search for Booth became the largest manhunt in American history up to that time. Thousands of soldiers scoured the countryside around Washington, following leads and chasing rumors. Booth had escaped into Maryland with David Herold, but his broken leg slowed him down and made him dependent on Confederate sympathizers for shelter.

For twelve days, Booth evaded capture while his leg healed and he tried to figure out how to escape to the South. He had expected to be hailed as a hero for killing Lincoln, but the reaction was much different from what he had imagined. Even many Confederate supporters were horrified by the assassination, seeing it as a cowardly murder rather than a heroic act.

Booth was finally tracked down to a tobacco barn in Virginia on April 26, 1865. When he refused to surrender, soldiers set the barn on fire to force him out. In the confusion, Sergeant Boston Corbett shot Booth, who died a few hours later. His last words were reportedly "Tell my mother I died for my country."

The other conspirators were quickly captured and put on trial before a military commission. Powell, Herold, Atzerodt, and Mary Surratt (who owned the boarding house where the conspirators met) were sentenced to death and hanged on July 7, 1865. Several other people who had aided the conspiracy received prison sentences.

Lincoln's funeral became a national event unlike anything America had ever seen. His body lay in state in the Capitol Rotunda, where thousands of mourners filed past his coffin. Then began a remarkable journey by train from Washington to Springfield, Illinois, where Lincoln would be buried. The funeral train stopped in major cities along the route, and at each stop, thousands of people gathered to pay their respects.

In Philadelphia, the line of mourners stretched for three miles. In New York, more than 120,000 people viewed Lincoln's body as it lay in state in City Hall. In Chicago, despite pouring rain, 125,000 people came to see the man who had saved the Union. The funeral train passed through small towns where entire communities gathered by the railroad tracks.

The Lincoln assassination had transformed the martyred president into something approaching a secular saint. The man who had been criticized and even hated by many Americans during his lifetime was now remembered as the Great Emancipator who had died for the cause of freedom. His death gave him a place in American memory that no living politician could ever achieve.

Lincoln's assassination also had immediate political consequences that would shape the nation's future. Vice President Andrew Johnson, who was now president, was a very different man with very different ideas about how to rebuild the South. The careful, patient approach that Lincoln might have taken to Reconstruction was replaced by Johnson's more confrontational style, setting up conflicts that would dominate American politics for years to come.

The man who might have guided America through the difficult transition from war to peace was gone, killed by someone who thought murder could change the course of history. Booth had succeeded in killing Lincoln, but he had failed utterly in his larger goal. The Union survived, the slaves remained free, and the Confederacy stayed dead. All Booth had accomplished was to deprive America of its greatest president at the moment when his leadership was most needed.

Chapter 12: Reconstruction: A Noble Attempt, A Tragic Failure

The assassination of Abraham Lincoln left America facing the most difficult challenge in its history. How do you put a nation back together after it has nearly destroyed itself?

This period, known as Reconstruction, would last from 1865 to 1877. It was America's first attempt to create a truly multiracial democracy, and for a brief, shining moment, it looked like it might succeed. Black men voted, held office, and enjoyed rights they had never known before. The Constitution was amended to establish the legal foundation for equality for all citizens.

But Reconstruction was also a story of broken promises and abandoned hopes. White resistance in the South, political exhaustion in the North, and the rise of violent organizations like the Ku Klux Klan eventually undid most of the progress that had been made. By 1877, the dream of racial equality was dead, and it would stay buried for nearly a century.

The Big Questions: How to Rebuild and What to Do with the Freedmen?

When the war ended, nobody really knew what to do next. The Constitution didn't say anything about how to handle states that had tried to leave the Union. Were they still states, or had they become conquered territories? Could they simply elect new governments and rejoin the Union as if nothing had happened? And what about the millions of formerly enslaved people who were now free but had no land, no money, and few skills beyond agricultural labor?

These weren't just legal questions—they were about what kind of country America was going to become. The war had settled the question of whether states could secede (they couldn't) and whether slavery would continue (it wouldn't). But it hadn't answered the deeper question of whether Black and White Americans could live together as equals in a single nation.

President Andrew Johnson, who had suddenly found himself in charge after Lincoln's assassination, had very different ideas about Reconstruction than many members of Congress. Johnson was a Tennessee Democrat who had remained loyal to the Union during the war, which was why Lincoln had chosen him as a running mate in 1864. However, Johnson also held deeply racist views and believed that America should remain under White political control.

Johnson's plan for Reconstruction was simple and lenient. Southern states could rejoin the Union as soon as they ratified the Thirteenth Amendment and repudiated their Confederate debts. Former Confederate leaders would be pardoned, and Southern states could organize new governments with minimal federal interference. Johnson believed that the fastest way to heal the nation was to get things back to normal as quickly as possible.

The ruins of Charleston, South Carolina, in 1865.[116]

Congress had other ideas. Republicans who controlled both houses believed that the South should be punished for the rebellion and that the federal government had a responsibility to protect the rights of freed slaves. They were horrified by Johnson's willingness to hand power back to the White Southern leaders who had started the war in the first place.

The conflict between Johnson and Congress came to a head over the "Black Codes"—laws passed by Southern states in 1865 and 1866 that severely restricted the rights of freed slaves. These laws varied from state to state, but they generally prohibited Black people from owning guns, traveling freely, or working in certain occupations. Some required freed slaves to sign yearly labor contracts with White employers, and those who couldn't prove they had jobs could be arrested for vagrancy and forced to work on chain gangs.

The Black Codes revealed the true intentions of many White Southerners. They had accepted military defeat but refused to accept social change. In Louisiana, the code prohibited Black people from living in towns or cities without special permits. In Texas, Black people who broke labor contracts could be arrested and forced to work without pay until their contracts expired.

These laws were designed to keep freed slaves in a condition as close to slavery as possible. Mississippi's code was particularly harsh, prohibiting Black people from renting or owning land and requiring them to have written proof of employment at all times. The law also stated that any Black person who quit a job before the end of their contract would forfeit all wages earned up to that point, making it almost impossible for workers to leave abusive employers.

South Carolina's code forbade Black people from working as anything other than farmers or servants unless they paid a special annual tax that most couldn't afford. The law also allowed any White person to arrest Black people who appeared to be unemployed and take them before a judge, who could sentence them to work on public projects or hire them out to private employers.

The enforcement of these codes was often brutal and arbitrary. Local sheriffs, most of them former Confederates, had wide discretion in interpreting the laws and frequently used them to intimidate Black people who showed any signs of independence. Black families who tried to move to find better work could be arrested for vagrancy. Black farmers who tried to negotiate better contracts could be jailed for violating labor agreements.

Perhaps most insidiously, the Black Codes often targeted Black children. Many states allowed White employers to "apprentice" Black children whose parents were deemed unable to support them. These apprenticeships were supposed to provide education and job training, but in practice, they were often a way to obtain free child labor. Parents who objected to having their children taken away could be arrested for interfering with legal contracts.

Northern Republicans were outraged by the Black Codes, seeing them as proof that the South hadn't really accepted defeat and was trying to restore slavery under a different name. They also pointed out that the codes made a mockery of the sacrifices that Union soldiers had made to win the war. Had 360,000 Union soldiers died just so that Black people could be kept in a new form of bondage?

It is important to mention that while the Black Codes were most systematic in the South, Black Americans faced discrimination throughout the country. Most Northern states had their own restrictions on Black voting, education, and employment. The difference was that Northern discrimination was often informal or local rather than written into state law. Northern Black people also had more legal recourse and political allies.

Congress responded by passing the Civil Rights Act of 1866, which declared that all people born in the United States (except Native Americans) were citizens with equal rights under the law. The act specifically prohibited the kind of discrimination codified in the Black Codes and gave federal courts the power to enforce these protections.

Johnson vetoed the Civil Rights Act, arguing that it gave too much power to the federal government and interfered with states' rights. His veto revealed his racial views clearly. He argued that the act discriminated against White people by giving Black people special protections, and he warned that it would lead to "a perfect equality of the white and black races."

Congress overrode Johnson's veto. This was the first time in American history that Congress had overridden a presidential veto on a major piece of legislation. The override vote showed how deep the split between Johnson and congressional Republicans had become. For the rest of his presidency, Johnson would be fighting a losing battle against a Congress determined to protect the rights of freed slaves.

The question of what to do with freed slaves—or "freedmen" as they were often called—was enormously complicated. Most had no education, no money, and no experience with freedom. They knew how to work the land, but they didn't own any land to work. They wanted to read and write, but there were few schools for Black children. They needed jobs, but many White employers refused to hire them for anything other than agricultural labor.

Some radical Republicans, led by Congressman Thaddeus Stevens of Pennsylvania, wanted to confiscate large plantations and redistribute the land to freed slaves. "Forty acres and a mule" became a rallying cry for those who believed that land ownership was essential to making freedom meaningful. Without economic independence, they argued, freed slaves would remain dependent on their former masters.

However, land redistribution was too radical for most Americans, including most Republicans. The idea of seizing private property, even from former Confederates, violated deeply held beliefs about property rights. Instead, Congress created the Freedmen's Bureau, a federal agency designed to help freed slaves transition to freedom by providing food, medical care, education, and assistance in finding jobs.

The Freedmen's Bureau did important work, establishing thousands of schools and helping to negotiate fair labor contracts between freed slaves and White employers. However, it was chronically underfunded and faced massive hostility from White Southerners who saw it as an unwelcome intrusion by the federal government. The Bureau's agents, many of them Union Army veterans, often found themselves in physical danger as they tried to protect the rights of freed slaves.

The fundamental problem was that most freed slaves wanted to own their own land, but most White Americans weren't willing to give them the resources to make that possible. The result was a system of sharecropping that trapped many Black families in poverty for generations. Under sharecropping, freed slaves would work a plot of land owned by a White landowner in exchange for a share of the crop. In theory, this gave freed slaves more autonomy than slavery had. In practice, it often meant that Black families remained economically dependent on White landowners who could manipulate contracts and prices to keep them in perpetual debt.

The Thirteenth, Fourteenth, and Fifteenth Amendments

While politicians argued about how to readmit Southern states to the Union, Congress was also working to amend the Constitution to protect the rights that the Union had fought to secure. Between 1865 and 1870, three constitutional amendments would fundamentally change American law and provide the legal foundation for equality, even though that promise would take generations to fulfill.

The Thirteenth Amendment, ratified in December 1865, was the most straightforward. It abolished slavery throughout the United States, making permanent what the Emancipation Proclamation had begun as a wartime measure. The amendment's language was simple and absolute. "Neither slavery nor involuntary servitude, except as a punishment for crime whereof the party shall have been duly convicted, shall exist within the United States, or any place subject to their jurisdiction."

The exception for criminal punishment would later be used by Southern states to create systems of convict labor that resembled slavery in many ways. But at the time, most Americans focused on the amendment's main purpose: ensuring that slavery could never again exist in the United States, no matter what future presidents or Supreme Court justices might decide.

The Fourteenth Amendment, ratified in July 1868, was much more complex and far-reaching. Its first section defined citizenship for the first time in the Constitution, declaring that "all persons born or naturalized in the United States, and subject to the jurisdiction thereof, are citizens of the United States and of the state wherein they reside." This directly overturned the Supreme Court's Dred Scott decision, which had ruled that Black people could never be American citizens. The amendment also prohibited states from denying any person "the equal protection of the laws" or depriving them of "life, liberty, or property, without due process of law."

The Fourteenth Amendment's second section tried to encourage Southern states to grant voting rights to Black men by threatening to reduce their representation in Congress if they didn't. States that denied voting rights to adult male citizens would have their representation reduced proportionally. This was a compromise measure. Republicans wanted to guarantee Black voting rights directly, but they didn't have enough support for such a radical step.

The amendment's third section temporarily barred most former Confederate leaders from holding federal or state office unless Congress voted otherwise. This was designed to prevent the same people who had led the rebellion from immediately returning to power in Southern state governments.

Andrew Johnson opposed the Fourteenth Amendment and encouraged Southern states to reject it. His opposition helped make the amendment a key issue in the 1866 congressional elections, which became a referendum on Reconstruction policy. Republicans campaigned on the need to protect freed slaves and ensure that the South truly accepted defeat. Democrats argued that Republicans were being vindictive and that Johnson's lenient approach would heal the nation faster.

The elections were a disaster for Johnson and the Democrats. Republicans gained overwhelming majorities in both houses of Congress, giving them the power to override Johnson's vetoes at will. The election also showed that Northern voters supported stronger federal action to protect the rights of freed slaves, at least for the time being.

With their new strength, Republicans passed a series of Reconstruction Acts in 1867 that divided the South into military districts and required Southern states to ratify the Fourteenth Amendment before they could rejoin the Union. The acts also required Southern states to hold new constitutional conventions with delegates elected by all adult males, including freed slaves.

The Fifteenth Amendment, ratified in February 1870, prohibited states from denying voting rights based on "race, color, or previous condition of servitude." This finally guaranteed Black men the right to vote, though it didn't address other potential barriers like literacy tests or poll taxes that would later be used to prevent Blacks from voting.

The amendment was controversial even among Republicans. Some wanted language that would have prohibited all barriers to voting, while others worried that federal control over voting rights went too far. Women's rights activists like Susan B. Anthony and Elizabeth Cady Stanton were furious that the amendment didn't extend voting rights to women as well.

Together, these three amendments represented a constitutional revolution that fundamentally changed the relationship between the federal government and the states. For the first time, the Constitution placed direct limits on what state governments could do to their own citizens. The federal government now had both the responsibility and the power to protect individual rights against state interference.

The progress that Black Americans made during Reconstruction was nothing short of revolutionary. For the first time in American history, Black men were voting in large numbers and winning political office at every level of government. In South Carolina, Black voters actually outnumbered White voters. More than 1,500 Black men held political office during Reconstruction, including two U.S. senators and fourteen members of the House of Representatives. Hiram Revels of Mississippi became the first Black senator in 1870, taking the seat once held by Jefferson Davis himself. P. B. S. Pinchback briefly served as governor of Louisiana, while Black men served as lieutenant governors in South Carolina and Mississippi. Every Southern state legislature included Black representatives, and some states had substantial Black representation in their lower houses.

The changes went beyond politics. Black communities established thousands of schools with help from the Freedmen's Bureau and Northern missionary societies, leading to dramatic increases in Black literacy rates. Some Black families managed to acquire land and start businesses despite enormous obstacles, while others became teachers, ministers, and skilled craftsmen. Black churches flourished as centers of community life and political organizing. For the first time since arriving in America, people of African descent were participating as full citizens in American democracy, and many were succeeding despite the challenges they faced.

However, constitutional amendments are only as strong as the political will to enforce them. As Northern enthusiasm for Reconstruction waned and Southern resistance intensified, the promise of these amendments would remain largely unfulfilled for nearly a century.

The Rise of the Ku Klux Klan and the End of Reconstruction

The most violent and effective opposition to Reconstruction came from a secret organization that started as a social club and became a terrorist army. The Ku Klux Klan was founded in Tennessee in 1866 by former Confederate officers who were looking for some way to fight back against what they saw as Northern oppression and Black advancement.

The Klan's first leader was Nathan Bedford Forrest, the brilliant Confederate cavalry general who had terrorized Union forces during the war. Under Forrest's leadership, the Klan spread rapidly across the South, recruiting thousands of members who were united by their determination to restore White supremacy and Democratic political control.

Klan members, known as "night riders," used terrorism to intimidate Black voters and White Republicans. They would ride to the homes of Black families in the middle of the night, wearing white robes and hoods to hide their identities. Sometimes, they would simply threaten their victims, warning them not to vote or send their children to school. Other times, they would whip, torture, or murder those who defied their demands.

The Klan's terrorism was incredibly effective because it was both random and systematic. Black families never knew when the night riders might come, but they knew that any sign of independence or political activity could make them targets. The psychological impact was devastating. Many Black voters stayed away from the polls rather than risk Klan violence against themselves or their families.

The Klan developed sophisticated methods of intimidation that went far beyond simple violence. They would leave threatening notes or symbols at the homes of their targets. They would burn crosses in front yards as warnings. They would parade through Black neighborhoods in full regalia, sometimes numbering in the hundreds, to demonstrate their power and organization. These displays were meant to show that the Klan was everywhere and that resistance was futile.

The Klan's targets weren't random. They focused on Black people who showed signs of economic success, political activity, or social independence. Black teachers, preachers, and political leaders were particularly vulnerable. So were Black families who owned their own land, started businesses, or sent their children to school. The message was clear: Black people who tried to rise above their assigned place in society would be punished.

The Klan also targeted White Republicans, especially those who worked with the Freedmen's Bureau or supported Black rights. Teachers at schools for Black children were particularly vulnerable, as were White politicians who depended on Black votes. Klan violence drove many White Republicans out of the South entirely, leaving Black communities with fewer allies and protectors.

Some specific incidents illustrate the Klan's brutal methods. In York County, South Carolina, the Klan murdered more than a dozen Black men and whipped hundreds more during 1870 and 1871. In Mississippi, the Klan assassinated a Black state legislator named Charles Caldwell on Christmas Day 1875, shooting him down in broad daylight as a warning to other Black politicians. In Alabama, Klan members dragged a Black teacher named Elijsha Davidson from his home and whipped him nearly to death for the crime of teaching Black children to read.

The federal government struggled to respond to Klan terrorism. Local law enforcement was often sympathetic to the Klan or too intimidated to act against it. State governments controlled by White Democrats had no interest in protecting Black citizens. That left the federal government as the only possible protector of civil rights, but federal resources were limited.

Congress passed several laws designed to combat the Klan, including the Ku Klux Klan Act of 1871, which made it a federal crime to conspire to deny anyone their civil rights. President Ulysses S. Grant, who had been elected in 1868, used these laws to authorize military action against the Klan in several states. Federal troops arrested thousands of Klan members, and the organization largely collapsed by 1872.

However, the victory over the Klan was temporary. As federal enforcement weakened and Northern interest in Reconstruction declined, new organizations arose to continue the work of terrorizing Black voters. Groups like the White League in Louisiana and the Red Shirts in South Carolina used the same tactics as the Klan but were more careful to avoid direct confrontation with federal authorities.

The end of Reconstruction came gradually and then suddenly. Northern voters grew tired of the expense and controversy of maintaining troops in the South. The economic depression that began in 1873 made people more concerned about their own problems than about protecting the rights of freed slaves. A new generation of political leaders, both Republican and Democratic, was more interested in economic development than in civil rights.

The decisive moment came with the disputed presidential election of 1876. Democrat Samuel Tilden appeared to have won the popular vote, but the electoral vote count was disputed in three Southern states where Republican governments were still in power. A special commission awarded all the disputed votes to Republican Rutherford B. Hayes, giving him the presidency by a single electoral vote.

But Hayes's victory came at a price. In exchange for Democratic acceptance of his presidency, Hayes agreed to withdraw the last federal troops from the South and end federal enforcement of civil rights laws. This "Compromise of 1877" marked the official end of Reconstruction and the beginning of nearly a century of legalized segregation and White supremacy in the South.

The results were immediate and devastating for Black Southerners. State governments across the South began passing new laws that denied Black people the right to vote, attend integrated schools, or use public accommodations. These "Jim Crow" laws created a system of legal segregation that would last until the 1960s.

Violence against Black people also increased dramatically after the end of Reconstruction. Lynching became a common form of terrorism used to enforce White supremacy. Between 1877 and 1950, more than four thousand Black people were lynched in the United States, most of them in the South. These murders were often public spectacles attended by hundreds of White spectators, including children.

The Reconstruction's failure had consequences that lasted for generations. The system of legal segregation and economic exploitation that replaced slavery kept most Black Southerners in poverty and denied them basic civil rights. The promise of equality that had been written into the Constitution during Reconstruction remained unfulfilled for nearly a century.

But Reconstruction wasn't a complete failure. The Thirteenth, Fourteenth, and Fifteenth Amendments remained part of the Constitution. The schools established by the Freedmen's Bureau and Black communities during Reconstruction created the foundation for Black education in the South. Most importantly, the idea that all Americans deserved equal rights regardless of race had been planted in the national consciousness, even if it would take decades to flower.

The Civil War and Reconstruction represent both the best and worst of the American experience. They showed that Americans could make enormous sacrifices to preserve their nation and extend freedom to those who had been denied it. However, they also showed how quickly progress could be reversed when political will weakened and violence was allowed to triumph over law.

Understanding this history is essential to understanding America today. The questions that divided Americans during Reconstruction—

about the role of the federal government, the meaning of equality, and the relationship between different racial groups—are still being debated. The failure of Reconstruction reminds us that democratic progress is never permanent and that each generation must work to fulfill the promises made by previous generations.

Conclusion:
Why We Still Remember

More than 150 years have passed since Robert E. Lee surrendered to Ulysses S. Grant at Appomattox Court House. The America of today would be unrecognizable to the soldiers who fought at Bull Run or the civilians who lived through Sherman's March to the Sea. We have smartphones in our pockets, cars in our driveways, and opportunities that people in 1865 couldn't have imagined. So why do we still talk about a war that ended before our great-great-grandparents were born?

The answer is simple. The Civil War created the America we live in today. Every major question about what kind of nation we are was forged in the fires of that conflict. The war didn't just preserve the Union; it transformed it into something entirely new.

But the Civil War also left behind unfinished business that we're still working on today. The promise of equality that was written into the Constitution during Reconstruction took another century to even partially fulfill. The tension between individual liberty and collective responsibility that drove Americans to war in 1861 still shapes our political debates today. Understanding the Civil War isn't just about understanding the past—it's about understanding ourselves.

When the war began in 1861, the United States was really more like a loose confederation of independent states that happened to share the same flag. People thought of themselves as Virginians or New Yorkers first, Americans second. The federal government was small and distant, touching most people's lives only through the post office and occasional tax collection. States made most of the important decisions about how people lived their daily lives.

The war changed all of that. By 1865, the federal government had demonstrated that it could draft soldiers, impose taxes, suspend civil liberties, and override state laws when necessary. The Union Army had become one of the largest and most effective military forces in the world. The federal bureaucracy had grown from a few thousand employees to more than 100,000. The federal government had also established the principle that national law trumped state law, and that some rights were too important to leave to local control.

This shift from state-centered to nation-centered government wasn't just about politics—it was about identity. Before the war, when Americans traveled abroad, they often identified themselves by their home states. After the war, they were Americans first and foremost. The phrase *United States* changed from plural to singular. Instead of saying "the United States are," people began saying "the United States is." It sounds like a small change, but it reflected a fundamental transformation in how Americans thought about their country.

The Civil War also established the principle that some moral questions are too important to compromise about. For decades before the war, American politicians had solved the slavery problem through deals and bargains that satisfied nobody completely but gave everybody something. The Missouri Compromise, the Compromise of 1850, and the Kansas-Nebraska Act were all attempts to find middle ground on an issue that, ultimately, had no middle ground.

Abraham Lincoln understood this when he said that a house divided against itself could not stand. Either slavery was right, or it was wrong. Either all men were created equal, or they weren't. Either America would become a nation dedicated to freedom, or it would remain a nation that denied freedom to millions of its people based on the color of their skin. The war decided these questions once and for all.

The cost of settling these questions was staggering. More than 600,000 Americans died in the war—more than in World War I and World War II combined. Entire regions of the country were devastated. Families were torn apart. The economic cost was enormous, creating debts that took decades to pay off. The psychological trauma affected an entire generation and was passed down to their children and grandchildren.

But the alternative might have been even worse. If the Union had let the Confederate states go peacefully, slavery would have continued indefinitely in the South. The Confederate Constitution explicitly protected slavery and made it almost impossible to abolish. Millions of Black Americans would have remained in bondage, and their children and grandchildren would have inherited that bondage. The example of a successful slaveholding republic might have encouraged other countries to reimplement, maintain, or even expand their own systems of forced labor.

The war also prevented the United States from becoming the kind of weak, divided nation that would have been easy prey for foreign powers. A split between two hostile countries on the same continent likely would have led to European interference. The British Empire might have allied with the Confederacy, the French might have supported the Union, and North America could have become another theater for European power struggles.

Instead, the Civil War created a united, powerful nation that could defend itself and project its values around the world. The same industrial capacity that won the war made America an economic powerhouse. The same organizational skills that mobilized millions of soldiers built transcontinental railroads, developed new technologies, and created modern corporations. The same democratic ideals that motivated Union soldiers also inspired reform movements that expanded rights to women, immigrants, and other marginalized groups.

The failure of Reconstruction reminds us that military victory doesn't automatically lead to social progress. Winning the war was only the first step toward creating a truly equal society. When the political will to enforce equality weakened, much of the progress made during Reconstruction was reversed. It took the civil rights movement of the 1950s and 1960s to revive the promise of equality that had been made a century earlier.

This history shows that democratic progress is never permanent. Each generation must work to fulfill the promises made by previous generations. The rights we take for granted today were won through struggle and sacrifice, and they can be lost if we don't remain vigilant. The same questions that divided Americans during the Civil War era—about the role of government, the meaning of equality, and the balance between majority rule and minority rights—continue to shape our political debates.

The Civil War also teaches us about the power of ordinary people to change history. The Union wasn't saved by a few great leaders making brilliant decisions. It was saved by millions of ordinary Americans—soldiers who enlisted despite the dangers, families who supported the war effort despite the hardships, freed slaves who seized their own liberation, and citizens who voted to continue fighting even when victory seemed impossible.

These ordinary Americans proved that democracy could survive its greatest test. They showed that a government "of the people, by the people, for the people" could mobilize the resources needed to preserve itself and extend its benefits to those who had been excluded. They demonstrated that Americans, despite their differences, shared common values that were worth fighting and dying for.

The story of the Civil War is ultimately a story about choices. Southerners chose to secede rather than accept limits on slavery's expansion. Northerners chose to fight rather than let the Union dissolve. Lincoln chose to make the war about ending slavery as well as preserving the Union. Millions of individual Americans chose to support their cause despite enormous personal costs.

These choices created the America we live in today—a nation where the federal government can protect civil rights, where all citizens are equal under the law (at least in principle), and where democracy has survived challenges that have destroyed other republics. The Civil War proved that the American experiment could endure and that the ideals proclaimed in the Declaration of Independence were worth whatever it cost to defend them.

We remember the Civil War because it was the moment when America became America. The nation that emerged from that conflict wasn't perfect—it took decades to fully live up to its ideals, and the work of perfecting the Union continues today. But it was a nation committed to the principle that all people are created equal and endowed with unalienable rights to life, liberty, and the pursuit of happiness.

That principle, tested in the fire of civil war and tempered by the struggles that followed, remains the foundation of American democracy. As long as people continue to believe in that principle and work to make it real for all Americans, the sacrifices made between 1861 and 1865 will not have been in vain. The Civil War generation passed the torch of freedom to us. Now it's our responsibility to keep that flame burning for future generations.

Here's another book by Matt Clayton that you might like

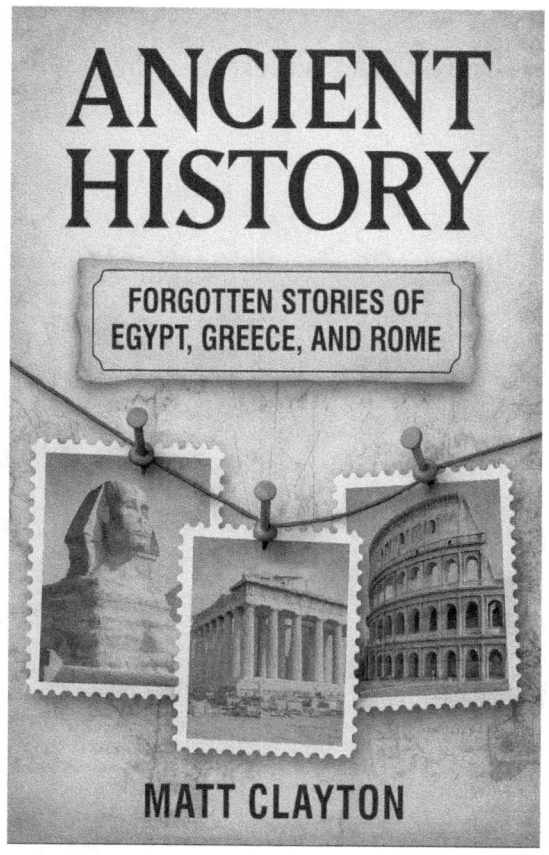

Free Bonus from Captivating History
(Available for a Limited time)

Hi History Lovers!

Now you have a chance to join our exclusive history list so you can get your first history ebook for free as well as discounts and a potential to get more history books for free!

Simply visit the link below to join.

Or, Scan the QR code!

captivatinghistory.com/ebook

Also, make sure to follow us on Facebook, X, and YouTube by searching for Captivating History.

Sources

Part 1: The History of the United States for Beginners

Anderson, Fred. Crucible of War: The Seven Years' War and the Fate of Empire in British North America, 1754-1766. New York: Alfred A. Knopf, 2000.

Arsenault, Raymond. Freedom Riders: 1961 and the Struggle for Racial Justice. New York: Oxford University Press, 2006.

Baker, Jean H. Sisters: The Lives of America's Suffragists. New York: Hill and Wang, 2005.

Beevor, Antony. The Second World War. New York: Little, Brown, 2012.

Berlin, Ira. Many Thousands Gone: The First Two Centuries of Slavery in North America. Cambridge: Harvard University Press, 1998.

Catton, Bruce. The Civil War. Boston: Houghton Mifflin, 1960.

Crosby, Alfred W. The Columbian Exchange: Biological and Cultural Consequences of 1492. Westport, CT: Greenwood Press, 1972.

Daniels, Roger. Coming to America: A History of Immigration and Ethnicity in American Life. 2nd ed. New York: HarperCollins, 2002.

DuBois, Ellen Carol. Suffrage: Women's Long Battle for the Vote. New York: Simon & Schuster, 2020.

Fagan, Brian M. Ancient North America: The Archaeology of a Continent. 4th ed. New York: Thames & Hudson, 2005.

Gaddis, John Lewis. The Cold War: A New History. New York: Penguin Press, 2005.

Halberstam, David. War in a Time of Peace: Bush, Clinton, and the Generals. New York: Scribner, 2001.

Hickey, Donald R. The War of 1812: A Forgotten Conflict. Urbana: University of Illinois Press, 1989.

Horn, James. A Land As God Made It: Jamestown and the Birth of America. New York: Basic Books, 2005.

Joseph, Peniel E. The Black Power Movement: Rethinking the Civil Rights–Black Power Era. New York: Routledge, 2006.

Katznelson, Ira. Fear Itself: The New Deal and the Origins of Our Time. New York: Liveright, 2013.

Keegan, John. The First World War. New York: Alfred A. Knopf, 1999.

——. The Second World War. New York: Viking, 1989.

Kennedy, David M. Freedom from Fear: The American People in Depression and War, 1929–1945. New York: Oxford University Press, 1999.

——. Over Here: The First World War and American Society. New York: Oxford University Press, 1980.

Kotkin, Stephen. Armageddon Averted: The Soviet Collapse, 1970–2000. New York: Oxford University Press, 2001.

Lepore, Jill. The Name of War: King Philip's War and the Origins of American Identity. New York: Alfred A. Knopf, 1998.

Mann, Charles C. 1491: New Revelations of the Americas Before Columbus. New York: Alfred A. Knopf, 2005.

——. 1493: Uncovering the New World Columbus Created. New York: Alfred A. Knopf, 2011.

McElvaine, Robert S. The Great Depression: America, 1929–1941. New York: Times Books, 1984.

McPherson, James M. Battle Cry of Freedom: The Civil War Era. New York: Oxford University Press, 1988.

Middlekauff, Robert. The Glorious Cause: The American Revolution, 1763–1789. New York: Oxford University Press, 1982.

Musicant, Ivan. Empire by Default: The Spanish–American War and the Dawn of the American Century. New York: Henry Holt, 1998.

Norton, Mary Beth. In the Devil's Snare: The Salem Witchcraft Crisis of 1692. New York: Alfred A. Knopf, 2002.

Okrent, Daniel. Last Call: The Rise and Fall of Prohibition. New York: Scribner, 2010.

Rhodes, Richard. The Making of the Atomic Bomb. New York: Simon & Schuster, 1986.

Richter, Daniel K. Facing East from Indian Country: A Native History of Early America. Cambridge: Harvard University Press, 2001.

Riis, Jacob. How the Other Half Lives: Studies Among the Tenements of New York. New York: Charles Scribner's Sons, 1890.

Silbey, David. A War of Frontier and Empire: The Philippine-American War, 1899-1902. New York: Hill and Wang, 2007.

Sitkoff, Harvard. A New Deal for Blacks: The Emergence of Civil Rights as a National Issue. New York: Oxford University Press, 1978.

Terborg-Penn, Rosalyn. African American Women in the Struggle for the Vote, 1850-1920. Bloomington: Indiana University Press, 1998.

Wood, Gordon S. The American Revolution: A History. New York: Modern Library, 2003.

———. Empire of Liberty: A History of the Early Republic, 1789-1815. New York: Oxford University Press, 2009.

Worster, Donald. Dust Bowl: The Southern Plains in the 1930s. New York: Oxford University Press, 1979.

Part 2: The American Revolution for Beginners

Anderson, Fred. *Crucible of War: The Seven Years' War and the Fate of Empire in British North America, 1754-1766.* New York: Alfred A. Knopf, 2000.

Bailyn, Bernard. *The Ideological Origins of the American Revolution.* Cambridge: Harvard University Press, 1967.

Beeman, Richard. *Plain, Honest Men: The Making of the American Constitution.* Random House, 2009.

Ellis, Joseph J. *Founding Brothers: The Revolutionary Generation.* Alfred A. Knopf, 2000.

———. *American Creation: Triumphs and Tragedies at the Founding of the Republic.* New York: Alfred A. Knopf, 2007.

———. *Revolutionary Summer: The Birth of American Independence.* New York: Alfred A. Knopf, 2013.

Ferling, John. *Almost a Miracle: The American Victory in the War of Independence.* Oxford: Oxford University Press, 2007.

Grainger, John D. *The Battle of Yorktown, 1781: A Reassessment.* Boydell Press, 2005.

Henretta, James A., and Gregory H. Nobles. *Evolution and Revolution: American Society, 1600-1820.* Lexington, MA: D.C. Heath, 1987.

Ketchum, Richard M. *The Winter Soldiers: The Battles for Trenton and Princeton.* Henry Holt and Company, 1973.

McCullough, David. *1776.* New York: Simon & Schuster, 2005.

Middlekauff, Robert. *The Glorious Cause: The American Revolution, 1763-1789.* New York: Oxford University Press, 1982.

Philbrick, Nathaniel. *Bunker Hill: A City, a Siege, a Revolution.* New York: Viking, 2013.

Richards, Leonard L. *Shays's Rebellion: The American Revolution's Final Battle*. University of Pennsylvania Press, 2002.

Taylor, Alan. *American Colonies: The Settling of North America*. New York: Penguin Books, 2001.

Wood, Gordon S. *The Radicalism of the American Revolution*. New York: Alfred A. Knopf, 1992.

Part 3: The Civil War for Beginners

Ballard, Michael B. *Vicksburg: The Campaign That Opened the Mississippi*. Chapel Hill: University of North Carolina Press, 2004.

Baptist, Edward E. *The Half Has Never Been Told: Slavery and the Making of American Capitalism*. New York: Basic Books, 2014.

Berlin, Ira. *Many Thousands Gone: The First Two Centuries of Slavery in North America*. Cambridge, MA: Belknap Press of Harvard University Press, 1998.

Catton, Bruce. *Grant Takes Command*. Boston: Little, Brown and Company, 1969.

Cooper, William J., Jr. *Jefferson Davis, American*. New York: Alfred A. Knopf, 2000.

Daniel, Larry J. *Shiloh: The Battle That Changed the Civil War*. New York: Simon & Schuster, 1997.

Davis, William C. *Battle at Bull Run: A History of the First Major Campaign of the Civil War*. Garden City, NY: Doubleday & Company, 1977.

Davis, Burke. *To Appomattox: Nine April Days, 1865*. New York: Rinehart & Company, 1959.

Detzer, David. *Allegiance: Fort Sumter, Charleston, and the Beginning of the Civil War*. New York: Harcourt, 2001.

Dew, Charles B. *Apostles of Disunion: Southern Secession Commissioners and the Causes of the Civil War*. Charlottesville: University of Virginia Press, 2001.

Donald, David Herbert. *Lincoln*. New York: Simon & Schuster, 1995.

Douglass, Frederick. *Narrative of the Life of Frederick Douglass, an American Slave*. Boston: Anti-Slavery Office, 1845.

Fehrenbacher, Don E. *The Dred Scott Case: Its Significance in American Law and Politics*. New York: Oxford University Press, 1978.

Foner, Eric. *Free Soil, Free Labor, Free Men: The Ideology of the Republican Party Before the Civil War*. New York: Oxford University Press, 1995.

Foner, Eric. *Reconstruction: America's Unfinished Revolution, 1863-1877*. New York: Harper & Row, 1988.

Good, Timothy S. *We Saw Lincoln Shot: One Hundred Eyewitness Accounts*. Jackson: University Press of Mississippi, 1995.

Holt, Michael F. *The Political Crisis of the 1850s*. New York: W. W. Norton & Company, 1978.

Holzer, Harold. *Lincoln President-Elect: Abraham Lincoln and the Great Secession Winter, 1860-1861*. New York: Simon & Schuster, 2008.

Kauffman, Michael W. *American Brutus: John Wilkes Booth and the Lincoln Conspiracies*. New York: Random House, 2004.

Litwack, Leon F. *Been in the Storm So Long: The Aftermath of Slavery*. New York: Alfred A. Knopf, 1979.

Marszalek, John F. *Sherman: A Soldier's Passion for Order*. New York: Free Press, 1993.

Marvel, William. *Lee's Last Retreat: The Flight to Appomattox*. Chapel Hill: University of North Carolina Press, 2002.

McCardell, John M., Jr. *The Idea of a Southern Nation: Southern Nationalists and Southern Nationalism, 1830-1860*. New York: W. W. Norton & Company, 1979.

McPherson, James M. *The Negro's Civil War: How American Blacks Felt and Acted During the War for the Union*. New York: Pantheon Books, 1965.

Potter, David M. *The Impending Crisis: America Before the Civil War, 1848-1861*. New York: Harper & Row, 1976.

Rable, George C. *But There Was No Peace: The Role of Violence in the Politics of Reconstruction*. Athens: University of Georgia Press, 1984.

Reynolds, David S. *John Brown, Abolitionist: The Man Who Killed Slavery, Sparked the Civil War, and Seeded Civil Rights*. New York: Alfred A. Knopf, 2005.

Rhea, Gordon C. *The Battle of the Wilderness, May 5-6, 1864*. Baton Rouge: Louisiana State University Press, 1994.

Richardson, Heather Cox. *The Death of Reconstruction: Race, Labor, and Politics in the Post-Civil War North, 1865-1901*. Cambridge, MA: Harvard University Press, 2001.

Sears, Stephen W. *Landscape Turned Red: The Battle of Antietam*. New Haven: Yale University Press, 1983.

Simpson, Brooks D. *Ulysses S. Grant: Triumph over Adversity, 1822-1865*. Boston: Houghton Mifflin, 2000.

Steers, Edward, Jr. *Blood on the Moon: The Assassination of Abraham Lincoln*. Lexington: University Press of Kentucky, 2001.

Trudeau, Noah Andre. *The Last Citadel: Petersburg, Virginia, June 1864–April 1865*. Boston: Little, Brown and Company, 1991.

Waugh, John C. *Reelecting Lincoln: The Battle for the 1864 Presidency*. New York: Crown Publishers, 1997.

Image Sources

1 User:Roblespepe, CC BY-SA 3.0 <https://creativecommons.org/licenses/by-sa/3.0>, via Wikimedia Commons, https://commons.wikimedia.org/wiki/File: Peopling_of_America_through_Beringia.png

2 https://commons.wikimedia.org/wiki/File:North_American_cultural_areas.png

3 Herb Roe, CC BY-SA 4.0 <https://creativecommons.org/licenses/by-sa/4.0>, via Wikimedia Commons, https://commons.wikimedia.org/wiki/File: Shriver_Circle_%26_Mound_City_solstice_sunrise_HRoe_2019sm.jpg

4 Richard Zietz, CC BY-SA 3.0 <https://creativecommons.org/licenses/by-sa/3.0>, via Wikimedia Commons, https://commons.wikimedia.org/wiki/File: Thirteencolonies_politics_cropped.jpg

5 Infrogmation of New Orleans, CC BY-SA 4.0 <https://creativecommons.org/licenses/by-sa/4.0>, via Wikimedia Commons, https://commons.wikimedia.org/wiki/File:Slave_shackle_-_1811_Kid_Ory_Historic_House,_LaPlace,_Louisiana_B.jpg

6 https://commons.wikimedia.org/wiki/File:Robert_Walter_Weir_-_Embarkation_of_the_Pilgrims_-_Google_Art_Project.jpg

7 https://commons.wikimedia.org/wiki/File:Salem_witch2.jpg

8 https://commons.wikimedia.org/wiki/File:Treaty_of_Penn_with_Indians_by_Benjamin_West.jpg

9 Pinpin, CC BY-SA 3.0 <https://creativecommons.org/licenses/by-sa/3.0>, via Wikimedia Commons, https://commons.wikimedia.org/wiki/File:Nouvelle-France_map-en.svg

10 https://commons.wikimedia.org/wiki/File:The_Boston_Massacre_MET_DT2086.jpg

11 https://commons.wikimedia.org/wiki/File:Boston_Tea_Party_Currier_colored.jpg

12 https://commons.wikimedia.org/wiki/File:Declaration_of_Independence_(1819),_by_John_Trumbull.jpg

13 https://commons.wikimedia.org/wiki/File:Surrender_of_Lord_Cornwallis.jpg

14 Made by User:Golbez., CC BY-SA 3.0 <http://creativecommons.org/licenses/by-sa/3.0/>, via Wikimedia Commons, https://commons.wikimedia.org/wiki/File:United_States_1789-08-1790-04.png

15 https://commons.wikimedia.org/wiki/File:Inauguration_of_George_Washington_by_Ramon_Elorriaga.jpg

16 https://commons.wikimedia.org/wiki/File:Battle_erie.jpg

17 William Morris, CC BY-SA 4:0 <https://creativecommons.org/licenses/by-sa/4.0>, via Wikimedia Commons, https://commons.wikimedia.org/wiki/File:Louisiana_Purchase.png

18 https://commons.wikimedia.org/wiki/File:Lewis_and_clark-expedition.jpg

19 https://commons.wikimedia.org/wiki/File:Trails_of_Tears_en.png

20 https://commons.wikimedia.org/wiki/File:Emanuel_Leutze_-_Westward_the_Course_of_Empire_Takes_Its_Way_-_Smithsonian.jpg

21 https://commons.wikimedia.org/wiki/File:Cotton_gin_EWM_2007.jpg

22 https://commons.wikimedia.org/wiki/File:Bombardment_of_Fort_Sumter.jpg

23 The copyright holder of this file, Adam Cuerden, allows anyone to use it for any purpose, provided that the copyright holder is properly attributed. Redistribution, derivative work, commercial use, and all other use is permitted. https://commons.wikimedia.org/wiki/File:Thure_de_Thulstrup_-_L._Prang_and_Co._-_Battle_of_Gettysburg_-_Restoration_by_Adam_Cuerden.jpg

24 https://commons.wikimedia.org/wiki/File:General_Robert_E._Lee_surrenders_at_Appomattox_Court_House_1865.jpg

25 https://commons.wikimedia.org/wiki/File:Assassination_of_President_Lincoln_(color)_-_Currier_and_Ives.jpg

26 https://commons.wikimedia.org/wiki/File:FreedmenVotingInNewOrleans1867.jpeg

27 https://commons.wikimedia.org/wiki/File:69workmen.jpg

28 https://commons.wikimedia.org/wiki/File:HaymarketRiot-Harpers.jpg

29 https://commons.wikimedia.org/wiki/File:State_Street,_north_from_Madison,_Chicago-LCCN2008678298.jpg

30 https://commons.wikimedia.org/wiki/File:Jacob_Riis,_Lodgers_in_a_Crowded_Bayard_Street_Tenement.jpg

31 https://commons.wikimedia.org/wiki/File:Arriving_at_Ellis_Island_LCCN2014710703.tif

32 https://commons.wikimedia.org/wiki/File:Immigrants1888.jpg

33 https://commons.wikimedia.org/wiki/File:Male_Carlisle_School_Students_1879.jpg

34 https://commons.wikimedia.org/wiki/File:Mary_Garrity_-_Ida_B._Wells-Barnett_-_Google_Art_Project_-_restoration_crop.jpg

35 Grastel, CC BY-SA 4.0 <https://creativecommons.org/licenses/by-sa/4.0>, via Wikimedia Commons, https://commons.wikimedia.org/wiki/File:Grand_Canyon_of_yellowstone.jpg

36 https://commons.wikimedia.org/wiki/File:Suffragists_Parade_Down_Fifth_Avenue,_1917.JPG

37 https://commons.wikimedia.org/wiki/File:San_Juan_Hill_by_Kurz_and_Allison.JPG

38 https://commons.wikimedia.org/wiki/File:U.S._Marines_during_the_Meuse-Argonne_Campaign.jpg

39 https://commons.wikimedia.org/wiki/File:Baker_Charleston.jpg

40 https://commons.wikimedia.org/wiki/File:Prohibition_agents_destroying_barrels_of_alcohol_(United_States,_prohibition_era).jpg

41 https://commons.wikimedia.org/wiki/File:Lange-MigrantMother02.jpg

42 https://commons.wikimedia.org/wiki/File:Pennsylvania_breaker_boys_1911.jpg

43 https://commons.wikimedia.org/wiki/File:The_USS_Arizona_(BB-39)_burning_after_the_Japanese_attack_on_Pearl_Harbor_-_NARA_195617_-_Edit.jpg

44 https://commons.wikimedia.org/wiki/File:American_troops_on_board_a_landing_craft_heading_for_the_beaches_at_Oran_in_Algeria_during_Operation_%27Torch%27,_November_1942._A12661.jpg

45 https://commons.wikimedia.org/wiki/File:Wright_R-1820_for_Douglas_SBDs.jpg

46 https://commons.wikimedia.org/wiki/File:First_Iwo_Jima_Flag_Raising.jpg

47 https://commons.wikimedia.org/wiki/File:C-54landingattemplehof.jpg

48 https://commons.wikimedia.org/wiki/File:NASA-Apollo8-Dec24-Earthrise.jpg

49 https://commons.wikimedia.org/wiki/File:Vietnam._As_the_second_phase_of_operation_%22Thayer,%22_the_1st_Air_Cavalry_Division_(airmobile)_is_having...-_NARA_-_530612.tif

50 https://commons.wikimedia.org/wiki/File:A_female_demonstrator_offers_a_flower_to_military_police_on_guard_at_the_Pentagon_during_an_anti-Vietnam_demonstration._Arlington,_Virginia,_USA.jpg

51 https://commons.wikimedia.org/wiki/File:JimCrowInDurhamNC.jpg

52 https://commons.wikimedia.org/wiki/File:Elizabeth_Eckford.jpg

53 https://commons.wikimedia.org/wiki/File:March_on_Washington_for_Jobs_and_Freedom,_Martin_Luther_King,_Jr._and_Joachim_Prinz_1963.jpg

54 https://commons.wikimedia.org/wiki/File:Gloria_Steinem_at_news_ conference,_Women%27s_Action_Alliance,_January_12,_1972.jpg

55 https://commons.wikimedia.org/wiki/File:Line_at_a_gas_station,_June_15,_1979.jpg

56 https://commons.wikimedia.org/wiki/File:Reagan_and_Gorbachev_signing.jpg

57 https://en.wikipedia.org/wiki/File:Gypsy_escortDN-ST-91-05966.jpg

58 Robert on Flickr, CC BY-SA 2.0 <https://creativecommons.org/licenses/by-sa/2.0>, via Wikimedia Commons, https://commons.wikimedia.org/wiki/File: North_face_south_tower_after_plane_strike_9-11.jpg

59 https://commons.wikimedia.org/wiki/File:Map_of_territorial_growth_1775.svg

60 https://commons.wikimedia.org/wiki/File:John_Dickinson_portrait.jpg

61 https://commons.wikimedia.org/wiki/File:The_Boston_Massacre_ MET_DT2086.jpg

62 https://commons.wikimedia.org/wiki/File:Boston_Tea_Party_w.jpg

63 https://commons.wikimedia.org/wiki/File:Joseph_Siffrein_Duplessis_-_Benjamin_Franklin_-_Google_Art_Project.jpg

64 https://commons.wikimedia.org/wiki/File:The_able_doctor,_or_ America_swallowing_the_bitter_draught_(NYPL_Hades-248165-425086).jpg

65 John Singleton Copley, CC0, via Wikimedia Commons, https://commons. wikimedia.org/wiki/File:Thomas_Gage_John_Singleton_Copley.jpeg

66 https://commons.wikimedia.org/wiki/File:The_Battle_of_Lexington.jpg

67 https://commons.wikimedia.org/wiki/File:Declaration_of_Independence_ (1819),_by_John_Trumbull.jpg

68 https://commons.wikimedia.org/wiki/File:William_Walcutt_statue_George_III.png

69 https://commons.wikimedia.org/wiki/File:Forcing_a_Passage_of_the_Hudson.jpg

70 https://commons.wikimedia.org/wiki/File:Washington_Crossing_the_ Delaware_by_Emanuel_Leutze,_MMA-NYC,_1851.jpg

71 https://en.wikipedia.org/wiki/File:The_Capture_of_the_Hessians_at_ Trenton_December_26_1776.jpeg

72 Hoodinski, CC BY-SA 4.0 <https://creativecommons.org/licenses/by-sa/4.0>, via Wikimedia Commons, https://commons.wikimedia.org/wiki /File:Burgoyne%27s_March_on_Albany,_1777.svg

73 https://commons.wikimedia.org/wiki/File:Sullivans-island-1050x777.jpg

74 https://commons.wikimedia.org/wiki/File:KingsMountain_DeathOfFerguson _Chappel.jpg

75 https://commons.wikimedia.org/wiki/File:Cowpens.jpg

76 https://commons.wikimedia.org/wiki/File:BattleOfVirginiaCapes.jpg

77 https://commons.wikimedia.org/wiki/File:Surrender_of_Lord_Cornwallis.jpg

78 https://en.wikipedia.org/wiki/File:Gilbert_Stuart_Williamstown_Portrait_ of_George_Washington.jpg

79 https://commons.wikimedia.org/wiki/File:DeborahSampson.jpg

80 https://commons.wikimedia.org/wiki/File:Evacuation_Day_and_ Washington%27s_Triumphal_Entry.jpg

81 https://commons.wikimedia.org/wiki/File:Scene_at_the_Signing_of_ the_Constitution_of_the_United_States.jpg

82 Júlio Reis, CC BY-SA 3.0 <https://creativecommons.org/licenses/by-sa/3.0>, via Wikimedia Commons, https://commons.wikimedia.org/wiki/File:US_Secession_map_1861.svg

83 https://commons.wikimedia.org/wiki/File:President-Jefferson-Davis.jpg

84 https://commons.wikimedia.org/wiki/File:Abraham_Lincoln_1860.jpg

85 https://commons.wikimedia.org/wiki/File:Gen._Pierre_Gustave_ Toutant_de_Beauregard,_C.S.A_-_NARA_-_528596.jpg

86 https://commons.wikimedia.org/wiki/File:Bombardment_of_Fort_Sumter.jpg

87 https://commons.wikimedia.org/wiki/File:Joseph_Johnston_(4x5_cropped).jpg

88 https://commons.wikimedia.org/wiki/File:Jackson-Stonewall-LOC.jpg

89 https://commons.wikimedia.org/wiki/File:Scott-anaconda.jpg

90 https://commons.wikimedia.org/wiki/File:George_B_McClellan_-_retouched,_cropped.jpg

91 https://commons.wikimedia.org/wiki/File:Robert_Edward_Lee_(3x4_cropped).jpg

92 Hlj, CC BY-SA 4.0 <https://creativecommons.org/licenses/by-sa/4.0>, via Wikimedia Commons, https://commons.wikimedia.org/wiki/File:Peninsula_Campaign_March-May_1862.png

93 Hlj, CC BY-SA 4.0 <https://creativecommons.org/licenses/by-sa/4.0>, via Wikimedia Commons, https://commons.wikimedia.org/wiki/File:Seven_ Days_Battles_overview.pdf

94 Hlj, CC BY-SA 4.0 <https://creativecommons.org/licenses/by-sa/4.0>, via Wikimedia Commons, https://commons.wikimedia.org/wiki/File: Maryland_Campaign_1862.pdf

95 https://commons.wikimedia.org/wiki/File:Thure_de_Thulstrup_-_Battle_of_Antietam.jpg

96 https://commons.wikimedia.org/wiki/File:Lincoln_at_Antietam.jpg

97 https://commons.wikimedia.org/wiki/File:Ambrose_Burnside2.jpg

98 Map by Hal Jespersen, www.posix.com/CW, CC BY 3.0 <https://creativecommons.org/licenses/by/3.0>, via Wikimedia Commons, https://commons.wikimedia.org/wiki/File:Fredericksburg-Overview.png

99 https://commons.wikimedia.org/wiki/File:Joseph_Hooker_-_Brady-Handy-- restored.jpg

100 https://commons.wikimedia.org/wiki/File:Battle_of_Chancellorsville.png

101 https://commons.wikimedia.org/wiki/File:Ulysses_S_Grant_as_ Brigadier_General,_1861.jpg

102 https://commons.wikimedia.org/wiki/File:Chickamauga.jpg

103 https://commons.wikimedia.org/wiki/File:Timothy_H._O%27 Sullivan_(American_-_A_Harvest_of_Death_-_Google_Art_Project.jpg

104 https://commons.wikimedia.org/wiki/File:Soldiers_White_Black_1861.jpg

105 https://commons.wikimedia.org/wiki/File:James_Longstreet.jpg

106 https://commons.wikimedia.org/wiki/File:George_G._Meade_Standing.jpg

107 https://commons.wikimedia.org/wiki/File:Thure_de_Thulstrup_- _L._Prang_and_Co._-_Battle_of_Gettysburg_-_Restoration_by_Adam_Cuerden.jpg

108 Map by Hal Jespersen, www.cwmaps.com, CC BY 3.0 <https://creativecommons.org/licenses/by/3.0>, via Wikimedia Commons, https://commons.wikimedia.org/wiki/File:Gettysburg_Campaign.png

109 Internet Archive Book Images, No restrictions, via Wikimedia Commons; https://commons.wikimedia.org/wiki/File:Makers_of_the_world%27s_history_and_t heir_grand_achievements_(1903)_(14596104027).jpg

110 Hlj, CC BY-SA 4.0 <https://creativecommons.org/licenses/by-sa/4.0>, via Wikimedia Commons, https://commons.wikimedia.org/wiki/File: Overland_Campaign_May-June_1864.pdf

111 Hlj, CC BY-SA 4.0 <https://creativecommons.org/licenses/by-sa/4.0>, via Wikimedia Commons, https://commons.wikimedia.org/wiki/File: Shenandoah_Valley_May-July_1864.pdf

112 https://commons.wikimedia.org/wiki/File:F.O.C._Darley_and_Alexander_ Hay_Ritchie_-_Sherman%27s_March_to_the_Sea.jpg

113 https://commons.wikimedia.org/wiki/File:New_York_Draft_Riots_-_fighting.jpg

114 https://commons.wikimedia.org/wiki/File:General_Robert_E._Lee_ surrenders_at_Appomattox_Court_House_1865.jpg

115 https://commons.wikimedia.org/wiki/File:Lincoln_assassination_slide_c1900_- _Restoration.jpg

116 https://commons.wikimedia.org/wiki/File:Broad_Street_Charleston_ South_Carolina_1865.jpg